UNDERSTANDING READERS' UNDERSTANDING
Theory and Practice

UNDERSTANDING READERS' UNDERSTANDING
Theory and Practice

edited by

ROBERT J. TIERNEY
Ohio State University

PATRICIA L. ANDERS
University of Arizona

JUDY NICHOLS MITCHELL
University of Arizona

LAWRENCE ERLBAUM ASSOCIATES, PUBLISHERS
1987   Hillsdale, New Jersey   Hove and London

Lawrence Erlbaum Associates, Inc., Publishers
365 Broadway
Hillsdale, New Jersey 07642

Library of Congress Cataloging-in-Publication Data

Understanding readers' understanding.

Bibliography: p.
Includes index.
1. Reading comprehension.   2. Reading, Psychology of.
3. Children — Books and reading.   I. Tierney, Robert J.
II. Anders, Patricia L.   II. Mitchell, Judy Nichols.
LB105.45.U529   1986   372.4   86-6266
ISBN 0-89859-911-3

Printed in the United States of America
10   9   8   7   6   5   4   3   2   1

CONTENTS

v

PART I

TEXT CONSIDERATIONS

Current reading research has directed relatively little attention to the investigation of text as written language. Much more emphasis has been placed on the role the reader plays in the encounter with text. This research imbalance may be appropriate for a field with the important goal of understanding readers' understandings; yet it seems obvious that text is a vital component of the process and hence worthy of study.

A contrast can be made regarding the study of spoken language. For centuries, philologists and linguists have identified and classified various forms and functions of speech: phonemes, morphemes, classes of words, particular types or genre of speech; prosodic features; intonation contours; syntactic patterns; sentence types; and semantic relationships. In more recent times, the study of language has included the description of differences among speakers, including registers, dialects, cultural and situational context, and pragmatic intent. Various theories of grammar have been offered to explain language as a rule-governed system, to account for the extensive linguistic knowledge of native speakers, and to describe the language acquisition process. Central to all such studies is the interest in some aspect of spoken language itself, rather than what speakers or listeners may do to comprehend spoken messages.

It is curious that written language has never been the object of such serious study. Linguists consider written text merely the result of secondary symbolic representation; researchers concerned with reading and writing are much more interested in such linguistic applications as the creation, use, and function of text. As a consequence, far more is known about spoken language than written language.

However, the study of text can contribute significant information about the application process of reading and writing. For example, more needs to be known about the features or characteristics of text, both those common to all texts and those that distinguish various text types. Further, information about how text is organized and how text is related to the reading strategies or processing of the reader will help to clarify our understanding of the links between reading and writing as processes.

The unifying theme of the chapters in this section is that they all contribute significantly to the understanding of text. Walter Kintsch's chapter provides an overview of the reader–text relationship by identifying several properties of text that influence the comprehension of readers. The concept of readability as an index of text difficulty is thereby clarified: According to the model, it is primarily the expectations of readers, text-based as well as knowledge-based, which affect their ability to inference.

The second chapter by Robert de Beaugrande approaches the study of text not only in terms of organization, but also in terms of attention and memory. He uses text world to describe relationships within the text, and linear intelligence to represent those capacities that enable readers to carry out complex processes over time. De Beaugrande's rich model has several levels, supported by experimental evidence from studies of perception, learning, attention, rehearsal, recognition and recall, thus providing a tangible illustration of the complexity associated with the reading act.

A third approach to text is offered by Bonnie Meyer, who explores both the structure of expository text and the ability of readers to use text structure as an aid to comprehension. What readers remember from a text appears to be dramatically influenced by the pattern of text relationships at the top level of the content structure. Further, readers also differ in their abilities to identify and use the organizational cues provided by an author to signal the top level of text.

Rand Spiro and Barbara Taylor introduce a theoretical scheme to classify text types. They suggest that labels such as *narrative* and *expository* are much too limited to explain the great diversity of text types. After a discussion of the ambiguities that result from traditional comparisons of text types, an outline of nine text dimensions is thoughtfully presented.

The section is concluded with Jim Mosenthal's chapter on the relationship of the reader's affective response to a narrative text's structural cohesion. The text-analytic methods are used to explain both the stylistic devices employed by the writer of the text and the interpretation, appreciation, and emotional response of the reader to the text—an interesting commentary concerning the triangular relationship of text structure, content, and response.

Individually and as a group, these chapters propose new ways to examine text and its role in the reading transaction. The chapters differ in their perspectives and in the questions they pose, but each presents a convincing argument that text is important to study for its own sake, as well as for the insights it contributes to reading research and classroom applications.

CONTRIBUTIONS FROM COGNITIVE PSYCHOLOGY

Walter Kintsch
University of Colorado

Building bridges is not an art but a technology. Teaching youngsters how to read and write and how to function as literates in our increasingly complex society is still an art. Will it ever become a technology, should it ever become one? There are a number of scientific disciplines that some day could provide a basis for an educational technology, among them cognitive psychology. What would such a technology look like, and what role might cognitive psychology play in it?

So far, pedagogical techniques derive almost exclusively from practical experience and common sense. It would be criminally foolish to denigrate either of these sources. They have served us well, they are the best we have, but perhaps they are no longer enough. In the days when formal education was reserved for the high and mighty who could afford a private tutor, traditional practices were surely sufficient. Even much later, when schools began to educate a substantial minority of the population (the bright ones, who came from a relatively high cultural and socio-economic background) educational techniques were adequate for the task. Many intelligent and dedicated teachers improved and modified these techniques, so that they kept pace with the changing view of human nature and new demands that society made on education. But, since truly universal education has become a reality in the most advanced parts of the world, we have reached a situation where the exclusive reliance on experience and intuition may no longer be possible.

There is somewhat of a crisis situation today in education, a dissatisfaction on the part of the general public with what schools achieve, best exemplified by the recurrent newspaper reports that some very high percentage of the children coming out of our schools "can't read." With many variations, most of them tiresomely familiar, schools are accused of doing a poor job. Clearly, we are at some sort of a limit: We have the schools, we have the teachers; for the most part these are working as well as they could be expected to under current conditions—so what is wrong? Obviously, problems like this are much too complex to permit a single or simple answer, but perhaps research in cognitive psychology can provide us with some insight into the situation. As yet, we do not even know what the problem really is. When it is said that 20% (or 30%) of eighth graders "can't read," what really is it that they can not do? Read, in the sense of word-decoding, or read in the sense of comprehending a newspaper or magazine article (an account of the last pro-football game, or an analysis of the energy crisis—which one?) or follow instructions on how to assemble and operate a lawnmower? In other words, to what extent do we have a reading problem as distinguished from a comprehension problem (could they get that lawnmower together if they listened to taped instructions?) If we had answers to these questions, then what could one do about our problem? Are there better teaching techniques that would make it possible that, say, 95% of the eighth graders function at a level that society expects of them? Or are we running at this point into limits of human intelligence, in that a substantial fraction of our population is not equipped genetically to perform cognitive tasks of a complexity required by our highly technological modern society? If so, can one adjust the demands of society to the realities of human nature?

Researchers are trying to find answers today to all of these questions. Educational common sense, at this point, needs to be supplemented by a concerted research effort to get us out of the crisis situation in which we find ourselves today. But one ought to be clear in one's own mind about what can and can not be expected from such a research effort.

Consider the following caricature. Suppose we had a fully worked out cognitive theory, and an equally well developed science of pedagogy. The latter would take some premises from the cognitive theory, and provide us with a chain of logical deductions that would terminate in some prescription, what Ms. Henderson should do on Monday morning with her second grade for example. Clearly, such a conjecture is ridiculous, given the complexity of Ms. Henderson and her class. Hence, it can not be the goal of cognitive psychology to develop a capability of telling the educator what to do in the classroom in any specific way. Indeed, there are few good examples where specific classroom practices were successfully introduced directly because of some basic research result. (There are some not so successful ones.) But it would be foolish to conclude from this that basic research is irrelevant to education. The relevance is merely a much more indirect one. Educators can not hope (fear?) that psychologists will tell them what to do. But psychologists might help educators to achieve a better understanding of what they do and why they are doing something, even to find new ways of doing things and improving old ways. All this could be the result of a better understanding of how man functions as a cognitive system—how we think, comprehend, learn, or why we fail. This, to me, appears to be the main contribution that cognitive psychology can make to education at this point: To supplement the educator's common sense and intuition—already well founded on rich practical experience—with a new, scientific understanding of human cognitive functioning. Sharpened intuitions about the learner as an information-processing system, with peculiar resource limitations and flexible strategies, might help us steer educational efforts into promising directions and overcome some of the frustrations that currently plague these efforts.

One of the recent findings in the area of text comprehension that has aroused a lot of interest among researchers in that field concerns the role of macrostructures on the comprehension process (I elaborate on this later, but see also the contribution of Meyer, this volume). Briefly, the point is that reading comprehension depends not only on the local properties of the text and the reader's decoding activities at the sentence and paragraph level, but also on the overall, between-paragraph organization of the text. A lot of evidence today points to the crucial role that macroprocesses ("getting the gist of it") plays in comprehension. How does that sort of discovery affect education? For the most part indirectly, in the sense that educators become aware of yet another facet of the process of text comprehension and ask themselves whether what they are doing takes into account macroprocesses. We do not know as yet enough about macroprocesses to develop precise ideas about training programs, but there are a number of things we can do. Obviously, students need to be given an opportunity to work with long enough texts in order to develop whatever skills are involved. Too much reading practice with short paragraphs, or even sentences, might develop bad comprehension habits that would be hard to break later on. Do comprehension questions encourage gist processing, or are they concerned with picky details (that often are a lot easier to score)? Do current tests evaluate these crucial macro-operations at all or are they preoccupied with more local processes? Furthermore, an educator might note that such and such a practice followed for a long time can suddenly be given a new theoretical rationale: What was done intuitively and because it seemed to work well, is now seen as playing a role in letting the reader learn about macroprocesses in comprehension. One can see this in some of the reports presented in this volume where practicing educators have developed the kind of programs present day cognitive theory would call for. They have done so on their own, but an improved understanding of the theoretical underpinnings of such programs might help them to continue and improve their work, and get others who are less perceptive involved in similar projects.

The point I wanted to make with this little homily on macroprocesses is that the effects that such research findings have on educational practice are significant and pervasive; it is shortsighted and narrow to claim that a basic research result is irrelevant to education because it has not resulted in a specific pedagogic prescription—the effects may still be there, but they may be indirect ones, less concrete but no less important.

I would like to sketch here very briefly the picture of comprehension processes that has emerged from the work done by our group at Colorado. It is still an incomplete picture and some of the detail is intolerably fuzzy. But the outlines are clear for a model of comprehension processes. This model, together with work done at other research centers (J. Anderson, 1976; R. Anderson & Pichert, 1978; Clark, 1977; Just & Carpenter, 1979; Schank & Abelson, 1977), has some strong implications for educational practice in the sense just described: It could help educators to better understand the process of understanding—and thereby make better pedagogic decisions.

The theory to be outlined here has been described more fully elsewhere, and the interested reader is referred to these sources for further detail (van Dijk & Kintsch, 1983; Kintsch & van Dijk, 1978; Kintsch & Vipond, 1979; Miller & Kintsch, 1980). The main goal of the theory is to account for the difficulty that readers experience with a text, and to describe what they remember after reading. Thus, the theory starts out with a given text and a characterization of the reader in terms of his or her goals and purposes. Actually, we do not deal with the text directly, but with a conceptual structure that represents the meaning of the text. This is achieved by handcoding the text into a sequence of propositions according to principles developed by Kintsch (1974).

There are a number of processing steps whereby the propositional representation of a text gets transformed into more and more abstract representations in conformance with the reader's goals that in our model are formalized as a control schema. The first level of processing that we are concerned with takes the list of input propositions and constructs from it a coherent whole. Thus, a text is no longer represented as a sequence of meaning elements (i.e., propositions) but as an interrelated, coherent structure. This process is psychologically interesting because of the inherent human processing limitations that make it necessary for the reader to form this structure piece by piece in a series of processing cycles, rather than all at once. The capacity of working memory is limited, so that not all the propositions in a text (many hundreds, even in a story only a few pages long) can be processed simultaneously. Instead, reading proceeds in a sequence of processing cycles, sentence by sentence. The propositions of one sentence are decoded and arranged in a coherent whole, and then the same is done for the next sentence. However, the two sentences must be interconnected, because the reader wants to understand the text as a whole—not as a series of unrelated sentences. Thus, in going from one sentence to the next, some information from the old sentence must be retained in the reader's short-term memory so that the new information can be integrated with the already known one. We know that the capacity of short-term memory is severely limited (for a full discussion of the cognitive psychology background of this work see Kintsch, 1977) and hence the reader can only hold over a few old propositions from the processing cycle to the next (estimates range from two to five propositions). This makes the whole thing interesting: The reader needs a good strategy on how to pick reasonable prospects to be held in short-term memory, for if he or she picks some unimportant detail, this very likely will be unrelated to whatever comes in the next sentence, and the process will be stuck. When that occurs, the reader in our model has two choices: either to just go on and leave the two pieces of text unrelated (but that results in an incoherent memory representation of the text, and as a consequence in poor understanding and poor memory), or our model reader can stop and try to undo the damage. He or she can go back and search the already read text for some proposition that does relate to the new input and that makes the text coherent. Sometimes, however, a text is written in such a way that it simply is incoherent, and bridging information can not be found in the text. In that case, the model has the choice of making an inference that can relate the two pieces of text.

All that backtracking (we call it a *reinstatement search*) and inferencing makes a text hard to read. There are of course other factors that long have been known to be involved in readability. Traditionally, the two most important ones have been sentence length and word frequency. However, readability formulas based on these factors and others like it have not been notably successful. In practice, they work to some extent, but because they lack theoretical motivation they tell us little about the reading process, and they are easily fooled, which severely limits their practical usefulness (e.g., see Kintsch & Vipond, 1979, for a discussion). It is of course true that word frequency and sentence length are important for readability. But there are many other important factors that may make a text easy or hard to read, even if we control for those two. In terms of our model, if readers do not understand the words used in a text, they will never be able to derive from it an adequate semantic representation, and hence all the higher order processes the model deals with will be impeded. Sentence length also enters the picture. Suppose a sentence is too long to be processed on a single cycle (what is too long depends, of course, on the reader, and whether he or she is skimming or reading carefully). In that case, the reader must form a processing chunk not based on a sentence boundary, but on some minor phrase boundary. Clearly, to find a suitable phrase boundary requires more of the readers' processing resources, and hence leaves less for the remaining operations that need to be performed, thus decreasing reading efficiency. Sentences, for optimal readability, should therefore be adjusted to the expected processing limits of the readers.

Now consider the reinstatement searches—occasions when a reader is forced to look for some piece of information in the text that is no longer in his active memory. These occasions are serious stumbling blocks, and we have found them to contribute substantially to the difficulty of a text. What produced these occasions? First, of course, poor writing. If an author organizes a text with little skill, it may happen that he or she refers back to an item of information that was last mentioned too far back in the text, and that is therefore no longer present in the reader's short-term memory at the point where it is needed. (Actually, this is not simply a question of how far back an item was last referred to; it also depends on the manner in which it was referred. Often some item in a text is clearly marked through its position in the semantic structure or even through such surface means as syntactic function or stress, and such marked items may be kept in short-term memory over very long stretches of a text). Reinstatement searches are not merely caused by deficiencies in the text, however. Rather, it is the text–reader interaction that is important. What is "too far back" depends crucially on the reader's short-term memory capacity. A beginning reader, whose short-term memory is occupied with processes that are quite automatic in an efficient reader, may have a much smaller effective memory capacity, and hence would be much more likely to be stopped by reinstatement searches. Thus, the same text may be easy for a reader with a large memory capacity, but hard for others. I repeat this point again in the section on the role of expectations and knowledge in understanding: Readability is not a property of a text, but a result of a reader–text interaction.

The role of "inferences" in reading is far from adequately understood at present. Many different types of inferences occur in reading, and they have many different functions. Here, we are concerned with only one type, the so-called bridging inferences that are necessary to connect two parts of a text that would otherwise be incoherent. Such inferences have been studied more extensively than others (e.g., Havilland & Clark, 1974; Keenan & Kintsch, 1974). Sometimes they are trivial as in
1.   John's car stalled. The carburetor was wet.
where there is no direct connection between the two sentences, requiring

the bridging inference that "A carburetor is part of a car." This is a piece of world knowledge widely shared and readily available. So readily, in fact, that we are not consciously aware of any inference at all, though Havilland and Clark have shown that even such relatively automatized bridging inferences require measurable processing time. On the other hand, consider

2.   John owns a lovely Kashan. The weft is made of blue silk.

which, if you are a connoisseur of Persian rugs, is just as readily understood as a coherent mini-text as (1). However, you have to have some rather specialized knowledge, which many people probably lack, that "a Kashan" is a particular kind of rug, and that rugs have wefts. Without this knowledge, (2) is either not understandable at all, or it is only partly understood and with a special effort (e.g., "a Kashan" must be something that has wefts, therefore it is some kind of textile). Thus, whether bridging inferences require processing resources, and hence make a text difficult to read, depends on whether the reader has the knowledge on which the inference is based readily available or not. In the right context, even if the requisite knowledge is missing entirely, inferences can be made with relative ease. For instance, even though a reader might not know anything about rugs, not even what a "weft" might be, if (2) occurs in the context of a description of John's rug collection, the reader will quite readily make the right kind of inferences, except that they will be context rather than knowledge-based inferences.

In a well-written text, inferences are invited by the context and occur without making great demands on the reader's processing capacities. That is, the reader is not only concerned with the coherence of the propositions in a text, but he or she also organizes them into units based on his world knowledge. We have called these units *facts*. The propositions of a text, in our theory, are grouped into a set of interrelated facts in comprehension. This fact organization is very important, because it is the basis on which the reader generates expectations about the text. Comprehension is a constructive process, and much of the construction is driven by the expectations that follow from the organization of the text propositions into fact units. If we say that "the old VW driven by Ms. X slid on the ice and smashed into a parked Cadillac," this is understood not merely as a (coherent) sequence of five propositions, but also as a fact about some accident. From this fact follow certain expectations that never need to be explicitly stated, but that nevertheless can play a decisive role in controlling the further processing of the text. For example, we are now ready to hear about the damage that occurred to the car, perhaps about an injury to the driver or passengers, that the police were called, that insurance will be involved. Thus, if the text continues with

3.   The insurance paid for all the damage.

the necessary bridging inferences are readily performed. We are trying to show experimentally how these expectations facilitate or mislead, as the case may be, text processing, but that is by no means their only effect. Others, for instance Goodman and Burke (1973), have traced the effects of expectations in the miscues that readers make, or in their eye movements (e.g., Just & Carpenter, 1980). There is still an enormous amount we have to learn about these processes and this aspect of our model needs to be worked out in much more detail than we have been able to do so far. But we need to know how to manipulate the reader's expectations if we want to devise effective teaching strategies.

Indeed, when it comes to teaching strategies, the most promising and most important level of comprehension is one concerned with the overall organization of the text, the gist processing (viz., the macrolevel).

Macrostructures, in our theory, are generated from a text by the reader and correspond to its gist, as expressed by a summary or abstract. Macrostructures are hierarchical. At the lowest level only the most irrelevant or redundant information is deleted or subsumed under some generalization. However, these operations of deletion and generalization are applied recursively, so that more and more concise abstracts are generated, until, at the highest level, only a title remains. It is useful to think of the fact representation as the lowest level of the macrostructure, containing everything that was in the text. The reader's control schema determines which of these facts are relevant to his or her goals and purposes, and the macro-operators then pick out from all of these facts those that are most relevant, frequently involving the construction of new propositions (generalizations, inferences) from the original ones. Note that this guidance by the schema is crucial and that the model would not work at all without it. We would not know how to apply the macro-operators. A macrostructure is always the product of some controlling schema and a text; if the same text is read by different subjects with different goals (and hence different schemata in control), the resulting macrostructures will be to some extent different. Indeed, if the same reader reads the same texts twice, the results can sometimes be enormously different. I sometimes labor through a research report on some topic X with some vague control schema ("examine this if there is anything interesting in it"), and it literally makes no impression upon me at all—I remember nothing. Months or years later, I may encounter the same report, but in the meantime I have found out that topic X is crucial for my present work. And now, what was difficult and obscure and utterly nonmemorable before, is suddenly perceived as an elegant and striking piece of research, practically unforgettable. The print is still the same, but the difference is in the control schema. The first time, I did not organize the material appropriately, because I never realized how this material fits into my personal cognitive structure (or perhaps, it really did not fit into it at that time). The second time, the macroprocesses are highly effective, because I know exactly what to look for, and what to do with what I find (how to relate it to my existing knowledge store).

At present, our model in certain controlled situations can generate macrostructures and hence summaries of texts. But, that is only a beginning. We still have much to learn, but there is a distinct promise that some of what we shall learn will be of practical pedagogical interest. As Kintsch and Vipond (1979) have argued, processes at the macrolevel may be much more important for readability, and indeed for the whole question of learning from texts, than semantic coding processes at the more local level. Psychologists, linguists (e.g., de Beaugrande & Dressler, 1981; van Dijk, 1977), and computer scientists (e.g., Bobrow & Winograd, 1977; Schank & Abelson, 1977) are working on these and related problems. I think it will be to their advantage if they do so in close interaction with educators, and if they accept the challenge offered by educational practice. And I think that educators, in turn, have something to learn from this modern work in cognitive science.

ACKNOWLEDGMENT

The research reported here was supported by Grant MH 15872–11 from NIMH and G–78–0172 from NIE.

REFERENCES

Anderson, J. (1976). *Language, memory and thought.* Hillsdale, NJ: Lawrence Erlbaum Associates.

Anderson, R. C., & Pichert, J. (1978). Recall of previously unrecallable information following a shift in perspective. *Journal of Verbal Learning and Verbal Behavior, 17,* 1–12.

de Beaugrande, R., & Dressler, W. (1981). *Introduction to text linguistics.* London: Longman.

Bobrow, D., & Winograd, T. (1977). An overview of KRL: A knowledge representation language. *Cognitive Science, 1,* 3–46.

Clark, H. H. (1977). Inferences in comprehension. In D. LaBerge & J. Samuels (Eds.), *Basic processes in reading: Perception and comprehension.* Hillsdale, NJ: Lawrence Erlbaum Associates.

van Dijk, T. A. (1977). *Text and context.* London: Longman.

van Dijk, T. A., & Kintsch, W. (1983). *Strategies of discourse comprehension.* New York: Academic Press.

Goodman, K., & Burke, C. (1973). *Theoretically based studies of patterns of miscues in oral reading performance.* Washington, DC: Health, Education & Welfare.

Just, M. A., & Carpenter, P. A. (1980). A theory of reading: From eye fixation to comprehension. *Psychological Review, 87,* 329–354.

Havilland, S. E., & Clark, H. H. (1974). What's new? Acquiring new information as a process in comprehension. *Journal of Verbal Learning and Verbal Behavior, 13,* 515–521.

Keenan, J. M., & Kintsch, W. (1974). The identification of explicitly and implicitly presented information. In W. Kintsch (Ed.), *The representation of meaning in memory.* Hillsdale, NJ: Lawrence Erlbaum Associates.

Kintsch, W. (1980). *The representation of meaning in memory.* Hillsdale, NJ: Lawrence Erlbaum Associates.

Kintsch, W. (1974). *Memory and cognition.* New York: Wiley.

Kintsch, W., & van Dijk, T. A. (1978). Toward a model of text comprehension and production. *Psychological Review, 85,* 363–394.

Kintsch, W, & Vipond, D. (1979). Reading comprehension and readability in educational practice and psychological theory. In L. G. Nilsson (Ed.), *Perspectives on memory research.* Hillsdale, NJ: Lawrence Erlbaum Associates.

Miller, J., & Kintsch, W. (1980). Recall and readability of short prose passages: A theoretical analysis. *Journal of Experimental Psychology: Human Learning and Memory, 6,* 335–354.

Schank, R., & Abelson, R. (1977). *Scripts, plans, goals, and understanding.* Hillsdale, NJ: Lawrence Erlbaum Associates.

2

TEXT, ATTENTION, AND MEMORY IN READING RESEARCH

Robert de Beaugrande
University of Florida

THE STATUS OF THE TEXT

A "text" can be defined as any communicative occurrence produced by a participant in discourse interaction within some temporal bounds. A set of mutually relevant texts may be termed a "discourse."[1] Although these notions are reasonably straightforward, their implications for research on language are still far from clear. Conventional linguistics has for decades pursued the project of describing language independently of its uses. Such a description has centered upon "virtual systems," i.e., repertories of available elements, whereas a text constitutes an "actual system," i.e., a configuration of elements selected from various virtual systems and thereby put to use (cf. de Beaugrande, 1980; de Beaugrande & Dressler, 1981; Hartmann, 1972; Luria, 1979).

The principles of "actualization" (putting repertories to use) need by no means be comparable to the principles whereby abstract (virtual) systems are organized. For example, the system of English phonemes has been defined in terms of simple oppositions like "voiced" versus "unvoiced" (cf. Jakobson & Halle, 1956). However, in actual speaking, the context heavily affects the vocal actions required to produce a particular phoneme at any moment (MacNeilage, 1970). Similarly, a dictionary or lexicon of word meanings may tell us very little about the complex ways in which meanings combine in context to yield the "sense" of a text (cf. Coseriu, 1955–1956). For reasons like these, the status of the text cannot

---

[1]These various notions are explicated with considerable literature in de Beaugrande (1980).

be defined in terms of old-style linguistics (e.g., simply as a unit bigger than a sentence or a paragraph, or as a sequence of well-formed sentences).

Instead, we need a "procedural" approach that describes texts in terms of how they are used in real communication. We must go beyond describing structures and explore the strategies, operations, and processes that reflect the activities of text users: their decisions, selections, controls, motivations, dispositions, and so forth. It is by virtue of these activities that any configuration of signs is indeed considered a text; it follows that textuality is not "in" the signs, but is rather the outcome of human processing acts. The following scheme seems to offer one means of factoring textuality in those terms (for details, see de Beaugrande, 1980; de Beaugrande & Dressler, 1981):

1. Cohesion is the principle whereby the occurrences of the "surface text" (the presented and perceived configuration of words) are organized into relational structures such as tone groups, utterances, phrases, clauses, and so on.[2]
2. Coherence is the principle whereby the possible meanings of words or phrases are organized into the "sense" of a text. The outcome is what I call a *text-world model,* as distinct from the surface text.
3. Intentionality subsumes the factors whereby the text producer's intentions control the operations of utilizing the text: that the presented configuration should be rendered cohesive and coherent; that discourse plans and goals are being forwarded; and so on.
4. Acceptability subsumes the factors whereby the text receiver's willingness to accept the presented configuration as cohesive, coherent, and relevant controls the operations of utilizing the text.
5. Situationality subsumes the factors that relate the occurrence of a text to a real or recoverable environment. For example, the text may serve to "monitor" the situation (i.e., provide a running linguistic account of what is going on); or else to "manage" it (i.e., steer things in such a way that the text producer's goals are likely to be attained).
6. Intertextuality subsumes the factors whereby the utilization of a given text depends on prior knowledge and experience gained from other texts. For example, communicative participants can rely on

---

[2]This notion is broader than the normal usage, e.g., Halliday and Hasan (1976), where only pro-forms, ellipsis, connection, and such devices are included. In principle, cohesion should encompass everything that "sticks" the text together, hence also the operations of syntactic structuring (as opposed to abstract syntax).

"defaults" assumed in absence of contrary specifications, or on "preferences" obeyed when choices must be made.

7. Informativity arises from the degree to which text occurrences were not known or expected prior to the moment of presentation. The resulting scale directly affects the amount of effort that participants must exert.

This scheme frees us from the hopeless disputes about the borderline between "texts" and "nontexts" inherited from the linguistic method of trying to stipulate all possible "sentences" of a language and to exclude all impossible ones. Many texts do not indeed meet the rules and standards of the language fully, as a recording of spontaneous speaking can easily show (cf. de Beaugrande, 1982a, 1984a; Fromkin, 1971; Maclay & Osgood, 1959). Yet these configurations are normally intended and accepted as texts. One major task of "psycholinguistics" was said to be an account of how and why communication ("performance") does not agree with grammar and logic ("competence"). This task was greatly impeded, however, by an unrealistic and empirically undemonstrable notion of "competence." For some time, the understanding of language was conveniently viewed as analogous to the procedures linguists use in analyzing sentences (cf. surveys in Clark & Clark, 1977; Levelt, 1978). Enormous care was lavished on the detailed syntax of isolated sentences during artificial tasks, and very little was expended upon real-life activities such as reading. Clark and Clark (1977) rationalized about this practice by asserting that "the studies of unrelated sentences tell us what to look for in 'normal' situations" (p. 157). The best refutation of this claim is the fact that after hundreds of these "studies," we still have little idea of "what to look for in normal situations."

Current models of understanding reveal quite a different approach (cf. survey in de Beaugrande, 1980–81). Researchers are wholly disenchanted with linguistic theories of syntax and look instead for means to represent configurations of knowledge conveyed via texts. The sentence is yielding to the network (cf. survey in Findler, 1979). Along the way, however, we are in danger of losing track of the surface text itself, in which words do after all appear in a certain sequence. We clearly need a new theory of syntax, stated not in terms of abstract grammars, but in terms of what I shall call *"linear intelligence"*: The capacities that make it possible to carry out complex processes in a time continuum. This chapter undertakes to propose one such approach by assembling and interpreting a variety of findings bearing on attention, memory, neurology (including aphasia), and discourse processing.

Consider now the "epistemological" implications of the network (cf. Brachman, 1979). We have a multi-directional "space" filled with nodes and links. The main operation of comprehension must involve means for identifying and accessing the nodes by traversing the links. By way of demonstration, we can model the reading of this brief passage (for a more complete treatment, cf. de Beaugrande, 1980):[3]

> (1) (1.1) A great black and yellow V-2 rocket 46 feet long stood in a New Mexico desert. (1.2) Empty, it weighed five tons. (1.3) For fuel it carried eight tons of alcohol and liquid oxygen.
> (2.1) Everything was ready. (2.2) Scientists and generals withdrew to some distance and crouched behind earth mounds. (2.3) Two red flares rose as a signal to fire the rocket.

One type of network can be designed for grammatical dependencies, e.g., that "rocket" is the head of a noun phrase including a number of modifiers. Figure 2.1 offers a graphic representation of such a network, with the links carrying labels to identify the nodes at either end. Another type of network can be designed for the conceptual dependencies, e.g., that "yellow" and "black" are the "attributes" of "rocket." Figure 2.2 would be a possible representation on this level, with the links now labeling the relations between concepts (rather than the grammatical dependencies). Notice that the two patterns are much the same, though the labels differ and the nodes are now not words, but concept names (cf. Turner & Greene, 1977). Some researchers would prefer to discard the words altogether in favor of some other designation. But the words are, in some psychologically non-trivial way, the real-time occurrences that activate concepts, and they should not be thrown out—even if we could agree (and so far we can not) on a method for replacing them with

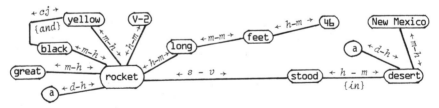

KEY: *cj*:conjunction; *d*:determiner; *h*:head; *m*:modifier; *s*:subject; *v*:verb; arrows point to the node described by the symbols.

Fig. 2.1.   A grammatical dependency network for a sentence.

---

[3]The sample is taken from McCall and Crabbs (1961), Booklet C, p. 8), reprinted by kind permission of the Teachers' College Press of New York. Compare its analysis in Kintsch and Vipond (1979). A simulation program for understanding and recalling the sample, based on my study (de Beaugrande, 1980), was written by Simmons and Chester (1979).

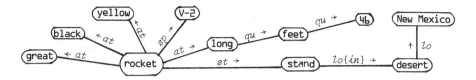

KEY: *at*:attribute of; *lo*:location of; *qu*:quantity of;
sp:specification of; *st*:state of

Fig. 2.2.   A conceptual dependency network for a sentence.

"primitives" or "semantic features" (cf. Schank, Goldman, Rieger, & Riesbeck, 1975; Wilks, 1977; Winograd, 1978).

As reading continues, each stretch of text would be converted into network format and added on to the already comprehended configuration. For our sample, the whole first paragraph (1.1) through 1.3) would give us the scheme shown in Fig. 2.3. The increment is simple because "rocket" remains the topic node of each stretch, and the coherence of the whole is thereby obvious. On the other hand, the second paragraph opens with material that is not explicitly related to what was read before. Inferencing is needed to relate "everything" to the previous state of affairs.[4] We can postulate that "everything" subsumes whatever is needed for the take-off of the "rocket"; and that "scientists and generals" were there for the purpose of observing the "rocket." If we put these inferences as nodes in square brackets, we get the pattern shown in Fig. 2.4.

This much serves to illustrate the still untouched issues I want to attack in this chapter. We have here a "text–world model" as a pattern of nodes and links that includes all concepts activated by words, plus relations specified on the links, and at least some inferences. But such a model is only a jumping-off point for a theory of reading, i.e., a point of orientation that serves in the kind of research program that older sentence syntax fails to provide. We need to explore how such a network is extracted from a text in real time, how it evolves or decays, and how all of that is stipulated by the nature of mental processes.

LINEAR INTELLIGENCE

We can begin by assuming that readers' resources are always limited and so must be strategically distributed among various possible tasks. Attention can only take in a certain amount of operations (Keele, 1973).

---

[4]These inferences were strongly confirmed when test subjects routinely recalled them as part of what they had read (de Beaugrande, 1980, p. 174f.). Kintsch and Vipond (1979, p. 345) postulate similar inferences. The usage of the term "inferencing" among various researchers is quite unstable (cf. survey in de Beaugrande, 1980–1981).

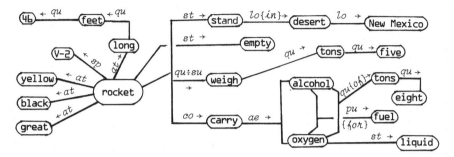

KEY: *ae*:affected entity; *at*:attribute of; *co*:containment of; *lo*:location of;
pu:purpose of; *qu*:quantity of; *sp*:specification of; *st*:state of;
su:substance of

Fig. 2.3. A conceptual dependency network for a paragraph.

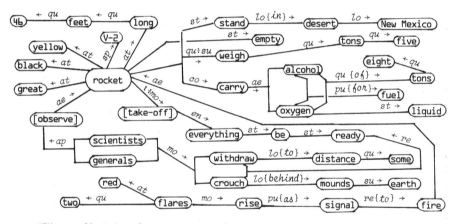

KEY: *ae*:affected entity; *ap*:apperception of; *at*:attribute of; *co*:containment
of; *en*:enablement of; *lo*:location of; *mo*:motion of; *pu*:purpose of;
qu:quantity of; *re*:reason of; *sp*:specification of; *st*:state of;
su:substance of; ε:entry; ι:initiation

Fig. 2.4. A conceptual dependency network for two paragraphs linked by inferences.

Memory can store and retain only a portion of one's experiences
(Kintsch, 1977; Loftus & Loftus, 1976). Time progresses both as real time
registered in constant units by clocks, and as psychological time created
by the scheduling operations of the human mind. The two kinds of time
are different in their organization, because in psychological time, events
can be prolonged, compressed, re-enacted, discarded before execution,
or interpreted in ways that real-time events can not. Most experiments
have abridged this issue by looking exclusively at real-time measure-
ments.

To ignore all of these limitations, as Chomsky (1965, pp. 3ff.) advises us to do, is to block any deeper insights into the processes of communication. "Studies of unrelated sentences" fail to capture "normal situations" for precisely this motive: as a rule, they artificially remove cognitive limitations by shutting out situational relevance, large-scale coherence, events competing for attention, and so forth. The findings predictably show people doing a much more thorough analysis of surface structure than would be done during continuous discourse—which I suppose psycholinguistics would find appealing. But in the long run, this "normal science" has been beset by anomalies, among which the most important is probably that people retain a strikingly inaccurate mental record of what they say, write, hear, or read. Indeed, memory at large appears disturbingly unreliable (Loftus, 1980).

A huge mass of evidence has accrued that memory storage does not possess a single unified character (cf. papers in Nilsson, 1979). Although it is quite plain that materials are not remembered equally well, disputes rage over how memory might be subdivided. One account is in terms of rehearsal: Materials are retained better if they are practised more (cf. Melton, 1963). Here, there are effects due to simple frequency (Ekstrand, Wallace, & Underwood, 1966). But more often, rehearsal improves recall because it encourages people to organize materials better by integration of internal relations or by elaboration with adding outside knowledge (Mandler, 1979). As Mandler (1979) points out, purely rote learning via repetition without organization is unfortunately overrated among writers who exercise a persistent and baleful influence on educational methods, such as Arthur Jensen.

Another account distinguishes range: a short-term sensory storage of about 1–2 second's duration, a short-term memory of about 20 seconds' duration, and a long-term memory of apparently unlimited duration (cf. Atkinson & Shiffrin, 1968). Each type of store has characteristic limitations not just in time, but also in capacity; each type seems to be best suited for dealing with certain kinds of materials. Still another account distinguishes "processing depths," where remembering is seen as a result of how "deeply" a presentation is processed (cf. Craik & Lockhart, 1972; Craik & Tulving, 1975; Mistler-Lachman, 1974). For example, meaning seems to be a "deeper" level than syntax.[5]

Finally, accounts can be set up in terms of processor contributions (cf. de Beaugrande, 1980–81; Royer, 1977). "Trace abstraction" involves

---

[5]Not everyone envisions this metaphor of "depth" in the same way. In my view, it is useful for designating the levels that move steadily further from the "surface text" (cf. de Beaugrande & Dressler, 1981). But in psychology, it tends to be linked with the durability of materials in memory, which, as I try to show, is a related but by no means identical consideration.

mere extracting of "traces" from the presented material, rather than adding one's own (cf. Gibson, 1971; Gomulicki, 1956). "Construction" entails integrating the understander's knowledge about language and the world at the very moment of comprehension (cf. Anderson & Ortony, 1975; Bransford, Barclay, & Franks, 1972). "Reconstruction" allows for entry of the understander's contributions not only during comprehension, but also during remembering (Spiro, 1977).

Skepticism and partisanship traditionally have been widespread among American psychologists. The conservative position, taken most spectacularly by Skinner (1978) but present in many schools of thought, is that what can not be observed with current instruments and statistically quantified is simply not evidence at all; one account should be able to deal with every aspect of human behavior. This stance can always count on support both from the general public (who like the simple and obvious) and from experimenters (who like easy ways to design their laboratory tests and "factor" their results). But it has been enormously impoverishing both in theory and method of language studies, and educational research needs a fundamentally new outlook (cf. de Beaugrande, 1984a, 1985).

Therefore, memory studies often have been rather narrow. Behaviorists would want to make everything a matter of repetitive rehearsal, i.e., of "conditioning." Supporters of processing depth wanted to deny both rehearsal effects and the distinctions of range in terms of stores (e.g., Craik & Lockhart, 1972; cf. the modifications in Craik & Tulving, 1975; and counter-arguments in Shallice, 1975). For a change, I would like to explore a model of reading in which all of these various dimensions are seen to interact. Findings on one dimension then do not constitute a denial of the existence of any other.

Even the most skeptical and restrictive researcher can see that reading is a linear activity, due to the medium of print as it moves across the page. Extremely detailed studies of eye movement (e.g., Gough, 1972) bear out this obvious fact: "with the exception of a small number of regressions the eye jumps from left to right across the page, stopping for a quarter of a second or so every one to five words" (Rumelhart, 1977a, p. 123). However, there is nothing at all obvious about what the mind is doing while this linear scanning is going on. Lashley (1951) already pointed out that the simplest models, in which the word sequence is described as a linear chain reaction, are clearly inadequate. There must be sophisticated "schemas" for imposing complex patterns on the actually presented and perceived series.

It is safe to divide the act of reading first according to real time, giving us the "prior text," the "current text," and the "subsequent text." The current text is whatever is held in working memory, a store that (in contrast to short- or long-term memory) can be defined not by range, but by its actions; working memory addresses ongoing input that demands processing in order to constitute comprehension. The time duration covered by working memory for a particular passage will vary according to the demands imposed by that passage in context. Thus, working memory shows a variable capacity, whereas that of short-term memory appears to be fixed. By strategic using of "chunking," considerable materials can be assembled in working memory—the limit is rather on the number of unrelated chunks (Miller, 1956).

The access to current text is provided by the momentary act of reading itself. Access to prior text is provided by "look-back," and to subsequent text by "look-ahead."[6] This simple scheme is shown in Fig. 2.5. Look-back is necessary for such needs as finding referents for pronouns, relatives, and the like (cf. Halliday & Hasan, 1976; Webber, 1980). Look-ahead arises from the heavily predictive nature of reading (cf. Goodman, 1976; Rumelhart, 1977b). The processing outcomes of reading can be correspondingly classified as "retrospective" for prior text, "perceptive" for current text, and "predictive" for subsequent text. We can show this in the scheme of Fig. 2.6, which resembles Fig. 2.5, but with an important distinction: The recovered and predicted materials are not the text, but a mental representation. It is plain that the representation differs substantially from the text. Readers are seldom able to give a verbatim account of what they have read just a few minutes before. Readers cannot predict the exact words they will be reading in a few minutes. But—and this conclusion is the most alarming—the representation is being consulted by the reader much more than the text. The actual confrontation with the text

	reader	
← look-back	↓	look-ahead →
P R I O R T E X T	CURRENT TEXT	S U B S E Q U E N T T E X T

Fig. 2.5.   Text divisions according to time.

	reader	
← look-back	↓	look-ahead →
RETROSPECTIVE REPRESENTATION OF PRIOR TEXT	PERCEPTION OF CURRENT TEXT	PREDICTIVE REPRESENTATION OF SUBSEQUENT TEXT

Fig. 2.6.   Cognitive divisions of the text and its representations.

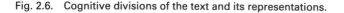

[6]On the various types of linear operations, consult de Beaugrande, 1984a, 1984b. They are all seen as working on all depths, rather like a "bus" that picks up different passengers going the same general direction.

itself (and perhaps with most human experiences) is comparatively brief and subject to the heavy limitations upon short-term sensory storage. If we add the three ranges of memory storage to our scheme, we obtain Fig. 2.7, with working memory gliding in accordance with current load.

There is some evidence that the processes responsible for the encounter with the surface text are at least partly dissociable from those of general understanding. In production, errors occur with the interpolation of sounds or letters in the immediate vicinity (cf. Boomer & Laver, 1968; Fromkin, 1971; MacNeilage, 1964). In reading, miscues demonstrate a comparable effect, as well as more extensive changes that match the text up to one's predictions (cf. Allen & Watson, 1976; Goodman & Burke, 1973). To account for such happenings, we must postulate that short-term sensory storage possesses some executor running very rapidly and projecting only 1 or 2 seconds backward and forward from the point of perception in the text. This executor is error-prone no doubt because it must not only take into account what is being expressed via the text, but also what is necessary in terms of neurological operations such as vision and articulation plus their feedback controls (cf. MacNeilage, 1970; Smith, McCrary, & Smith, 1960). Resource limitations naturally lead to what Norman and Bobrow (1975) call "degradation," where an operating system sacrifices some of its accuracy, and thoroughly for the sake of efficiency.

Where do miscues come from? Sometimes, as in (2), miscues create non-words; whereas in (3), they create perfectly acceptable sequences

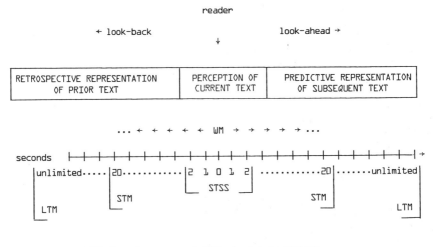

Fig. 2.7.   Cognitive divisions of the text with memory factors.

that just do not happen to be what is written on the page (all samples from Goodman & Burke, 1973, pp. 246f.):

> *queen exmotter*
(2)What a queer experiment

> *he climbed up on it.*
(3)Pulling the kitchen stepladder out into the hall and climbing up on it,

It seems justified to postulate that short-term memory, like short-term sensory storage, also has a predictive as well as a recovering component, but extending up to 20 seconds into the future. This component does not deal with actual sounds or letters of words, but it tries to anticipate the layout of surface structure, as shown in (3). Miscues arise when this anticipation is not synchronized with short-term sensory execution, although self-corrections prove that readers can notice the discrepancy and seek a remedy. However, if one tries with great effort to read without any miscues, comprehension suffers (see section on Dissociation and Reconciliation).

Finally, we can complete the scheme of range with a long-term predictive memory akin to the well-documented long-term retrospective memory. This store has no obvious limits on its range. In return, it is probably not very specific in regard to what the text will talk about. For example, readers have been shown to use large-scale story schemas with slots for actions and outcomes (cf. survey in Norman, 1979; Rumelhart, 1980; Thorndyke & Yekovich, 1980).[7] The schema will not dictate the exact words in which a particular event will be narrated, though, as argued by de Beaugrande and Colby (1979), particular words and phrases may well serve to mark event boundaries and thereby be useful in foreshadowing the story. We thus have the scheme shown in Fig. 2.7, where three ranges of memory have both predictive and retrospective components.

Armed with this much, we can turn to the matter of processing depths. These can be seen as different "levels" upon which a text can be processed, as demonstrable in different modes of comprehension and recall. The "deepest" level should presumably be that of goals: how a discourse fits into someone's intention to attain a goal (cf. Allen, 1979; Austin, 1962; Cohen, 1978; Grice, 1975, 1978; Schank & Abelson, 1977; Searle, 1969). At this depth, a text constitutes one or more "discourse actions" that affect the evolution of the participants' situation: by "in-

---

[7]A measure for "density" could be, for example, the ratio of propositions to words (Kintsch & Keenan, 1973).

forming" them of new material, or by "invoking" known material; by "monitoring" or "managing" the situation itself; and so on. This depth thus relates to the already expanded notions of intentionality, acceptability, and situationality.

Another depth concerns the conveying of ideas, being global configurations of concepts and relations that make up the topic, gist, or theme of a text (cf. van Dijk, 1979; Jones, 1977; Kintsch, 1975; Meyer, 1975). The next depth would be the detailed, developed configurations of concepts and relations along the lines illustrated in Fig. 2.2 through 2.4, with attributes, locations, quantities, and so forth (compare Frederiksen, 1977; Kintsch & van Dijk, 1978; Norman & Rumelhart, 1975; Schank et al., 1975). We thus have two depths for coherence that are distinguished on the grounds that the ideas routinely function in comprehension and recall much more prominently than do detailed concept/relation configurations.

For cohesion, we can identify three steadily shallower levels: syntax (structure of phrases and clauses), words (choice and formation of lexical items), and letters (individual written symbols) or sounds (individual articulated symbols). These three depths are by far the best explored in conventional linguistics, no doubt because they offer the most solid basis for agreement. The surface text itself can be tapped as a representation, whereas researchers will disagree about how to designate and represent concepts, ideas, and goals. However, linguistics has not made much headway on such questions as how these shallow depths are utilized along with deeper ones in continuous, everyday discourse. To describe sentences in an abstract grammar, to list words in a lexicon, or to set up sound repertories for a whole language, are quite distinct activities from explaining the formation and recognition of sentences, words, and sounds/letters in an act such as reading.

We can plot the six depths onto our continuum, thereby obtaining something like Fig. 2.8. This diagram suggests that all depths are at least potentially operating in all three ranges of memory storage, a supposition that requires some defense. Early models of understanding often foresaw sequential stages in which each depth was processed independently and then relayed its final results to the next deeper one (compare Chomsky, 1965; Craik & Lockhart, 1972; Gibson, 1971). In the cognitive science paradigm at least, the consensus is now heavily in favor of parallel stages whose results continually interact (cf. survey in de Beaugrande, 1980–81). That outlook is supported both by experimentally observed behavior (e.g., Marslen-Wilson, 1975) and by the simulation of comprehension (e.g., Walker, 1978; Woods et al., 1976; Woods, 1978). Any single depth is likely to be replete with potential ambiguities and alternatives that can be readily reduced or eliminated by consulting the other depths. For example, the "it" in (1.2), in terms of syntax alone, might refer to "desert" as

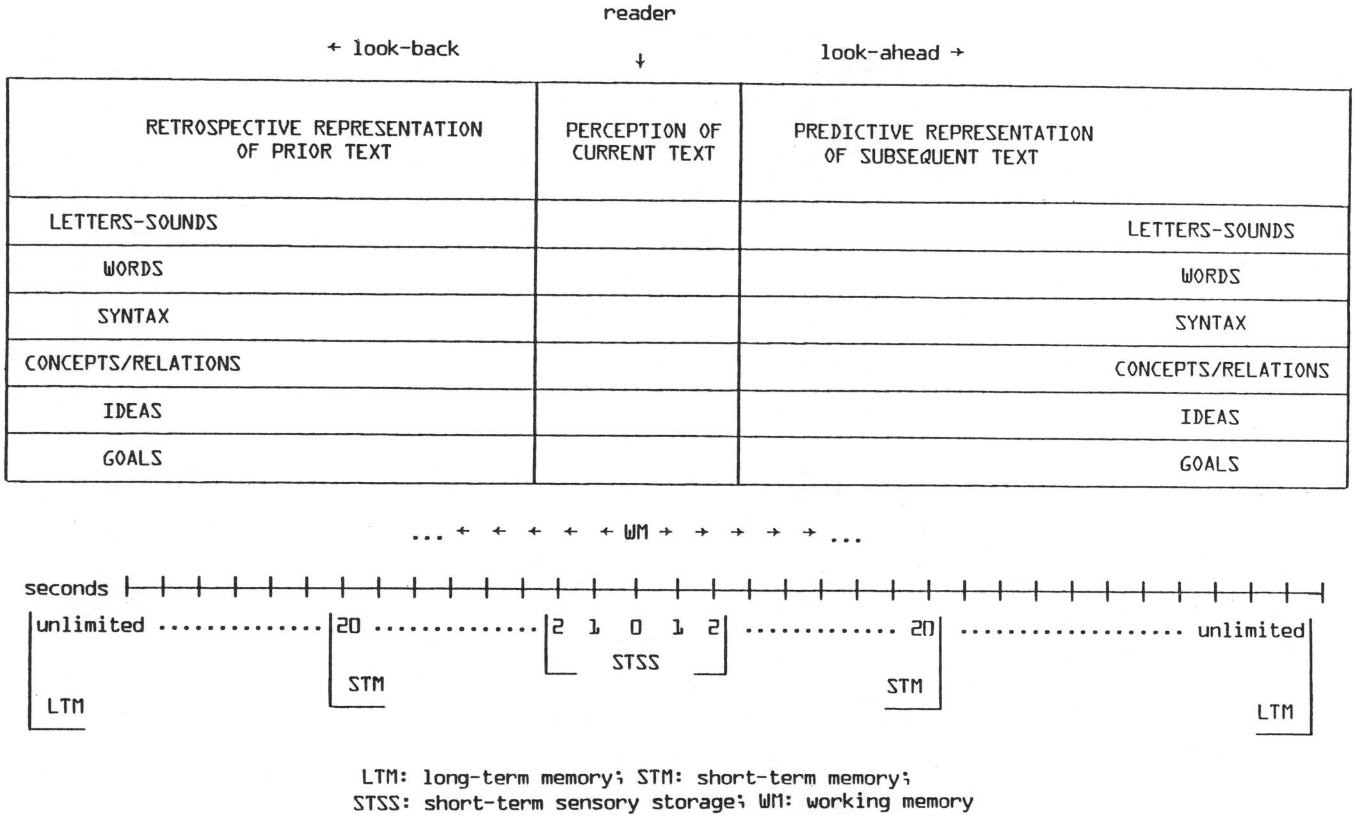

reader

← look-back   ↓   look-ahead →

RETROSPECTIVE REPRESENTATION OF PRIOR TEXT	PERCEPTION OF CURRENT TEXT	PREDICTIVE REPRESENTATION OF SUBSEQUENT TEXT
LETTERS-SOUNDS		LETTERS-SOUNDS
WORDS		WORDS
SYNTAX		SYNTAX
CONCEPTS/RELATIONS		CONCEPTS/RELATIONS
IDEAS		IDEAS
GOALS		GOALS

... ← ← ← ← ← WM → → → → → ...

seconds

unlimited ·········· 20 | STM | 2 | STSS | 2 1 0 1 2 | STSS | 20 ·········· unlimited | STM |

| LTM | | LTM |

LTM: long-term memory; STM: short-term memory;
STSS: short-term sensory storage; WM: working memory

Fig. 2.8. Cognitive divisions of the text with memory and processing depth.

well as "rocket"; but conceptually, it is at once assigned to "rocket," because the weight of a "desert" is hardly likely to be given, and because "rocket" belongs to the main idea of the text, "rocket flight."

There is plenty of evidence that the various depths are not equally prominent in the several types of memory store. In general, short-term sensory storage favors the most shallow levels of sound/letter and word. Long-term memory favors the deepest levels of goal and idea. In short-term memory, the syntactical and conceptual/relational depths are handled in some detail (cf. Johnson-Laird & Stevenson, 1970; Sachs, 1967). To capture these differences, we can use heavy shadings for the prominent depths and sparse ones for shallow depths, thus getting the scheme in Fig. 2.9. The normal trend will be to prefer the prominent depths when allotting cognitive resources. Limitations should be respected at the expense of the non-prominent ones. For example, if you read in a great hurry, you will tend to retain in long-term storage only the general goal and idea of the text, and the details of the surface organization will be lost (cf. Masson, 1979). However, an important factor in what I am calling *"linear intelligence"* is the ability to distribute resources such that limitations do not actually disturb the operations of the various levels beyond a reasonable threshold.

Finally, we must consider the diffuseness of the depths of processing. In the current text, the depths are very closely tied together. As a reader moves further away, either backward or forward in time, the depths become more diffuse. Hence, it becomes steadily harder to render the ideas or concepts/relations in the same surface format that can be found in the text; in contrast, recalling or predicting the exact words just before or after the immediate point of reading is much less taxing. We can represent diffuseness by squeezing together the short-range stores and spreading out the longer-range ones, attaining the final scheme of Fig. 2.10. We can now turn to a survey of evidence that could be construed as support for this on-line model.

OPERATIONAL ASPECTS

Several methods could be applied in weighing the merits of the kind of model seen in Fig. 2.10. First, such a model should capture the operational aspects of an activity such as reading, as determined both by our intuitions and by the findings obtained in simulation or human experiments. Second, it should allow us to dissociate its components by consulting cases where one component behaves differently from the others under specified conditions (cf. Shallice, 1979). Third, it should reconcile a wide range of proposals and findings by being able to account

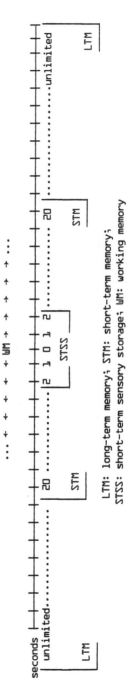

Fig. 2.9.   Cognitive divisions of the text with memory specialized to depths.

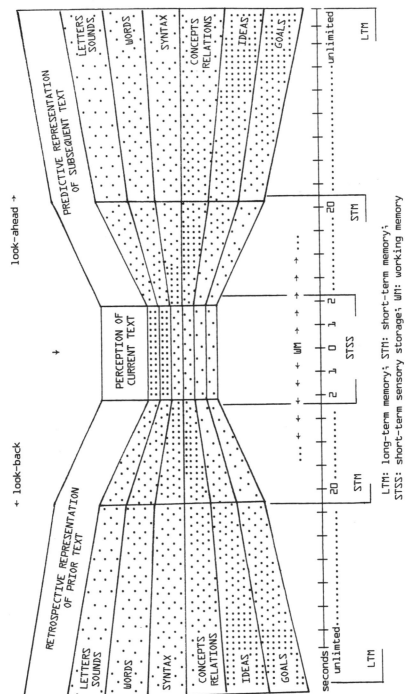

LTM: long-term memory; STM: short-term memory;
STSS: short-term sensory storage; WM: working memory

Fig. 2.10.   Cognitive divisions of the text according to diffuseness.

for the diverse occasions established by prior research at least as well as the theories or models of that time (cf. Estes, 1979; Tulving, 1979). Whether such a model could be conclusively "proven" by tests that set it apart from every other possible model seems arduous and doubtful, at least with the current methods of demonstration. At best, we could hope for an eventual clarification of the anomalies that simpler models fail to address or predict and for a reasonably good fit to the obtainable data of both everyday and laboratory observations.

In the operational perspective, several factors deserve consideration. We know that resources are indeed limited, but that reading normally runs fairly well despite the obvious complexity of the act. We also know that different texts present different degrees of difficulty and that different reader groups react in characteristic ways on this count. The "readability" of texts has been analyzed over and over, but nearly all "formulas" address the shallow levels of words and syntax, ignoring the deeper ones (cf. surveys in Klare, 1963, 1974–1975; critiques in Kintsch & Vipond, 1979; Rothkopf, 1976). Plainly, any realistic model of reading demands both unity and flexibility to capture such differences within one general framework.

If we view the text as an actual system, then the processes of producing or understanding the text must have a systemic character, i.e., there must be a powerful organization that assigns functions strategically. I have argued that the cybernetic system that organizes and regulates itself is a useful analogy (de Beaugrande, 1980; cf. Schweizer, 1979). The various demands that the reader must meet and juggle are all fed into some central control that is responsible for scheduling operations (i.e., determining order) and for allotting resources. Some processes can be done simultaneously, whereas others run successively (cf. Das, Kirby, & Jarman, 1979). The more difficult an operation is, the less suited it becomes for being carried out at the same time with any others.

The various degrees of difficulty that a particular reader might experience for a given text can thus be envisioned in terms of the loading that the system shown in Fig. 2.10 must support. All factors that contribute to greater exertion—such as informativity, salience, or density[8]—can accordingly be subsumed under the notion of "heaviness" (cf. de Beaugrande, 1984a, 1984b). The fact that everyday reading involves miscues and inaccurate recall suggests that reading operates at a rather heavy load, such that overloading is never very far away. It is the task of linear intelligence to reduce overloading and to combat its more serious effects.

---

[8]Levy (1977) found that articulatory interference (a counting task) affects the retention of sentences when presented visually, but not acoustically. Apparently, readers can recode from visual to acoustic, but if necessary, can also bypass this step (cf. also Posner, 1978).

The "graceful degradation" noted by Norman and Bobrow (1975) is a good illustration: The system does not just fall apart or break down, but rather accepts certain thresholds of approximation or error that do not seriously damage the effectuality of processing. For example, people pressed for time can get a good idea of the gist by skim-reading (Masson, 1979), and the major purpose of the communication is upheld. If they concentrated on surface details, or selected words at random, the purpose would be defeated.

The dimension of time is thus a key factor. It was argued previously that the encounter with the surface text is of very brief duration, just a second or two behind or ahead of the point where the eye is focused; all the rest must be handled in memory storage alone. It follows that the readability of a text results from the nature of the demands that its organization imposes on memory. The familiarity of words should affect the speed with which their underlying concepts are activated. The complexity of clauses should decide the load that the depth of syntax places on short-term memory. The organization at the depth of ideas decides how the major concepts are kept active or else "reinstated" as the text unfolds (Kintsch & Vipond, 1979, p. 348).

The use of "reading time" as a dependent variable in so many experiments reflects the belief that difficult tasks must be done more slowly. But the reasons why this should be so are still poorly explained. On many tasks, simple practice brings a direct increase in speed; presumably, the repetition gives the processor a chance to test various ways of scheduling and resource allotment and eventually settle on an advantageous one. The "resource limitations" imposed by processing contingencies rather than by the nature of the materials ("data"), as postulated by Norman and Bobrow (1975), can thereby be reduced. An important and plausible contributor to the improvement is the rescheduling of successive processes as simultaneous ones: as strategic routines develop, the drain on resources decreases to the point where a given activity can be done along with others. In the sense of LaBerge and Samuels (1974), the activity becomes automatic and no longer draws away one's attention (cf. also Posner & Snyder, 1975). However, if a reader finds the text unusually difficult—even the best of us have trouble, say, with *Finnegan's Wake*—then processes would be re-scheduled back to successive operation, and reading time increases. Luria (1972) shows that a patient with severe aphasia carried this effect to a startling extreme.

Eye movement studies indicate that there is a pause principle of great impact upon reading. Carpenter and Just (1977, p. 110) distinguish between "fixations" (the eye at rest) and "saccades" (the eye in motion), with the former taking some 90% of the total time of reading. They survey the experimental findings that suggest "a relation between eye fixations and the underlying comprehension processes": selective fixation on pronoun referents, and intense fixation on words that trigger inferences or help to sort out old versus new knowledge (p. 136). They also note the intriguing fact that comprehension is not greatly altered if readers are prevented from looking back at the prior text—lending support to my assumption that a memory representation readily supplants the surface text as a point of orientation.

My own experiments with filmed writing (de Beaugrande, 1984a) indicate that production pauses reflect activities at all depths, and look backward as well as forward. One motive for believing that the mental representation rather than the surface text serves for orientation is the inefficiency that the latter would entail. To look back over the text in search of the referent of a pronoun, for example, would be very clumsy: One would have to read over a large number of words that are not likely candidates at all. Unless one reads backwards, which seems a bit odd, one would have to keep jumping from one place to another, scanning clauses all over again that were comprehended before. Carpenter and Just (1977) were able to demonstrate that referent search is in fact highly selective, zeroing in on the nouns that were most reasonable candidates. In our sample (1.2), the "it" can readily be related to "rocket" because the latter activates the topic concept.

The surface text also is not suitable because it favors shallow depths—because it decays rather rapidly from short-term storage—and because it is not available for look-ahead very far. Consequently, we may assume that reading (along with other processes of cognition and communication) does not rely directly on the surface presentation except during the brief ascendancy of short-term sensory storage. The mental representation which supplants it otherwise ought to have a format fitting for its uses. The network as a pattern of access from one state to the next, with directions for passing control (shown by arrows in Fig. 2.1 through 2.4), therefore might be a much closer rendition of that representation. For example, the topic node would be immediately obvious because it has the largest number of pathways going in and out. When a "reinstatement" must be done, the processor would easily zoom in on these conspicuous nodes as those most likely to be needed. The "leading edge" strategy described by Kintsch and Vipond (1979, pp. 347ff.) favors "superordination" (where the dominant node is sought directly) and "recency" (where the search follows the shortest pathways in the immediately accruing network—not in the actual sequence of printed words!).

The question should then be whether there is a single, multi-purpose network for all depths, or a separate one for each. If we accept the plausibility of parallel processing, a set of separate networks hardly seems reasonable. On the other hand, a single network would ignore the many ways in which the patterns of the various depths are not identical. There is the factor of asymmetry: different ways of pursuing a goal, developing an idea, expressing a concept. Similarly, redundancy enters wherever a selected element of a deeper level is realized by several elements (each of which would be sufficient as a signal) on a shallower one (de Beaugrande, 1980, p. 208). No doubt the whole system can reduce overload not just by rescheduling and pausing but also by increasing redundancy. Therefore, we would not want to postulate a fixed network that gives the same patterning to all depths.

The best solution, I believe, is the one worked out in the "cascading networks" of Woods (1978) and co-workers. There are networks for each of the depths, but they are all built interactively, consulting each other's results and—of crucial importance here—combining the operations whenever the configurational pattern of two or more depths would look much the same. Thus, the similarity between the graphs for cohesion (Fig. 2.1) and coherence (Fig. 2.2) can lead to important savings in on-line processing (cf. also Bobrow, 1978). The full representation for text processing would be an inordinately intricate graph with cascading networks passing control impulses to each other's strategic nodes. Fig. 2.11 shows what such a graph could look like just for the short stretch "A rocket stood in a desert." For the whole "rocket"-text, the graph would be alarmingly cumbersome, but probably still too simple for the true complexity of reading. For one thing, these networks arise and fade at different rates, and may be simplified or rearranged to offset overloading. Apparently, nodes or pathways that decay (or are never set up in the first place) are easily supplanted by others, so that impression of cohesion and coherence is preserved even for highly inaccurate recall (de Beaugrande, 1980, pp. 234–240). Here again, the self-regulating nature of the text-system is revealed. On the other hand, if an access route is cut off, then whatever was connected to it will not be recoverable (unless special inferences are able to bridge the gap; Kintsch & Vipond, 1979, p. 356). This effect explains why cued recall routinely gives more complete results than free recall; a point of entry into a sub-graph is provided in the former case. A real-life example is the way stage actors can remember a forgotten line just from being prompted with the first word or so.

The requirements of navigating in a network suggest the need for a "core-and-adjunct principle" (de Beaugrande, 1984a, 1984b). This function establishes the control centers from which access can be set up for peripheral elements. On the depth of syntax, the core could be the head of a noun or verb phrase, and the modifiers the adjuncts; or the core could be the main clause, and the adjuncts the dependent clause. On the depth of concept/relation, the cores would usually be events, actions, objects, or situations, whereas adjuncts could be locations, causes, times. On the

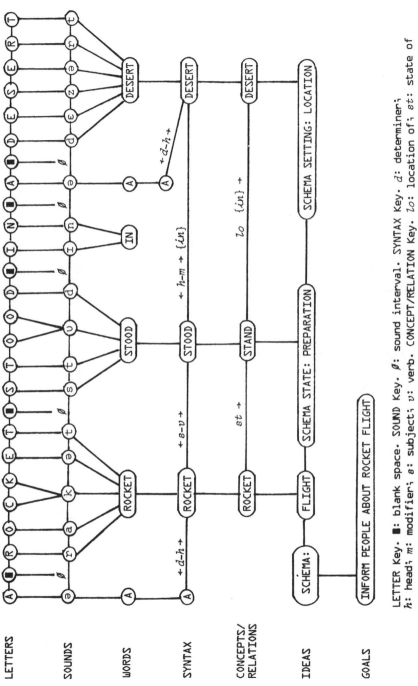

Fig. 2.11. Cascading networks for processing depths of a sentence.

LETTER Key. ■: blank space. SOUND Key. ∅: sound interval. SYNTAX Key. *d*: determiner; *h*: head; *m*: modifier; *s*: subject; *v*: verb. CONCEPT/RELATION Key. *lo*: location of; *st*: state of

depth of goals, the core might be the main goal and the adjuncts the plan steps that create necessary preconditions. Load can be reduced by sacrificing adjunts, especially in surface structure (cf. O'Regan, 1975; Schank, Lebowitz, & Birnbaum, 1978); forgetting should also favor them (e.g., many readers forgot that the "rocket" of (1.1) was "black and yellow").

The importance of cores in reading comprehension was noted by Fillmore (1977) for sentences like:

(4a) I smeared the wall with paint.
(4b) I smeared paint on the wall.

The implication that the whole wall was covered is strong only in (4a) because the word "wall" is given the core-slot of direct object, whereas in (4b), it figures as a prepositional phrase adjunct. The lines from Krishnamurti's poem *The Spirit's Odyssey* depicting the moment of encountering a "sudden truth" run this way:

(5a) Now fierce and sudden-truth'd/ She smites me, sabre-tooth'd:/
      As sunlight, snarling, crawls/ Into the bower and mauls/
      The waker, slumber-sooth'd.

A group of students were persistently unable to interpret the lines until I gave them a version in which the "sudden truth" was expressed in core, not adjunct format:

(5b) Her fiercely sudden truth/ Now smites me sabre-tooth'd

Apparently, the adjunct "sudden-truth'd" was ignored as a key for the interpretation.

Our scheme in Fig. 2.10 expressly suggested that the load of reading is prone to stretch the resource capacities of the processing system. This factor might explain why two readers of a text (or the same reader for two different texts) might well behave in dissimilar ways, depending on prior knowledge, skill level, interest, and available time or attention. Thus, any model of reading should allow considerable freedom for individual variation. The researchers whose models are compared in de Beaugrande (1980–1981) agreed on this point, but a clarification of the factors involved is only just beginning, e.g., reader age (Meyer & Rice, 1980).

The ultimate question is how reading might be improved; among the various ways of reading a text, not all can be equally effectual. Skilled readers are evidently able to navigate complex or poorly organized texts without severe impairment of understanding, whereas many others reveal symptoms of overloading, disorientation, and low recall. Such problems could be attacked either by better educational training in reading or by improving the readability of the texts themselves (Bormuth, 1975). Readability formulas usually consider only very shallow depths (word and syntax), whereas the entire memory load must in fact be considered. Specifically, we need to explore the ways in which that load might be either reduced or else redistributed. Many children's texts reflect the belief that a simple reduction is the key: short, simple words and sentences, trivial concepts and ideas, and so on, are the order of the day. Paradoxically, however, there is a threshold where reading ease also causes degradation because attention falters for lack of interest. This trade-off is apparently built into the human processing system as a self-regulatory feature.

Therefore, much greater care should be directed to the possibility of redistributing rather than just reducing the reader's load. What should be eliminated is not the expenditure of effort, but only the needless or wasteful expenditure. A case in point is the trend toward nominalization as a tactic for seeming formal and impressive in one's written style (cf. critique in Flesch, 1972; Halliday, 1967). Passages like these are pointlessly hard to read (from Halliday, 1967, pp. 8, 10):

(6) main burner oil feed adjustment cover retaining screw
(7) police drink test tables review
(8) tourist holiday coach death crash enquiry verdict appeal decision sensation

The reason is that the core-adjunct principle has been set aside on the depth of syntax, throwing an unusual strain onto that of concept/relation. Compare the more readable version of (6):

(9) This screw retains the cover on the mechanism that adjusts oil feed into the main burner.

But note than an undue simplification soon becomes less readable:

(10) This screw retains a cover. The cover is located over a mechanism. That device adjusts oil flow. The main burner receives this flow.

Obviously, an increase in redundancy improves readability only if it is strategically correlated with a degree of informativity that maintains attention. In (9), the reading load is less than (6) because of the redistribution within the depth of syntax, following the core-adjunct principle. In (10), any such gain is offset by the overall loss of attention that a boring presentation will elicit. Many children's books overlook this danger.

Ambiguities, such as are noticeable in (7), are another case of needless loading. The interaction of various depths eliminates many possible ambiguities of the kind linguists are fond of inventing in order to support transformational theories, e.g.,

(11) Lecturing grammarians can be utterly useless.

What readers do here is not to "transform" the passage into its "syntactic deep structures," but to consult the deeper levels (concept/relation, idea, goal) to decide which reading is most plausible: who's saying what to whom, and why. There must be a "disambiguation principle" in discourse processing that specializes in removing such obstacles because they increase processing load without any communicative benefits (unless intended for puns, jokes). The need to distribute resources over multiple readings dilutes the ability to address any one. The ensuing disturbance can on occasion be observed experimentally (MacKay, 1966).

Non-parallelism is also an unnecessary obstacle. Casually written texts are replete with passages like these (from my students' papers):

(12) People fall into two groups: the workers and those who depend on others.
(13) Congressional leaders couldn't decide whether to increase American involvement or if they should withdraw.

Processing is wasted because different formats on the depth of syntax conceal the similar organization on the depth of concept/relation. A reader has to make a new parsing, whereas in parallel versions, the same parsing could be reused at once, while still in short-term memory:

(14) People fall into two groups: those who work and those who depend on others.
(15) Congressional leaders couldn't decide whether to increase American involvement or to withdraw.

Note that the old readability formulas miss this kind of distinction: (14) would be judged less readable for being longer and more complex than (12). Yet aside from syntax, (12) is misleading in that "workers" suggests a class of people, rather than the action that should be in focus; (13) creates a needless obscurity about who "they" might be (probably not the "leaders," but the "Americans" who are "involved" abroad).

One major source of low readability in texts is easy to uncover. There is a trade-off between the effort exerted by a writer and that demanded of a reader. The producers of (12) and (13) were respecting only their own convenience by short-sighted formatting, seizing on commonplace phrasing ("workers," "American involvement"). They did not consider the audience's effort or take the trouble to revise. Indeed, the model in Fig. 2.10 would predict that proofreading one's own texts is likely to be ineffectual. Either the deepest levels are already clearly stored in memory, in which case nominalizations, ambiguities, and non-parallelism appear to present no obstacles at all. Or else the deepest levels are not yet clearly organized, in which case they drain resources away from the shallow ones and impede proper care toward the surface text. It follows that writing skills can improve only if training in specialized proofreading methods is also provided (cf. de Beaugrande, 1985c for applications).

DISSOCIATION AND RECONCILIATION

Earlier, I remarked that the model shown in Fig. 2.10 could be supported in three ways. So far, we have looked at some operational aspects that seem at least intuitively necessary, e.g., scheduling, resource allotment, load, time, pausing, redundancy, and obstacles. The model suggests that reading skill and readability hinge crucially on these aspects, because overloading is imminent and wasted effort is therefore costly.

Taking another tack, we should inquire whether the components of the model can be identified as individually necessary, as compared to the simpler models that did not make so many distinctions in the past. In older linguistics, for example, the term "sentence" was used rather indiscriminately for a grammatical format, an utterance, an assertion, a proposition, a speech-act, and so on (cf. de Beaugrande, 1980, pp. 10–16; O'Connell, 1977). In this manner, a purely grammatical approach could be misconstrued as an account of language as a whole, at least for a while.

Shallice (1979) meets the denials from the depth-of-processing camp against different-range memory stores by means of dissociation. If variations can be observed for operation A but not for operation B—if a task or a specific test group is exchanged—then the two operations cannot be identical. For example, there could be two classes of aphasics, one whose performance is impaired only for A, the other only for B. The capacities of short-term memory can indeed be dissociated from those of long-term memory, as Shallice demonstrates.

If we postulate a reading model with varied ranges and depths, we need to show that its components can be, under stated conditions, independently affected. Some experimental literature can be used here, even though it was not gathered for the model advocated in this chapter. Beginning at the shallow end, we need to dissociate the depth of letters/sounds from that of words. After all, letters or sounds do not normally confront communicative participants except in words, so that the motives for setting up distinct processing depths might be denied. One class of evidence bearing on the point concerns the perception of letters versus words. There is a clear superiority of letters in words over letters in non-word strings, both in perception (Miller, Bruner, & Postman, 1954; cf. Norman, 1979) and in recognition (Reicher, 1969). Reicher's study in fact indicates that perception for every single letter inside a word is better than for only one isolated letter. This knowledge applies both to the position of a letter in an array and to the relative ordering of letters (cf. Estes, 1975; Johnston & McClelland, 1973; Rumelhart & Siple, 1974). However, these effects seem to depend on presenting a visual mask (a different, confusing array) immediately after the target array (McClelland, 1976); the mask cancels short-term sensory stores enough that the word-format is crucially in demand as a guideline. Also, if readers are placed under great time pressure, they evidently switch to a shallower depth where isolated letters fare better than those in words (Polf, 1976).

I have noted the emerging consensus that language processing on various depths runs in parallel rather than in a discrete sequence of stages. This outlook is quite plausible for the two depths of sound/letter versus word (cf. especially Posner, 1978). Thus, readers can and normally do use word knowledge actively in recognizing letters, unless, as in Polf's (1976) study, their resources are drastically cut down. Experiments on speech perception suggest that word knowledge renders comprehension fairly impervious against disturbances due to missing sounds (Warren, 1970) or mispronunciation (Marslen-Wilson & Welsh, 1978); in exchange, hearers may misperceive words through relying on their own constructions (Bond & Garnes, 1980). The depths of syntax and concept/relation also play a role: larger contexts aid perception more than briefer ones (Pollack & Pickett, 1964); meaningful and/or grammatical contexts are more helpful than nonsensical and/or ungrammatical ones (Miller & Isard, 1963). These effects obtain also for the presentation of written texts (Tulving, Mandler, & Baumal, 1964).

It might be justified to subdivide the shallowest depth into two: a very shallow one for visual processing of letters, and a less shallow one for recoding the letters into some sound-based representation (cf. Gough, 1972; Posner, 1978, pp. 76ff.). The interactions of these two possible depths with the depth of the word might be distinctive. For example, Foss, Harwood, and Blank (1980) suggest that words are first looked up and then used to identify phonemes, but that under certain conditions, that identification could run instead directly from a very shallow perception unaffected by meaning. Also, some simulations of language comprehension (e.g., Reddy, Erman, Fennell, & Neely, 1973) foresee a division between visual and acoustic/phonetic processing. On the other hand, the recognition and recall of words does not seem to depend significantly on whether the visual or acoustic presentation is used (Bray & Batchelder, 1972; Hintzman, Block, & Inskeep, 1972; Kintsch, Kozminsky, Streby, McKoon, & Keenan, 1975). Therefore, the impact of the surface mode of the input upon issues like readability or learning may not be of great import.

Dissociating the word depth from the syntax depth is easy, thanks to the wealth of syntactic studies contributed by psycholinguistics. In general, the utilization of a word in comprehension reflects its syntactic status in the processing of clauses and sentences (e.g., Kimball, 1973). Words appearing in the latest clause or sentence are favored over earlier ones both in recall (Jarvella, 1970, 1971) and recognition (Caplan, 1972). More words can be remembered if sentences are presented rather than mere word lists (cf. Marks & Miller, 1964)—the same dissociation already noted between letters in words versus non-words. Reading can be facilitated by placing each constituent in a visually separate space (Graf & Torrey, 1966). Probe-response word pairs fair better in tests where they have been presented within the same constituent (Ammon, 1968). In all these findings, the impact of syntax over that of mere word processing is quite plain.

The dissociation of the depth of syntax from that of concept/relation was for some time obscured by an enormous over-estimation of the role of syntax in language processing, a view inherited from the predominantly syntactic studies of linguistics at the time. The tendency was to suppose that meaning was added as an after-the-fact "interpretation," and that the central operations addressed syntactic structure. In practice, however, the meaning or propositional content was simply treated as identical with the syntax—hence the term *sentence comprehension* instead of the more precise term *comprehension of propositions underlying sentences* (or any other surface unit). This conflation is no less rampant in philosophical discussions. It is a natural confusion, considering that propositions are normally presented, both to the researcher and to the normal human being, as sentence-like expressions.

The already cited experiment of Miller and Isard (1963) indicated the superior memory for meaningful sequences over syntactically normal but meaningless ones. Readers will notice changes in the meaning of what they have read but not in the syntactic format (Bransford, Barclay, & Franks, 1972; Sachs, 1967). The reliability of memory for syntax decays much faster than that for concept/relation (Begg & Wicklegren, 1974; Garrod & Trabasso, 1973; cf. Anderson, 1974). Skill in recognizing exact wording seems unrelated to conceptual/relational comprehension (Begg, 1971). Aphasics with short-term memory deficits can paraphrase sentences they cannot repeat (Saffran & Marin, 1975).

The dissociation of concept/relation from word also is a troublesome issue, because concepts so rapidly bring words to mind. However, Kintsch and Keenan (1973) found that reading time varies according to the number of underlying propositions rather than to the number of words in a text. Moreover, the conceptual/relational organization of a text contains a fair amount that was not expressed in words, but supplied by inferencing. And mental imagery certainly does not have to be organized in words (Paivio, 1975), yet figures prominently in conceptual understanding. The problem here is not whether words and concepts should be dissociated, but rather how to represent concepts independently of words. So far, most proposals involve something like "primitives" that are concepts of special status; they constitute the basic meaningfulness of more complex concepts (e.g., Lehnert, 1978; Schank et al., 1975; Wilks, 1977), but they too must be named with words. Thus, the best solution may be to retain the words of a text within our models of reading, but to bear in mind their different status as concept names, rather than surface occurrences with a sound/letter aspect.

The concept/relation depth can be dissociated from the depth of ideas in at least two ways. First, the superiority of recall for main ideas over the configuration of concepts and relations is well documented (e.g., Kintsch, 1974; Meyer, 1975). The more time that elapses after reading, the more pronounced this effect becomes (Kintsch & van Dijk, 1978). If two texts have the same number both of words and propositions, the one whose conceptual organization is centered around a few main ideas takes less reading time than one with many minor ideas (Kintsch et al., 1975). The second line of argument is that aphasics can lose control over one depth, but not the other. Luria (1979, pp. 284–287) describes how one patient recalled the main ideas of the story but replaced the detailed content, whereas another recalled detailed content but could not remember the main ideas—this finding was traced back to different locations of brain tumors.

Finally, the relationship of the planning depth to the other depths needs defining. In one perspective, it is intuitively plain enough that one's actions, intentions, and goals are not identical with either the form or the meaning of what one says, writes, reads, or hears. A well-known illustration is found in the "conversational implicatures" explored by Grice (1975, 1978); and, for well-defined situations, in the distinction between the "propositional" aspect of a message and its "illocutionary" and "perlocutionary" aspects (cf. Austin, 1962; Searle, 1969). Schweller, Brewer, and Dahl (1976) found that people can remember the "illocutionary" and "perlocutionary" aspects of an utterance as an action with an effect, even after forgetting the content. Spiro (1977) showed how beliefs and motives led readers to convert a story over some weeks. But, as Spiro himself remarked, laboratory studies that take people's attitudes and goals into account are regrettably rare. If, as I am suggesting, the "pragmatic" level is the deepest, then such an omission gravely limits our insight into the dynamics of communicative processes.

In another perspective, the control and operations of all depths can be seen as goal-oriented actions. The writer and reader plan out the message, and cohesion and coherence are maintained only by means of appropriate mental acts, including the intending and accepting of communicative standards. This perspective is too broadly inclusive to be very helpful, except as a corrective measure against the conventional linguistic tendency to view language (words, grammars, sentences) as timeless objects with independent existence (cf. critique in Morgan, 1975), thereby ignoring many vital questions about cognition and communication. The first perspective in which plans and goals reasonably can be dissociated from other depths therefore seems preferable.

Having looked at some evidence indicating that the depths of the model in Fig. 2.10 can have some operational identity of their own under certain conditions, we should now consider whether the model can be reconciled with alternative models of simpler design. For example, earlier research implied that each type of memory storage was specialized for a single scope: short-term sensory storage for sounds and letters, short-term memory for syntax, and long-term memory for meaning. We would then have a straightforward design such as that suggested in Fig. 2.12. The passage of time would only lead to a transfer from one distinctive storage plus depth to another. However, this design cannot accommodate the findings that sensory perception does have some immediate access to meaning (e.g., Raser, 1972; Shulman, 1970). For example, dyslexics have more difficulty reading abstract than concrete words, independent of word frequency or spelling regularity (Marshall & Newcombe, 1973; Shallice & Warrington, 1975). In the "Stroop" effect, identifying print color is confounded if the word is the name of a different color (Dyer,

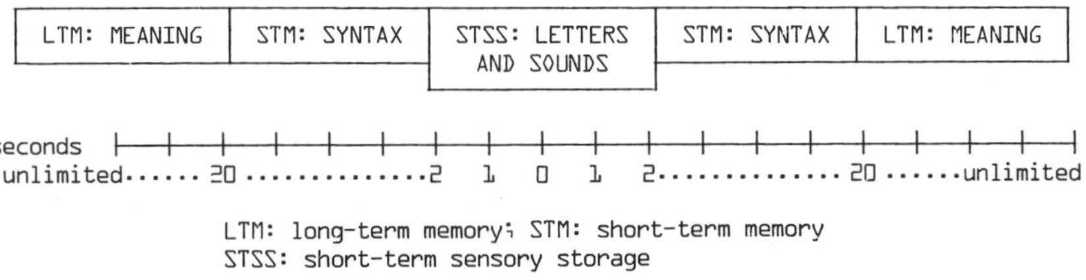

LTM: MEANING	STM: SYNTAX	STSS: LETTERS AND SOUNDS	STM: SYNTAX	LTM: MEANING

```
seconds   |—+—+—+—+—+—+—+—+—+—+—+—+—+—+—+—+—+—|
unlimited...... 20 .............2  1  0  1  2............. 20 ......unlimited
```

LTM: long-term memory; STM: short-term memory
STSS: short-term sensory storage

Fig. 2.12. A simplified model of memory specialization.

1973). In all these cases, readers must be contacting the concept/relation depth almost at the very instant of the visual encounter with the surface text. Erdelyi's (1974) study of "perceptual defense" (where objectionable words are simply rejected before reading them) points, moreover, to an immediate access to the depth of goals. It is clearly possible, therefore, that very shallow depths can consult very deep ones without having to pass through a fixed pathway from shallow to deep (cf. Craik & Lockhart, 1972) or from earlier to later in an item list (cf. Waugh & Norman, 1965) or a rehearsal schedule (cf. Atkinson & Shiffrin, 1968).

Similarly, long-term memory is not exclusively devoted to the deepest levels. In the already cited studies of visual versus acoustic presentation in list learning (Bray & Batchelder, 1972; Hintzman, Block, & Inskeep, 1972), people could remember for up to 15 minutes (long after short-term storage would have decayed) which modality the surface of the language items had possessed, even though modality did not affect capacities for recognition or recall; it made no difference whether or not people were warned to attend to modality or not. Verbatim recall of a passage, though certainly not the rule, can be attained over considerable periods of time (cf. Kintsch, 1974, pp. 257ff.). We might assume that what seems to be direct verbatim recall is in fact a reconstruction working back from a deeper representation, especially when there are very few possible expressions for the concepts involved, e.g., "black and yellow rocket" (which was so often reported by readers of the "rocket" sample (1.1). But Kintsch (personal communication, July, 1978) points out that not all memory for surface features can be explained in this way.

It seems safe, in view of these various findings, to reject the simple model of specialized stores for each depth as shown in Fig. 2.12 in favor of the gradated model already shown in Fig. 2.10. Short-term sensory storage favors shallow depths, and long-term memory favors deeper ones; but other depths appear to be represented at both ends in reduced capacities (Kintsch, 1974, p. 98; cf. Shallice, 1975). Those capacities can be markedly altered by a special assignment of resources, notably of time and attention. For example, memorizing the surface text is not impossible if the reader is willing to expend vastly increased effort—the impulse to do so must come from the depth of goals (e.g., one must carry out a school assignment; one needs to repeat someone's exact words in a later situation).

In this connection, the effects of rehearsal can be reconciled with the model under consideration. It is striking that rehearsal improves recognition of items, but not recall (i.e., not if test persons have to supply a memory record without re-encountering what they saw or heard; cf. Kintsch, 1970; McCormack, 1972; Woodward, Bjork, & Jongewald, 1973). The behaviorist tenet that simple frequency controls learning has yielded to the view that the organizing processes performed on rehearsed materials are the crucial factor (cf. Dark & Loftus, 1976; Darley & Glass, 1975; Hogan & Kintsch, 1970; Mandler, 1979). Yet these and other researchers still disagree about the nature of those processes. Craik and Tulving (1975) suggested that repetition aids learning if done on deeper levels. Mandler (1979) has for some time categorized rehearsal according to whether it improves internal organization of the material ("integration") or whether it enriches the external context ("elaboration"). These views, like a number of others, pose grave difficulties for finding experimental proof.

In a typical recognition test, some distractor words are conceptually related to the correct ones (e.g., Underwood & Freund, 1968). Obviously, a person needs to direct unusually great attention to the shallowest levels, so that synonyms, for example, will not be mistaken for previously encountered words (cf. Anisfeld & Knapp, 1968). That attention can be freed partly because the deepest levels of idea and goal are scarcely being tapped in any way comparable to real-life discourse. One benefit is seen in the enormous numbers of words people can recognize even after one exposure (Shepard, 1967). With repetitive rehearsal, this effect is intensified as the deep levels become steadily less relevant, and informativity drops. Thus, there is a particularly good pathway for shallow depths to enter long-term memory.

In a recall test, on the other hand, these shallow levels are far less helpful, because they are very cumbersome for purposes of chunking. One could sort a word list according to whether items are long or short, nouns or verbs, and still end up with categories too vague to be supportive of memory; the same applies to classifying sentences according to their surface structure. The deeper levels, in contrast, are vastly better for chunking; a list organized into conceptual categories is thus much easier to recall, but hardly easier to recognize (Kintsch, 1968). If the effects described previously are true, then rehearsal can not be expected to improve recall, because of the reduction in deeper level processing. That defect can be offset only if deeper organizational strategies, such as depicted by Mandler (1979), can find effectual chunking methods in the alloted time. There is nothing built into simple repetition that compels any such thing to happen. Recall would be better served if the effort were spent instead on relating the materials to a context (cf. Anderson & Reder, 1978; Thomson, 1972).

The dimension of trace abstraction, construction, and reconstruction deserves mention here. The entry of traces from the actual presentation into long-term memory is by no means excluded from the multi-level, multi-store model advocated in this chapter, but cannot assume the dominance assigned to it by researchers like Gibson (1971). Readers tend to focus more heavily on traces in the laboratory setting, yielding a disproportionate picture (Spiro, 1975); rehearsal should intensify that trend still more. But the deeper levels—even syntax (see literature on missing or distorted sounds)—are still treated constructively, because that is the condition of textuality. This same activity is again carried out during recall, giving us a "re-construction" that cannot be divorced from text production (cf. de Beaugrande, 1984a). Whether the outcome is an accurate version of the original depends on the relationship of its deep-level content to what readers already know, and what they may have learned in the interim since they read the text (Spiro, 1977, p. 139).[9]

An intriguing case is found when readers are given a chance to peruse the text again and yet do not profit thereby. Kay's (1955) readers stuck to their own, often inaccurate versions, and the opportunity to study the materials again went unused. One study of mine suggested that mental imagery is a powerful force (de Beaugrande, 1984a, pp. 137–138). Students read and studied a text (without time pressure) in which a New England scene was depicted. I then asked them for visual details, most of which had not been specified in the text (e.g., what a house or a room looked like, how tall the trees were). They responded at once, and with surprising agreement (e.g., over 90% averred that the trees were much taller than the house, though the text said nothing of the kind). More striking yet was the treatment of the "red brick schoolhouse" mentioned in the text. One made it "white," and a few changed it into "wood"; other readers made the hero's house, the general store, even the barn out of brick, for which there was no authority—and all the while, the text was sitting under their noses for free consultation! Such results lend support to the already voiced assertion that readers rely on their mental representation most of the time, apart from a brief encounter with the surface text. That representation obviously includes an image component. Thus, the distinction between "traces" and "constructions" (or "reconstructions") seems hardly sensible if we take the text alone as our point of departure.

For some years, researchers have recognized a distinction between episodic memory ("what happened to me") and semantic or conceptual memory ("what I know about the world and how it all fits together") (Kintsch, 1980; Ortony, 1975; Rumelhart, 1977a; Tulving, 1972). Kintsch (1977, p. 284) notes that psychological experiments are heavily concentrated on episodic memory. His remark holds best for tests involving recognition and trace abstraction; recall and construction depend on conceptual memory for the discovery of organizational patterns (e.g., for purposes of chunking content around the main ideas). Indeed, without

---

[9]A network designated a "world-knowledge correlate" is proposed for representing this matter (de Beaugrande, 1980, pp. 99ff.), but empirical support is still lacking.

conceptual memory, the episodes of our experience would in general not make much sense to us. It therefore does not appear justified to equate shallow-level processing with episodic, and deep-level processing with conceptual memory. Both personal experience and overall world knowledge are involved at every level of understanding, in accord with the factor of intertextuality: reading a text presupposes both experience with other texts and some kind of systematic generalizations about the nature and purpose of texts. The virtual system for each depth—the alphabet, the phoneme inventory, the lexicon of words, the typology of sentence formats, the catalogue of common situations or goals—enters conceptual memory via episodic memory in a transfer that never ceases as long as the reader learns by reading. Conversely, expectations drawn from conceptual memory heavily determine one's outlook on any specific episode; this effect is especially likely in very rich systems of significance, such as reading.

Along another dimension, one might want to reduce a model of reading to the distinction between attentional and automatic processing. Both kinds are plainly involved in reading (LaBerge & Samuels, 1974). However, such an approach would in effect give us no model at all, because the threshold involved can be reset for any particular occasion of reading (Keele & Posner, personal communications, 1981). Automatic processing is by no means restricted to very shallow levels. Rather, the predictable, routine activities on all levels are good candidates for automaticity. Attention is prone to address whatever seems novel, informative, difficult, or problematic, regardless of level—bizzare misspellings, rare words, displaced syntax, odd groupings of concepts or ideas, and mysterious plans or goals, will all draw attention. Of course, these classifications depend on the reader's own experience and world-knowledge, on the text type (e.g., science fiction versus science textbook), situational setting (e.g., religious sermon vs. courtroom testimony), and so forth. These confounding factors make it very hard to isolate attentional processing from automatic in direct experimentation.

Ideally, a reader should focus attention on what matters most. In part, that postulate is carried out to the degree that main ideas are most often processed and remembered (Kintsch & Vipond, 1979). But more detailed concepts are hardly ever of the same importance within a text-world model, and readers may not foresee what they may need to know later on. An indiscriminate attention to details is likely to cause a degradation of overall coherence, as was the case with Luria's (1968) famous memory expert. Interesting materials may not be relevant, e.g., when students recalled the anecdotes best from a classroom lecture (Kintsch & Bates, 1977). Ambiguities may demand attention, even though, in most text types, they are wasted effort.

More for motives of design than of empirical evidence, I suggested that attention may be alloted according to "power" (de Beaugrande, 1980–1981). On each level, the powerful categories or operations are those that most readily identify any specific occurrence as the instantiation of a general type. For example, on the concept/relation level, "motion" is more powerful than "walk," "run," "amble." The loss of detail that a recall protocol assumes in comparison to the presented text would then be due in part to higher powered processing (e.g., many of my readers recalled the rocket's "motion" but not its "speeding," "plunging." The greater the strain, the more likely readers would be to work with high-power. This effect would explain "graceful degradation": performance is reorganized to sacrifice lower-powered operations so that the overall processing system can still keep going. The limited supply of attention would be wisely invested at the higher degree of power (which would yield such findings as those of Bransford, Barclay, & Franks, 1972).

A crucial difficulty for experiments on reading is that, by definition, automatic processes run concurrently with others and yet do not interfere. Hence, they need not show up in real time at all, at least not additively, and our observations might well pick up on other activities done at the same time. At most, automatic actions are located in psychological time created by the scheduling operations of the mind, an issue researchers have barely envisioned so far. As asserted by Posner (1978, p. 7) "modern cognitive psychology" is based on "the idea that mental processes are embedded in real time." At the risk of being an alarmist, I would surmise that this idea needs proof in its own right, and cannot be assumed in that a priori fashion.[10] It is conceivable (though, with conventional techniques, hardly demonstrable) that psychological time is not linear (or not exclusively), nor are its units constant under all conditions. Instead, the mind may construct its own packaging according to the tasks it receives and the resources available for the occasion. For example, boring tasks seem to the performer to consume more time than interesting ones, irrespective of the real time used up.

Before this section is concluded, one final dimension deserves note. It might be contended that short-term sensory storage should be collapsed with short-term memory, so that we have only a two-range scheme (e.g., of "primary" vs. "secondary" memory). This simplification would undercut my contention that the exposure to the surface text is extremely brief, on the order of one to four seconds. However, the existence of a transitory store based on the perceived properties of the presented text,

---

[10]Chronometric studies like Posner's are not in themselves such a proof, because the supposition is part of his argument—the proof would be circular. At most, we know that some operations add to performance time under some conditions.

as distinct from a longer lasting store for representing phrases or clauses and their content, is indicated by some significant findings: Sperling's (1960) work with letter arrays, Eriksen and Collins' (1967) tactic of superposing individually presented dot patterns to create a nonsense syllable, and Crowder and Morton's (1969) explorations of an acoustic sensory store. The impact of masking (McClelland, 1976) certainly demands account. The capacities uncovered in such studies seem of a different order than those of short-term memory (e.g., Sachs, 1967).

I have now pursued an assortment of findings and issues that bear upon the design which a model of on-line reading should adopt. I have argued that the model proposed here, with a differentiation of both ranges and depths, cannot be simplified, though it can be reconciled with many findings brought forth in support of simpler models in the past. I suspect that this simplicity was attained by assuming that a particular store or process was exclusively devoted to one factor, whereas it is only predominantly so. Skepticism and parsimony are not always productive in research. A more complex model can offer more regarding what Estes (1979) considers "the measure of success in moving toward scientific explanation: the degree to which a theory brings out relationships between otherwise distinct and independent clusters of phenomena" (p. 47).

BACK TO SCHOOL

After so much emphasis on theories and experiments, I would like to conclude with a short note on educational practices. The unfortunate impact of behaviorist theories of learning (if we can even use that term despite Skinner, 1950) on school practices arose mainly from the poverty of the accepted models. The insistence upon quantifying outward behavior as the only possible evidence led to total preoccupation with shallow depths and total disregard for deep ones. Indeed, the behaviorist is in principle incapable of telling the difference between the most superficial activities and cognitively effectual ones. In consequence, children are stuffed with "facts" for rote recitation on an endless series of high-pressure tests, but the more crucial task of finding a coherent and meaningful framework without which no fact is useful, is left mostly up to the learner. The outcome—young people leaving school with no integrated understanding either of the world or their own lives—is painfully evident.

In the model I am advocating, any occurrence on any depth is related to a host of others on the same or on different depths. The networks are intended to illustrate issues of continuity and access for this very reason. Whether the memory for one occurrence must be retrieved by the "cues" that accompanied its original processing—the "encoding specificity" hypothesis of Tulving and Thomson (1973)—can only be decided if we have a much better notion of these complex interactions. Perhaps the hypothesis is not testable at all, as Mandler (1979, p. 305) says, at least not with the usual experiments. But the practicing teacher needs to know what can be done to promote learning from texts.

Consider for instance the notion of rehearsal as applied to text processing. To the behaviorist, repetition of an event (e.g., a word list) is simply that: the same thing happening over and over, gradually becoming cemented in the learner's mind, given proper "reinforcement." In the model set forth here, repetition has different aspects and effects for each depth of processing. On the shallowest levels, the repetition of letters/sound and words does not normally draw attention, being a trivial condition of language, unless clearly marked patterns are used (e.g., alliteration and rhyme in poetry; frequent use of rare words). Thus, the benefits of rehearsal for recall are so slight. The repetition of syntactic formats in parallelism supports reading ease. The repetition of concepts and relations is necessary for coherence, whether or not the same concept names return in the surface text; often, recurring concepts/relations will be construed as main ideas and be well remembered. Recurring goals can guide reading at such a deep level that their boundaries in terms of segments of text are very hard to establish. Who can say, for example, where the *Declaration of Independence* ceases to be a narrative of past events and starts to be a call for future actions? The impression created by much work on "speech acts" that every sentence is exactly one such act is certainly wrong.

Ideally, children should learn from reading a text both the main ideas and at least some more specific terms or concepts. The main ideas are likely to be retained in any event, provided the children can relate them to previous knowledge. That effect is a simple improvement of rehearsal at greater depths (cf. Craik & Tulving, 1975). But specific terms and concepts will normally require an added allotment of attention to guarantee their relevance for the main ideas or goals. The average learning text leaves this matter mostly up to chance, shifting the responsibility from the educator to the child.

I recently undertook to design a research textbook (de Beaugrande, 1980) in a format that might reduce this chance factor. All main terms are defined at first encounter, and used consistently throughout. Cross-referencing, both within the running text and in an elaborate index, enables readers to assemble ideas apart from the order of presentation. For this purpose, paragraph numbers were taken as superior to page numbers; moreover, subordination of several paragraphs to a predecessor can be signalled by adding a decimal place to the subordinates. For example, paragraph I.3.4 announces that texts have different status from sentences, and I.3.4.1 through I.3.4.10 offer motives for this claim (de Beaugrande, 1980, pp. 11–14). In addition, main terms are printed in BLOCK CAPITALS, so that *italics* can be used for emphasis. This differentiation of the shallowest level should encourage an immediate distribution of attention favorable to recognition and recall; and for later search, the upper case print is at once discoverable on the page. The reaction to these usages has been mixed. The paragraph numbering in particular has been misconstrued, even by prominent researchers on memory and readability, as a hindrance or even an intimidation of the reader.

It is worth asking whether contemporary print is a conducive vehicle for learning at all. In past centuries, it was commonplace in English prose to capitalize at least the first letter of important words, a tendency which, interestingly enough, children writers still adopt today (and are usually discouraged from continuing). Perhaps even more radical distinctions might prove helpful, such as harnessing the Stroop effect by printing associated concept names in distinctive colors, or setting chunks of discourse in visually distinctive space (Graf & Torrey, 1966), or introducing more print sizes to set off major topics from minor ones, or central ideas from inessential ones. Anything that could be done to guide shallow processing toward desired deeper results deserves a try, provided we have some way to model the correspondence involved.

At the reader's end, training tasks such as summarizing, supplying titles or endings, or filling in content should further deep processing by impelling children to construct and apply large configurations of content. The texts in use should be more challenging than what we find in school readers. Far from improving skills, dull passages may well encourage a degradation by reducing the overall attention that children are willing or able to invest in the task. In my experience, it is far easier to underestimate the capacities of children than to overestimate them.

REFERENCES

Allen, J. (1979). *A plan-based approach to speech act recognition.* Unpublished doctoral dissertation, University of Toronto.

Allen, P., & Watson, D. (Eds.). (1976). *Findings of research in miscue analysis.* Urbana: National Council of Teachers of English.

Ammon, P. (1968). The perception of grammatical relations in sentences. *Journal of Verbal Learning and Verbal Behavior, 7,* 869–875.

Anderson, J. R. (1974). Verbatim and propositional representation of sentences in immediate and long-term memory. *Journal of Verbal Learning and Verbal Behavior, 13,* 149–162.

Anderson, J. R., & Reder, L. M. (1978). Elaborative processing of prose material. In L. Cermak & F. Craik (Eds.), *Levels of processing in human memory*. Hillsdale, NJ: Lawrence Erlbaum Associates.

Anderson, R., & Ortony, A. (1975). On putting apples into bottles—A problem of polysemy. *Cognitive Psychology, 7*, 167–180.

Anisfeld, M., & Knapp, M. (1968). Association, synonymity, and directionality in false recognition. *Journal of Experimental Psychology, 77*, 171–179.

Atkinson, R. C., & Shiffrin, R. M. (1968). Human memory: A proposed system and its control processes. In K. Spence & J. Spence (Eds.), *The psychology of learning and motivation* (pp. 89–195). New York: Academic Press.

Austin, J. (1962). *How to do things with words*. Cambridge: Harvard.

de Beaugrande, R. (1980). *Text, discourse, and process: Toward a multidisciplinary science of texts*. Norwood, NJ: Ablex; London: Longman.

de Beaugrande, R. 1980–1981). Design criteria for process models of reading. *Reading Research Quarterly, 16*, 261–315.

de Beaugrande, R. (1982a). Psychology and composition: Past, present, future. In M. Nystrand (Ed.), *What writers know* (pp. 211–267). New York: Academic Press.

de Beaugrande, R. (1982b). General constraints on process models of language. In J. F. le Ny & W. Kintsch (Eds.), *Language and comprehension* (pp. 179–192). Amsterdam: North Holland.

de Beaugrande, R. (1984a). *Text production*. Norwood, NJ: Ablex.

de Beaugrande, R. (1984b). The linearity of reading: Fact, fiction or frontier? In J. Flood (Ed.), *New issues in reading comprehension*. Newark, DE: International Reading Association.

de Beaugrande, R. (1985c). *Writing step by step*. New York: Harcourt Brace Jovanovich.

de Beaugrande, R. & Colby, B. N. (1979). Narrative models of action and interaction. *Cognitive Science, 3*, 43–66.

de Beaugrande, R. & Dressler, W. (1981). *Introduction to text linguistics*. London: Longman.

Begg, I. (1971). Recognition memory for sentence meaning and wording. *Journal of Verbal Learning and Verbal Behavior, 10*, 176–181.

Begg, I., & Wickelgren, W. (1974). Retention functions for syntactic and lexical versus semantic information in recognition memory. *Memory and Cognition, 2*, 353–359.

Bobrow, R. (1978). The RUS system. In B. Webber and R. Bobrow (Eds.), *Research in natural language understanding* (Tech. Rep. 3878). Cambridge: Bolt, Beranek & Newman.

Bond, Z. S., & Garnes, S. (1980). Misperceptions of fluent speech. In R. Cole (Ed.), *Perception and production of fluent speech*. Hillsdale, NJ: Lawrence Erlbaum Associates.

Boomer, D., & Laver, J. (1968). Slips of the tongue. *British Journal of Disorders of Communication, 3*, 2–11.

Bormuth, J. (1975). Reading literacy: Its definition and assessment. In J. Carroll & J. Chall (Eds.), *Toward a literate society*. New York: McGraw-Hill.

Brachman, R. (1979). On the epistemological status of semantic networks. In N. Findler (Ed.), *Associative networks*. New York: Academic Press.

Bransford, J., Barclay, J. R., & Franks, J. (1972). Sentence memory: A constructive versus interpretative approach. *Cognitive Psychology, 3*, 193–209.

Bray, N., & Batchelder, W. (1972). Effects of instructions and retention interval on memory of presentation mode. *Journal of Verbal Learning and Verbal Behavior, 11*, 367–374.

Caplan, D. (1972). Clause boundaries and recognition latencies for words in sentences. *Perception and Psychophysics, 12*, 73–76.

Carpenter, P., & Just, M. (1977). Reading comprehension as the eye sees it. In M. Just & P. Carpenter (Eds.), *Cognitive processes in comprehension* (pp. 109–139). Hillsdale, NJ: Lawrence Erlbaum Associates.

Chomsky, N. (1965). *Aspects of the theory of syntax.* Cambridge: MIT Press.

Clark, H., & Clark, E. (1977). *Psychology and language.* New York: Harcourt Brace Jovanovich.

Cohen, P. (1978). *On knowing what to say: Planning speech acts.* Unpublished doctoral dissertation, University of Toronto.

Coseriu, E. (1955–1956). Determinación y entorno. *Romanistisches Jahrbuch, 7,* 29–54.

Craik, F., & Lockhart, R. (1972). Levels of processing. *Journal of Verbal Learning and Verbal Behavior, 11,* 671–684.

Craik, F., & Tulving, E. (1975). Depth of processing and the retention of words in episodic memory. *Journal of Experimental Psychology: General, 104,* 268–294.

Crowder, R., & Morton, J. (1969). Precategorical acoustic storage. *Perception and Psychophysics, 5,* 365-373.

Dark, V., & Loftus, G. (1976). The role of rehearsal in long-term memory performance. *Journal of Verbal Learning and Verbal Behavior, 15,* 479–490.

Darley, C., & Glass, A. (1975). Effects of rehearsal and serial list position on recall. *Journal of Experimental Psychology: Human Learning and Memory, 1,* 453–458.

Das, J., Kirby, J., & Jarman, R. (1979). *Simultaneous and successive cognitive processes.* New York: Academic Press.

van Dijk, T. (1979). *Macro-structures.* Hillsdale, NJ: Lawrence Erlbaum Associates.

Dyer, F. (1973). The Stroop phenomenon and its use in the study of perceptual, cognitive, and response processes. *Memory and Cognition, 1,* 106–120.

Ekstrand, B., Wallace, W., & Underwood, B. A. (1966). A frequency theory of verbal discrimination learning. *Psychological Review, 73,* 566–578.

Erdelyi, M. (1974). A new look at the new look: Perceptual defense and vigilance. *Psychological Review, 81,* 1–25.

Eriksen, C., & Collins, J. (1967). Some temporal characteristics of verbal perception. *Journal of Experimental Psychology, 74,* 476–484.

Estes, W. K. (1975). The locus of inferential and perceptual processes in letter identification. *Journal of Experimental Psychology: General, 1,* 122–145.

Estes, W. K. (1979). On the descriptive and explanatory functions of theories of memory. In L. G. Nilsson (Ed.), *Perspectives on memory research.* Hillsdale, NJ: Lawrence Erlbaum Associates.

Fillmore, C. (1977). The case for case reopened. In P. Cole & J. Sadock (Eds.), *Syntax and semantics VIII: Grammatical relations.* New York: Academic Press.

Findler, N. (Ed.). (1979). *Associative networks.* New York: Academic Press.

Flesch, R. (1972). *Say what you mean.* New York: Harper & Row.

Foss, D., Harwood, D., & Blank, M. (1980). Deciphering decoding decisions: Data and devices. In R. Cole (Ed.), *Perception and production of fluent speech* (pp. 165–199). Hillsdale, NJ: Lawrence Erlbaum Associates.

Frederiksen, C. (1977). Semantic processing units in understanding text. In R. Freedle (Ed.), *Discourse production and comprehension* (pp. 57–87). Norwood, NJ: Ablex.

Fromkin, V. (1971). The non-anomalous nature of anomalous utterances. *Language, 47,* 27–52.

Garrod, S., & Trabasso, T. (1973). A dual-memory information processing interpretation of sentence comprehension. *Journal of Verbal Learning and Verbal Behavior, 12,* 155–167.

Gibson, E. (1971). Perceptual learning and the theory of word perception. *Cognitive Psychology, 2,* 351–368.

Gomulicki, B. (1956). Recall as an abstractive process. *Acta Psychologica, 12,* 77–94.

Goodman, K. (1976). Reading: A Psycholinguistic guessing game. In H. Singer & R. Ruddell (Eds.), *Theoretical models and processes of reading* (pp. 497–518). Newark, DE: International Reading Association.

Goodman, K., & Burke, C. (1973). *Theoretically based studies of patterns of miscues in oral reading performance.* Washington, DC: U.S. Dept. of Health, Education & Welfare.

Gough, P. (1972). One second of reading. In J. Kavanagh & I. Mattingly (Eds.), *Language by ear and by eye* (pp. 331–358). Cambridge: MIT Press.

Graf, R., & Torrey, J. (1966). Perception of phrase structure in written language. *American Psychological Association Convention Proceedings, 83–84.*

Grice, P. (1975). Logic and conversation. In P. Cole & J. Morgan (Eds.), *Syntax and semantics III: Speech acts.* New York: Academic Press.

Grice, P. (1978). Further notes on logic and conversation. In P. Cole (Ed.), *Syntax and semantics IX: Pragmatics.* New York: Academic Press.

Halliday, M. A. K. (1967). *Grammar, society, and the noun.* London: Lewis.

Halliday, M. A. K., & Hasan, R. (1976). *Cohesion in English.* London: Longman.

Hartmann, P. (1972). Text, Texte, Klassen von Texten. In W. A. Koch (Ed.), *Strukturelle Textanalyse.* Hildesheim: Olms.

Hintzman, D., Block, R., & Inskeep, N. (1972). Memory for mode of input. *Journal of Verbal Learning and Verbal Behavior, 11,* 741–749.

Hogan, R., & Kintsch, W. (1970). Differential effects of study and test trials on long-term recognition and recall. *Journal of Verbal Learning and Verbal Behavior, 10,* 562–567.

Jakobson, R., & Halle, M. (1956). *Fundamentals of language.* The Hague: Mouton.

Jarvella, R. (1970). Effects of syntax on running memory span for connected discourse. *Psychonomic Science, 19,* 235–236.

Jarvella, R. (1971). Syntactic processing of connected speech. *Journal of Verbal Learning and Verbal Behavior, 10,* 409–416.

Johnson-Laird, P. N., & Stevenson, R. (1970). Memory for syntax. *Nature, 227,* 412.

Johnston, J. C., & McClelland, J. L. (1973). Visual factors in word perception. *Perception and Psychophysics, 14,* 365–370.

Jones, L. (1977). *Theme in English expository discourse.* Lake Bluff, IL: Jupiter.

Kay, H. (1955). Learning and retaining verbal material. *British Journal of Psychology, 46,* 81–100.

Keele, S. (1973). *Attention and human performance.* Pacific Palisades: Goodyear.

Kimball, J. P. (1973). Seven principles of surface structure parsing in natural language. *Cognition, 2,* 15–47.

Kintsch, W. (1968). Recognition and free recall of organized lists. *Journal of Experimental Psychology, 78,* 481–487.

Kintsch, W. (1970). Models for free recall and recognition. In D. Norman (Ed.), *Models of human memory* (pp. 331–373). New York: Academic Press.

Kintsch, W. (1974). *The representation of meaning in memory.* Hillsdale, NJ: Lawrence Erlbaum Associates.

Kintsch, W. (1975). Memory representations of text. In R. Solso (Ed.), *Information processing and cognition* (pp. 269–294). Hillsdale, NJ: Lawrence Erlbaum Associates.

Kintsch, W. (1977). *Memory and cognition.* New York: Wiley.

Kintsch, W. (1980). Semantic memory: A tutorial. In R. Nickerson (Ed.), *Attention and performance VIII* (pp. 595–620). Hillsdale, NJ: Lawrence Erlbaum Associates.

Kintsch, W., & Bates, E. (1977). Recognition memory for statements from a classroom lecture. *Journal of Experimental Psychology: Human Learning and Memory, 3,* 150–159.

Kintsch, W., & Dijk, T. van. (1978). Toward a model of text comprehension and production. *Psychological Review, 85,* 363–394.

Kintsch, W., & Keenan, J. (1973). Reading rate and retention as a function of the number of propositions in the base structure of the text. *Cognitive Psychology, 5*, 257–274.

Kintsch, W., Kozminsky, E., Streby, W., McKoon, G., & Keenan, J. (1975). Comprehension and recall of text as a function of content variables. *Journal of Verbal Learning and Verbal Behavior, 14*, 257–274.

Kintsch, W., & Vipond, D. (1979). Reading comprehension and readability in educational practice. In L. G. Nilsson (Ed.), *Perspectives on memory research*. Hillsdale, NJ: Lawrence Erlbaum Associates.

Klare, G. (1963). *The measurement of readability*. Ames: Iowa State University.

Klare, G. (1974–1975). Assessing readability. *Reading Research Quarterly, 10*, 62–102.

LaBerge, D., & Samuels, S. J. (1974). Toward a theory of automatic information processing in reading. *Cognitive Psychology, 6*, 293–323.

Lashley, K. S. (1951). The problem of serial order in behavior. In L. Jeffress (Ed.), *Cerebral mechanisms in behavior* (pp. 112–136). New York: Wiley.

Lehnert, W. (1978). *Representing physical objects in memory* (Department of Computer Sciences Research Report 131). New Haven: Yale University.

Levelt, W. J. M. (1978). A survey of studies in sentence perception, 1970-1976. In W. J. M. Levelt & G. Flores d'Arcais (Eds.), *Studies in the perception of language*. New York: Wiley.

Levy, B. (1977). Speech processes during reading. *Journal of Verbal Learning and Verbal Behavior, 16*, 623–638.

Loftus, E. (1980). *Memory: Surprising new insights into how we remember and why we forget*. Reading, MA: Addison-Wesley.

Loftus, G., & Loftus, E. (1976). *Human memory: The processing of information*. Hillsdale, NJ: Lawrence Erlbaum Associates.

Luria, A. (1968). *The mind of a mnemonist*. New York: Basic Books.

Luria, A. (1972). *The man with a shattered world*. New York: Basic Books.

Luria, A. (1979). Neuropsychology of complex forms of human memory. In L. G. Nilsson (Ed.), *Perspectives on memory research*. Hillsdale, NJ: Lawrence Erlbaum Associates.

MacKay, D. (1966). To end ambiguous sentences. *Perception and Psychophysics, 1*, 426–436.

Maclay, H., & Osgood, C. E. (1959). Hesitation phenomena in spontaneous English speech. *Word, 15*, 19–44.

MacNeilage, P. (1964). Typing errors as clues to serial ordering mechanisms in language behavior. *Language and Speech, 7*, 144–159.

MacNeilage, P. (1970). Motor control and serial ordering of speech. *Psychological Review, 77*, 182–196.

Mandler, G. (1979). Organization and repetition: Organizational principles with special reference to rote learning. In L. G. Nilsson (Ed.), *Perspectives on memory research*. Hillsdale, NJ: Lawrence Erlbaum Associates.

Marks, L. E., & Miller, G. A. (1964). The role of semantic and syntactic constraints in the memorization of English sentences. *Journal of Verbal Learning and Verbal Behavior, 3*, 1–5.

Marshall, J. C., & Newcombe, F. (1973). Patterns of paralexia: A psycholinguistic approach. *Journal of Psycholinguistic Research, 2*, 175–198.

Marslen-Wilson, W. (1975). Sentence perception as an interactive parallel process. *Science, 189*, 226–228.

Marslen-Wilson, W., & Welsh, A. (1978). Processing interactions and lexical access during word recognition in continuous speech. *Cognitive Psychology, 10*, 29–63.

Masson, M. (1979). *Cognitive processes in skimming stories* (Tech. Rep. No. 84-ONR). Boulder: University of Colorado, Institute for the Study of Intellectual Behavior.

McCall, W., & Crabbs, L. (1961). *Standard test lessons in readability*. New York: Teachers' College Press.

McClelland, J. (1976). Preliminary letter identification in the perception of words and nonwords. *Journal of Experimental Psychology: Human Perception and Performance, 2*, 80–91.

McCormack, P. D. (1972). Recognition memory: How complex a retrieval system? *Canadian Journal of Psychology, 26*, 19–41.

Melton, A. (1963). Implications of short-term memory for a general theory of memory. *Journal of Verbal Learning and Verbal Behavior, 2*, 1–21.

Meyer, B. J. F. (1975). *The organization of prose and its effects on memory*. Amsterdam: North Holland.

Meyer, B. J. F., & Rice, G. E. (1980). *The amount, type, and organization of information recalled from prose by young, middle, and old adult readers* (Dept. of Educational Psychology Tech. Rep.). Tempe: Arizona State University. Presented at the 1980 annual meeting of the American Psychological Association, Montreal.

Miller, G. A. (1956). The magic number seven, plus or minus two. *Psychological Review, 63*, 81–97.

Miller, G. A., Bruner, J., & Postman, L. (1954). Familiarity of letter sequences and tachistoscopic identification. *Journal of Genetic Psychology, 50*, 129–139.

Miller, G. A., & Isard, S. (1963). Some perceptual consequences of linguistic rules. *Journal of Verbal Learning and Verbal Behavior, 2*, 217–228.

Mistler-Lachman, J. L. (1974). Depth of comprehension and sentence memory. *Journal of Verbal Learning and Verbal Behavior, 13*, 98–106.

Morgan, J. (1975). Some remarks on the nature of sentences. In R. Grossman, J. San, & T. Vance (Eds.), *Papers from the parasession on functionalism*. Chicago: CLS.

Nilsson, L. G. (Ed.). (1979). *Perspectives on memory research*. Hillsdale, NJ: Lawrence Erlbaum Associates.

Norman, D. (1979). Perception, memory, and mental processes. In L. G. Nilsson (Ed.), *Perspectives on memory research*. Hillsdale, NJ: Lawrence Erlbaum Associates.

Norman, D., & Bobrow, D. (1975). On data-limited and resource-limited processes. *Cognitive Psychology, 7*, 44–64.

Norman, D., & Rumelhart, D. (1975). *Explorations in human cognition*. San Francisco: Freeman.

O'Connell, D. (1977). One of many units: The sentence. In S. Rosenberg (Ed.), *Sentence production* (pp. 307–313). Hillsdale, NJ: Lawrence Erlbaum Associates.

O'Regan, J. K. (1975). *Structural and contextual constraints on eye movements in reading*. Unpublished doctoral dissertation, Cambridge University.

Ortony, A. (1975). How episodic is episodic memory? In R. Schank & B. Nash-Webber (Eds.), *Theoretical issues in natural language processing*. Cambridge: Bolt, Beranek & Newman.

Paivio, A. (1975). Perceptual comparisons through the mind's eye. *Memory and Cognition, 3*, 635–647.

Polf, J. (1976). *The word superiority effect: A speed-accuracy analysis and test of a decoding hypothesis*. Unpublished doctoral dissertation, University of Oregon.

Pollack, I., & Pickett, J. (1964). Intelligibility of excerpts from fluent speech: Auditory vs. structural content. *Journal of Verbal Learning and Verbal Behavior, 3*, 79–84.

Posner, M. I. (1978). *Chronometric explorations of mind*. Hillsdale, NJ: Lawrence Erlbaum Associates.

Posner, M. I., & Synder, C. (1975). Attention and cognitive control. In R. Solso (Ed.), *Information processing and cognition* (pp. 55–85). Hillsdale, NJ: Lawrence Erlbaum Associates.

Raser, G. A. (1972). Recoding of semantic and acoustic information in memory. *Journal of Verbal Learning and Verbal Behavior, 11,* 692–697.

Reddy, D. R., Erman, L. D., Fennell, R. D., & Neely, R. B. (1973). The HEARSAY speech understanding system: An example of the recognition process. *Proceedings of the Third International Joint Conference on Artificial Intelligence,* Stanford.

Reicher, G. (1969). Perceptual recognition as a function of meaningfulness of stimulus materials. *Journal of Experimental Psychology, 81,* 274–280.

Rothkopf, E. Z. (1976). Writing to teach and reading to learn: A perspective on the psychology of written instruction. *Yearbook of the National Society for the Study of Education, 75,* 91–129.

Royer, J. (1977). Remembering: Constructive or reconstructive? In R. Anderson, R. Spiro, & W. Montague (Eds.), *Schooling and the acquisition of knowledge* (pp. 167–173). Hillsdale, NJ: Lawrence Erlbaum Associates.

Rumelhart, D. (1977a). *Introduction to human information processing.* New York: Wiley.

Rumelhart, D. (1977b). Toward an interactive model of reading. In S. Dornic (Ed.), *Attention and performance VI.* Hillsdale, NJ: Lawrence Erlbaum Associates.

Rumelhart, D. (1980). Schemata: The building blocks of cognition. In R. Spiro, B. Bruce, & W. Brewer (Eds.), *Theoretical issues in reading comprehension* (pp. 33–58). Hillsdale, NJ: Lawrence Erlbaum Associates.

Rumelhart, D., & Siple, P. (1974). Process of recognizing tachistoscopically presented words. *Psychological Review, 81,* 99–118.

Sachs, J. S. (1967). Recognition memory for syntactic and semantic aspects of connected discourse. *Perception and Psychophysics, 2,* 437–442.

Saffran, E., & Marin, O. (1975). Immediate memory for word lists and sentences in a patient with deficient auditory short-term memory. *Brain and Language, 2,* 420–433.

Schank, R., & Abelson, R. (1977). *Scripts, plans, goals, and understanding.* Hillsdale, NJ: Lawrence Erlbaum Associates.

Schank, R., Goldman, N., Rieger, C., & Riesbeck, C. (1975). *Conceptual information processing.* Amsterdam: North Holland.

Schank, R., Lebowitz, M., & Birnbaum, L. (1978). *Integrated partial parsing* (Dept. of Computer Sciences Research Report 143). New Haven: Yale University.

Schweizer, H. (1979). *Sprache und Systemtheorie.* Tübingen: Narr.

Schweller, K., Brewer, W., & Dahl, D. (1976). Memory for illocutionary forces and perlocutionary effects of utterances. *Journal of Verbal Learning and Verbal Behavior, 15,* 325–337.

Searle, J. (1969). *Speech acts.* London: Cambridge.

Shallice, T. (1975). On the contents of primary memory. In P. Rabbitt & S. Dornič (Eds.), *Attention and performance V* (pp. 269–280). London: Academic Press.

Shallice, T. (1979). Neuropsychological research and the fractionation of memory systems. In L. G. Nilsson (Ed.), *Perspectives on memory research.* Hillsdale, NJ: Lawrence Erlbaum Associates.

Shallice, T., & Warrington, E. (1975). Word recognition in a phonemic dyslexic patient. *Quarterly Journal of Experimental Psychology, 27,* 187–199.

Shepard, R. (1967). Recognition memory for words, sentences, and pictures. *Journal of Verbal Learning and Verbal Behavior, 6,* 156–163.

Shulman, H. G. (1970). Encoding and retention of semantic and phonetic information in short-term memory. *Journal of Verbal Learning and Verbal Behavior, 9,* 499–508.

Simmons, R. F., & Chester, D. (1979). *Relating sentences and semantic networks with clausal logic* (Dept. of Computer Sciences Tech. Rep.). Austin: University of Texas.

Skinner, B. F. (1950). Are theories of learning necessary? *Psychological Review, 57,* 193–216.

Skinner, B. F. (1978). Why I am not a cognitive psychologist. In B. F. Skinner, *Reflections on behaviorism and society*. Englewood Cliffs, NJ: Prentice-Hall.

Smith, W., McCrary, J., & Smith, K. (1960). Delayed visual feedback and behavior. *Science, 132*, 1013–1014.

Sperling, G. (1960). The information available in brief visual presentations. *Psychological Monographs, 74*, 1–29.

Spiro, R. (1975). *Inferential reconstruction in memory for connected discourse* (Tech. Rep. 2). Urbana: University of Illinois Laboratory for Cognitive Studies in Education.

Spiro, R. (1977). Remembering information from text: The "state of schema" approach. In R. Anderson, R. Spiro, & W. Montague (Eds.), *Schooling and the acquisition of knowledge* (pp. 137–165). Hillsdale, NJ: Lawrence Erlbaum Associates.

Thomson, D. M. (1972). Context effects in recognition memory. *Journal of Verbal Learning and Verbal Behavior, 11*, 497–511.

Thorndyke, P., & Yekovich, F. (1980). A critique of schemata as a theory of human story memory. *Poetics, 9*, 23–49.

Tulving, E. (1972). Episodic and semantic memory. In E. Tulving & W. Donaldson (Eds.), *Organization of memory* (pp. 381–403). New York: Academic Press.

Tulving, E. (1979). Memory research: What kind of progress? In L. G. Nilsson (Ed.), *Perspectives on memory research*. Hillsdale, NJ: Lawrence Erlbaum Associates.

Tulving, E., Mandler, G., & Baumal, R. (1964). Interaction of two sources of information in tachistoscopic word recognition. *Canadian Journal of Psychology, 18*, 62–71.

Tulving, E., & Thomson, D. (1973). Encoding specificity and retrieval processes in episodic memory. *Psychological Review, 80*, 352–373.

Turner, A., & Greene, E. (1977). *The construction of a propositional text base* (Tech. Rep. 63). Boulder: University of Colorado Institute for the Study of Intellectual Behavior.

Underwood, B., & Freund, J. (1968). Errors in recognition, learning, and retention. *Journal of Experimental Psychology, 78*, 55–63.

Walker, D. (Ed.). (1978). *Understanding spoken language*. Amsterdam: North Holland.

Warren, R. M. (1970). Perceptual restoration of missing sounds. *Science, 167*, 392–393.

Waugh, N., & Norman, D. (1965). Primary memory. *Psychological Review, 72*, 89–104.

Webber, B. (1980). Syntax beyond the sentence: Anaphora. In R. Spiro, B. Bruce, & W. Brewer (Eds.), *Theoretical issues in reading comprehension* (pp. 141–164). Hillsdale, NJ: Lawrence Erlbaum Associates.

Wilks, Y. (1977). Good and bad arguments about semantic primitives. *Communication and Cognition, 10*, 181–221.

Winograd, T. (1978). On primitive prototypes and other semantic anomalies. *Theoretical Issues in Natural Language Processing, 2*, 25–32.

Woods, W. (1978). Generalizations of ATN grammars. In W. Woods & R. Brachman, *Research in natural language understanding* (Tech. Rep. 3963). Cambridge: Bolt, Bernek & Newman.

Woods, W. Brown, G., Bruce, B., Cook, C., Klorstad, J., Khoul, J., Nash-Webber, B., Schwartz, R., Wolf, J., & Zue, V. (1976). *Speech understanding systems* (Tech. Rep. 3438). Cambridge: Bolt, Bernek & Newman.

Woodward, A., Bjork, R., & Jongewald, R. (1973). Recall and recognition as a function of primary rehearsal. *Journal of Verbal Learning and Verbal Behavior, 12*, 608–617.

3

FOLLOWING THE AUTHOR'S TOP-LEVEL ORGANIZATION: AN IMPORTANT SKILL FOR READING COMPREHENSION

Bonnie J. F. Meyer
University of Washington

An important reading skill identified by a number of educators involves following the author's organization of a text. For example, Davis (1944) identified eight reading comprehension skills through a factor analytic method. Two of these factors were following the structure of a passage and recognizing the author's purpose. In addition, the work of Niles (1965) states that children must learn to follow the author's pattern of thought. Spearritt (1972) identified four separate skills in reading comprehension and they also included following the structure of the passage and recognizing the author's purpose.

Little research has been conducted on these two skills (e.g., Carroll, 1971; Caterino, 1977; Horowitz, 1985). In addition, few long-standing programs have been developed to teach these skills. Programs (Gainsburg, 1967; Niles, 1965; Sack & Yourman, 1972) that do exist have not been formally evaluated for their success in teaching these skills nor for the relationship between improvement in these skills and overall improvement in comprehension.

Examining the strategies and skills involved to follow the author's structure and purpose appeared in 1976 to be a logical next step for my research effort. My earlier research (Meyer, 1971, 1975, 1977a, 1977b; Meyer & McConkie, 1973); examined the effects of structure in text on what people remember from it. One of the findings of this earlier research was that information located at the top levels of a hierarchical structure of the content of text (main ideas) is recalled and retained better than the information at lower levels in this content structure (details). This effect of structure has been found with various types of materials, recall tasks, and subjects (Kintsch & Keenan, 1973; Mandler & Johnson, 1977; Meyer, 1977a; Thorndyke, 1977). A second finding (Meyer, 1975) of this earlier work relates more closely to the skill described by educators as following the author's structure. The pattern of relations at the top levels of the content structure was found to dramatically influence which ideas located at the top level in the structure would be remembered, while the pattern of relationships low in the structure had no influence on recall. A third finding (Meyer & Freedle, 1984) showed that manipulating the extreme top-level structure in text affected recall and retention of the text.

These findings point to the importance of the top-level structure in prose in influencing what and how much is learned from reading. The structure at the lower levels in the content structure or microstructure was not found to be important in predicting recall. These results have important practical implications. A detailed structural analysis (Meyer, 1975) of text is very time consuming and an impractical task for reading teachers. However, an analysis of the top levels of text is less involved and could be performed to assist educators in constructing equivalent forms of reading tests and preparing lessons to teach reading and writing skills.

Few studies have examined the skills involved in identifying the structure of text and the author's purpose due to a lack of tools to objectively identify the structure of text and the author's message. In recent years, a number of prose analysis systems have been developed by psychologists (Frederiksen, 1975; Kintsch, 1974; Meyer, 1975) based on developments in linguistics (van Dijk, 1976; Grimes, 1975; Halliday, 1967). The various prose analysis systems have similarities and differences; some are better suited to certain research questions than others (Meyer, 1985a; Meyer & Rice, 1984). My approach (Meyer, 1975, 1985a) appeared well-suited for examining the skills in question.

The top level in the content structure recovered by an analysis of a text depicts the major rhetorical relation used by the author to organize his or her text. Classroom text can be classified into different types of expository text on the basis of differences in this top-level structure. My colleagues and I have studied four types of text (Bartlett, 1978; Brandt, 1978; Elliott, 1980; Meyer, 1977a; Meyer & Freedle, 1984; Meyer, Freedle, & Walker, 1978). The top-level rhetorical structures examined include: *problem/solution* which relates a problem (or question) to a solution (or answer), *comparison* which relates what did happen to what did not, or a favored view to an opposing view, *causation* which relates an antecedent condition to its consequent, and *description* which relates a collection of attributes or more specific information to an event or idea. The research with college students (Meyer & Freedle, 1984) showed that comparison and causation structures yielded better recall and retention than description structures. In addition, the purpose of the author can be identified by examining the content and relationships at the extreme top levels in the content structure; the idea units at this level of the structure embody the author's message. Thus, the top-level structure leads readers directly to the main idea of the text.

Tools are now available to investigate further these reading comprehension skills identified by educators. This area of investigation is of potential value not only for its practical applications, but for clarification of aspects in the reading comprehension process.

THE RELATIONSHIP BETWEEN USE OF THE TOP-LEVEL STRUCTURE AND A MODEL OF READING COMPREHENSION

Schema-Theoretic Model

The model of reading comprehension based on schema theory as proposed by Rumelhart (1977) explains reading comprehension as the process of choosing and verifying conceptual schemata for the text. Rumelhart's model and the schema-theoretic model of Adams and Collins (1979) stress both bottom-up (from the text) and top-down (from the reader) processing of text. This view explains that schemata of various levels of generality and abstractness operate in coordination during reading comprehension. The skilled reader uses bottom-up and top-down processing simultaneously and at all levels of analysis as he or she proceeds through the text.

Top-down processing is the particular concern of this chapter. It is hypothesized that skilled readers have a finite number of abstract, superordinate schemata that are used in text comprehension. The story schema used to comprehend narratives has been discussed quite extensively (van Dijk & Kintsch, 1977; Rumelhart, 1975). Schemata used in classroom text of an expository nature have been studied less often. They would apply to the four text types described in research by Meyer and co-workers. This type of schema is more abstract and general than schemata for such things as a restaurant, a fact, or building a house that are more concrete and specific. In their outline of schema theory, Rumelhart and Ortony (1977) explained that schemata are stereotyped knowledge structures that vary in their level of abstraction, have variables, and can embed to form networks. The described top-level structures of text meet these requirements of schemata. Anderson (1977) appears to concur since he stated that "the structures by which an author gives a high level organization to a text . . . are schemata, as are the complementary ones by which readers detect this organization and use it as ideational scaffolding for detailed information" (p. 416).

In this view, the skilled reader is one who approaches a text with knowledge of how texts are organized. The reader selects from her or his repertoire the schemata that best matches the text to be processed. Aspects of the text structure and signaling (Meyer, 1975) suggest which schema can be best employed; Figure 3.1 (taken from Meyer, 1984a) presents a model for this process. The schema employed to comprehend the text functions like an outline. For example, if the reader brings the problem/solution schema to the text he or she will be looking for content to fill in for the variables of a problem with its description, antecedents, and consequences and a solution with attributes that will block at least one of the causes of the problem. When recalling text, the skilled reader activates the same kind of superordinate schema that was used in encoding and retrieves the information stored in memory about the text through a top-down search.

Reading as a Conversation Between Author and Reader

The schema-theoretic model of reading comprehension is compatible with the view of reading as a conversation between an author and a reader (Grice, 1967). In order for the interaction between the author and the reader to be productive, it should follow the pragmatic constraints of conversational behavior (Grice, 1967). That is, there must be cooperation between the author and the reader. There are a number of considerations dealing with audience that an author must make (e.g., Flower & Hayes, 1977). However, this discussion focuses on the reader, and he or she must be a good listener. The conversation will be more successful if the reader has a general idea of the author's purpose (Bruce, 1980). Thus, if the reader recognizes the author's organization or top-level structure of a passage, the conversation will be more successful and the reader will get the author's message.

Once the author's message is comprehended, the reader may disagree and argue back at the author. In fact, in a study (Meyer, 1984a) with 50 proficient adult readers, 49% reported arguing back at the author when reading; most of these readers (84%) recognized and utilized the author's top-level structure when they recalled text.

Extent of the Applicability of the Proposed Reading Strategy

An assumption underlying my research, and recommendations of reading specialists, is that an important strategy for reading comprehension is the ability to identify and use the top level structure of text for both encoding and retrieval. That is, the skilled reader will be capable of using the same

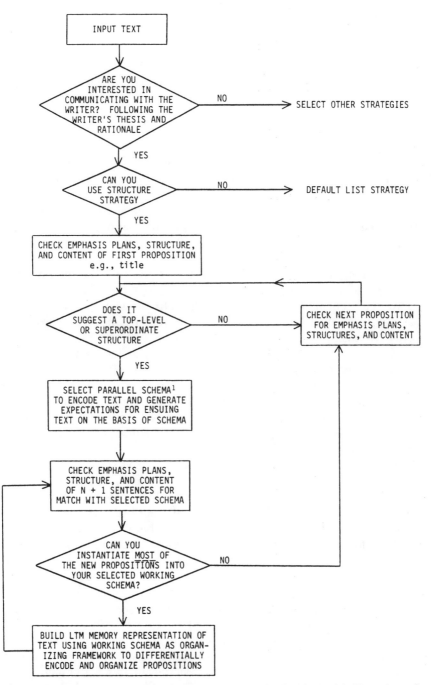

INPUT TEXT

ARE YOU INTERESTED IN COMMUNICATING WITH THE WRITER? FOLLOWING THE WRITER'S THESIS AND RATIONALE

NO → SELECT OTHER STRATEGIES

YES

CAN YOU USE STRUCTURE STRATEGY

NO → DEFAULT LIST STRATEGY

YES

CHECK EMPHASIS PLANS, STRUCTURE, AND CONTENT OF FIRST PROPOSITION e.g., title

DOES IT SUGGEST A TOP-LEVEL OR SUPERORDINATE STRUCTURE

NO → CHECK NEXT PROPOSITION FOR EMPHASIS PLANS, STRUCTURES, AND CONTENT

YES

SELECT PARALLEL SCHEMA[1] TO ENCODE TEXT AND GENERATE EXPECTATIONS FOR ENSUING TEXT ON THE BASIS OF SCHEMA

CHECK EMPHASIS PLANS, STRUCTURE, AND CONTENT OF N + 1 SENTENCES FOR MATCH WITH SELECTED SCHEMA

CAN YOU INSTANTIATE MOST OF THE NEW PROPOSITIONS INTO YOUR SELECTED WORKING SCHEMA?

NO

YES

BUILD LTM MEMORY REPRESENTATION OF TEXT USING WORKING SCHEMA AS ORGAN-IZING FRAMEWORK TO DIFFERENTIALLY ENCODE AND ORGANIZE PROPOSITIONS

[1]Type of schema selected here influences processes of selection and buffer rehearsal.

Fig. 3.1. Model for getting text into organized schemata in memory.

type of superordinate schema as that used by the author in writing the text. In reading exposition, readers will search for the superordinate logical relationships that underlie it; they will look for the use of comparative, descriptive, causative, and problem solving type schemata used by authors to organize their ideas.

Classroom Situations.   In most school situations and many learning situations outside of school, a person wants to know exactly what an author said. The reader needs to pick up as much of the information presented as possible as well as to retain the author's message or main ideas. For reading situations of this type, it seems reasonable that the most efficient strategy for a reader is to utilize the organization of the writer and store in memory the text's information in the same type of schema as that used by the writer. Using the top-level structure of text provides the learner with a way to organize the text. In addition, the reader does not have to search his or her memory for an alternative and appropriate schema nor does he or she have to reorganize the ideas in the passage to fit this different schema while reading; instead, the reader saves processing time by utilizing the same schema as that of the author and organizing the information in the same way as the author (for some empirical support see Meyer, Rice, and Vincent, 1986).

Of course, there are times when using schema of the same type as the author is not efficient. One such time would be when the reader's purpose is simply scanning an article for a specific detail. Another time would be when the reader strongly disagrees with the schema of the author. Data relating to this alternative strategy have been collected by Meyer and Freedle (1984) from school teachers reading a passage with a problem/solution schema. The solution in this passage was "immediate dismissal of athletic coaches by school boards"; the teachers tended not to report this solution in their recall protocols and did not organize their recall in terms of the author's problem/solution format, but instead organized their recall protocols with comparative or descriptive schemata. In addition, often a reader must integrate information by a number of authors on one topic. The first reading of the articles would probably be most efficient with the proposed strategy of utilizing the same type of schema as that of the author, but later integration and comparison would require restructuring with different schemata provided by the reader.

Thus, it is not being proposed that readers become recorders only looking at things in the same way as authors. Instead, it is posited that before readers start arguing with or restructing an author's content, they should first learn how the author views the situation and pick up as much of the information as possible. In summary, the ability to utilize the author's top-level structure to process text is seen as a basic prerequisite skill for the competent reader.

Texts Varying in Quality of Organization.   This position holds for well-organized texts. With prose that has been scrambled or lacks organization, skilled readers would certainly improve their comprehension by providing a schema to organize the input; Kintsch, Mandel, and Kozminsky (1977) found that this is, in fact, what college students do with scrambled stories.

The research of Meyer and co-workers shows that even seemingly well-organized text materials differ in quality of organization which, in turn, affects quantity recalled. When diagrammed, the comparison, causation, and problem/solution structures have an extra link of relationship over the description structure. According to an application of the Anderson (1976) model, recall of the information related together by the three structures providing extra linkage should be superior to that of the descriptive structure.

The same predictions for recall would be made from a schema theory orientation. All four of the text types are used in expository text and convey to a learner that some ideas will be presented about a topic. However, the comparison, causation and problem/solution patterns provide the learner with additional schemata. For example, a comparison passage tells the learner that in addition to the passage presenting ideas about a topic these ideas presented will be opposing on one or more dimensions (see Meyer & Freedle, 1984, for specification of the differences in the organizational components of the different text types). A reasonable expectation is that recall from the texts with more organized structures will be significantly greater than that from the less organized descriptive structure.

Data from two studies with adults relate to these predictions. In the first study (Meyer & Freedle, 1984) the predictions were confirmed in part in that the comparative and causative top-level structures facilitated greater recall and retention than the descriptive structure. The second study (Meyer, 1983, 1984b; Meyer, Freedle, & Walker, 1978) showed that although graduate students perform better with the contrastive structure, retired adults with low vocabulary performance (average age = 80 years) do not effectively utilize this superior top-level structure in text and recalled more after reading a text with the list-like descriptive top-level structure. A more recent listening study (Meyer, Rice, & Vincent, 1986) was conducted with young, middle-aged, and old adults with three levels of performance on the vocabulary subtest of the WAIS (high, high-average, and average). Adults from all age groups with high-average and above vocabulary scores recalled more from comparative than descriptive structures. However, no differences in recall from the two structures were found for average scoring adults.

The Poor Reader.   Poor readers may not come to text with knowledge that authors organize text with such structures as comparative or causative top-level structures. The primary expectation of some poor readers when approaching expository text may be that the text lists some things to remember. These readers may not be able to utilize a superior structure like the comparative structure, and may perform better on the descriptive structure that better fits the list-like schema they bring to the text.

Advantages for Skilled Readers With Well-Organized Text.   Readers utilizing the top-level structure of well-organized text will have advantages over readers not using this strategy at both the encoding and retrieval stages. For example, readers using a comparative schema in their top-down processing of text will look for the two opposing views presented, contrast them on their points and counterpoints, and try to evaluate why one is favored over the other by the author. Readers using this scheme should be processing the information more deeply than readers trying to recall a list of ideas stated by the author or some other schema which fits the input less adequately. In addition, at retrieval poor readers who use a list-like strategy will search memory for descriptions of the topic of the passage. Recalling one attribute will not necessarily cue another. In contrast, the readers that use a comparative schema will have a more systematic retrieval plan. Using the comparative schema insures the reader of recalling both views presented in the text, as well as many stored subordinate propositions located in a top-down search at retrieval. In addition, if they recall one point for one view, it will often facilitate the retrieval of the corresponding point for the other view or prompt the reconstruction of the point if the exact details have been forgotten.

Utilizing the same top-level structure as that used in the text should be of even more assistance as time passes after reading a text. Immediately after reading a passage, vivid content from propositions low in the hierarchical structure will be more readily available for recall than after a delay of a week (Meyer, 1975). Readers using this systematic retrieval plan should show an increased advantage over readers not using this approach on delayed recall tasks when these low-level details have been subsumed in memory.

EMPIRICAL STUDIES WITH NINTH GRADERS EXAMINING THE USE OF THIS STRATEGY

Several studies conducted with ninth graders have empirically examined these notions concerning the value of following the author's top-level structure in text. Each of these studies is discussed in the remaining section of this chapter.

First Exploratory Study.   The first study (Meyer, Brandt, & Bluth, 1980) examined the use of the top level structure in text by ninth graders gauged as high, average, and low comprehenders on standardized reading comprehension tests. The texts selected were two well-organized passages; one with a comparative top-level structure and one taken from a junior high magazine with a problem/solution top-level structure.

A with-signaling and without-signaling (Meyer, 1975) version of each passage was written. In the with-signaling version, the top-level rhetorical structure was explicitly stated and in the without-signaling version, it was not. For example, the with-signaling version of the problem/solution passage on the topic of supertankers began with "A problem of vital concern is the prevention of oil spills from supertankers," whereas the without-signaling version did not include the words problem and solution and began with "Prevention is needed of oil spills from supertankers." In addition, in the with-signaling version, the three-fold solution was explicitly pointed out to the reader whereas it was not in the without-signaling version.

Use of the same top-level structure or schema as the author used in the text was measured by assessing the top-level structure of the free recall protocols written by the students immediately and one week after reading the passages. (The reliability coefficients for this technique for three independent raters ranged from .95 to .98.) A recognition test also was given at the delayed testing.

The data revealed four important findings related to ninth graders' use of the author's top-level structure. First, slightly less than 50% of the ninth graders sampled utilize this strategy in their reading. Second, most ninth graders rated by their teacher and standardized tests as high in reading comprehension use the same top-level structure for organizing their recall protocols as the author of the passage, whereas most students with low reading comprehension do not. Third, students who employ this structure strategy recall much more information from passages than those who do not; use of the author's top-level structure accounted for an average of 44% of the variance in recall immediately after reading passages and 68% of the variance in recall one week later. Use of this strategy was a better predictor of recall than vocabulary test scores or comprehension test scores. Fourth, the recognition task indicated that students who use this strategy can discriminate better between information consistent with the semantics of the passage and intruded information on the same topic than students who do not employ this strategy.

There was no overall effect of signaling. It did not assist high comprehenders who could apparently identify and utilize the top-level structure of the text regardless of whether or not it was explicitly stated by the author. Signaling did not influence low comprehenders who were unable to use the top-level structure of text in either signaling condition. However, it facilitated use of the top-level structure and amount of information remembered after reading by the ninth graders identified as under-achievers; these students had comprehension subtest scores on the Stanford Achievement Test at least one stanine below their vocabulary subtest scores.

The major findings of this study are supportive of the facilitative properties hypothesized for the systematic, top-down process of retrieval used by readers utilizing the top-level structure in text. The top-down search should provide superior recall of information at all levels of the content structure and particularly that information at the top-levels of the structure where the retrieval process begins. The content structure of the passages used in the Meyer, Brandt, and Bluth (1980) was divided into three levels to examine any differences in processing different types of information between students who did and did not utilize the top-level structure of text.

A Closer Look at the Type of Information Recalled by Students Who Differ on the Use of This Strategy.   Levels one and two in the content structures of the passages were most crucial to the overall meaning of the text and labeled the message. For example, the message from the problem/solution passage on the topic of supertankers can be paraphrased as "A problem of vital concern is the prevention of oil spills from supertankers. Because . . . The solution to the problem is not to immediately halt the use of supertankers. Instead the solution lies in the training of officers, the building of better tankers, and installing ground control stations." The major details were found from levels three and four in the content structure and the minor details were located in levels five and lower.

The following depicts the message, major details, and minor details from the passage with the comparative top-level structure on the topic of loss of water from the body. The capitalized words are the message (levels one and two in the content structure). The underlined words are the major details (levels three and four); the words in italics are the minor details (levels lower than four). The top levels of the content structure of this passage are shown in Fig. 3.2.

VIEWS CLASH ON LOSS OF BODY WATER

THE LOSS OF WATER FROM THE BODY IS <u>frequently</u> RE-QUIRED by coaches of wrestlers, boxers, judo contestants, karate contestants, and 150-pound football team members SO THAT they will REACH specified body weights for a sports event. These

Body Water Passage:

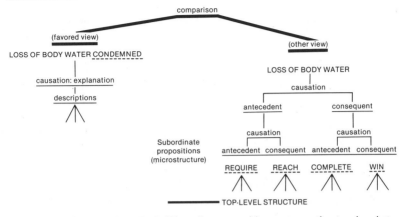

Fig. 3.2.   Top levels of the Body Water Passage with a comparative top-level structure.

specified weights *are much below the athletes' normal weights.* THIS REQUIREMENT ALLOWS athletes to COMPETE in lower "weight classes" AND WIN. *Coaches take this position due to the fact that winning teams* bring *recognition and money to the schools and the individual athletes who may become rich and famous.*

IN CONTRAST TO THE ACTION TAKEN BY COACHES, THE LOSS OF BODY WATER IS strongly CONDEMNED BY THE AMERICAN MEDICAL ASSOCIATION. THEY CONDEMN LOSS OF BODY WATER DUE TO THE FACT THAT it HARMS the body. MORE SPECIFICALLY, *a loss of three percent of body water* hurts *physical performance, and a loss of five percent* results *in heat exhaustion. Moreover, a loss of seven percent of body water* causes *hallucinations. Losses of ten percent or more of body water* result *in heat stroke, deep coma and convulsions; if not treated death will result.*

Use of the top-level structure yielded significantly superior recall for message units, major details, and minor details for both passages immediately and one week after reading. Numbers in the passage were analyzed as part of the previous groupings and separately; numbers appear to be unusually well recalled regardless of position in the content structure (Meyer, 1971) due to the von Restorff effect. Use of the top-level structure as a production strategy had no effect on numbers recalled. However, use of this strategy was particularly crucial for recall of the message. For both passages there was a highly significant information type x use of structure interaction ($p < .0001$). Those who used the author's top-level structure experienced little forgetting of the author's message over the week retention interval; this was not the case for those who did not use this strategy. Thus, those who used this strategy had a much better criterion on the delayed recognition test for judging whether or not an item on the same topic as the text had actually been stated in the text. It is plausible that those who use the top-level structure of the text on the immediate recall task but not on the delayed task would surpass the performance of those who use it consistently due to the former group integrating the information with different prior knowledge structures. However, the data from both passages revealed that those who used the top-level structure immediately but not a week later performed very similarly on the immediate free recall test to the group that consistently used the top-level structure and on the delayed test performed like the group that never used the strategy. This finding argues that use of the top-level structure is particularly important for facilitating a systematic top-down retrieval strategy.

LATER STUDIES EXAMINING
THE RELATIONSHIP BETWEEN USE OF THE TOP-LEVEL
STRUCTURE AND RECALL

Across Various Ages.   The strong relationship between amount of information remembered from a text and use of the text's top-level structure has been found in a number of studies with elementary school children (Bartlett, Turner, & Mathams, 1981; Taylor, 1980), junior high students, junior college students, and older adults (Meyer, 1983). A study with graduate students reading the passages used by Meyer, Brandt, and Bluth showed that all of the students utilized the author's top-level structure; 50% of a group of junior college students tested used the strategy on more difficult materials (Meyer, Rice, Bartlett, & Woods, 1978).

Across Various Topics.   With over 300 ninth graders tested on seven different passages (Bartlett, 1978; Brandt, 1978; Meyer, Brandt, & Bluth, 1980; Swanson, 1979), the variance accounted for in recall by use of the author's top-level structure ranges from 36% to 52% immediately after reading passages to 68% to 80% one week after reading. The content of these seven passages taken from junior high school magazines and textbooks involved topics such as supertankers, loss of water from the body, and the history of railroads. However, on a highly familiar topic (Brandt, 1978) the amount of variance accounted for immediately was 22% and 30% one week later. On this delayed recall test there were no recall differences among students with high, average, and low scores on the comprehension subtest of the Stanford Achievement Test. The topic was killer whales and the students had just finished a science unit on oceanography and were planning a field trip to Sea World during the week of the delayed testing. It seems plausible that use of the top-level structure would be a less crucial strategy for this highly familiar content. With high prior knowledge of a topic, the content from the passage is integrated with existing propositions. The rich network on the topic provide many cues and links (Anderson, 1976) that facilitate recall independent of the use of the author's top-level structure. Although the magnitude of the effect of this strategy was reduced for this highly familiar topic, students who used the strategy still performed better than their peers who did not use the strategy.

INVESTIGATING A CAUSAL RELATIONSHIP BETWEEN USE OF THE TOP-LEVEL STRUCTURE AND INCREASED RECALL

The correlational data from the previous studies strongly suggested the possibility of a causal relationship between following and utilizing the author's top-level structure in text and how much and what can be remembered from it. Dissertations by two of my students were designed to investigate this causal relationship, and are described below:

Increasing Use of the Strategy With Advance Organizers.   One of the dissertations (Brandt, 1978) examined whether or not an advance organizer focusing on the top-level structure of text would facilitate recall of comparative and descriptive passages. Ninth graders with high, average, and low reading comprehension skills were placed in three groups. One group received text explaining the structure of the passage to be read as well as a diagram of the passage's top-level structure in an outline format. A second group was instructed to use a structure different from that of the passage (comparison for the descriptive passage and description for the comparative passage). This different structure also was presented in text and outline; the passage content could be reorganized by the reader to fit this different organizational structure. The third group worked on mathematics prior to reading the passage and served as the control group. All groups read two passages and recalled them immediately after reading them and 1 week later.

The data showed that prior knowledge of the author's structure or any other structure had no effect on the ninth grader's learning and retention of the passages. Use of the author's structure was the best predictor of recall, supporting the findings of the original study. Although the main effects were not significant, three important findings emerged from this dissertation. First, there was a significant interaction between text type and comprehension level of the readers; high and average comprehenders remembered more from the comparative version of the passage than the descriptive version, whereas the effects were reversed for low comprehenders. The second finding relates to the group asked to reorganize the passage with a top-level structure different from the author's. Although most students ignored these inconsistent instructions, high comprehenders were more likely to follow the instructions when the better comparative structure was to be employed with the poorer descriptive passage than when instructed to use the descriptive schema on the comparative passage. Third, the magnitude of the correlation between use of the author's top-level structure and recall was somewhat less for the descriptive versions (50% of variance accounted for) than the comparative versions (65% of the variance).

A possible explanation for the lack of main effects in this dissertation is that this type of advance organizer given to facilitate use of the top-level structur did not provide enough information to bridge the gap between the top-level structure of the passage and the ninth graders' cognitive structure related to strategies for learning text. Perhaps an advance organizer of this type would be helpful for more sophisticated readers on more difficult passages, but for these students it was not effective. Thus, for ninth graders, an extensive training program on identifying different types of top-level structures found in classroom text appeared to be the next step since the advance organizer, by definition a brief treatment, was not effective.

Increasing Use of the Strategy With a Week-Long Training Program.   The second dissertation (Bartlett, 1978) examined the effects of teaching ninth graders to recognize commonly found top-level structures on their ability to identify and use these structures in their own recall protocols and the amount of information they could remember. The duration of the instruction was one class period a day for five consecutive days. The instruction focused on how to identify and use four commonly found top-level structures in classroom text; these structures were comparison, causation, problem/solution and description. Special aids for identifying the top-level structure were faded out over the week of instruction and the passages studied increased in complexity; most of the instruction passages were taken from textbooks written for junior high school students.

Students in the training group and control group read and recalled passages prior to the training, one day after the training program, and three weeks after the completion of the program. The instruction resulted in significantly increased use and identification of the top-level structure of passages and in the amount of information recalled. The amount of information remembered from passages by the instructed group on each of the posttest sessions was nearly double that of both their pre-instruction scores and the scores for the control group for all testing sessions. The instruction benefited students with high, average, and low vocabulary scores on the Stanford Achievement Test (SAT). The effects of instruction were maintained three weeks after the training program by nearly all of the students except those with SAT vocabulary scores below the 12th percentile on national norms (2% of the students given the training); these students showed an initial benefit from instruction but it was not maintained three weeks later. Thus, the study shows that use of the top-level structure in prose is an important reading strategy and can be taught to most ninth graders.

An adaptation of this training program (Meyer & Bartlett, 1985) is currently being evaluated with old and young adults (Meyer, 1985b; Meyer, Young, & Bartlett, 1986). The strategy group is compared with a group who received practice on the same texts without direct instruction to use the top-level structure and a group who received no treatment. The first two instructional sessions defined five top-level structures: description, sequence, causation, problem/solution, and comparison, gave examples, and presented signaling words for the structures. The last three involved modeling and practicing a reading and recalling strategy for using the top-level structure to facilitate encoding and retrieval. It appears that the last three sessions were critical. Just teaching the structures (an extensive version of Brandt's advanced organizers) is not sufficient; readers must be shown how to use the structure when reading and remembering information from text.

Summary

The research studies discussed have shown empirically the importance of following and utilizing the top-level structure in text for reading comprehension. The data provide insight into the cognitive processes involved in reading comprehension. In addition, the findings and text analysis procedures have important practical implications for educators teaching reading comprehension. Further research could be profitably employed by examining the use of this strategy with different prose forms of various difficulty levels as well as looking at the use of this strategy with readers of different ages.

ACKNOWLEDGMENT

This research was supported in part by a Faculty Grant-in-Aid provided by Arizona State University.

REFERENCES

Adams, M. J., & Collins, A. (1979). A schema-theoretic view of reading. In R. O. Freedle (Ed.), *Discourse processing: Multidisciplinary perspectives*. Norwood, NJ: Ablex.

Anderson, J. R. (1976). *Language, memory and thought*. Hillsdale, NJ: Lawrence Erlbaum Associates.

Anderson, R. C. (1977). The notion of schemata and the educational enterprise. In R. C. Anderson, R. J. Spiro, & W. E. Montague (Eds.), *Schooling and the acquisition of knowledge* (pp. 415–431). Hillsdale, NJ: Lawrence Erlbaum Associates.

Bartlett, B. J. (1978). *Top-level structure as an organization strategy for recall of classroom text*. Unpublished doctoral dissertation, Arizona State University.

Bartlett, B. J., Turner, A., & Mathams, P. (1981, April). *Top-level structure: A significant relation for what fifth graders remember from classroom reading*. Paper presented at the annual meeting of the American Educational Research Association, Los Angeles.

Brandt, D. M. (1978). *Prior knowledge of the author's schema and the comprehension of prose*. Unpublished doctoral dissertation, Arizona State University.

Bruce, B. C. (1980). Plans and social actions. In R. J. Spiro, B. C. Bruce, & W. F. Brewer (Eds.), *Theoretical issues in reading comprehension* (pp. 367–384). Hillsdale, NJ: Lawrence Erlbaum Associates.

Carroll, J. B. (1971). *Learning from verbal discourse in education media: Review of the literature* (Final Report Project 7–1069). Princeton, N.J.: Educational Testing Service.

Caterino, L. C. (1977). *Adjunct structure and reading comprehension*. Unpublished doctoral dissertation, Arizona State University.

Davis, F. B. (1944). Fundamental factors of comprehension in reading. *Psychometrika, 9*, 185–197.

van Dijk, T. A. (1976). Narrative macrostructures: Logical and cognitive foundations. *PTL: A Journal for Descriptive Poetics and Theory of Literature, 1*, 547–568.

van Dijk, T. A., & Kintsch, W. (1978). Cognitive psychology and discourse: Recalling and summarizing stories. In W. V. Dressler (Ed.), *Current trends in text linguistics*. New York-Berlin: de Gruyter.

Elliott, S. N. (1980). *Effect of prose organization on recall: An investigation of memory and metacognition*. Unpublished doctoral dissertation, Arizona State University.

Flower, L. S., & Hayes, J. R. (1977). Problem solving and the writing process. *College English, 39*, 449–461.

Frederiksen, C. H. (1975). Representing logical and semantic structure of knowledge acquired from discourse. *Cognitive Psychology, 7*, 371–457.

Gainsburg, J. C. (1967). *Advanced skills in reading*. New York: Macmillan.

Grice, H. P. (1967). *Logic and conversation*. The William James Lectures, Harvard University.

Grimes, J. (1975). *The thread of discourse*. The Hague: Mouton.

Halliday, M. A. K. (1967). Notes on transitivity and theme. *Journal of Linguistics, 3*, 37–81; 199–244.

Horowitz, R. (1985). Text patterns: Part II. *Journal of Reading, 28*, 534–541.

Kintsch, W. (1974). *The representation of meaning in memory*. Hillsdale, NJ: Lawrence Erlbaum Associates.

Kintsch, W., & Keenan, J. M. (1973). Reading rate as a function of the number of propositions in the base structure of sentences. *Cognitive Psychology, 5*, 257–274.

Kintsch, W., Mandel, T. S., & Kozminsky, E. (1977). Summarizing scrambled stories. *Memory and Cognition, 5*, 547–552.

Mandler, J. M., & Johnson, N. S. (1977). Remembrance of things parsed: Story structure and recall. *Cognitive Psychology, 9*, 111–151.

Meyer, B. J. F. (1971). *Idea units recalled from prose in relation to their position in the logical structure, importance, stability and order in the passage*. Unpublished master's thesis, Cornell University.

Meyer, B. J. F. (1975). *The organization of prose and its effects on memory*. Amsterdam: North Holland.

Meyer, B. J. F. (1977a). The structure of prose: Effects on learning and memory and implications for educational practice. In R. C. Anderson, R. Spiro, and W. E. Montague (Eds.), *Schooling and the acquisition of knowledge* (pp. 179–208). Hillsdale, NJ: Lawrence Erlbaum Associates.

Meyer, B. J. F. (1977b). What is remembered from prose: A function of passage structure. In R. O. Freedle (Ed.), *Discourse production and comprehension* (pp. 307–336). Norwood, NJ: Ablex.

Meyer, B. J. F. (1983). Text structure and its use in studying comprehension across the adult life span. In B. Hutson (Ed.), *Advances in reading/language, Vol. 2* (pp. 9–54). Greenwich, CT: JAI Press.

Meyer, B. J. F. (1984a). Text dimensions and cognitive processing. In H. Mandl, N. L. Stein, & T. Trabasso (Eds.), *Learning from texts* (pp. 3–51). Hillsdale, NJ: Lawrence Erlbaum Associates.

Meyer, B. J. F. (1984b). Organizational aspects of texts: Effects on reading comprehension and applications for the classroom. In J. Flood (Ed.), *Reading comprehension* (pp. 113–138). Newark, DE: International Reading Association.

Meyer, B. J. F. (1985a). Prose analysis: Purposes, procedures and problems. In B. K. Britton & J. Black (Eds.), *Understanding expository text* (pp. 11–64, 269–304). Hillsdale, NJ: Lawrence Erlbaum Associates.

Meyer, B. J. F. (1985b). Using text structure to increase reading comprehension: A description of an instructional program and its evaluation. *Keynote addresses of the 11th Australian Reading Association Conference*. Brisbane, Australia: Australian Reading Association.

Meyer, B. J. F., & Bartlett, B. J. (1985). *A plan for reading: A strategy to improve reading comprehension and memory for adults*. Research Report No. 14 Prose Learning Series, Arizona State University.

Meyer, B. J. F., Brandt, D. M., & Bluth, G. J. (1980). Use of the top-level structure in text: Key for reading comprehension of ninth-grade students. *Reading Research Quarterly, 16*, 72–103.

Meyer, B. J. F., & Freedle, R. O. (1984). The effects of discourse types on recall. *American Educational Research Journal, 21*, 121–143.

Meyer, B. J. F., Freedle, R. O., & Walker, C. H. (1978). *Effects of discourse on the recall of young and old adults*. Unpublished manuscript, Arizona State University.

Meyer, B. J. F., & McConkie, G. (1973). What is recalled after hearing a passage? *Journal of Educational Psychology, 65*, 109–117.

Meyer, B. J. F., & Rice, G. E. (1984). The structure of text. In P. D. Pearson (Ed.), *Handbook of research in reading* (pp. 319–352). New York: Longman.

Meyer, B. J. F., Rice, G. E., Bartlett, B., & Woods, V. (1978). *Facilitative effects of passages with the same structure and different content on prose recall.* Unpublished manuscript, Arizona State University.

Meyer, B. J. F., Rice, G. E., & Vincent, J. P. (1986). *Effects of discourse type on recall by young, middle, and old adults with high, high-average, and average vocabulary scores.* Unpublished manuscript, Arizona State University.

Meyer, B. J. F., Young, C. J., & Bartlett, B. J. (1986). *A prose learning strategy: Effects on old and young adults.* Unpublished manuscript, Arizona State University.

Niles, O. S. (1965). Organization perceived. In H. H. Herber (Ed.), *Perspectives in reading: Developing study skills in secondary schools* (p. 76). Newark, DE: International Reading Association.

Rumelhart, D. E. (1975). Notes on a schema for stories. In D. G. Bobrow & A. M. Collins (Eds.), *Representation and understanding.* New York: Academic Press.

Rumelhart, D. E. (1977). Understanding and summarizing brief stories. In D. LaBerge & J. Samuels (Eds.), *Basic processes in reading: Perception and comprehension.* Hillsdale, NJ: Lawrence Erlbaum Associates.

Rumelhart, D. E., & Ortony, A. (1977). The representation of knowledge in memory. In R. C. Anderson, R. J. Spiro, & W. E. Montague (Eds.), *Schooling and the acquisition of knowledge* (pp. 99–136). Hillsdale, NJ: Lawrence Erlbaum Associates.

Sack, A., & Yourman, J. (1972). *The Sack–Yourman developmental reading course.* New York: College Skills Center.

Spearritt, D. (1972). Identification of subskills of reading comprehension by maximum likelihood factor analysis. *Reading Research Quarterly, 8,* 92–111.

Swanson, C. (1979). *The effects of readability and top-level structure on ninth graders' recall of textual materials.* Unpublished doctoral dissertation, Arizona State University.

Taylor, B. M. (1980). Children's memory for expository text after reading. *Reading Research Quarterly, 15,* 399–411.

Thorndyke, P. (1977). Cognitive structures in comprehension and memory of narrative discourse. *Cognitive Psychology, 9,* 77–110.

4

ON INVESTIGATING CHILDREN'S TRANSITION FROM NARRATIVE TO EXPOSITORY DISCOURSE: THE MULTIDIMENSIONAL NATURE OF PSYCHOLOGICAL TEXT CLASSIFICATION[1]

Rand J. Spiro
University of Illinois at Urbana-Champaign

Barbara M. Taylor
University of Minnesota

In recent years, considerable research attention has been directed to the psychology of prose processing (see Goetz & Armbruster, 1980; Reder, 1978; Spiro, 1980, for reviews). However, most of this work, especially that investigating children's performance, has focused on the comprehension and recall of narrative (Baker & Stein, 1978). Our resulting lack of knowledge about the way children process expository material (e.g., content area texts) is particularly unfortunate given that reading such material becomes so increasingly prominent a part of school experience after the third grade or so. Although at the time this was written we were able to locate only a few preliminary empirical studies comparing children's performance on narrative and expository material (e.g., Dixon, 1979), the ubiquity of the observation that children find the latter more difficult than the former (Baker & Stein, 1978; Freedle & Hale, 1979; Hall, Ribovich, & Ramig, 1979; Harris & Smith, 1976; Lapp & Flood, 1978) seems sufficient warrant for addressing why that might be the case.

This chapter is primarily concerned with ambiguities that result from traditional comparative analyses of text types. To take one example, hypotheses about why children have greater difficulty with expository

[1]This chapter was published as Center for the Study of Reading Technical Report No. 195 in December, 1980. Limitations of time have prevented us from attempting any revision based on developments over the last few years. There has been a substantial increase in the volume of research on expository text, and it obviously would have been desirable to make some changes in the details of our arguments if that had been possible. The general form of our argument, however, is one that we believe has retained its relevance.

than with narrative prose frequently invoke some variation on a "fit to prior experience" theme (e.g., Harris & Smith, 1976). That is, narrative is easier because children have more pre-reading and beginning reading linguistic experience with narrative forms, especially stories. Such accounts suggest many questions of clarification. For example: Do prior experiences with stories facilitate later comprehension of written narrative because children learn how narratives are typically organized (i.e., a "story schema" is available) or because children develop more efficient processing mechanisms to deal with material processing the characteristics of the more familiar narrative form (e.g., processes for encoding and retrieving temporally organized information)? Or does form follow function, with the common superficial story structures really reflecting the fact that stories usually deal with people and their goals whereas expository structures must adapt to a greater variety of topics? Children's stories might then be easier not because of familiarity with the form, but rather because of familiarity related to their content. What aspects of relative familiarity relate to intrinsic rather than actuarial characteristics of narrative and exposition? Is it, in fact, even the case that children have more experience with narrative than expository forms? Intuitively, it seems that children hear stories less often than they hear responses to questions like "Why is the sky blue?" Similar questions could be addressed to the other hypotheses offered to account for the difficulty of exposition, e.g., ideational density and complexity (Aulls, 1978; Baker & Stein, 1978; Freedle & Hale, 1979; Hall et al., 1979); for one thing, differences in ideational difficulty must be actuarial rather than intrinsic— every story written by Kafka involves more complex ideas than *You and Ohio*—the important question is what makes an idea difficult, and difficult in what way.

Our contention is that the ambiguity involved in interpreting differences in text difficulty has a very basic origin: the text classification scheme itself. As long as greatly diverse texts are lumped in overly subsuming categories like exposition and narrative, uniform conclusions regarding the nature of processing difficulties are not likely to be forthcoming. For one thing, it is difficult to classify texts within traditional taxonomies; there is no uniform agreement on what constitutes a narrative versus an expository text. For example, Freedle and Hale's (1979) expository passage, so classified because of its hypothetical nature (exemplified by the use of modal auxiliaries of theoretical possibility—"[to] get his stubborn horse into the barn . . . the farmer can go into the barn and hold out some sugar . . ."), would be a narrative in Brewer's (1980) classification scheme because of its underlying temporal organization. Despite the fact that many frequently occurring psychological properties of narrative and expository texts, respectively, can be identified, it can be demonstrated that any proposed psychological characteristic of exposition or narrative can be represented in varying degrees (or not at all) or be of varying importance for specific instances of both types of text. Structural familiarity is an example. Although many expository structures are less well known to children than story structures, some (e.g., lists) are relatively familiar. As Freedle and Hale (1979) and Stein (cited in Center for the Study of Reading, 1978) have pointed out, there are similarities between the structures of even more conventional exposition and narrative. For example, goals frequently have similar structural importance in exposition and narrative. Given such problems of partial overlap between the text types, is it reasonable to question whether a particular expository text still would be relatively difficult if those nonintrinsic properties typically found in exposition and associated with processing difficulty were absent and built into a narrative instead? If not, attention should not then be devoted to the properties and not to the traditionally classified text form that frequently but not necessarily possesses those properties? Because many correlated psychological properties are subsumed under the conventional text-type labels, the resultant confounding of possible causes of processing difficulty makes identification of specific difficulty loci methodologically problematic and conclusions expressed generally for a given text-type likely not to be replicated from text to text as underlying dimensions vary in uncontrolled mix.

Our primary thesis, then, can be expressed as follows. Difficulties children have with texts are attributable to specific psychological properties of the texts (and the contexts in which they are encountered). General labels of text-types only represent actuarially common (but not always present) conglomerates of text properties. Because whatever power a text-type label possesses for the prediction of text processing difficulty inheres in the specific and confounded dimensions the label imperfectly substitutes for, our recommendation is a simple one: Abandon the overly general and sometimes misleading conventional text-classification schemes as they are currently applied and, instead, characterize a text according to its psychologically relevant properties. The next section proposes, in preliminary fashion, a general outline that might guide the development of such a text classification scheme. Only when the many dimensions of intrinsic or actuarial difference between (conventionally labeled) narrative and exposition are deconfounded will specific and psychologically valid answers to the question of the difficulty of exposition be forthcoming. And only then will instruction differentially directed as a function of type of reading material be more than a well-intentioned shot in the dark.

A PRELIMINARY SKETCH OF A MULTIDIMENSIONAL
TEXT- AND CONTEXT-CLASSIFICATION SCHEME

The following is an outline of some of the psychological dimensions on which texts (and readers) may differ. The discussion is organized to inform an understanding of the phenomenon that was our point of departure: The difficulty children frequently manifest in making the transition from children's stories to content area texts.

Before proceeding, some caveats. Our list of dimensions is not orthogonal nor is it intended to be exhaustive. Within each general dimension many sub-dimensions are scattered. Also, precise measurement along some of the dimensions is beyond current capabilities—so the ultimate goal of uniquely identifying a point in the multidimensional space that corresponds to a given text for a given reader in a given situation must remain for the present a futuristic vision. We are not offering a "how to" manual. Rather, our intention is to illustrate the complexity of the text-classification problem and to suggest directions more complete schemes may follow. It is hoped that further developments of the multidimensional space will permit the kind of clarity found, for example, in the multidimensional space for differentiating oral and written discourse developed by Rubin (1980). Finally, it is recognized that multidimensional classification will frequently vary within a given text. Ideally, the scheme would be applied to text segments that are uniformly describable by the same values on the various dimensions, where the size of such segments may vary from parts of sentences to entire passages. In fact, the frequency and extensiveness of changes in the multidimensional space within a single text also may relate to processing difficulty.

Underlying Structure

Texts vary in terms of underlying organizational structure. A text can be comprised of a sequence of events in time or it can be organized in some other, nontemporal manner. In the case of a sequential underlying structure, the presentation of events often matches the representation of event, such as in a typical, well-formed story. This is especially true in children's stories, which rarely have flashbacks. In contrast, in a nontemporally structured text, as often is found in content area material, the sequential presentation of ideas necessitated by linguistic expression does not correspond to the mental representation of those ideas. This may produce an advantage for children's stories, given that temporal congruity between presentation and representation of events facilitates comprehension of a story (Baker, 1978; Mandler, 1978; Stein & Nezworski, 1978; Thorndyke,

1977). Mnemonic advantages of temporal sequence are further indicated by the commonly observed phenomenon of imposing temporal order in the recall of nontemporally ordered text (Gomulicki, 1956).

A mismatch between presentation and representation of ideas could present processing difficulties for children in a number of ways. It may be more difficult to discern the structural organization of content area text if the underlying representation of ideas does not correspond to their order in the surface structure of the text. Also, comprehension of content area text may be impaired if substantial amounts of processing capacity are required for the restructuring of nontemporally organized text from its sequential order of input to its underlying organization, leaving less capacity for other comprehension processes, such as following a recursive pattern of superordinate and subordinate ideas in content area text. Finally, the demands for integration may be different. The necessity of text being presented as a linear sequence of segments has the virtue, already mentioned, of correspondence with the chaining together of episodes in stories. The underlying ideas in some content area texts, on the other hand, may be more holistic in nature. In such cases, the sequential and segmented nature of language may inhibit synthetic processes.

To the extent that the underlying organization of children's stories is hierarchical as well as sequential, characteristics of superordinateness tend to differ in the two text-types. It may be that goals, so frequently superordinate in children's stories, are more salient and thus more readily apprehended (thus facilitating apprehension of the entire structure) than, for example, the subsuming abstract ideas commonly superordinate in content area text. (This is an obvious example of the promised nonorthogonality of the dimensions with, in this case, structural and content variables interacting. Actually, we consider superordinateness to be more of a semantic variable than an organizational one.)

A mismatch between presentation and representation of ideas in content area text may conflict with test demands. For example, if children are asked to recall a hierarchically organized segment of content area text, they might have difficulty retransforming this information back into a sequence of ideas (a kind of output interference). A recall of a story, in contrast, would probably be easier to produce simply because the surface organization of the story would more closely match the underlying representation of the story in memory. Here characteristics of underlying organization may interact with type of test (see the section on Subsequent Use of Text Information), with the mismatch just described having more serious consequences for the complete reproduction of a text than for probe-type questions.

Relevance of Preexisting Structural Knowledge

Recently, a great deal of theoretical and empirical work has focused on the use of story schemata by children and adults (Mandler & Johnson, 1977; Rumelhart, 1977; Stein & Glenn, 1979; Thorndyke, 1977). Basically, this work suggests that children and adults possess information about how stories are typically organized which, independent of content or input sequence, is used to facilitate comprehension and recall of children's stories and inform decisions on what constitutes a well-formed story. In contrast with the story schema research, much less empirical work has focused on schemata for content area discourse. However, Meyer (1975) has identified a number of content area patterns, such as problem–solution or cause–effect (naturally, this topic has received considerable attention in such disciplines as rhetoric; see Brewer, 1980).

Children may have difficulty with content area material because they do not possess structural schemata for content area text that are as well formed as those they possess for stories. They may have trouble selecting the appropriate content area schemata for a particular text from their available pool of content area schemata, given that content area forms are not as limited as children's story forms. Also, content area text more often may require the concurrent use of more than one structural schema, a further potential source of difficulty.

Digressing briefly, we believe that the importance of structural schemata has been exaggerated. As we indicated earlier, it seems likely that the common structural forms associated with children's stories result from the common content of children's stories: people, their goals, and their actions to attain goals. Expository material has a greater variety of structures because it tends to be about a greater variety of things, with different structures best fitting each thing (this is not to say that stories are only about people and their goals, but that common central concerns are much more likely to be found in stories than subject-area texts). Thus, results apparently attributable to structural story schemata really may be due to availability of a common core of content schemata, whereas requisite content knowledge for content area text more often may be unavailable.

Form of Linguistic Expression

Relevant language characteristics include traditional readability measures as well as several other less frequently considered variables. Readability formulas have traditionally been used to determine the relative difficulty of texts (e.g., Flesch, 1949). In general, these formulas are based on some measure of vocabulary difficulty, such as word length, and some measure of sentence difficulty, such as sentence length and syntactic complexity. Although these measures produce a global indication of the difficulty of a text, the inadequacies of this simplistic approach to readability have been stressed (e.g., Kintsch & Vipond, 1977). Factors omitted include most of the potential dimensions of difficulty discussed in this chapter. Nevertheless, it has been pointed out, based on readability formulas, that children's content textbooks in school often are written at a more difficult level than their basal reader stories (Hall et al., 1979). Children may have more difficulty with content area selections than stories, in part, because of more difficult vocabulary and longer sentences in the former type of text. Content area texts may contain more complex syntax (e.g., greater relative use of passive than active voice, more embedding, etc.) and less familiar cohesion producing connectives (e.g., in other words, this shows that, for example, as well as less transparent anaphoric reference). However, it should be kept in mind that more complex forms may sometimes promote comprehension (see Pearson, 1974–1975, for example).

In addition to vocabulary difficulty and sentence complexity, texts may vary in their use of figurative language. This variation may involve not only the frequency of occurrence of figurative language, but also its communicative function (Ortony, 1975). For example, metaphors could be used merely to repeat or to embellish information conveyed elsewhere literally, or they could carry exclusive communicative responsibility. Furthermore, metaphor and analogy often play a pivotal role in the elucidation of central concepts in content area texts (especially in the sciences). In children's stories, metaphor seems more often to serve peripheral functions, such as ancillary description. To the extent that figurative language is more difficult than literal language, and that content area texts contain more pivotal and unsupported use of figurative language, such texts may accordingly increase in difficulty.

Finally, oral and written language differ in many respects (Rubin, 1980; Schallert, Kleiman, & Rubin, 1977). To the extent that a written text utilizes oral language conventions congruously, the text may be easier. Consider the frequent incidence of dialogue in children's stories (but note the novel punctuation that must be introduced, perhaps adding compensating difficulty).

CONTENT AND SEMANTIC ORGANIZATION

Texts can differ along many interrelated content dimensions. Texts may be relatively abstract or concrete and imageable, with abstract text more difficult (Thorndyke, 1977). They may differ in their density of ideas versus events. If events are described, they may be real or hypothetical, contain substantial action content or be relatively peaceful, resolve rapidly or linger in unresolved suspense. Variability along these lines may affect children's processing; for example, children tend to assign great importance to action (Brown & Smiley, 1977). The number of ideas (or concept load) in texts of the same length may vary; some texts may frequently repeat (explicitly or implicitly) the same propositions whereas others frequently introduce new propositions, perhaps increasing text difficulty (Kintsch, Kozminsky, Streby, McKoon, & Keenan, 1975; for a detailed model that may permit measurement of a text's psychological processing difficulty along these lines, see Kintsch & van Dijk, 1978). The concepts discussed in a text may themselves vary in complexity. To take a simple example, the concept of "selling" is psychologically more complex than the concept of "giving," because the former entails the additional component of money transfer (Gentner, 1975).

Texts differ in the type and complexity of semantic relationships between ideas they contain. In stories, actions have to be pragmatically interpreted as to their relationship to goals of the characters (Bruce, 1980). More logical sorts of interrelating operations are frequently required in content area text (e.g., relating concepts to their attributes, categorization, and so on—see also the parallel distinction between common sense and logical modes of analysis in the section on Text Evaluation). Once again, however, such characteristics are not universally associated with a given type of text. It has been pointed out that some content area text is characterized by goal structures similar to those of stories (Freedle & Hale, 1979). It might be added that stories do not always have goal structures (stories about the random and purposeless activities of people can be very good stories—some existentialist philosophers might even say the only kind of stories that would really capture the nature of modern experience). This once again illustrates the misleading nature of the general text labels "exposition" and "narrative," as a common characteristic of one type may sometimes be absent from that type and present in the other.

Inferencing is another aspect of processing for which logical versus pragmatic semantic operations may be differentially required across texts. The information implicit in text but necessary for coherent understanding may need to be generated by pragmatic inferences (Brewer, 1977) relatively more in children's stories and by logical inferences more in content area text; children may have greater difficulty making logical than pragmatic inferences (Hildyard, 1979). Likewise, relationships affecting the importance of ideas in text may more often be determined on pragmatic grounds in stories and have a logical basis in content area text. Because pragmatically based semantic processes make more demands than logical processes on content knowledge (see the next section), we once again have a demonstration of interrelatedness within the dimensional space.

Finally, content may be of varying interest to readers. However, because of the relation of interest to prior knowledge, this topic is taken up in the next section.

Relevance and Availability of Preexisting Content Knowledge

Meaning is not conveyed solely by the linguistic content of text. Rather, meaning is constructed, using the text as a point of departure. The constructive process utilizes various kinds of contextual information, most prominent of which is the topic-related knowledge already possessed by the reader (see R. Anderson, 1977; Bartlett, 1932; Bransford & McCarrell, 1975; Dooling & Lachman, 1971; Spiro, 1977). One's knowledge structures (schemata, frames, scripts) are organized to enable such basic comprehension activities as inferencing, generating expectations, and imparting thematic connectedness (Collins, Brown, & Larkin, 1980; Rumelhart & Ortony, 1977; Schank & Abelson, 1977). Schemata have been shown to support memory for details (Anderson, Spiro, & Anderson, 1978), reconstruction (Bartlett, 1932; Spiro, 1977) and retrieval (Anderson & Pichert, 1978) of text information, determination of the relative importance of text information (Pichert & Anderson, 1977), and identification of information that requires less processing and explicit memorial representation as a function of its future derivability from other information (Spiro & Esposito, 1977; Spiro, Esposito, & Vondruska, 1978). Furthermore, if prior knowledge includes information about the typical or natural order of events, this may enhance the mnemonic advantages of temporally over nontemporally organized information (Baker, 1978; Schank & Abelson, 1977; see the earlier section on Underlying Structure).

To the extent that one's knowledge structures are derived from personal experience, employing them in understanding text may permit greater empathic involvement. Also, it is part of conventional wisdom that there are advantages to learning things directly from character rather than indirectly from instruction (but see Ausubel, 1968, p. 467). Perhaps the ability to personally simulate what one is reading about (and thereby "live" it in a sense) might be enhanced.

Prior knowledge may affect one's expectations concerning the interestingness of classes of text materials, such as stories versus subject-area texts, although it is not clear whether interest affects performance because of motivational factors or because one tends to be more interested in things one knows about (i.e., the knowledge, not the interest, produces the effect; see Asher, 1980).

The extent to which the various advantages of conceptually driven processes will apply is a function of characteristics of texts and of readers' knowledge. In virtually all texts some information is omitted by the author on the assumption that it is available to the reader and may easily be supplied (Clark & Haviland, 1977; Grice, 1975). Texts will vary in the extent to which this is the case, some texts being relatively more self-contained than others. For texts that are less self-contained, there will be differences in the burden placed on the individual to construct new knowledge structures rather than merely instantiating existing generic knowledge structures; that is, some structures may be permanently represented in memory as "pre-compiled" wholes whereas others need to be assembled when and as needed (Schank, 1979; Spiro, 1980). Additionally, texts will vary in their facilitation of conceptually driven processes, some providing clear explicit cues as to which preexisting knowledge is relevant, for how long it should be maintained as an adjunct to understanding the text, and when it should yield to other knowledge.

Further constraints on prior-knowledge-based processes result from reader characteristics. Most obviously, schemata presupposed by an author must be possessed by the reader. However, schema availability by itself is insufficient. Among other necessary accompanying processes (see Spiro, 1979), schemata must be efficiently accessed, at an appropriate level of specificity, and accurately applied to the text. Finally different individuals' schemata for the same concept may vary in their suitedness for achieving the advantages of knowledge-based processing. For example, mere familiarity with a situation will not enable increased recall of details unless the schema for the situation is sufficiently differentiated and constrained (Anderson et al., 1978). That is, feelings of familiarity may be generated by knowledge structures of varying states of development.

Discourse Function

Numerous taxonomies of the purpose or "force" of discourse have been proposed. For example, Brewer (1980) suggests that a text may be written to entertain, persuade, inform, or aesthetically please. Whatever the specific taxonomy, functions or purposes of reading may differ in their ease of satisfaction. In general, children may be more eager to read stories written for entertainment than content textbooks written to inform. Furthermore, it is clear that texts may be written, assigned during instruction, and read for a variety of purposes; the outcomes of comprehension may then differ accordingly. Common sense would suggest that when these purposes are not in agreement for the author, teacher, and student, adequacy of perceived comprehension outcomes can be seriously influenced.

Subsequent Use of Text Information

Related to the functions of a text are the uses to which it will later be put. Will understanding have to be demonstrated at a later time? Will such demonstrations be informal or formal? For how long will information have to be held in memory prior to the demonstration? It may be the case that story understanding in schools tends to be assessed informally (e.g., in class discussions) fairly soon after reading, whereas understanding of content area material is more often assessed formally, by written tests and after relatively longer delays (Dixon, 1979). In the simplest case, content area material may appear to cause difficulty just because more is expected for demonstrating its understanding. Furthermore, the standards by which a text is to be evaluated may tend to differ for stories and subject-area texts; judgments of conformity to common sense experience more often may be applied to the former ("Could this really happen?"; "What would you do in this situation?"; etc.), whereas the latter are subject to a "literate bias" according to which they stand or fall as a function of the adequacy and internal consistency of their logical arguments (Olson, 1977).

The child is expected to learn from content area text, to update his or her knowledge by integrating new information with topically related old information, sometimes to be able to transfer the newly acquired information (i.e., apply it in some novel context). Stories, on the other hand, are not supposed to be assimilated to other similar stories. Stories are complete; different fairy tales are supposed to be differentiated, whereas, at least below the college level, the different texts in which information about the Revolutionary War is received are not supposed to maintain their particular identity (Spiro, 1980). Of course, as with all dimensions, these are just tendencies; children may be expected to learn from the morals of stories, and, in later schooling, prose fiction will become a topic of study where knowledge updating will become relatively more important.

It is worth noting that educational ideals and testing realities frequently conflict, perhaps indirectly contributing a measure of difficulty with content area text for some children. Optimal transfer potential may be promoted by constructing trans-situationally integrated knowledge structures, but examinations usually test just the last acquisition situation and emphasize accurate memory. For such a test, compartmentalization of knowledge is frequently the best strategy (Spiro, 1977). Some children who appear to be having trouble with content area text may be confused as to what to expect, given that their teacher teaches one way and then, for convenience purposes, tests another. Such children might actually be acquiring important knowledge, but in a way not well adapted to test demands. Other children, apparently having little difficulty with content area text (given adequate test performance), may not, in any useful way, be learning at all.

Contextual Relevance

A child's oral language experience typically includes considerable contextual support; it frequently involves things that are going on in the child's life, quite often the immediate physical environment (Rubin, 1980). Children's early oral experience with expository types of information tend to be of this contextually (and personally) relevant kind ("What's that?"; "Please explain why what just happened to me happened that way?"). The child passes a tree and asks why leaves are green. It is probably less often the case that somebody says to the child, "Let's learn about why trees are green" when there are no trees around. Children's stories, on the other hand, almost always come "out of the blue"—one typically does not wait for situations to arise involving glass slippers, pumpkin carriages, or creative mice before reading Cinderella to a child. Rather than the context of stories, it is the activity of reading itself that tends to be situationally relevant (e.g., before going to bed is a time to read stories). It may be, then, that some children are less prepared by their oral language experience for school situations that involve contextually irrelevant, "out of the blue" written presentation of expository material. On the other hand, contextual discontinuity may seem less unnatural with stories.

Extra-Textual Support

Text is frequently supplemented in various ways to enhance understanding or interest. Depending on how they are used, adjunct questions (Anderson & Biddle, 1975), advance organizers (Mayer, 1979), and illustrations (Schallert, 1980), among other devices (see T. Anderson, 1980, for a review), may all result in some decrease in text difficulty. Because the applicability of such support devices will depend on the types of difficulty they are intended to overcome, this aspect does not constitute an independent dimension within the scheme. Rather, it requires a recursive analysis of the extra-textual aid and its relation to a specific text in terms of all the preceding dimensions.

CONCLUDING REMARKS

Obviously, the classification scheme as presented is not even close to completely formed. Surely important dimensions have been overlooked. It is clear that the dimensions (and sub-dimensions) require more precise differentiation and, in some cases, development of reliable methods of measurement. Calibrating the various measurement metrics will present further problems. However, because our goal was nothing so ambitious as the construction of a complete model, we will be satisfied if three of our modest goals were attained. First, we hoped to demonstrate the complexity of the web of psychological properties that distinguish the processing of one text from another and, thereby, the need to abandon simplistic traditional classifications of text as a basis for investigating the differential difficulty texts may present. Second, we wanted to offer preliminary suggestions that might provide useful directions for the development of a complete and practical method of multidimensional text classification.

Third, we intended that our discussion of text classification, however embryonic, would provide a framework for the design and interpretation of empirical studies that less ambiguously identify sources of difficulty in children's transition to subject-area reading. The discussion of psychological text properties, besides aiming toward a text-classification logic, is a collection of hypotheses about why that transition may be difficult for some children; that is, the scheme suggests dimensions to include in multivariate correlational studies of the transition phenomenon using existing texts and to control when constructing texts for experimental investigations. A caveat: The demands of rigorous experimental control, by extirpating properties from those with which they typically co-occur, may produce artificial texts artificially responded to—a measure of ability to adapt to ecologically invalid reading situations would likely be of little utility. Another caveat: processing difficulty along any of the dimensions can lead to comprehension failure; care should be taken to identify individuals whose apparently equivalent degrees of disability may be measuring very different sources of disability. The same caveat may even apply for the same individual across types of text; for example, a child experiencing difficulty with whatever is read may be having different problems with stories than with subject-area texts.

Identifying psychological dimensions of text processing difficulty would only be the first step. One would still want to know why some text property caused difficulty. Is it a problem of initial understanding? Of remembering? Might the transition problem result from cognitive capacity limitations on the number of dimensions of difficulty that can be dealt with in the same text? (In which case the strategy of manipulating one dimension at a time may be unrevealing.) Are certain kinds of processes inherently easier, or is it more a matter of fit to prior oral or written language experience? If the latter, does experience at some level of a text dimension produce positive transfer to stories or negative transfer to subject-area texts? Would the source of such effects be experiences in school, out of school, or both?

Finally, the outcomes of research such as we have proposed would have obvious instructional implications. For example, they could serve as a framework to guide further research aimed at developing strategies for overcoming difficulty along the various dimensions. More ambitiously, development of the multidimensional text-classification scheme could permit investigation of alternative sequences of phasing in subject-area text by gradually increasing the number of dimensions with difficulty that they contain, perhaps ultimately developing procedures for identifying instructionally optimal sequences of text transitions suited to individual needs.

ACKNOWLEDGMENTS

The research reported herein was supported in part by the National Institute of Education under Contract No. HEW-NIE-C-400-76-0116 to the Center for the Study of Reading, and in part by Grant AP Sloan Fdn #79-4-8 to Yale University.

Portions of this chapter were written while the first author was on leave at the Yale University Cognitive Science Program. The gracious hospitality of Roger Schank and Robert Abelson is much appreciated.

The authors gratefully acknowledge helpful discussions with Robert Kantor, Jana Mason, Andrew Ortony, David Pearson, David Rumelhart, and Nancy Stein. Comments by Larry Guthrie and Peter Johnston on an earlier version of this chapter were also very useful.

REFERENCES

Anderson, R. C. (1977). The notion of schemata and the educational enterprise. In R. C. Anderson, R. J. Spiro, & W. E. Montague (Eds.), *Schooling and the acquisition of knowledge*. Hillsdale, NJ: Lawrence Erlbaum Associates.

Anderson, R. C., & Biddle, W. B. (1975). On asking people questions about what they are reading. In G. Bower (Ed.), *Psychology of learning and motivation* (Vol. 9). New York: Academic Press.

Anderson, R. C., & Pichert, J. W. (1978). Recall of previously unrecallable information following a shift in perspective. *Journal of Verbal Learning and Verbal Behavior, 17*, 1–12.

Anderson, R. C., Spiro, R. J., & Anderson, M. C. (1978). Schemata as scaffolding for the representation of information in discourse. *American Educational Research Journal, 15*, 433–440.

Anderson, T. H. (1980). Study strategies and adjunct aids. In R. J. Spiro, B. C. Bruce, & W. F. Brewer (Eds.), *Theoretical issues in reading comprehension*. Hillsdale, NJ: Lawrence Erlbaum Associates.

Asher, S. R. (1980). Effects of interest on children's reading comprehension. In R. J. Spiro, B. C. Bruce, & W. F. Brewer (Eds.), *Theoretical issues in reading comprehension*. Hillsdale, NJ: Lawrence Erlbaum Associates.

Aulls, J. (1978). *Developmental and remedial reading in the middle grades*. Boston: Allyn & Bacon.

Ausubel, D. P. (1968). *Educational psychology: A cognitive view*. New York: Holt, Rinehart & Winston.

Baker, L. (1978). Processing temporal relationships in simple stories: Effects of input sequence. *Journal of Verbal Learning and Verbal Behavior, 17*, 559–572.

Baker, L., & Stein, N. J. (1978, September). *The development of prose comprehension skills* (Tech. Rep. No. 102). Urbana: University of Illinois, Center for the Study of Reading. (ERIC Document Reproduction Service No. ED 159 663).

Bartlett, F. C. (1932). *Remembering*. London: Cambridge University Press.

Bransford, J. D., & McCarrell, N. S. (1975). A sketch of a cognitive approach to comprehension. In W. B. Weimer & D. S. Palermo (Eds.), *Cognition and the symbolic processes*. Hillsdale, NJ: Lawrence Erlbaum Associates.

Brewer, W. F. (1980). Literary theory rhetoric, stylistics: Implications for psychology. In R. J. Spiro, B. C. Bruce, & W. F. Brewer (Eds.), *Theoretical issues in reading comprehension*. Hillsdale, NJ: Lawrence Erlbaum Associates.

Brewer, W. F. (1977). Memory for the pragmatic implications of sentences. *Memory and Cognition, 5*, 673–678.

Brown, A. L., & Smiley, S. S. (1977). Rating the importance of structural units of prose passages: A problem of metacognitive development. *Child Development, 48*, 1–8.

Bruce, B. C. (1980). Plans and social actions. In R. J. Spiro, B. C. Bruce, & W. F. Brewer (Eds.), *Theoretical issues in reading comprehension*. Hillsdale, NJ: Lawrence Erlbaum Associates.

Center for the Study of Reading. (1978). *The analysis of texts and tasks* (Report submitted to the National Institute of Education). Urbana: University of Illinois, Center for the Study of Reading.

Clark, H. H., & Haviland, S. E. (1977). Comprehension and the given-new contract. In R. O. Freedle (Ed.), *Discourse production and comprehension*. Norwood, NJ: Ablex.

Collins, A. M., Brown, J. S., & Larkin, K. (1980). Inference in text understanding. In R. J. Spiro, B. C. Bruce, & W. F. Brewer (Eds.), *Theoretical issues in research comprehension*. Hillsdale, NJ: Lawrence Erlbaum Associates.

Dixon, C. N. (1979). Text type and children's recall. In M. Kamil & A. Moe (Eds.), *Reading research: Studies and applications*. Clemson, SC: National Reading Conference.

Dooling, D., & Lachman, R. (1971). Effects of comprehension on retention of prose. *Journal of Experimental Psychology, 88*, 216–222.

Flesch, R. F. (1949). *The art of readable writing*. New York: Harper.

Freedle, R., & Hale, G. (1979). Acquisition of new comprehension schemata for content area prose by transfer of a narrative schema. In R. Freedle (Ed.), *New directions in discourse processing*. Norwood, NJ: Ablex.

Gentner, D. (1975). Evidence for the psychological reality of semantic components: The verbs of possession. In D. A. Norman, D. E. Rumelhart, & LNR Research Group, *Explorations in cognition*. San Francisco: Freeman.

Goetz, E., & Armbruster, B. (1980). Psychological correlates of text structure. In R. J. Spiro, B. C. Bruce, & W. F. Brewer (Eds.), *Theoretical issues in reading comprehension*. Hillsdale, NJ: Lawrence Erlbaum Associates.

Gomulicki, B. R. (1956). Recall as an abstractive process. *Acta Psychologica, 12,* 77–94.

Grice, H. P. (1975). Logic and conversation. In P. Cole & J. L. Morgan (Eds.), *Syntax and semantics (Vol. 3): Speech arts.* New York: Academic Press.

Hall, M. Ribovich, J., & Ramig, C. (1979). *Reading and the elementary school child* (2nd ed.). New York: Van Nostrand.

Harris, L. A., & Smith, C. B. (1976). *Reading instruction: Diagnostic teaching in the classroom* (2nd ed.). New York: Holt, Rinehart & Winston.

Hildyard, A. (1979). Children's production of inferences from oral text. *Discourse Processes, 2,* 33–56.

Kintsch, W., & van Dijk, T. A. (1978). Toward a model of text comprehension and production. *Psychological Review, 85,* 363–394.

Kintsch, W., Kozminsky, E., Streby, W. J., McKoon, G., & Keenan, J. M. (1975). Comprehension and recall of text as a function of content variables. *Journal of Verbal Learning and Verbal Behavior, 14,* 196–214.

Kintsch, W., & Vipond, D. (1977). *Reading comprehension and readability in educational practice and psychological theory.* Paper presented at the Conference on Memory, University of Upsala, Sweden.

Lapp, D., & Flood, J. (1978). *Teaching reading to every child.* New York: Macmillan.

Mandler, J. M. (1978). A code in the node: The use of a story schema in retrieval. *Discourse Processes, 1,* 14–35.

Mandler, J. M., & Johnson, N. S. (1977). Remembrance of things parsed: Story structure and recall. *Cognitive Psychology, 9,* 111–151.

Mayer, R. E. (1979). Can advance organizers influence meaningful learning? *Review of Educational Research, 49,* 371–383.

Meyer, B. J. F. (1975). *Organization of prose and its effects on memory.* Amsterdam: North Holland.

Olson, D. (1977). The languages of instruction: On the literate bias of schooling. In R. C. Anderson, R. J. Spiro, & W. E. Montague (Eds.), *Schooling and the acquisition of knowledge.* Hillsdale, NJ: Lawrence Erlbaum Associates.

Ortony, A. (1975). Why metaphors are necessary and not just nice. *Educational Theory, 1,* 45–54.

Pearson, P. D. (1974–1975). The effects of grammatical complexity on children's comprehension, recall, and conception of certain semantic relations. *Reading Research Quarterly, 10,* 155–192.

Pichert, J. W., & Anderson, R. C. (1977). Taking different perspectives on a story. *Journal of Educational Psychology, 69,* 309–315.

Reder, L. (1978, November). *Prose comprehension: A literature review* (Tech. Rep. No. 108). Urbana: University of Illinois, Center for the Study of Reading. (ERIC Document Reproduction Service No. ED 165 114).

Rubin, A. D. (1980). A theoretical taxonomy of the differences between oral and written language. In R. J. Spiro, B. C. Bruce, & W. F. Brewer (Eds.), *Theoretical issues in reading comprehension*. Hillsdale, NJ: Lawrence Erlbaum Associates.

Rumelhart, D. E. (1977). Understanding and summarizing brief stories. In D. LaBerge & S. J. Samuels (Eds.), *Basic process in reading: Perception and comprehension*. Hillsdale, NJ: Lawrence Erlbaum Associates.

Rumelhart, D. E., & Ortony, A. (1977). The representation of knowledge in memory. In R. C. Anderson, R. J. Spiro, & W. E. Montague (Eds.), *Schooling and the acquisition of knowledge*. Hillsdale, NJ: Lawrence Erlbaum Associates.

Schallert, D. L. (1980). The role of illustrations in reading comprehension. In R. J. Spiro, B. C. Bruce, & W. F. Brewer (Eds.), *Theoretical issues in reading comprehension.* Hillsdale, NJ: Lawrence Erlbaum Associates.

Schallert, D. L., Kleiman, G. M., & Rubin, A. D. (1977, April). *Analysis of differences between oral and written language* (Tech. Rep. No. 29). Urbana: University of Illinois, Center for the Study of Reading. (ERIC Document Reproduction Service No. ED 144 038).

Schank, R. C. (1979). *Reminding and memory organization: An introduction to MOPS* (Research Rep. No. 170). New Haven: Yale University Department of Computer Science.

Schank, R. C., & Abelson, R. P. (1977). *Scripts, plans, goals, and understanding.* Hillsdale, NJ: Lawrence Erlbaum Associates.

Spiro, R. J. (1977). Remembering information from text: The "state of schema" approach. In R. C. Anderson, R. J. Spiro, & W. E. Montague (Eds.), *Schooling and the acquisition of knowledge.* Hillsdale, NJ: Lawrence Erlbaum Associates.

Spiro, R. J. (1979). Etiology of reading comprehension style. In M. Kamil & A. Moe (Eds.), *Reading research: Studies and application.* Clemson, SC: National Reading Conference.

Spiro, R. J. (1980). Constructive aspects of prose comprehension and recall. In R. J. Spiro, B. C. Bruce, & W. F. Brewer (Eds.), *Theoretical issues in reading comprehension.* Hillsdale, NJ: Lawrence Erlbaum Associates.

Spiro, R. J., & Esposito, J. (1977, December). *Superficial processing of explicit inferences in text* (Tech. Rep. No. 60). Urbana: University of Illinois Center for the Study of Reading. (ERIC Document Reproduction Service No. ED 150 545).

Spiro, R. J., Esposito, J., & Vondruska, R. (1978). The representation of derivable information in memory: When what might have been left unsaid is said. In D. Waltz (Ed.), *Theoretical issues in natural language processing II.* New York: Association for Computing Machinery and Association for Computational Linguistics.

Stein, N. L., & Glenn, C. G. (1979). An analysis of story comprehension in elementary school children. In R. Freedle (Ed.), *New directions in discourse processing.* Norwood, NJ: Ablex.

Stein, N. L., & Nezworski, T. (1978). The effects of organization and instructional set on story memory. *Discourse Processes, 1,* 177–194.

Thorndyke, P. W. (1977). Cognitive structures in comprehension and memory of narrative discourse. *Cognitive Psychology, 9,* 77–110.

THE READER'S AFFECTIVE
RESPONSE TO NARRATIVE TEXT

James H. Mosenthal
National College of Education

The purpose of this chapter is to argue for the importance of the reader's affective response to narrative text in comprehending narrative text. It is an emphasis meant to complement structure-based explanations of comprehension of narrative (i.e., the story grammar perspective). This chapter uses Halliday and Hasan's (1976) concept of lexical cohesion as a tool for analysis. From the outset, it must be emphasized that the concept of lexical cohesion is not understood to operate independent of content, nor is a lexical cohesion analysis understood as a psychologically real determinant of a reader's affective response to narrative, nor is it a concept recommended for use by the teacher in the classroom. Rather, its use in this chapter is as a text-analytic tool for isolating stylistic choices of a writer relevant to discussion of affective response to narrative text. In the following pages, I discuss the role of affective response in comprehension, give an example of the potential power of affective response in comprehension, and conclude with a section on implications for teaching.

THE ROLE OF AFFECTIVE RESPONSE IN
COMPREHENSION

I make several assumptions about the concepts affective response and narrative text. Narrative texts are stories intended by the writer to emotionally involve the reader, as it is the reader's intention to be so involved. Use of the term *narrative text* assumes these complementary intentions. Affective response is the reader's involvement, his or her interpretation and appreciation of a writer's theme(s). Theme is to be regarded as the author's affective, felt purpose for writing. This affective domain in narrative cannot be broken down into parts of a whole and analyzed—it can not be perceived as structure. I present the notion that affective response to narrative text is potentially as powerful a determinant of comprehension as the canonical order of story parts.

As background to these claims, the work of Halliday (1977) and Halliday and Hasan (1976) on textual cohesion, the story grammar work of Thorndyke (1977), Stein and Glenn (1979), Mandler and Johnson (1977), and Rumelhart (1975), and van Dijk's work (1977, 1979) on textual relevance and textual coherence are discussed.

Halliday and Hasan (1976) state in their introduction to *Cohesion in English* that they are concerned with the concept of text and define text as any sequence of sentences, spoken or written, which functions as a coherent whole. Halliday (1977) describes a text-linguistic system with a textual component made up of thematic (unrelated to the definition of theme in this chapter), informational, generic structural, and cohesive subsystems. Only cohesion deals with non-structural, linguistic elements of text that signal continuity across sentences. I have adopted as an analytical tool Halliday and Hasan's (1976) concept of lexical cohesion, a subpart of the cohesion subsystem.

Non-structural cohesive relations, or ties, are defined by Halliday and Hasan as instances of reference, substitution, ellipsis, conjunction, or lexical cohesion. For example, a writer's use of intersentential referential items (*he, she, it, this, those*, etc.) or sentential conjunctives (*therefore, however, but, and*, etc.) explicitly signal relationship in text. Lexical cohesion, however, is the consequence of the use of reiteration (repetition of a word) and collocation (use of words that tend to appear together as a consequence of the particular topic addressed).

In this chapter, the identification of instances of reiteration and collocation serves as a means of isolating lexical choices of the writer that serve the writer's affective intentions but are not a consequence of the structural characteristics of the text. As a result, aspects of thematic development can utilize lexically cohesive items that, while participating in relatively low-level structural nodes, call up thematically superordinate concepts.

Story grammarians are concerned with the generic structure of narrative text. The intent of the story grammarians is clear. Stein and Glenn (1979) state that they mean to describe "the underlying structures used to comprehend the information units in a story and the relations which occur between them" (p. 1). Mandler and Johnson (1977) speak of a

story schema (referring) to an idealized internal representation of the parts of a typical story and the relationships among those parts. It is claimed that people use this type of representation of stories to guide comprehension during encoding and as a retrieval mechanism during recall. (p. 111)

Rumelhart (1975) speaks of a story grammar as describing the internal structure of a story analogous to the internal structure of sentences. And Thorndyke (1977) states that the intent of a story grammar is to define the structure of a narrative separate from its content. He describes a story grammar and comprehension model "that assumes a hierarchical organizational framework of stories in memory, determined by the grammar, representing the abstract structural components of the plot" (p. 77).

Consider Thorndyke's story grammar. His story grammar represents an approximation to a reader's schema for narrative. This schema is characterized by recursive rules of the grammar that define such categories as setting, theme, plot, and resolution. The setting includes the optional and subordinate subcategories of time, place, and character. Plot has an episodic structure varying in complexity depending on the specific narrative, with each episode having subordinate subgoal, attempt, and outcome categories. The complex of categories is hierarchical, governed by a set of grammatical rules, and represents the reader's internalized schema for making sense out of stories. The schema, or set of expectations for organizing a story, allows the reader to enter and remain situated in a story.

A problem with approaching comprehension of narrative text from the story grammar perspective is that comprehension is regarded as a measurable performance variable defined by the recall of structural elements of narrative text. However, if comprehension of narrative text contains an affective component independent of structural characteristics, then structural considerations alone will not adequately explain or predict comprehension. As stated previously, aspects of thematic development can contain lexically cohesive items that, while participating in relatively low-level structural nodes, call up thematically superordinate concepts. An example of this phenomenon is given later on.

The importance of affective response is discussed by van Dijk (1979) in terms of the reader's assignment of relevance in discourse comprehension. Relevance is defined by van Dijk as "degree of importance" (p. 113). He distinguishes between textual and contextual relevance:

Textual relevance is defined in terms of textual structures, such that certain structures are assigned a higher degree of relevance than others on general structural grounds. Contextual relevance is the assignment of a relevance value on the basis of any kind of contextual criterion such as the interest, attention, knowledge, wishes etc., of the reader. (p. 113)

Textual relevance is essentially determined by the structure described by a story grammar. Such a grammar describes what van Dijk calls global relevance, as opposed to the relevance assigned in sentential structure. Textual relevance is invariant with respect to context and operates as a type of "semantic background" against which the assignment of contextual relevance takes place (p. 119).

For van Dijk, contextual relevance assignment is equivalent to "the cognitive (and social, communicative) context defining what elements of a text are found important by a reader" (p. 119). Van Dijk describes contextual relevance assignment as a reader-based process that can be used to "upgrade" or "downgrade" information slotted in the structural description of the narrative (p. 122). This grading process occurs independently of the assignment of events to nodes in a structural representation of a story, and is in itself highly flexible, dependent on the current state of a reader's cognitive set.

AN EXAMPLE OF THE POTENTIAL POWER OF
AFFECTIVE RESPONSE: A THEME OF ALIENATION

In the rest of this chapter I look closely at the sixth chapter of *A Hero Ain't Nothin But a Sandwich,* by Alice Childress (1974). The chapter is a brief one narrated by the hero of the novel, Benjie Johnson. A propositional display of the chapter is given in Fig. 5.1. This chapter develops a theme of alienation and is referred to as the alienation chapter. The chapter is examined in an attempt to explore the relationship between affective response and comprehension.

A Hero was chosen for discussion because of its possible presence in an elementary or junior high school classroom. Pedagogical implications of the importance of affective response in comprehension are not clear. Potentially, a teacher's appreciation of a student's appreciation of a story need not be based primarily on the student's ability to recall its generic structure. Affective response determines an involvement with the text that is not necessarily tapped by questions and activities demanding accurate recall of character, and plot. Therefore, it may be beneficial for the student if the teacher devised methods of eliciting the more idiosyncratic responses a student has about the text. A reader's appreciation of a story can be as much a reflection of the author's choice of words as it is a reflection of the author's development of plot.

In narrative text, thematic concerns of the author will control word choice. Lexically cohesive items can be thought of as a means of the writer to signal the presence and importance of a motif set up by the writer within the general context of his or her thematic concerns. For example, take the reiterative use of the word 'chile.' When the use of an item such as 'chile' reiterates the previous use of 'chile,' this use is a cohesive use. Examples of reiteration in a given text define types of coreference. Halliday and Hasan (1976) describe four types: same referent ('chile$_1$' and 'chile$_2$' are used to refer to the same individual); inclusive (in a 'chile$_1$' 'chile$_2$' pair, 'chile$_2$' is used to refer to a class of children that includes the 'chile$_1$'); exclusive (in a 'chile$_1$' 'chile$_2$' pair 'chile$_2$' is used to refer to a class of children that excludes the 'chile$_1$'); and unrelated (in a 'chile$_1$' 'chile$_2$' pair 'chile$_2$' is used to refer to a class of children that does not obviously include or exclude the 'chile$_1$').

The reiterative use of 'chile' in the alienation chapter extends outside of the chapter and helps establish theme and the reader's affective response to the chapter. The word 'chile' is first used reiteratively in the opening chapter of the novel:

> Now I thirteen, but when I was a chile, it was hard to be a chile because my block is a tough block and my school is a tough school. I'm not trying to cop out on what I do or don't do cause man is man and chile is chile, but I ain't a chile no more. (p. 9)

No assertion is being made about the conscious, complex, literary use of 'chile.' What is asserted is the purposeful, therefore meaningful, reiterative use of the expression 'chile.' By using 'chile' in a factually inclusive but personally exclusive sense, the writer has Benjie generalize the notion of his early youth into a kind of abstraction from which he is alienated. It is precisely the sense of alienation from a time past that makes 'chile' appropriate for the voice of Benjie. There is no familiarity in the use of 'chile.' And much of Benjie's feel for his alienation is communicated in the use of 'chile.'

The reader's feeling for Benjie's alienation is most fully articulated in the alienation chapter. In the chapter, Benjie describes, and in so doing, asserts the only happiness he ever knew, the happiness of being a 'chile' cared for by his mother. By virtue of Benjie's alienation from that happiness there is a tension in the chapter embodied in the 'chile' motif. The happiness of being a 'chile' is memory and the pain of separation and addiction is Benjie's reality. The feel for this alienation is not something easily articulated by an adolescent reader (nor is it a response typically requested in recall measures). Yet, it is the essence of the reader's appreciation of the chapter.

It is important to note that inferences generated by the reiterative use of the word 'chile' are a product of the reiteration of a single lexical item used to refer to a concept or motif important in a specific thematic environment. The importance of the reiterative use of 'chile' is not of structural importance, but, in the terms of van Dijk, of contextual relevance defined by the individual reader's own involvement with the narrative.

Sentence #	Proposition #	
1	1.	When I was a chile,
	2.	me and my mother was cool with each other,
	3.	got along just fine,
	4.	also got along with my grandmother,
	5.	who was a classic dancer
	6.	when she was young.
2	7.	My mother used to help
	8.	go over my homework
	9.	and we be watchin our TV too:
	10.	Do little homework,
	11.	then look up
	12.	and dig TV
	13.	when the chase go on,
	14.	or the mystery bout to be solve
	15.	and the bad guy caught.
3	16.	I had me a happy childhood.
4	17.	Mama and me used to go for a walk on Satday night,
	18.	go to the newstand bout ten o'clock
	19.	and buy the Sunday newspaper with funnies in it,
	20.	then we go to the candystore
	21.	and buy us two little boxes of hand-dip ice cream, one for her and one for me
	22.	each gonna have our own box
	23.	to eat outta
	24.	while we read our papers.
5	25.	Sometimes Mama say,
	26.	"Let's go all the way!"
6	27.	Then she laugh
	28.	and we go to the bakery shop
	29.	and buy coffee ring
	30.	to have early Sunday mornin.
7	31.	I never did dig coffee
	32.	to drink
	33.	but it smell fine
	34.	when it perkin on Sunday.
8	35.	We be eatin our coffee cake with the raisins inside and nuts on top,
	36.	and I have cold milk with mine.
9	37.	Sometime we don't have coffee cake,
	38.	and Grandma make a bacon pancake.
10	39.	First she fry your piece-a bacon
	40.	till it's criss,
	41.	then she pour pancake batter topa that,
	42.	so your pancake gonna come out with a piece-a criss bacon stuck in the middle of it.
11	43.	Back in them days, we used to know
	44.	when we was happy
	45.	and didden have to be talkin it out
	46.	to see

	47.	if we was.
12	48.	Mama used to have a happy look right on her face.
13	49.	Grandma used to sing
	50.	a hymn call "Will There Be Any Stars in My Crown?"
	51.	-sing it on Sunday mornin
	52.	while makin our bacon pancakes.
14	53.	Mama say,
	54.	"When you gonna dance for us?
15	55.	Benjie, your grandma ain't never danced for me in her life."
16	56.	Then I tease Grandma,
	57.	"I don't believe
	58.	you can dance!"
17	59.	My grandmother take hold the end of her skirt
	60.	and say, "A-one, and a-two and a-three!"
18	61.	Then laugh
	62.	and say,
	63.	"Fooled you,
	64.	didden I!"
19	65.	She really didden fool nobody
	66.	because we knew
	67.	she wasn't gonna dance.
20	68.	Grandma say,
	69.	"My dancin days over."
21	70.	Christmas time we had a nice tree and plenty fruit and candy.
22	71.	I'd get games and new clothes.
23	72.	Only time Mama look sad
	73.	is when
	74.	she say,
	75.	"It's terrible
	76.	for a woman to be alone."
24	77.	I look at her
	78.	and ask,
24	79.	"How you alone
	80.	if you got me?
25	81.	You got me, Mama!"
26	82.	She smile
	83.	and say,
	84.	"Sure have.
27	85.	You mine
	86.	and I'm yours."
28	87.	All that was back
	88.	when I was six, seven and eight,
	89.	back before Butler took over
	90.	and stole my mother.
29	91.	Back in days before Nigeria Greene pulled the big double cross.
30	92.	I'm sorry
	93.	I ever had him for a teacher.
31	94.	He really ratted.

FIG. 5.1:   List of propositions for the alienation chapter in *A Hero Ain't Nothin But a Sandwich.*

With all that is brought to bear on the 'chile' motif a theme of alienation is developed underlying Benjie's predicament as a young adolescent. This theme comes to dominate the message of the alienation chapter, overcoming the force of Benjie's happy memories as a 'chile.' The foreboding character of this movement is indicated by the use of several other reiterative items. For example, the word 'days' is used three times in the alienation chapter.

> Back in them *days,* we used to know when we was happy and didden have to be talking it out to see if we was. (propositions 43–47)

> Grandma say, 'My dancin *days* are over.' (propositions 68–69)

> Back in *days* before Nigeria Greene pulled the big double cross. (proposition 91)

'Days,' in propositions 43 and 91, is an example of same-referent reiteration, and, in relation to the use of 'days' in proposition 69, an example of exclusive reiteration. It is significant that Grandma's "dancin days are over," for the happiness of those "dancin days," and the youthfulness of those days (Grandma "was a classic dancer when she was young" [propositions 5–6]), are past. Grandma's situation, expressed lightheartedly, does recall Benjie's own situation.

All the reiterative uses of 'days' are put in a context that nullifies the happiness of being a 'chile.' Childress' stylistic decision to include reiterative uses of 'days' carries with it an affective consequence. Together, the three uses of 'days' have a reinforcing power that complements the considerable knowledge already brought to bear on the opening time statement, "when I was a chile." Such reinforcement generates an affective appreciation for the tension between days before and days after. This tension further characterizes Benjie's feeling of alienation.

The reiterative use of the word 'back' complements the reiterative use of 'days':

> *Back* in them days, we used to know when we was happy and didden have to be talkin it out to see if we was. (propositions 43–47)

> All that was *back* when I was six, seven and eight, *back* before Butler took over and stole my mother. *Back* in the days before Nigeria Greene pulled the big double cross. (propositions 87–91)

In the first and fourth instances 'back' is used conjunctively as well as reiteratively. The reiterative use of 'back' reinforces the alienation theme. It helps put in a thematic context Benjie's description of his happy days of being a 'chile.'

Examples of collocation in the alienation chapter are, for the most part, related to Benjie's memory of Saturday nights and Sunday mornings spent with his mother. For Benjie there are deep feelings of security in his memories of his Saturday night/Sunday morning experiences. It can be argued that the reader also has access to prior knowledge of Saturday night/Sunday morning experiences that provides him or her with a powerful means for making inferences about Benjie's weekend memories (the reader identifies with Benjie's weekend happiness). In reading a novel those inferences are felt inferences. The prior knowledge allows emotional and conceptual entry into the schema Benjie instantiates. The power of the description, its contextual relevance, is not structural and is not easily articulated in recall.

Halliday and Hasan (1976) state that a group of terms are used collocationally if they have a tendency to be used in similar contexts. 'Saturday,' 'Sunday,' and 'weekend' are words often used concurrently and therefore are used in a collocationally cohesive way. Halliday and Hasan say that such words are regularly used in the same lexical environment. The following examples of collocational chains (a series of terms related to a common concept) are related to Benjie's memory of the Saturday nights and Sunday mornings spent with his mother:

Concept: weekend

Satday night (proposition 17) . . . Sunday newspaper (19) . . . Sunday mornin (30) . . . Sunday (34) . . . Sunday mornin(51)

Concept: food shared as a child with mother on weekend

candystore (20) . . . hand dip ice cream (21) . . . bakery shop (28) . . . coffee ring (29) . . . coffee (31) . . . coffee cake (35) . . . raisins and nuts (35) . . . cold milk (36) . . . bacon pancake (38) . . . bacon (39) . . . pancake batter (41) . . . pancake (42) . . . bacon (42) . . . bacon pancakes (52)

Concept: newspaper read on weekend

newstand (18) . . . Sunday newspaper (19) . . . funnies (19) . . . read (24) . . . papers (24)

These concepts are used to help develop a feeling of nostalgia and remembered happiness, love, and security that is not explained by structural characteristics of the text.

At a more general level, Benjie talks in detail about the times he <u>has</u> with his mother, the times they <u>shared</u>, the things they <u>bought</u> together, the places they went <u>together</u>, the things they did together. The underlined words constitute a collocational chain used to communicate the notion of shared possession. The shared possession motif in Benjie's narration is dominating in the alienation chapter. There is a lot of 'having' and 'sharing' going on. It is 'my mother,' 'my grandmother,' 'I had me a happy childhood,' 'buy the newspaper,' 'buy the ice cream . . . one for her and one for me, each gonna have our own to eat outta while we read our paper.' Suddenly, it is 'stole.' When Benjie says Butler 'stole' his mother, the use of 'stole' calls up and contextualizes a theft the reader experiences. Thematically, it is Benjie's interpretation of when and how he 'lost' his childhood.

What is important in the previous discussion is the fact that the chapter is viewed as intending to invoke affective response. Such response is not based on structural conditions, yet it is a form of comprehension. The idea of affective comprehension or response complements the emphasis of the work of the story grammarians in asserting an independent source affecting comprehension.

This complementarity has not been noted by the story grammarians. Thorndyke states that "recall probability of any individual proposition from a story passage (is) a function of its structural centrality as determined by the grammar" (p. 105). However, given the alienation chapter, propositions 84 and 85 ("You mine and I'm yours") have no structural centrality. However, they have great thematic or contextual relevance given the possession and chile motifs described previously. Such a proposition has strong potential for being 'upgraded' and having an effect on the reader's appreciation of the chapter. That effect is reinforced through other reiterative uses or adaptations of propositions 84–85. In chapter 26 Benjie recalls how Butler said to his mother "you got him" and she replied "yes, he's mine and I'm his" (page 92). In chapter 20 Butler Craig says "I went off cause he wasn't mine" (p. 110). In chapter 21 Butler tells the social worker—with sarcasm for the worker and love for Benjie—"let's put it this-a-way, I am who he has got for a father, that is sufficient to make him mine and me his" (p. 112). All that has been discussed leads to this fact, that a structurally subordinate proposition can be contextually upgraded and made more important or relevant than a structural analysis may reflect.

Overall, although a story grammar does provide an orienting schema for stories and can predict comprehension of plot, it does not solely define the nature of the reader's comprehension of the story. It is complemented by the affective, contextually relevant aspects of comprehension.

IMPLICATIONS FOR THE CLASSROOM

In the classroom the question could be asked, "Why did Benjie have it in for Butler?" The correct answer: "Because he stole Benjie's mother away from Benjie." This is a correct answer. However, with the concern for theme described in this chapter, it can be recommended that the teacher attempt to have the reader come to terms with Benjie's feeling of loss, and not be satisfied with the answer, "because he stole Benjie's mother."

As another example, in discussing the Saturday night/Sunday morning experiences, a teacher can have students talk about their own Saturday night/Sunday morning experiences rather than ask only "What did Benjie do on the weekends?" Such a question keys into the structural node "go for a walk with his mother" (proposition 17) without equal concern for the reader's appreciation of theme.

Ultimately, the teacher can pay more attention to what is contextually relevant to the reader. He or she can pay more attention to the reader's affective appreciation of the story and not simply demand right answers for questions keying into structural considerations of the story. In the case of *A Hero,* the teacher can allow the student to generate responses about his or her own understanding of and feeling for alienation. These responses can in turn be used to develop an understanding of Benjie's alienation.

This approach to a discussion of the alienation chapter in the classroom is not presented as one distinct from a discussion emphasizing plot. The two approaches interact. In truth, an appreciation of theme can not happen unless the reader knows what has happened in the story. The point is that mere concern for plot on the part of the teacher denies the student the opportunity to attempt to articulate his or her appreciation for a story's theme. For it is this theme that is the writer's purpose in writing, and the experience of it is the reader's goal for reading. The teacher must consider this affective response and encourage its articulation.

REFERENCES

Childress, A. (1974). *A hero ain't nothin but a sandwich.* New York: Avon.

van Dijk, T. A. (1977). *Text and context: Explorations in the semantics and pragmatics of discourse.* New York: Longman.

van Dijk, T. A. (1979). Relevance assignment in discourse comprehension. *Discourse Processes, 2,* 113–126.

Halliday, M. A. K. (1977). Text as semantic choice in social contexts. In T. A. van Dijk & J. S. Petofi (Eds), *Grammars and descriptions* (pp. 176–225). New York: de Gruyter.

Halliday, M. A. K., & Hasan, R. (1976). *Cohesion in English.* London: Longman.

Mandler, J. M., & Johnson, N. S. (1977). Remembrance of things parsed: Story structure and recall. *Cognitive Psychology, 9,* 111–151.

Rumelhart, D. E. (1975). Notes on a schema for stories. In D. G. Bobrow & A. Collins (Eds.), *Representation and understanding: Studies in cognitive science* (pp. 211–236). New York: Academic Press.

Stein, N. S., & Glenn, C. G. (1979). An analysis of story comprehension in elementary school children. In R. O. Freedle (Ed.), *Advances in discourse processes (Vol. 2): New directions in discourse processing* (pp. 53–120). Norwood, NJ: Ablex.

Thorndyke, P. (1977). Cognitive structures in comprehension and memory of narrative discourse. *Cognitive Psychology, 9,* 77–110.

PART II

LANGUAGE, KNOWLEDGE OF THE WORLD, AND INFERENCE

Over the past two decades we have seen an upsurgence of activity and interest in applying language learning theories to classroom reading instruction. In the 1960s and 1970s, the psycholinguistic models of Goodman (1967) and Smith (1970) challenged instructional practices that served no "real-world" function and that emphasized decontextualized letter and word identification. In the mid-70s, cognitive theories began emerging as the dominant view from which needed developments in the teaching of reading comprehension might be derived. For example, in 1975, a panel for the National Institute of Education nominated a schema-theoretic perspective as the most viable as the basis for a language-learning model from which issues related to reading comprehension might be examined. The celebrity status that schema theory subsequently acquired is now history. Numerous doctoral theses based on a schema-theoretic perspective were derived as well as several articles dealing with classroom applications. The chapters in this section should force us to take stock of the viability of these popularized notions and translations.

At the same time as they clarify and extend our notions of the reading act, these chapters do much to establish a view of schema theory that is contextually richer and more dynamic than most contemporary conceptualizations. In the first chapter, Iran-Nejad questions the structural orientation of several contemporary schema theorists and raises issue with the bridled view of information storage and processing they have prompted. The chapter by Pappas presents a view of reading comprehension based on a description of the nature of world knowledge that is derived from an amalgamation of schema theory with the research of

Rosch, Chafe, and Head. Pappas presents a detailed discussion of the protypical rather than definitional nature of world knowledge as well as the relevance of these notions to individual differences among comprehenders. The notion of protypicality is also at the heart of a discussion of readers' use of pragmatic conventions by Beach and Brown. Using selected examples of readers' responses to text they illustrate the role of context and pragmatic conventions and develop a model of discourse conventions based on their research and the work of literary theorists and pragmatists such as Grice, Searle, and Labov. Altwerger and Strauss review the research on metaphor and suggest that studies of metaphors using decontextualized presentations offer little that is worthwhile. In their stead they posit a call for research that is grounded in psycholinguistic theory. The issue of context reemerges in the next chapter by Carey and Harste who question selected schema-theoretic views of comprehension that disregard context and its transactional nature. In accordance with this transactional view, the last chapter in the set by Tierney, LaZansky, Raphael, and Cohen explores the view that reading involves transactions along two dimensions—readers with authors and readers with his or her "other self."

The chapters individually and as a set represent a rich and thoughtful repertoire of ideas that are both diverse and complimentary. They are diverse in the nuances they address; they are complimentary in their depiction of reading as interpersonal, ideational, dynamic and transactional.

6

THE SCHEMA: A LONG-TERM MEMORY STRUCTURE OR A TRANSIENT STRUCTURAL PHENOMENA

Asghar Iran-Nejad
University of Michigan

Currently, dominant theories of comprehension and cognition are schema theories. They all assign a central role in comprehension to high-level, domain-specific cognitive structures variously referred to as *frames* (Minsky, 1975), *scripts* (Schank & Abelson, 1977), *schemata* (Rumelhart, 1978; Rumelhart & Ortony, 1977), or *macrostructures* (Kintsch & van Dijk, 1978).

Indubitably, the notion of schema is a useful one. It not only refers to elements and relations in the conceptual network (Ortony, 1978, p. 54), but also underscores the patterning aspect of cognition (Anderson, 1977). Schemata further draw attention to the domain-specific nature of knowing. More specifically, in contrast with traditional information processing theories that emphasize processing, storage, retrieval, and utilization of knowledge in general, schema-based research concentrates predominantly on knowledge of particular domains.

Domain specificity is clearly a relevant issue. This is because cognition and comprehension seem to operate in terms of particular domains and in particular situations. Research based on the notion of schema and related concepts has demonstrated that comprehension of the same textual material varies from one domain of knowing (one schema) to another. To cite some specific example, it makes a difference whether or not people know that the passage they are about to read is, for instance, about "washing clothes" (e.g., Bransford & Johnson, 1972), whether they know what they are reading is about eating in a fancy restaurant as opposed to shopping at a supermarket (e.g., Anderson, Spiro, & Anderson, 1977), buying as opposed to burglarizing a home (e.g., Anderson & Pichert, 1978), breaking out of jail as opposed to wrestling (Anderson, Reynolds, Schallert, & Goetz, 1977), or finally, whether they find out later that the female character of the passage they have read is a lesbian or a heterosexual (Snyder & Uranowitz, 1978). Furthermore, people become experts in specific domains. There are no such things as experts per se. Rather, there are expert tennis players, expert readers, expert clinicians, and so forth. It is perhaps this realization that renders the use of nonsense syllables as (domain-independent) experimental material nonsensical. In short, if common denominators concerning cognitive functioning in general are to be discovered, they ought to be sought where they are actually operative, (that is, in terms of specialized domains of knowing).

Thus, conceptually a schema is a domain-specific relational cluster. Beyond this, however, the concept of schema remains, theoretically, disturbingly vague. One reason for this is that the metaphors cognitive scientists use (e.g., "link," "association," "connection," "pointer") to refer to the relations among schema constituents are purely conceptual. The question of the real nature of cognitive patterning has not as yet been addressed, although the reality of mental schemata is generally assumed. In fact, given the current state of the art, the issue of the reality of schemata remains a remote problem. The purpose of this chapter is to discuss one way in which cognitive patterning is actually possible.

The term actual is meant to refer to the physical plausibility of the concepts used in theorizing about cognitive schemata. It is assumed that the issue of the physical reality of cognitive patterns is as inevitable as it is urgent. That the physical plausibility of the concepts under investigation is a necessary precondition for scientific progress is evident from many instances in the history of science. The concept of the light bulb, for instance, must have started as a physically plausible notion. In other words, the usefulness of conceptual metaphors is contingent on the scientist's belief in their physical possibility as well as on some "thinkable" basis for the belief. Purely conceptual metaphors with mysterious or abstract characteristics are logical shuttles that only serve to delay the thought and investigation. (It was Edison's unshakable belief in the physical possibility of the light bulb, and a more or less clear notion about the nature of this possibility, which led to its reality, that is, to the actual construction of the light bulb). Without this belief in physical reality, the abstract concept would have been worth nothing.

Early in this chapter I stated what I believe schemata are. Before discussing their nature, it must be also clarified what I think schemata are not. The following section is aimed at this issue.

UNEXPLAINING THE CONCEPT OF SCHEMA

The Schema as a Structural Construct

For many theorists who use it, the term *schema* has come to be synony-mous with the term *long-term memory structure*. The schema-is-a-struc-ture assumption is clearly evident in the cognitive scientific literature and needs no elaboration. What is perhaps not as obvious is what the term *structure* (schema) is meant to represent. I will attempt to clarify this issue by looking at the metaphors cognitive scientists often use to qualify or describe the notion of schema and by considering the contrast often made between the terms *structure* and *process*.

First, schemata are generally claimed to be pre-existing knowledge structures stored in some location in the head. A schema is said to be a collection of concepts and associative links (e.g., Ortony, 1978, p. 54) or "a cognitive template against which new inputs can be matched and in terms of which they can be comprehended" (Rumelhart & Ortony, 1977, p. 131). Moreover, like any stored or storable entity, schemata are said to be "searched," "found," "utilized," and "stored again." The following excerpts from some often-cited sources in the literature of cognitive science clearly illustrate this point:

> The reader brings a large repertoire of knowledge structures to the under-standing task . . . Rumelhart puts the matter very well when he says, "the process of understanding a passage consists in finding a schema which will account for it." (Schank & Abelson, 1977, p. 10) According to "schema theories" all knowledge is packaged into units. These units are the sche-mata. (Rumelhart, 1978, p. 3)

> The entire memory system contains an enormous number of schemata and memories. At any one time only a few of them are required and no procedure of random search could possibly lead to their efficient discovery. The search for likely candidate schemata must, therefore, be somehow guided and it must be sensitive to the context. . . . (Rumelhart & Ortony, 1977, p. 128)

> The building block of the model is the "State of Schema." The SOS is a representation of the subset of the information hypothesized to be stored in a schema (or a set of related schemata). (Spiro, 1977, p. 151)

The preceding paragraphs clearly reflect a belief that schemata are relatively permanent structures (at least as permanent as the long-term memory), that they are brought to the comprehension situation somewhat ready-made, and that they are capable of being stored, searched, retrieved, and so forth. One may also note the passive static character of these cognitive templates, though some theorists might argue otherwise.

That the term *structure* refers to the relatively permanent and static aspect of cognition is evident from the fact that cognitive scientists often contrast it with the term *process* (see, e.g., Bobrow & Norman, 1975; Collins & Loftus, 1975, pp. 411–413; Rumelhart & Ortony, 1977, p. 100, pp. 127–128), which points to the more transient and dynamic aspect of cognition. In this sense the term *process* falls in the same category as the word *function*.

Bartlett (1932), for instance, contrasted *structure* with *function* instead of *process*. For Bartlett, it is live biological structures that function rather than object-like knowledge or mental structures. He finds no necessity in appealing to mental structures in his account of remembering. He states:

> Everything in this book has been written from the point of view of a study of the conditions of organic and mental functions, rather than from that of an analysis of mental structure. It was, however, the latter standpoint which developed the traditional principles of association. The confusion of the two is responsible for very much unnecessary difficulty in psychological discussion. (p. 304)

And indeed it is. The slight difference in terminology reflects a fundamental difference in theoretical perspective. The term *function* as a verb is intransitive. For Bartlett, live biological structures *act*. They do not *act upon* some object-like entity. His is not an industrial-plant metaphor. This is why Bartlett's functional schema theory can do away with the notion of storage entirely (p. 200). Clearly, whereas structural schema theory cannot survive without it, the verb *process* is transitive; it requires an object, that is, some entity to get processed.

The Schema as an Explanatory Construct

Although this chapter is centered around the idea that the patterning aspect of cognition must be treated as a problem to be resolved, many theorists have used the schema as an explanatory construct. Schemata often are said to be "employed in the process of interpreting sensory data, (both linguistic and non-linguistic) in retrieving information from memory, in organizing actions, in determining goals and sub goals, in allocating resources and generally in guiding the flow of processing in the system" (Rumelhart, 1980, pp. 33–34). In short, "theorists have tended to regard schemata as a panacea . . ." (Ortony, 1978, p. 54). Because it is not clear how the concept of schema is capable of performing these "wondrous things," as Rumelhart calls them (p. 34), one feels compelled to suggest that the term *schema* only be used to refer to the purely pattern-ing aspect of cognition and even then as a problem to be resolved. I repeat the question posed early in this chapter: Just how is patterning actually possible? Or, as Bartlett (1935) stated, "first, . . . how are the organized patterns of psychological and physiological material formed? . . . [And] second, what are the conditions and laws of construction in the mental life? These are urgent psychological problems, not outside the experimen-talist's scope" (p. 226).

THE STRUCTURAL ASSUMPTION AND THE PROBLEM
OF PATTERNING

The Nature of the Problem

The idea that schemata are long-term memory knowledge structures (cognitive building blocks, cognitive templates) with permanent internal connections becomes paradoxical when the issue of the physical reality of cognition is considered. This is because one can assert with confidence that there is no single element in the entire cognitive network that can be said to belong, or be uniquely connected to, one and only one schema. It is more likely that element E is a component of schema A at one time and an element of B, C, or D at some other time. But if this is the case, in what sense can it be claimed that E is more an element of A than an element of B, C, or D? In other words, what does it mean to say that elements of A form a long-term memory associative knowledge cluster?

In order to conceptualize the magnitude of the problem, consider the metaphors often used to refer to knowledge networks. "Encyclopedia," and "dictionary" are among the most common. Imagine, now, the extent of crisscrossing of associations necessary to represent in structural network form an encyclopedia of everything a particular average college student, for instance, might know. Even if such a representation were possible, which is clearly questionable, it would constitute a static repre-sentation. Hardly anyone, however, would doubt the idea that the human cognitive network is a highly plastic, highly dynamic network; the rela-tions involved are constantly in a state of change. As Bartlett (1932) states, "since many 'schemata' are built of common materials, the images and words that mark some of their salient features are in constant, but explicable change" (p. 214). Truely, the number of possible connections and combinations (i.e., schemata) is indefinitely large. As long as purely conceptual metaphors such as "link," "association," and "pointer," etc. are used, the problem remains masked. At a physical level a structural cognitive network seems impossible to imagine, if not simply impossible.

It is because of the requirement of "continuous change" in the face of constantly novel situations that the idea of schemata as pre-existing long-term memory structures becomes paradoxical. As Anderson (1977) points out,

> It could not be that people have stored a schema for every conceivable scene, event sequence, and message. . . . Even if the nominal stimuli in two situations were the same, people change. They come to similar situations with different perspectives and different intentions; they play different roles. It follows that people do not function by selecting the right template from a great mental warehouse of templates abstracted from prior experience. The process must be more dynamic. (p. 421)

Neither can it be said that a schema is a collection of discrete concepts. In an associative cluster, if the link with one of the elements is missing, the remaining fragment may preserve the pertinent characteristics. It seems more reasonable to assume that a schema is an emergent transient gestalt. In this sense, *combine* might be a better metaphor than *link* or *associate*. The whole can be more than the collection of its elements because it does not *consist* of elements; rather, it is *generated* by the elements (John Stuart Mill, 1843/1965). If oxygen is taken out of water, the property of "waterness" is lost, because this property is not independently present in the components. Similarly, if an element of a cognitive pattern is taken out or replaced by another element, the resulting combination gives rise to a different pattern with its unique properties. "Opening a door" is not the same as "opening a bottle," "opening one's mouth," "opening a discussion," or "opening a can of worms." If Wittgenstein is right, words like "open," and "game," do not probably depend on a common underlying structural core whether it be called "a core meaning," "a schema," or something else (see Anderson & Ortony, 1975; Goetz, Anderson, & Schallert, 1979).

The Relationship Between the Neuronal Network and the Cognitive (Conceptual) Network

Sooner or later, theories of cognition will have to deal with the problem of the relationship between the neuronal network and the conceptual network. However, given the structural assumption and the overly complicated picture of the conceptual network it provides, the issue seems as remote as the equally ignored problem of the phenomenal aspect of patterning. This is perhaps why some ingenious attempts at building psychoneural models, as made by Hebb (1949), have remained largely ignored.

Some cognitive scientists, however, have demonstrated a willingness to speak in neural terms. Collins and Loftus (1975), for instance, consider their semantic network model quasi-neurological (p. 411). This is perhaps because they use neuronal terms such as *activation, threshold,* and *summation* in the context of their structural conceptual network. A cogent summary of their model is given in the following paragraph from Ortony (1978).

> In their recent modification and improvement of the Quillian (1968) network model of semantic memory, Collins and Loftus (1975) introduce some additional processing assumptions. The first is that when a concept is processed activation spreads from it in a decreasing gradient; the second is that release of activation from a concept continues at least as long as that concept is processed; and a third relates to decrease of activation over time. The fourth addition is that activation from different sources summate and that there is a threshold which determines whether or not an intersection is found. Added to these are two additional structural features. First, that semantic similarity plays a larger role in the organization of the network, and second that the names of concept, i.e., words, are stored in a lexical network, which is to some extent independently "primable." (p. 55)

Quasi-neurological semantic network models, therefore, speak of activation spreading in a structural conceptual network. However, it is possible that cognition can be characterized without the need to hypothesize such associationistic networks. As Bartlett (1932) suggests, this would also eliminate a great deal of "unnecessary difficulty in psychological discussion" (p. 304). Whatever the case may be, the relationship between the neuronal, phenomenal, and the conceptual aspects of the mind must be theoretically clarified before neurophysiological concepts can be used in the psychological domain.

TOWARD A SOLUTION TO THE PROBLEM OF THE NATURE OF COGNITIVE PATTERNING

The Schema as a Functional-Phenomenal Pattern

Underlying cognitive patterns are, according to the structural assumption just discussed, relatively permanent, frame-like, knowledge structures with long-term internal connections. Counterintuitive as it may seem at first, it is entirely conceivable, however, that the patterning aspect of cognition is a transient functional-phenomenal, rather than a long-term memory structural, organization. The question of the organizational nature of cognitive clusters may be posed in the following manner: Given schemata A and B which share elements (e.g., the schema for "supermarket" and the schema for "restaurant"), is it the case that when A is in a state of functioning (activation) B is also preserved (stored?) in some intact structural form?

A structural assumption, it seems, is committed to an affirmative answer to this question. In fact, schema theorists assert that even in cases where the same generic schema is used in comprehension of a particular passage, that is, in schema-theoretic terms, when an instantiated copy of a generic schema is constructed, "what gets stored in memory is, in effect, a copy or partial copy" of the instantiated schema (Rumelhart & Ortony, 1977, p. 116).

By contrast, if it is assumed that the patterning aspect of cognition is functional-phenomenal in nature, the need does not arise for preservation of multiple long-term memory copies. Furthermore, there will be no need for hypothesizing an *independent* frame-like structure corresponding to each and every *independent functional-phenomenal* pattern. The following section is intended to elaborate on these ideas.

An Analogy

In order to clarify the functional-structural distinction, I will use what I hereafter refer to as the *light-constellation analogy*. The problem is how to conceptualize an actual system that generates "functional-phenomenal" patterns without postulating long-term frame-like entities. Imagine a room containing a few hundred color-coded light bulbs. In this simple system, every time a subset or a constellation of the light bulbs goes on, it generates what might be called a transient functional pattern. Here *transient* means when the light bulbs go off the pattern of light no longer exists, and the constellation maintains no corresponding frame-like form; *functional* means generative—some kind of apparatus functions and this leads to some emergent phenomenon (light). Now, when a given cluster of lights goes off, some of its component lights can participate in some other cluster to generate another unique functional pattern. Thus, between two patterns that must share elements, when one is functional the other cannot exist and vice versa.

If, on the other hand, one assumes that the cluster-like aspect of the system is structurally based and long term, the only way that the system could be actually possible would be by introducing a new long-term cluster for every different pattern that must emerge. This would mean, of course, that multiple copies of the same structural entities (light bulbs) would be required which would, in turn, require storage and working space accommodation for an infinite number of long-term clusters.

The light-constellation analogy is deceptively simple. Even at the elementary level just outlined, it has tremendous explanatory power if applied to the psychological domain. First, it clearly illustrates how an indefinite number of functional-phenomenal patterns could be generated based on a limited number of long-term memory *elements*. (In reference to the analogy, functional corresponds to the burning of discrete light bulbs and phenomenal corresponds to the global pattern of light.) Secondly, there is no need for an independent storage mechanism. Thirdly, for each emergent phenomenal pattern, the whole is clearly greater than (or rather different from) the sum of individual component parts: the global color generated by a given constellation of light bulbs will be different from that generated by each of the individual light bulbs. And, most importantly, there will be no need for an independent structural long-term memory pattern corresponding to each distinguishable functional-phenomenal pattern. In this fashion, the light constellation analogy makes it possible to conceptualize the physical (i.e., neuronal), dynamic (i.e., functional), and experiential (i.e., phenomenal) aspects of cognition.

However, a functional assumption need not imply that there is necessarily no independent structural basis underlying a given functional-phenomenal pattern. All it says, I reiterate, is that (a) there is no long-term frame-like structural entity corresponding to each distinguishable cognitive pattern above and beyond the structure of the physical and physiological hardware and (b) there is no one-to-one correspondence between any complex mental pattern (e.g., a concept) and any localized physiological structure. A single element, for instance, might signal the activation of a constellation of elements, or vice versa. Such single elements could provide one way for the system to keep record of past functional-phenomenal patterns. For instance, a single element specialized to respond to the activity of a particular constellation of elements (A) could, in turn, signal activation of a second constellation (B) generating, "Oh, yes! This is old. I recognize it." And this could, in principle, happen every time A got activated.

Cognition as a Functional-Phenomenal Reality

The structural–functional distinction may be further clarified by considering two distinct meanings of the term *cognition*. The first meaning could be represented by such terms as *perceiving, attending, knowing, understanding,* and *remembering.* The second meaning would refer to the products of such acts. The product of the act of *knowing,* for instance, is *knowledge.* The functional approach would be concerned directly with the first meaning: What sort of live biological elements (analogous to the lights in our constellation apparatus) give rise to these acts? How do the elements interact? What causes the initiation and cessation of functioning in the elements (the turning on and the turning off of the lights)? How, when, and why do new elements enter the scene? The functional approach assumes that knowledge, as a product, "is created" by the neuronal elements functioning in unison. When the functioning of a set of elements creating a particular phenomenal experience ceases or when the elements participate in some other combination, the previous pattern is no longer in existence; though it can, of course, be recreated. In short, based on the functional assumption, the mind is a functional-phenomenal reality and as such the conceptual network as a whole remains an abstraction—only portions of it can be said to actually exist at different times but never the network as a whole.

The structural approach, on the other hand, concentrates on the product. It raises a different set of questions: How is knowledge processed, retrieved, and stored? How is it organized in long-term memory? And so forth.

I used a light-constellation analogy to demonstrate how unique mental patterns may emerge. The analogy may be extended, for the sake of comparison, to encompass the structural assumption. What is needed is a camera to take a picture of each unique pattern that is generated. Only then the need would arise for a storehouse for the pictures; and only then one may speak of searching, finding, retrieving and so on. The organization of the pictures in the storehouse would then create a problem; and only then one might speak of copies and originals or tokens and types.

The constellation analogy, without necessarily suggesting inherent correspondence with the human cognitive system, demonstrates how a highly generative physical system is possible. It does this without appealing to such independent conceptual constructs as "network," "storage," "link," "token," "pointer," and "comparison," (which are deep-seated remnants of associationism). I consider this a major advantage of the functional approach. Bartlett (1932) argued against this tradition and pointed out that "the force of the rejection of associationism depends mainly upon the adoption of a functional point of view" (pp. 307–308). Bartlett also prophetically stated:

> In various senses, therefore, associationism is likely to remain, though its outlook is foreign to the demands of modern psychological science. It tells us something about the characteristics of associated details, when they are associated, but it explains nothing whatever of the activity of the conditions by which they are brought together. (p. 308)

Bartlett used the term *remembering* to emphasize the functional aspect of the influence of the past on the present. Unfortunately, with few exceptions (e.g., Bransford, McCarrell, Franks, & Nitsch, 1977), Bartlett has been generally misunderstood. This is perhaps due to the deep-seated influence of structural (as opposed to functional-phenomenal) metaphors such as the above (e.g., network). It may still take many direct attacks like that of Bransford et al. to unexplain these metaphors and many years before they are annihilated, roots and all. Nevertheless, the doom of associationism has never been so clearly in sight as it appears today.

However, the application of the light-constellation analogy may strike some readers as too mechanistic to be meaningful with respect to the human cognitive system. Admittedly, this feeling is somewhat justified. Clearly, metaphors present both desirable and undesirable aspects. Therefore, caution must be exercised in their use and interpretation. The analogy was introduced here to allow a clearer conceptualization of how "patterning" is actually possible. To the extent that it has served this purpose, the analogy has been useful. It must also be noted, on the other hand, that the metaphor can also safely permit an overall picture of the cognitive system in a most revealing fashion. Whether it will develop into a mechanistic perspective will largely depend on the details that will have to be filled in. We are told that the "pump" metaphor helped physiologists to conceptualize the functioning of the blood circulation system. It can be seen now that the metaphor did not reduce the latter, an amazingly flexible and complex system, to the status of the former, a highly rigid mechanistic apparatus.

HISTORICAL OVERVIEW

It is fashionable among current cognitive scientists to credit Bartlett (1932) for the notion of schema as a structural construct. The following illustrative excerpts were chosen to reiterate what may be obvious to many readers:

> A central theme in work of the kind referenced above is the postulation of interacting knowledge structures which . . . we shall call "schemata." The term finds its way into modern psychology from the writings of Bartlett (1932) and it is to him that most workers acknowledge their debt (Rumelhart & Ortony, 1977, p. 100).

> He [Bartlett] hypothesized that to-be-remembered (TBR) information is assimilated into *pre-existing holistic cognitive structures* (schemata) in such a manner as to lose particular identity. (Spiro, 1975, p. 4; italics added)

> Building upon Bartlett's (1932) original work . . . several story grammars have been constructed to describe the structural basis of story understanding. . . . The theoretical assumptions of these grammars specify that memory for stories is a constructive process, resulting from the interaction between incoming information and preexisting cognitive structures, or schemata, containing knowledge about the generic characteristics of stories. (Stein & Nezworski, 1978, p. 2)

I believe it is worth considering just how representative of Bartlett's work this current trend in cognitive science is. The following quotations should provide a clue:

> Schemata are data structures for representing the generic concepts *stored in memory*. (Rumelhart & Ortony, 1977, p. 101; italics added)

> What is stored, given that *reconstruction must be based upon some stored information?* Some details from discourse are specifically stored. . . . (Spiro, 1977, p. 157; italics added)

I suspect that Bartlett would have greatly disliked to see such metaphors as "stored" or even "memory" used in reference to his theory. In fact he washed his hands of them when he objected to Head's (1920) use of these concepts in the following fashion:

> Head gives away far too much to earlier investigators when he speaks of the cortex as a "storehouse of past impressions." . . . A storehouse is a place where things are put in the hope that they may be found again when they are wanted exactly as they were when first stored away. The schemata are, we are told, living, constantly developing, affected by every bit of incoming sensational experience of a given kind. The storehouse notion is as far removed from this as it well could be. (p. 200)

The nature of conceptual metaphors used is an issue of utmost importance in scientific exposition. Scientists' use of concepts represents the way they perceive the world. It is the difference between "seeing" the apple fall and "seeing" the earth attract the apple. The first is a routine incident of no significance. The second is a scientific discovery. Conceptual metaphors do not merely assign perspectives. They also modulate the level of vagueness tolerated in scientific expositions or the distance between scientific theories and the actual phenomena under investigation. Metaphors are further used in the interpretation of existing theories. Of special relevance here is Neisser's (1967) application of the dinosaur reconstruction analogy in his interpretation of Bartlett's idea of schema reconstruction, as it is illustrated in the following quotation from Spiro (1980):

> What has already been read is not remembered as it was originally understood; rather, inferences about what must have transpired are made from what is known about later developments. A parallel may be drawn with the activities of a paleontologist who inferentially reconstructs a dinosaur utilizing an assortment of bone fragments (bits of stories) and knowledge about the anatomy and physiology of other dinosaurs (prototypic knowledge about the situations described in a given story). See Bartlett (1932) for further discussion of the reconstruction notion. (p. 5)

Neisser's concept of *reconstruction* is much closer to the literal meaning of the term than to Bartlett's notion of reconstruction. For Neisser, bone fragments are needed because reconstruction must be based on stored information. The light-constellation analogy showed that this is not necessarily the case. Elements participating in reconstruction are active in themselves. They re-create a global phenomenal experience. Similarly, for Bartlett, reconstruction means fresh re-creation. Activation of a few elements generates a global attitude, a momentary setting directed toward a more and more coherent phenomenal experience. Bartlett states, "As I have shown, to serve the needs of biological adaptation interests are all the while increasing in diversity, in narrowness and in definiteness. So our range of search, when we have to attempt recall, tends to get more and more refined" (pp. 312–313). Thus, for Bartlett, reconstruction is a live biological function. The notion of dead dinosaur "bone fragments" is as far removed from this as it can be. In fact, Bartlett disliked the term *schema* fearing that it might lead to the very same type of interpretation. He stated:

> I strongly dislike the term "schema." It is at once too definite and too sketchy. The word is already widely used in controversial psychological writing to refer generally to any rather vaguely outlined theory. It suggests some persistent, *but fragmentary, "form of arrangement,"* [italics added] and it does not indicate what is very essential to the whole notion, that the organized mass results of past changes of position and posture are actively *doing* something all the time; are so to speak, carried along with us, complete, though developing, from moment to moment. Yet it is certainly very difficult to think of any better single descriptive word to cover the facts involved. It would probably be best to speak of "active, developing patterns"; but the word "pattern," too, being now very widely and variously employed, has its own difficulties. . . . (pp. 200–201)

I suspect what Bartlett actually meant by the term *schema* can be more accurately described by the phrase *"schema-of-the-moment,"* which he sometimes used. The latter denotes, somewhat more accurately, the transient functional-phenomenal aspect of cognitive patterns. However, the term *transient* need not indicate fleeting, momentary experiences isolated from the past and the future. On the contrary, the schema-of-the-moment is ordinarily very stable. It lasts as long as it continues to be created and upheld by the underlying physiology. It inherits the influence of the past en masse and cumulatively and builds upon it from moment to moment.

Thus, the distance between Bartlett's concept of schema and that of the current cognitive scientist, is vast indeed. This became evident to me quite by chance when I began to draw excerpts from the literature bearing on the notion of schemata as structural constructs for the purpose of citing in this chapter. Surprisingly, in a close reading of Bartlett's discussion of the notion of schema (pp. 186–238, 301–313), I failed to locate a paragraph that would confidently suggest that Bartlett meant schemata to be long-term memory patterns. On the contrary, I found plenty of evidence suggesting that Bartlett used the concept of schema in the functional-phenomenal sense. These paragraphs are cited as examples:

> If Head is right, "schemata" are built up chronologically. Every incoming change contributes its part to the total "schema" of the moment in the order in which it occurs. That is to say, when we have movements a, b, c, d, in this order, our "plastic postural model" of ourselves at the moment d is made depends, not merely upon the direction, extent and intensity of a, b, c, d, but also upon the chronological order in which they have occurred. Suppose, for the moment, that a "model," to continue to use this picturesque phraseology, is completed, and all that is needed is its maintenance. Since its nature is not that of a passive framework, or patchwork, but of an activity, it can be maintained only if something is being done all the time. So in order to maintain the "schema" as it is—though this is rather inaccurate language—a, b, c, d must continue to be done, and must continue to be done in the same order. (p. 203)

> There is, however, an obvious objection to all this. So far as the "schema" is directly responsible for the attitude, it looks as if the latter must itself be predominantly determined by the last incoming incident of the mass of past reactions. But remembering often pretends to be of an incident remote in time, and that incident is not, as in the rote recapitulation method, now reconstructed by going through a whole chronological series in order. If "schemata" are to be reconstructed after the fashion that seems to be demanded by the phenomena of recall, somehow we have to find a way of individualizing some of the characteristics of the total functioning mass of the moment. (p. 208)

It is important to note that Bartlett makes no pretense about knowing how this functional mass of the moment comes about. More specifically, unlike many current cognitive scientists who take the patterning aspect of cognition for granted, Bartlett sees it as a problem to be solved. "Again I wish I knew precisely," he points out, "how it is brought about and again I can make only a few tentative suggestions" (p. 209). And the latter are along the following lines:

> In the clearest and most definitely articulated cases, there first occurs the arousal of an attitude, an orientation, an interest. Then specific detail, either in image or in direct word form, tends to be set up. Finally there is a construction of other detail in such a way as to provide a rational, or satisfactory setting for the attitude. (pp. 304–305)

As we have seen, one possible way to describe how the construction phenomenon may happen is to use the light-constellation terminology. Then one can imagine that (under the influence of Bartlett's prerequisite global orientation) some "lights" go on, some gain in brightness, some go off, and still others gain in dimness. The final product is a more or less coherent mass of the moment.

Bartlett emphasizes, and here I use the chemistry analogy again, that in addition to the composition aspect, there is yet a second fundamental aspect, i.e., decomposition:

> If any marked further advance is to be achieved, man must learn how to resolve the "scheme" into elements and how to transcend the original order of occurrence of these elements. This he does, for he learns how to utilize the constituents of his own "schemes," instead of being determined to action by the "schemes" themselves, functioning as unbroken units. He finds how to "turn round his own schemata. (Bartlett, 1932, p. 301)

The "decomposition" aspect of Bartlett's theory has not been appreciated by researchers who have found the phrase "turning round upon one's schema" unclear (e.g., Oldfield & Zangwill, 1942–1943). The problem, I suspect, has arisen not because of some inherent vagueness in Bartlett's theory, but because of researchers' failure to comprehend his functional approach. In functional terms, because relations are assumed to be actually transient, composition and decomposition become relatively easier to conceptualize.

In order for the reader to get an intuitive feeling for the type of functional reorganization just discussed, I present here a summary of one of the passages that I have used in my experiments concerning this intriguing phenomenon. As the reader goes through the summary, I suggest he or she keep the light-constellation analogy in mind. True, at this level of complexity the analogy is rather unrealistic and could be misleading. Nevertheless, I believe it does provide the intended general framework with the reader filling in any necessary details.

The story, adopted from Thurmond (1978), is about a nurse, named Marilyn, who leaves the hospital where she works to go home after a late-night shift. The hospital is presumably in the downtown of a large city. When on the freeway, she notices that she is running out of gas and becomes terrified. She remembers the recent surge in muggings, beatings, and so on in the area. Finally, she decides to go to Gabriel's gas station for gas. Gabriel has always seemed to her to be a pleasant person and she knows him by going to his station for gas.

Gabriel fills the tank, returns the change, and, as she is ready to leave, he suddenly asks her to go inside the station office with him to see some birthday present he has recently received. Marilyn refuses, but Gabriel insists. She finally agrees. She parks the car out of the way at his request in front of the office window and follows him inside the office.

Once inside, Gabriel quickly locks the door and pulls a gun out of the drawer. She becomes terrified and begins experiencing the symptoms of shock. She sees Gabriel walking toward her. His lips are moving but she cannot hear. She cannot defend herself and she yields to the pressure of Gabriel's hand on her shoulder forcing her to the floor. Gabriel is still looking out of the window with the gun clutched in his hand.

Finally, she begins to hear what he is saying: "Sorry I had to scare you like that. I was scared myself when I saw that dude on the floor in the back of your car."

There are perhaps many different ways to describe the somewhat instantaneous reshuffling involved in the comprehension of this story. But, I believe, the present functional approach presents the most straightforward conceptualization.

SUMMARY AND CONCLUSIONS

Many psychologists would agree that patterning is a fact of cognition. But the physical and phenomenal nature of mental patterns presents a difficult problem. This is because, in order to avoid postulating multiple copies of the same cognitive elements, patterns must share elements. As Bartlett put it:

> This complexity of "schematic" formulation means that many objects, many stimuli, many reactions, get organized simultaneously into different "schemes," so that when they recur, as, in the world we know they are bound to do, they tend to set into activity various cross-streams of organizing influence. (p. 302)

But sharing elements means breaking the relations in the pattern. One way to solve this problem, and it may be the only way, is to postulate transient relations. And one type of transient relation, and again this may be the only type, is the functional relation of the sort described in this chapter. Those who agree with these statements would also note that structural theories of cognition and comprehension are likely to run into unresolvable problems of organization when, and if, they come to deal with the issues of physical and phenomenal nature of cognition.

Some readers may argue that we are still far from dealing with the physical and phenomenal nature of mental schemas and that there are more immediate problems to be resolved and more sophisticated techniques to be developed. This type of argument I consider procrastination in the face of a difficult problem rather than scientific logic. Means develop in response to needs; and it is unlikely that one gets closer to a problem by simply avoiding it.

Unfortunately much psychological theory and research has been based on a great amount of tolerance for vagueness. At the risk of repetition, I present the following paragraph, part of which was quoted earlier. It is a clear but by no means an isolated example of vagueness:

> For all of the aforementioned authors, schemata truly are *the building blocks of cognition*. They are the fundamental elements upon which all information processing depends. Schemata are employed in the process of interpreting sensory data, (both linguistic and nonlinguistic) in retrieving information from memory, in organizing actions, in determining goals and sub goals, in allocating resources and generally in guiding the flow of processing in the system. *Clearly, any device capable of all these wondrous things must be powerful indeed. Moreover, since our understanding of none of these tasks which schemata are supposed to carry out has reached maturity, it is little wonder that a definitive explication of schemata does not yet exist and that skeptics view theories based on them with some suspicion* [italics added]. (Rumelhart, 1980, pp. 33–34)

The tolerance for vagueness characteristic of much psychological literature is only partially justified by the difficulty of the problem. One thing is certain: Tolerance for vagueness is detrimental to progress.

I have argued that cognition is a functional-phenomenal reality directly created by the neuronal network. Based on this perspective, the complex problem of the organization of long-term memory schemas in some purported long-term memory storehouse disappears. There will be no long-term structural organization other than the neuronal organization. Does this mean that in order to learn about cognition, one would have to open the head and directly examine the neuronal organization? Not ncessarily. Obviously, inferences concerning the neuronal network, its organization, and how it functions to create cognitive acts such as perceiving, knowing, remembering, comprehending, and thinking may be made based on observable products of these functions (e.g., linguistic performance).

Viewing knowing as a functional-phenomenal reality, rather than as the storing of abstract structural frames, raises some fundamental questions. With respect to research on reading comprehension, for instance, at least two approaches are possible: (a) concentrating exclusively on the analysis of the features of the text or (b) concentrating on the conditions under which functional-phenomenal experiences are created, maintained, uti- lized, and revised. In the past, text and story grammarians have done the former. There are serious problems with such an approach. First, as we saw earlier, there is no limit on the possible number of functional patterns. Secondly, even if common denominators were to be found, as one hopes they would be, they may not map the characteristics of the system which should be of ultimate concern. Analyzing the features of the pictures a camera takes may never tell anything about what the camera itself is like. Text and story grammarians need to seriously consider these problems.

ACKNOWLEDGMENTS

I would like to thank Larry Guthrie, William S. Hall, Anne Roalef, and Peter Winograd for their valuable comments on an earlier version of this paper. I am also greatly indebted to Rita Gaskill and Michael Nivens for their assistance at various stages in the preparation of the typescript. The research reported herein was supported in part by the National Institute of Education under Contract No. US-NIE-C-400-76-0116 and by a National Institute of Mental Health social psychology grant (MH15801) to the University of Michigan.

REFERENCES

Anderson, R. C. (1977). The notion of schemata and educational enterprise: General discussion of the conference. In R. C. Anderson, R. J. Spiro, & W. E. Montague (Eds.), *Schooling and the acquisition of knowledge* (pp. 415–431). Hillsdale, NJ: Lawrence Erlbaum Associates.

Anderson, R. C., & Ortony, A. (1975). On putting apples into bottles: A problem of polysemy. *Cognitive Psychology, 7,* 167–180.

Anderson, R. C., & Pichert, J. W. (1978). Recall of previously unrecallable information following a shift in perspective. *Journal of Verbal Learning and Verbal Behavior, 17,* 1–12.

Anderson, R. C., Reynolds, R. E., Schallert, D. L., & Goetz, E. G. (1977). Frameworks for comprehending discourse. *American Educational Research Journal, 14,* 367–381.

Anderson, R. C., Spiro, R. J., & Anderson, M. C. (1977, March). *Schemata as scaffolding for the representation of information in connected discourse* (Tech. Rep. No. 24). Urbana: University of Illinois, Center for the Study of Reading. (ERIC Document Reproduction Service No. ED 136 236).

Bartlett, F. C. (1932). *Remembering: A study in experimental and social psychology.* Cambridge, England: Cambridge University Press.

Bartlett, F. C. (1935). Remembering. *Scientia, 52,* 221–226.

Bobrow, D. G., & Norman, D. A. (1975). Some principles of memory schemata. In D. G. Bobrow & A. M. Collins (Eds.), *Representation and understanding: Studies in cognitive science* (pp. 131–149). New York: Academic Press.

Bransford, J. D., & Johnson, M. K. (1972). Contextual prerequisites for understanding. *Journal of Verbal Learning and Verbal Behavior, 11,* 717–726.

Bransford, J. D., McCarrell, N. S., Franks, J. J., & Nitsch, K. E. (1977). Toward unexplaining memory. In R. E. Shaw & J. D. Bransford (Eds.), *Perceiving, acting and knowing: Toward an ecological psychology* (pp. 431–466). Hillsdale, NJ: Lawrence Erlbaum Associates.

Collins, A. M., & Loftus, E. F. (1975). A spreading activation theory of semantic processing. *Psychological Review, 82,* 407–428.

Goetz, E. T., Anderson, R. C., & Schallert, D. L. (1979, September). *The representation of sentences in memory* (Tech. Rep. No. 144). Urbana: University of Illinois, Center for the Study of Reading.

Head, H. (1920). *Studies in neurology.* London: Oxford University Press.

Hebb, D. O. (1949). *The organization of behavior.* New York: Wiley.

Kintsch, W., & van Dijk, T. A. (1978). Toward a model of text comprehension and production. *Psychological Review, 85,* 363–394.

Mill, J. S. (1965). *On the logic of moral sciences.* New York: Bobbs-Merrill. (Originally published 1843).

Minsky, M. (1975). A framework for representing knowledge. In P. H. Winston (Ed.), *The psychology of computer vision* (pp. 211–277). New York: McGraw-Hill.

Nasser, U. (1967). Cognitive psychology. New York: Appleton, Century-Croft.

Oldfield, R. C., & Zangwill, O. L. (1942–1943). Head's concept of the schema and its application in contemporary British psychology. *British Journal of Psychology, 32,* 267–286; *33,* 58–64, 113–129, 143–149.

Ortony, A. (1978). Remembering, understanding, and representation. *Cognitive Science, 2,* 53–69.

Quillian, M. R. (1968). Semantic memory. In M. Minsky (Ed.), *Semantic information processing* (pp. 227–270). Cambridge, MA: MIT Press.

Rumelhart, D. E., & Ortony, A. (1977). The representation of knowledge in memory. In R. C. Anderson, R. J. Spiro, & W. E. Montague (Eds.), *Schooling and the acquisition of knowledge* (pp. 99–135). Hillsdale, NJ: Lawrence Erlbaum Associates.

Rumelhart, D. E. (1980). Schemata: The building blocks of cognition. In R. J. Spiro, B. C. Bruce, & W. F. Brewer (Eds.), *Theoretical issues in reading comprehension: Perspectives from cognitive psychology, linguistics, artificial intelligence, and education* (pp. 33–58). Hillsdale, NJ: Lawrence Erlbaum Associates.

Schank, R., & Abelson, R. (1977). *Scripts, plans, goals, and understanding.* Hillsdale, NJ: Lawrence Erlbaum Associates.

Snyder, M., & Uranowitz, S. W. (1978). Reconstructing the past: Some cognitive consequences of person perception. *Journal of Personality and Social Psychology, 36,* 941–950.

Spiro, R. J. (1975, October). *Inferential reconstruction in memory for connected discourse* (Tech. Rep. No. 2). Urbana: University of Illinois, Laboratory for Cognitive Studies in Education. (ERIC Document Reproduction Service No. ED 134 927).

Spiro, R. J. (1977). Remembering information from text: The "state of schema" approach. In R. C. Anderson, R. J. Spiro, & W. E. Montague (Eds.), *Schooling and the acquisition of knowledge* (pp. 137–165). Hillsdale, NJ: Lawrence Erlbaum Associates.

Spiro, R. J. (1979, August). *Prior knowledge and story processing: Integration, selection, and variation* (Tech. Rep. No. 138). Urbana: University of Illinois, Center for the Study of Reading.

Stein, N. L., & Nezworski, T. (1978, January). *The effects of organization and instructional set on memory* (Tech. Rep. No. 68). Urbana: University of Illinois, Center for the Study of Reading. (ERIC Document Reproduction Service No. 149 327).

Thurmond, P. J. (1978). If cornered, scream. *Ellery Queen's Mystery Magazine, 71,* 66–68.

THE ROLE OF "TYPICALITY" IN READING COMPREHENSION

Christine C. Pappas
University of Kentucky

Recently, reading research has focused upon the relationship between text structure and information recalled (e.g., Mandler & Johnson, 1977; Marshall & Glock 1978-1979; Meyer, 1975) in an attempt to provide some insights into the reading comprehension process. Despite some progress in this venture, still more basic questions concerning the mechanisms or strategies underlying comprehension have been left unattended and unanswered. It has been argued (Rumelhart, 1980; Smith, 1982; Spiro, 1980) that what people know about the world is necessarily related to their comprehension of a text. Nevertheless, most traditional definitions of categories defined in terms of logical conjunctions of discrete criterial attributes (Bourne, 1968), have neither reflected this world-knowledge nor indicated how this world-knowledge might be utilized by readers. For example, F. Smith (1975, 1982) has proposed that knowledge of categories, part "of the theory of the world in our heads," enables readers to predict and hypothesize about meanings expressed in text. Yet it is difficult to speculate how these categories—in his view, defined in terms of criterial sets of features—become transformed into directive or predictive processing strategies in comprehension. Perhaps another view of categories may offer a more consistent way to explain the gap between readers' formation and knowledge of categories and the manner in which readers might process and comprehend them.

Briefly, the alternative view presented here involves an analog, rather than a digital, model of categories in which natural categories are characterized by an "internal structure" or a "core meaning" (Rosch, 1975a). The prototype, as the clearest cases or the best examples of a particular category, is seen to reflect this "internal structure." Other category members, then, are seen to "surround" this prototype; they are of decreasing similarity to the prototype that results in a corresponding decrease in their degree of membership.

The most documented case for the prototype is in the domain of color. Although physical properties of light are not discrete but of continuous variation, certain "focal points" in color space appear to be so perceptually salient as to be selected as the best examples for various color terms by individuals from diverse languages (Berlin & Kay, 1969). Rosch's work (1975a), which has demonstrated that very young children were able to match focal colors more accurately than nonfocal colors and that Dani speakers—whose language contains only two color terms—were able to learn the names of focal colors better than those of the nonfocal ones, provides further evidence for the importance of the notion of prototypes as an underlying perceptual-cognitive factor in the formation and reference of linguistic categories.

I argue that "typicality"—as an underlying processing mechanism or strategy—may have a major role in reading comprehension. However, before talking about the ways in which typicality may be involved, two general kinds of background information are required: First, we need to get a better idea of what typicality is by examining how it has been used. Second, because typicality has been used for the most part in the area of speech production, we need to show its applicability to comprehension, or, more to the point, its applicability to reading comprehension. Consequently, the first section will provide both kinds of background information.

The second section of this chapter examines how typicality may be involved in reading comprehension by addressing two themes:

1. Typicality as a processing mechanism can account for individual difference in the knowledge of categories among readers. As a result, it may explain better—better than word frequency, for example,—a reader's ease or difficulty in comprehending and/or acquiring new information from a particular text.

2. Intrinsically related to the concept of typicality is the notion of codability in categorization. When an idea of a particular object in a category, for example, is considered to be close to the prototype of that category, then that idea is highly codable; when an idea of an object is considered to be less typical, then it is of lower codability. The high to low codability aspects in categorization have direct consequences in both oral and written text. I argue that readers utilize these codability features as representations of semantic distance information in comprehending a text.

GENERAL BACKGROUND

Traditional approaches to concept formation (e.g., Bourne, 1968; Bruner, Goodnow, & Austin, 1966) have assumed two general characteristics about categories: They are well-defined and their attributes can be specified arbitrarily. Recent work in conceptual development and semantic memory is a departure from the traditional approach because of its emphasis on natural categories (e.g., Anglin, 1977; Carey, 1978; Miller & Johnson-Laird, 1976; Nelson, 1974; Rosch, 1973a, 1973b; Rosch, Mervis, Gray, Johnson, & Boyes-Broem, 1976; Smith, Rips, & Shoben 1974; Smith, Shoben, & Rips, 1974). From this new perspective, several "prototype" approaches have evolved (Anglin, 1977; Bowerman, 1978; Bridges, Sinha, & Walkerdine, 1981; Chafe, 1977a, 1977b; Rosch, 1973a, 1973b, 1975a, 1975b; Rosch & Mervis, 1975; Rosch et al., 1976; Smith, Rips, & Shoben, 1974; Smith, Shoben, & Rips, 1974). Research on prototypes makes two alternative assumptions about categories: (a) categories or concepts in natural languages rarely have well-defined boundaries, and (b) following from (a), the process of differentiating one category from another involves underlying probability principles.

In my discussion of the prototype approach, I primarily rely on the work of three researchers—Rosch, Anglin, and Chafe. Rosch's work (1973a, 1973b, 1975a, 1975b; Rosch & Mervis, 1975; Rosch et al., 1976) is used to review the major characteristics of the prototype approach. The works of Rosch (1973b; Rosch et al., 1976) and Anglin (1977) are used to explain how the prototype is involved in the child's acquisition or formation of categories and the linguistic symbols that refer to those categories. Chafe's work (1977a, 1977b) is used to show how the category processes fit in the broader framework of verbalization or discourse.

Underlying Rosch's view is a way of looking at the world. According to Rosch, there has been a tendency in psychology and anthropology to view the world as entirely unstructured. The task in these disciplines, then, is to focus on how children learn to segment such a world into "separate things" and on what the effects are of having a label or a name for some segment. Categories or separate things are based on an unstructured view of the world and are formed on an originally arbitrary segmentation. In contrast to this view, Rosch (Rosch et al., 1976) has argued that

> the world does contain "intrinsically separate things." The world is structured because real-world attributes do not occur independently of each other. Creatures with feathers are more likely also to have wings than creatures with fur, and objects with the visual appearance of chairs are more likely to have functional sit-on-ableness than objects with the appearance of cats. That is, combinations of attributes of real objects do not occur uniformly. Some pairs, triples, or ntuples are quite probable, appearing in combination sometimes with one, sometimes another attribute; others are rare; others logically cannot or empirically do not occur. (p. 383)

Categories of the concrete world, therefore, are structured, for they are based upon a structured world. Furthermore, these categories within taxonomies of concrete objects possess an internal structure so that there is one level of abstraction—a level that she calls the 'basic object level'—at which most boundaries are established; that is, the level at which categories are most differentiated from one another. Rosch et al. (1976) have demonstrated that basic objects or categories also are the most inclusive ones, whose members can be characterized in four ways: (a) they possess significant numbers of attributes in common, (b) they have similar motor programs, (c) they have similar shapes, and (d) they can be identified from averaged shapes of members of the class.

The notion of a prototype is directly related to Rosch's concept of basic objects in that some members of a basic level category will "reflect the redundancy structure of the category as a whole" (Rosch et al., 1976, p. 433). Thus, these particular members of a particular category are seen as having an exaggeration of structures—they have the most attributes, the most motor programs, and so forth. These members are the typical or focal cases of a particular category. For example, "robin" and "sparrow" have been reliably rated as typical birds; whereas "chicken" and "duck" have been considered as atypical ones (Rips, Shoben, & Smith, 1973; Rosch, 1973a; Smith, Shoben, & Rips, 1974). Moreover, people frequently use different hedges (Lakoff, 1972) when talking about the typical versus atypical birds: A "robin" will be considered a "true" bird while a "chicken" will be viewed as a bird, "technically speaking" (Smith, Shoben, & Rips, 1974).

This example represents the sharp contrast that exists between the prototype approach and the traditional digital category approach (Rosch, 1975a). The former is a schema or analog representation of categories where some members—the prototypes ("robin" or "sparrow")—are better examples of the bird category. Because the prototype view rests upon correlational real-world attributes, membership in a category is a "matter of degree." In the digital view, on the other hand, each instance of a particular category (e.g., a "robin," a "sparrow," a "chicken," a "duck") reflects a criterial set of all the possible attributes of that category so that each is equal in membership. As a result, category membership is orthogonal in the digital perspective; it is an "all-or nothing" matter.

Both basic objects and the prototype are central to the child's conceptual and linguistic development. For example, Rosch (et al. (1976) has explicitly extended these notions to such development as follows:

Basic objects are shown to be the most inclusive categories for which a concrete image of the category as a whole can be formed, to be the first categorization made during perception of the environment, to be the earliest categories sorted and earliest named by children, and to be the categories most codable, most coded, and most necessary in language. (Rosch, p. 382)

Rosch presents an attractive case for the potential utility of prototypes as a processing mechanism or strategy. Because the prototype is an exaggeration of category structure, it may be potentially useful in cognitive processes (like reading). Matching to a prototype in categorization would allow humans to make use of their knowledge of the world in order to predict and eliminate unlikely alternatives—to use Frank Smith's words (1982)[1]—"without the laborious process of computing and summing validities of individual cues" (Rosch et al., 1976, p. 434). In addition, because basic prototypes represent exaggerations of structure, they provide additional explanatory support for the developmental iconic representation stage postulated by Bruner et al., (1966) and for the strong concrete imagery effect found in Paivio's work (1971).

Anglin (1977) also has suggested a prototype-like mechanism in the child's conceptual/linguistic development. He describes the prototype of a category as a generalized conception, a central tendency. More specifically, his research indicates that there is no unidirectional progression—either general-to-specific or vice versa—in the acquisition of category labels. Anglin, therefore, has suggested that vocabulary development can be better described in terms of complementary kinds of differentiation and hierarchic integration such as Werner and Kaplan (1963) have proposed for development in general. Although both Rosch and Anglin admit to differences between child and adult conceptual systems, they also emphasize underlying continuities between the adult and child.

This notion of prototypes fits nicely into the current theory of speech production set forth by Chafe (1973, 1974, 1976, 1977a, 1977b). According to Chafe, verbalization or discourse consists of three major kinds of processes: (a) those that deal with the organization of content, (b) those that deal with the speaker's consideration of the addressee's current consciousness and processing capacities with a particular context of discourse—what Chafe calls "packaging processes," and (c) those that deal with syntactic processes. These three major processes represent semantic, psychological, and linguistic concerns as they converge upon the prototype in categorization. The emphasis here, however, is on the semantic or content aspects with some reference to psychological factors, but with little regard to any syntactic concerns.

Within the first class of processes, the content-related ones, Chafe has

---

[1]Rosch's role of the prototype in categorization is quite similar to Frank Smith's view of comprehension in many respects. Rosch's view, however, is not a feature theory, although some semantic feature models (e.g., Smith, Rips, & Shoben, 1974; Smith, Shoben, & Rips, 1974) have incorporated some prototype-like aspects.

distinguished three sub-processes: subchunking, framing or propositiona-lizing, and *categorizing*. Categorization is the point in verbalization or discourse at which a speaker must decide upon the specific words to convey the ideas of an event, a situation, or an object already decided upon during the other two content-related processes. In order to convey these ideas, the speaker has to categorize these ideas; the speaker "must decide to interpret the object or event as an instance of some category, which in the favorable case will then provide him with a word that will more or less satisfactorily convey what he has in mind" (Chafe, 1977b, p. 277). Now, how does prototype fit this account of categorization? Some ideas of particular events, situations, objects, and individuals are easier to categorize than others. The ease of categorizing ideas is related to the notion of codability. More specifically, to say that an idea of a particular object, for example, is highly codable is to say that "its experiential content matches that of the *prototype* or focus of the category quite closely" (Chafe, 1977a, p. 50; italics added). Conversely, if a speaker interprets that a particular idea to be conveyed is not the typical case of the category, it will be more difficult for the speaker to categorize it because that idea is of lower codability. Describing a "good" red versus an "off" red illustrates this phenomenon. A prototypical red is easily categorized whereas a less typical red will result in descriptions like "orangish-red" or "reddish-purple."

To sum up, categories reflect real-world correlational structure. This perspective supports the assumption expressed by Deese (1976) that many of the categories of perception are basically the same as the categories of cognition. Thus, although the typicality notion has evolved from speech production research, it is plausible to propose that it must also hold for comprehension. Indeed, evidence from recall protocols in several discourse studies (e.g., Bartlett, 1932; Bransford & Franks, 1976; Bransford & Johnson, 1973; Frederiksen, 1975; Mandler & Johnson, 1977) indicates that readers expect or assume that this kind of real-world structure will be expressed in the text they read. Typicality is not only part of this expectancy, but also is a mechanism or strategy that readers utilize when they try to make sense of written text. But, how does typicality play a role in reading comprehension?

INDIVIDUAL DIFFERENCES IN THE COMPREHENSION OF CATEGORIES

In cognitive tasks, such as reading, many categories may be processed in terms of internal structure rather than in terms of the attributes of their formal definitions (the traditional category approach). A category defined by its internal structure will be characterized by its core meaning, its focal or typical cases, and, as such, will operate more as a psychological unit than as a formally defined category (Rosch, 1973b). We have seen that the structure of categories is based on learning the co-occurrence contingencies of the world, the "out there" structure. "Out there" structure is not a metaphysical speculation, but, more importantly, an empirical claim that includes a knower. That is, "given a knower who can perceive the complex attributes of feathers, fur and wings, it is an empirical fact 'out there' that wings co-occur with feathers more than with fur" (Rosch et al., 1976, p. 429). Furthermore, provided a person has the capacity to perceive some set of attributes and that this set of attributes possesses correlational structure in the world, then it follows that any one individual's knowledge may be different from the potential existing in the world either by ignoring (or being indifferent or inattentive to) or by exaggerating this correlational structure. Such a view provides a basis for individual differences in the knowledge of categories and sets the stage for the discussion of its implications in reading comprehension. Differences among individuals in general, including those between the child and the adult and/or between individuals of different cultures or sub-cultures, can be accounted for by the basic object-prototype approach; because the basic objects of individuals are a result of the *interaction* between the potential structure existing in the world and the particular emphases—heavily influenced by the social environment (Halliday, 1975, 1978; Shields, 1978; Wells, 1981)—and the state of knowledge of the people who are doing the categorizing (Karmiloff-Smith, 1979; Rosch et al., 1976). The emphasis here is on the universality of the process of category formation rather than on the content of the categories. In reading this universal process regarding categories can be expressed as follows: Although the content of what readers know may be different, how readers will use what they know will be the same.

What makes the prototype a useful strategy in reading comprehension is that it enables the reader to generate expectancies about present and future meanings expressed in the text. Expectancy here operates in a fashion similar to F. Smith's prediction (1975); consequently, many of the points made may appear to be familiar. However, the present perspective does differ from his in that it will not be cast into an information-processing paradigm. Instead, the expectancy perspective rests upon a view that describes written discourse as a schema-nested hierarchy. Category schemas are nested within frame or propositional contexts (Anderson & Ortony, 1975; Anderson, Pichert, Goetz, Schallert, Stevens, & Trollip, 1976; Chafe, 1977a, 1977b). The frame contexts are, in turn, nested within higher order or larger "chunks" of schema (Chafe, 1977a, 1977b) or "episodes" (Johnson & Mandler, 1979; Rumelhart, 1977). In such a hierarchical schemata, there can be a combination or simultaneity of both bottom-up and top-down processing (Rumelhart & Ortony, 1977) or of focal and global predictions (F. Smith, 1982).

Briefly, this expectancy perspective describes the expectancies of a reader as the search for invariant relations against a flux of constant change (M. Jones, 1976, 1978; Neisser, 1976). Seeking consistent patterns is the most efficient heuristic for coping with any environment (Karmiloff-Smith, 1979) and typicality is the functional means by which readers can organize and seek conceptual patterns realized in texts. Expectancies are relative predictions about present and future meanings based on proto-typic cognitive/linguistic structures that conform to patterns of real world events and objects. The expectancies generated by readers are considered as pattern-conserving procedures in that they recognize positive in-stances. Simply speaking, at the category level, a reader exaggerates existing structures in such a way that attributes, motor programs, and shapes characteristic of only some members of a category are thought to be characteristic of all. Using typical cases of a category in this way, the reader can satisfactorily, albeit partially, comprehend a text even though real world experience may be limited (as is the case of a child, for example). If concepts in a text are extremely far away from a reader's prototype (or knowledge base), his or her generated expectancy encoun-ters very few confirmations and too many exceptions so that very little is comprehended. In this case, too large of a deviation exists between what the text may have afforded in terms of semantic patterns and what the readers's expectancies may have been able to pick up about these patterns. Real-life experiences on which the textual concepts are based may be necessary before such a reader is able to comprehend the text in question. However, other reading experiences (namely, reading a text on the same subject matter or of the same genre, or perhaps even reading the same text) may also facilitate the reader's acquisition of new information. Each time, the prototype might be interpreted as a "selection" (Fre-deriksen, 1975) or "mediating meaning" (F. Smith, 1982) mechanism in the acquisition of semantic information from discourse. Each time, the reader generates expectancies that result in smaller and smaller devia-tions so that what was initially incomprehensible is now more readily comprehended and, as a result, the reader is now considered to be "fluent" in the Marshall and Glock (1978-1979) sense. The degree of deviations in expectancies reflects the individual reader's relative diffi-culty or ease in comprehending a particular text.

An example of the process of typicality in action can be found in Bartlett (1932). Bartlett indicated that in his subjects' reproductions some "particular" or item of recall from a story was, in his words, "trans-formed immediately into a more familiar character." Thus, 'canoe' be-came 'boat,' 'paddling' became 'rowing,' 'Kashim' (a proper name for a shelter) became 'cabin,' and so forth. "Familiar character" in Bartlett's terms can be seen as synonymous with typicality. It could be argued that word frequency accounts for Bartlett's transformation phenomena; however, word frequency cannot explain how people learn from "novel" and "new" texts by generating expectancies based on their present knowledge bases. Moreover, word frequency could not predict why an individual's relative ignorance or expertise in specific subject matter should make a difference in comprehension. Furthermore, word frequency cannot explain why the same individual is able to "shift" prototypes in recall protocols (Freedle, Naus, & Schwartz, 1977) in order to take into account what the listener or reader knows about categories.

What individuals know about objects—that is, their relative ignorance or expertise—will certainly affect their own classification scheme. What exactly is involved when individuals become "experts" in certain areas of a taxonomy? An airplane mechanic, for example, would list a different and larger set of attributes for airplanes, would produce different motor programs, and would visualize a different average shape for airplanes (undersides and engines, etc.) than that of an average individual (Rosch et al., 1976). Particular expertise in the area of fixing engines of certain kinds of airplanes has resulted in what I call a *shift* of the basic level of abstraction and, consequently, in a different prototype. But, what is important to point out is that the airplane mechanic "could take the role of the average person and list attributes common to all airplanes, and could imagine an average airplane shape from the outside" (Rosch et al., 1976, p. 430). With respect to the mechanic's ease or difficulty in comprehending some hypothetical airplane reading material, certain predictions could be made: If the airplane reading material was found in *Newsweek* and thus was directed toward a lay audience, comprehension would be extremely easy—in fact, reading probably would be boring. If the airplane reading material was found in *Mechanic's Illustrated*, it probably would be relatively easy to comprehend, and, what is more, interesting. If the reading material was found in the *Journal of Aeronautics*, it would be more difficult for the mechanic to comprehend because the mechanic's expertise with airplanes is reflected in a different part of the taxonomy from that of an engineer. Thus, the readability and comprehensibility of these three kinds of reading materials, in expectancy terms, correspond to small, somewhat larger, and very large deviations, respectively, from the mechanic's prototype.

These comprehension differences also hint at other aspects converging upon the typicality processes, namely, "packaging" (Chafe, 1976, 1977a, 1977b) and/or psychosocial factors (Bruce, 1980; Freedle et al., 1977). In recent work on written discourse, various kinds of packaging features have been emphasized in various ways: as rhetorical predicates (Grimes, 1975; Meyer, 1975), as staging effects (Marshall & Glock, 1978-1979; Meyer, 1975), and as cohesion (Halliday, 1978; Halliday & Hasan, 1976).

Making inferences about a reader's comprehension based on recall protocols is inherently risky business. Frequently, what individuals know about objects is related to what they believe that their listener–reader knows about objects. Bartlett (1932) frequently emphasized that individual differences reflected in reproductions were based on his subjects' acknowledging the social membership of their audience. Freedle et al. (1977) specifically examined discourse along this line. Using what they called "a new communicative psychosocial paradigm" for the study of prose, they attempted to analyze the protocols of individuals whose intended listener was either an adult or a child. Differences in categorization were evident: If the speaker expected the listener to be an adult, "Victorians" and "myths" were used; if the speaker expected the listener to be a child, "people who lived 100 years ago" and "very old stories" were used to express the ideas comprehended from the prose the subjects read. So, what the listener is likely to know also appears to be a determining factor involved in any discourse experiment in which a subject is attempting to comprehend categories expressed in prose.

In summary, individual differences in reading comprehension involve a processing mechanism or strategy which incorporates prototypes. These prototypes enable the reader to generate expectancies which are in essence an interaction or convergence of: (a) the categories expressed in the text; (b) the packaging aspects built in by the writer; and (c) depending on the recall or retelling conditions of an experiment (or of a school setting, as well), certain psychosocial factors.

CODABILITY ASPECTS INVOLVED IN THE COMPREHENSION OF CATEGORIES

Intrinsically related to the concept of typicality is the notion of codability. The relative distance of an idea (of a particular object, for example) from the category's prototype is related to its codability which, in turn, is associated with a writer's or speaker's difficulty in categorizing that idea. Both oral and written discourse reflect several consequences of these variable codability aspects. For example, if an idea is highly codable for a speaker or writer (close to the prototype), then it can be expressed by a single word; whereas, if it is of lower codability (farther away from the prototype), then that idea might have to be expressed by including adjectives, relative clauses, and other modifiers (Chafe, 1977a, 1977b). Another symptom of low codability is that the speaker–writer will tend to call an idea of lower codability something different on different occasions. Moreover a speaker may hesitate in verbalization (Chafe, 1977a, 1977b) or may tend to use nonverbal gestures (such as found in the "talk with your hands" phenomenon) in order to describe an object.

An extreme example of low codability can be seen in some types of aphasia. Head (1926), for example, described a certain kind of aphasia in which the patient's speech was characterized as having verbal defects. Because of this "defective word-formation," such a patient was "unable to find the words" required in ordinary conversations (p. 221). Apparently, in the beginning of this kind of aphasia, a patient was unable to categorize at all. But, as recovery progressed and the patient regained a considerable vocabulary, there was still a residue of the defect. As Head described it, "syntax was not fundamentally affected, but the patient was frequently compelled by want of a word to go back and reconstruct the sentence on a different plan" (p. 222). As a result, frequent substitutions of metaphorical expressions, "dig it up" for "remember," or longer phrases, "strong-willed and strong-headed" for "headstrong," were used by the patient when unable to "access" the word(s) for the ideas to be conveyed on some particular occasion. What is interesting is that the patient was able to interpret that a particular idea of an object, event, or situation was an instance of a category, but was unable to find, in a satisfactory way, the words to approximate that idea. As recovery progressed, the aphasic patient became quite good at categorizing highly codable items but was still having difficulty with less codable ones. Hence, the patient had to "go back and reconstruct the sentence on a different plan."

Although the aphasia example was presented in oral text terms, writing that lacks precision, a consequence of codability, may be a salient characteristic that affects a reader's comprehension of a text. When readers are generating their expectancies about the meanings expressed in the text, they are using these codability consequences just described as semantic distance information. The following studies in which the semantic aspects have been examined in spatial terms support this view.

Wickens (1972), using a procedure called *release from proactive inhibition* (PI), has demonstrated the superiority of semantic over physical or syntactic attributes of words in recall experiments. Briefly, the paradigm entails presenting a successive set of words within a particular category— for example, the names of fruits—which usually results in a subject's progressively poor recall. Then, as words of a different category are presented, perhaps flowers, marked improvement in recall occurs. This shift from poorer to much better recall defines release from PI. Wickens (1972) concludes that:

> the individual is sensitive to . . . a large number of aspects of words, but is
> also insensitive to certain other aspects. He is particularly reactive to

semantic attributes of words, mildly reactive to the method of their physical representation and essentially impervious to their syntactical characteristics. (p. 213)

This research indicates that individuals are extremely sensitive to semantic aspects of words. For our purposes, this research provided some initial support for the speculation that individuals also are sensitive to semantic distance aspects, for the release from PI procedure itself was concerned with ascertaining between-category differences, that is, determining the semantic distance between fruits and vegetables versus, or relative to, the distance between fruits and flowers.

Evidence for semantic distance as it functions along degrees of typicality (high, medium, or low) also has been provided by Smith, Shoben, and Rips (1974). They have proposed that semantic decisions are involved in individual's determinations as to whether some particular test instance belongs to a target category. The first stage of their model is a typicality resolution stage supported by several empirical techniques—typicality ratings, multidimensional space representations of these ratings, and acceptability judgments of sentence substitutions. This research again confirms the typicality proposal argued here because typicality decisions may include some semantic distance quality that can be spatially expressed, as in the case of the multidimensional solutions.

That some semantic decisions may induce subjects to utilize some spatially relevant strategy has been reported in experiments in which subjects have been asked to solve linear syllogisms (Handel, London, & DeSoto, 1968; Huttenlocher, 1968; S. Jones, 1970; Scholz & Potts, 1974). Explanations as to exactly how syllogisms are comprehended and solved by subjects, however, have been a controversial matter. Huttenlocher (1968), for example, has proposed that subjects invoke spatial images in order to solve three-term syllogisms. On the other hand, Clark (1969) and S. Jones (1970), although not denying that the majority of subjects may make use of spatial axes in solving syllogisms, argue that it is more parsimonious to explain problems solutions "in terms of language comprehension, as formulated by deep structure theory, without recourse to speculations based on spatial imagery" (S. Jones, 1970, p. 213). What is argued here is that spatial imagery versus deep structure explanations is not an either/or matter and that parsimony is beside the fact. As Richardson (1974) points out, Clark's deep structure explication of syllogism solutions, in fact, includes a lexical marking system [± polar] that can be seen to be directly derived from spatial imagery. Moreover, Clark (1973) has explicitly argued a spatial imagery thesis (namely, a Cartesian coordinate system) to account for the child's conceptual/linguistic acquisition process.

The purpose here is not to solve the syllogism dilemma[2], but to contend that each of these theories lends support to the major thesis argued here. Many linguistic symbols express or map real-world correlational structure and individuals' strategies to comprehend those linguistic symbols (and/or solve syllogisms) are frequently rooted in their knowledge of the world. These studies lend credence to the contention that semantic distance is psychologically real for human beings. Is it not reasonable to suppose that the codability consequences in texts reflecting that distance would be utilized concomitantly by readers in generating their expectancies about meaning, that is, in comprehending a text?

THE TYPICALITY THEORY IN PERSPECTIVE

The typicality perspective offered here can be seen as an example of one of the invariants expressed in text and, more importantly, as a suggestion regarding how readers may use this invariant in comprehending a text. One advantage of this view is that it accounts for and relates expectancies, content relations, packaging notions, and psychosocial and context functions.

The discussion of how the categorization processes fit in Chafe's larger framework of verbalization was included in order to be remindful of a larger perspective. In generating expectancies about meanings expressed in a text, readers are simultaneously utilizing typicality aspects with their concomitant coding consequences, as well as many other discourse elements or invariants. What has been emphasized is that although individual differences will be a factor involved in the expectancies generated for a particular reader and a particular text, the fact that readers do generate expectancies will be universal. Therefore, generating expectancies in this view is an active and directive process in the way Bartlett (1958) has described thinking.

Conceptualizing category membership in terms of distance from, or closeness to, a stored prototype also is consistent with more higher order schema conceptualizations of discourse (e.g., Anderson, Spiro, & Anderson, 1978; Rumelhart, 1977). The typicality perspective parallels recent attempts to explain the gradual abstraction processof children learning

---

[2]One may wonder what the spatial imagery or the deep structure theory of syllogism-solving has to do with reading. Of course, it might be argued that since both reading and the solving of syllogisms are cognitive tasks, they are already related. However, each theory has also been more *directly* applied to reading. For example, Richardson (1974) has proposed that dyslexia may be attributed to the lack of an internal visual Cartesian frame of reference. And Mosenthal (1976-1977) has proposed that H. Clark's deep structure theory of syllogism solving can adequately describe silent reading comprehension competence.

the orthographic structure of words (Gibson, 1977). Furthermore, in a more general way, the prototype or analog perspective has been prominent in neural models of human memory and learning (Anderson, 1977). Regarding our memorial system, Anderson suggests that "we have a system that loses the details of particular events, but has the capacity to generalize and to abstract common parts of separate events. Yet the loss and gain are two facets of the same process, one inversely related to the other. Perhaps this balance between memory detail and memory for generality is struck everywhere in the central nervous system" (p. 54). In a similar way, the prototype will provide answers to some of the basic questions regarding the comprehension process: It is the explanatory mechanism for bridging the gap between "what people know about the world" and *how* they generate predictions or expectancies in *reading comprehension*.

ACKNOWLEDGMENTS

I am indebted to Victor M. Rentel for his comments on an earlier version of this paper and to Rob Tierney for his useful editorial feedback. Any errors that remain are my own.

REFERENCES

Anderson, J. A. (1977). Neural models with cognitive implications. In D. LaBerge & S. J. Samuels (Eds.), *Basic processes in reading: Perception and comprehension* (pp. 27-90). Hillsdale, NJ: Lawrence Erlbaum Associates.

Anderson, R. C., & Ortony, A. (1975). On putting apples into bottles: A problem of polysemy. *Cognitive Psychology, 7,* 167-180.

Anderson, R. C., Pichert, J. W., Goetz, E. T., Schallert, D. L., Stevens, K. V., & Trollip, S. R. (1976). Instantiation of general terms. *Journal of Verbal Learning and Verbal Behavior, 15,* 667-679.

Anderson, R. C., Spiro, R. J., & Anderson, M. C. (1978). Schemata as scaffolding for the representation in connected discourse. *American Educational Research Journal, 15,* 433-440.

Anglin, J. (1977). *Word, object and conceptual development.* New York: Norton.

Bartlett, F. (1958). *Thinking: An experimental and social study.* New York: Basic Books.

Bartlett, F. C. (1932). *Remembering.* Cambridge, England: Cambridge University Press.

Berlin, B., & Kay, P. (1969). *Basic color terms: Their universality and evaluation.* Berkeley: University of California Press.

Bourne, L. E. (1968). *Human conceptual behavior.* Boston: Allyn & Bacon.

Bowerman, M. (1978). The acquisition of word meaning: An investigation into some current conflicts. In N. Waterson & C. E. Snow (Eds.), *The development of communication* (pp. 263-287). New York: Wiley.

Bransford, J. D., & Franks, J. J. (1976). Toward a framework for understanding learning. In

G. Bower (Ed.), *Psychology of learning and motivation* (Vol. 10, pp. 93-125). New York: Academic Press.

Bransford, J. D., & Johnson, M. K. (1973). Some problems of comprehension. In W. G. Chase (Ed.), *Visual information processing* (pp. 383-438). New York: Academic Press.

Bridges, A., Sinha, C., & Walkerdine, V. (1981). The development of comprehension. In G. Wells (Ed.), *Learning through interaction: The study of language development* (pp. 116-156). Cambridge: Cambridge University Press.

Bruce, B. C. (1980). Plans and social actions. In R. J. Spiro, B. C. Bruce, & W. F. Brewer (Eds.), *Theoretical issues in reading comprehension: Perspectives from cognitive psychology, linguistics, artificial intelligence, and education* (pp. 367-384). Hillsdale, NJ: Lawrence Erlbaum Associates.

Bruner, J. S., Goodnow, J., & Austin, G. (1966). *A study of thinking.* New York: Wiley.

Carey, S. (1978). The child as a word learner. In M. Halle, J. Bresnan, & G. A. Miller (Eds.), *Linguistic theory and psychological reality* (pp. 264-293). Cambridge, MA: MIT Press.

Chafe, W. (1973). Language and memory. *Language, 49,* 261-281.

Chafe, W. (1974). Language and consciousness. *Language, 50,* 111-133.

Chafe, W. (1976). Giveness, contrastiveness, subjects and topics. In C. N. Li (Ed.), *Subject and topic* (pp. 27-55). New York: Academic Press.

Chafe, W. (1977a). Creativity in verbalization and its implications for the nature of stored knowledge. In R. O. Freedle (Ed.), *Discourse production and comprehension* (pp. 41-55). Norwood, NJ: Ablex.

Chafe, W. (1977b). The recall and verbalization of past experience. In R. W. Cole (Ed.), *Current issues in linguistic theory* (pp. 215-246). Bloomington: Indiana Press.

Clark, H. H. (1969). Linguistic processes in deductive reasoning. *Psychological Review, 76,* 387-404.

Clark, H. H. (1973). Space, time, semantics, and the child. In T. E. Moore (Ed.), *Cognitive development and the acquisition of language* (pp. 27-63). New York: Academic Press.

Deese, J. (1976). Semantics: Categorization and meaning. In C. C. Carterette & M. P. Friedman (Eds.), *Handbook of perception* (Vol. VII, pp. 265-297). New York: Academic Press.

Fredericksen, C. H. (1975). Acquisition of semantic information from discourse: Effects of repeated exposures. *Journal of Verbal Learning and Verbal Behavior, 14,* 158-169.

Freedle, R. O., Naus, M., & Schwartz, L. (1977). Prose processing from a psychosocial perspective. In R. O. Freedle (Ed.), *Discourse production and comprehension* (pp. 175-192). Norwood, NJ: Ablex.

Gibson, E. J. (1977). How perception really develops: A view from outside the network. In D. LaBerge & S. J. Samuels (Eds.), *Basic processes in reading: Perception and comprehension* (pp. 155-173). Hillsdale, NJ: Lawrence Erlbaum Associates.

Grimes, J. E. (1975). *The thread of discourse.* The Hague, Holland: Mouton.

Halliday, M.A.K. (1975). *Learning how to mean: Explorations in the development of language.* London: Edward Arnold.

Halliday, M.A.K. (1978). *Language as social semiotic.* London: Edward Arnold.

Halliday, M.A.K., & Hasan, R. (1976). *Cohesion in English.* London: Longman.

Handel, S., London, M., & DeSoto, C. (1968). Reasoning and spatial representations. *Journal of Verbal Learning and Verbal Behavior, 7,* 351-357.

Head, H. (1926). *Aphasia and kindred disorders of speech* (Vol. 1). New York: Hafner.

Huttenlocher, J. (1968). Constructing spatial images: A strategy in reasoning. *Psychological Review, 75,* 550-560.

Johnson, N. S., & Mandler, J. M. (1979). *A tale of two structures: Underlying and surface forms in stories* (Tech. Rep. No. 80). LaJolla, CA: University of California-San Diego, Center for Human Information Processing.

Jones, M. R. (1976). Time, our lost dimension: Toward a new theory of perception, attention, and memory. *Psychological Review, 83,* 323-355.

Jones, M. R. (1978). Auditory patterns: Studies in the perception of structure. In E. D. Carterette & M. P. Friedman (Eds.), *Handbook of perception* (Vol. VIII, pp. 255-288). New York: Academic Press.

Jones, S. (1970). Visual and verbal processes in problem-solving. *Cognitive Psychology, 1,* 201-214.

Karmiloff-Smith, A. (1979). *A functional approach to child language: A study of determiners and reference.* Cambridge: Cambridge University Press.

Lakoff, G. (1972). Hedges: A study in meaning criteria and the logic of fuzzy concepts. *Papers from the eighth regional meeting. Chicago Linguistics Society.* Chicago: University of Chicago Linguistics Department.

Mandler, J. M., & Johnson, N. S. (1977). Remembrance of things parsed: Story structure and recall. *Cognitive Psychology, 9,* 111-151.

Marshall, N., & Glock, M. D. (1978-1979). Comprehension of connected discourse: A study into the relationships between the structure of the text and information recalled. *Reading Research Quarterly, 14,* 10-56.

Meyer, B. J. (1975). *The organization of prose and its effects on memory.* Amsterdam: North Holland.

Miller, G. A., & Johnson-Laird, P. N. (1976). *Language and perception.* Cambridge, MA: Harvard University Press.

Mosenthal, P. (1976-1977). Psycholinguistic properties of aural and visual comprehension as determined by children's abilities to comprehend syllogisms. *Reading Research Quarterly, 12,* 55-92.

Neisser, V. (1976). *Cognition and reality.* San Francisco: Freeman.

Nelson, K. (1974). Concept, word and sentence: Interrelations in acquisition and development. *Psychological Review, 81,* 267-285.

Paivio, A. (1971). *Imagery and verbal processes.* New York: Holt, Rinehart & Winston.

Richardson, G. (1974). The Cartesian frame of reference: A structure unifying the description of dyslexia. *Journal of Psycholinguistic Research, 3,* 15-63.

Rips, L. J., Shoben, E. J., & Smith E. E. (1973). Semantic distance and the verification of semantic relations. *Journal of Verbal Learning and Verbal Behavior, 12,* 1-20.

Rosch, E. H. (1973a). Natural categories. *Cognitive Psychology, 4,* 328-350.

Rosch, E. H. (1973b). On the internal structure of perceptual and semantic categories. In T. E. Moore (Ed.), *Cognitive development and the acquisition of language* (pp. 111-144). New York: Academic Press.

Rosch, E. H. (1975a). Universals and cultural specifics in human categorization. In R. Brislin, S. Bochner, & W. Lonner (Eds.), *Cross-culural perspectives on learning* (pp. 177-206). New York: Sage/Halsted.

Rosch, E. (1975b). Cognitive reference points. *Cognitive Psychology, 7,* 532-547.

Rosch, E., & Mervis, C. B. (1975). Family resemblances: Studies in the internal structure of categories. *Cognitive Psychology, 7,* 573-605.

Rosch, E., Mervis, C. B., Gray, W. D., Johnson, D. M., & Boyes-Broem, P. (1976). Basic objects in natural categories. *Cognitive Psychology, 8,* 382-439.

Rumelhart, D. E. (1977). Understanding and summarizing brief stories. In D. LaBerge & S. J. Samuels (Eds.), *Basic processes in reading: Perception and comprehension* (pp. 265-303). Hillsdale, NJ: Lawrence Erlbaum Associates.

Rumelhart, D. E. (1980). Schemata: The building blocks of cognition. In R. J. Spiro, B. C. Bruce, & W. F. Brewer (Eds.), *Theoretical issues in reading comprehension: Perspectives from cognitive psychology, linguistics, artificial intelligence, and education* (pp. 33-58). Hillsdale, NJ: Lawrence Erlbaum Associates.

Rumelhart, D. E., & Ortony, A. (1977). A representation of knowledge in memory. In R. C. Anderson, R. J. Spiro, & W. E. Montague (Eds.), *Schooling and the acquisition of knowledge* (pp. 99-135). Hillsdale, NJ: Lawrence Erlbaum Associates.

Scholz, K. W., & Potts, G. R. (1974). Cognitive processing of linear orderings. *Journal of Experimental Psychology, 102,* 323-326.

Shields, M. M. (1978). The child as psychologist: Construing the social world. In A. Lock (Ed.), *Action, gesture and symbol: The emergence of language* (pp. 529-556). New York: Academic Press.

Smith, E. E., Rips, L. J., & Shoben, E. (1974). Semantic memory and psychological semantics. In G. H. Bower (Ed.), *The psychology of learning and motivation* (Vol. 8, pp. 1-45). New York: Academic Press.

Smith, E. E., Shoben, E., & Rips, L. J. (1974). Structure and process in semantic memory: A featural model for semantic decisions. *Psycholgical Review, 81,* 214-241.

Smith, F. (1975). *Comprehension and learning.* New York: Holt, Rinehart & Winston.

Smith, F. (1982). *Understanding reading* (3rd ed.). New York: Holt, Rinehart & Winston.

Spiro, R. J. (1980). Constructive processes in prose comprehension and recall. In R. J. Spiro, B. C. Bruce, & W. F. Brewer (Eds.), *Theoretical issues in reading comprehension: Perspectives from cognitive psychology, linguistics, artificial intelligence, and education* (pp. 245-278). Hillsdale, NJ: Lawrence Erlbaum Associates.

Wells, G. (Ed.). (1981). *Language through interaction: The study of language development.* Cambridge: Cambridge University Press.

Werner, H., & Kaplan, B. (1963). *Symbol formation.* New York: Wiley.

Wickens, D. D. (1972). Characteristics of word encoding. In A. W. Melton & E. Martin (Eds.), *Coding processes in human memory* (pp. 191-215). New York: Winston.

DISCOURSE CONVENTIONS
AND LITERARY INFERENCE:
TOWARD A THEORETICAL MODEL

Richard Beach
University of Minnesota

Robert Brown
University of Minnesota

Any discussion of pragmatics raises all of the critical, highly political field-defining and methodological issues in the recent history of linguistic theory. Or if it doesn't, it should. That history is alternately characterized by unrecognized theoretical assumptions determining the outcomes of empirical research, and theorizing innocent of empirical data. We do not try to correct these meta-theoretical problems here—Levinson (1983), and Leech (1983) summarize them nicely—though we do hope to operate from a consistent theoretical position, suggesting the direction such a correction might take. Some of our guiding questions:

- What apparatus (we are reluctant to commit to its nature) do speakers bring to text-forming and text-interpreting situations? The question of pragmatic competence(s).
- What is the nature of each of the components of this competence? The question of ontology—rules, conventions, strategies, heuristic procedures, and mutual knowledge: what's what?
- What analytical methods and formal representations serve us best?

We touch on these questions in our various analyses, and we hope to suggest our position on some of them. But we will not claim to answer them definitively.

A homely, but interesting example, taken from everyday conversation, and recorded by one of the authors, Speaker A:

SCENE: A fast-food restaurant. Speaker A enters, stands for a few moments in the 'public' space just inside the door to unbutton his long, blue Air Force-surplus overcoat, and to check his wallet. He then approaches the counter, entering the understood 'customer' space, and causing Speaker B—a teen-age restaurant worker—to initiate the conversation:

Text:
B: Can I help you over here?
A: Ah, yeah, I'd like a Whaler, by itself, please.
B: By itself? You mean you don't want it wrapped? No bag?
A: Oh sure I want it wrapped. I want a bag. I just meant I want a Whaler and nothing else.
B: (into the microphone on the counter) Drop a Whaler. (to A) Ninety-eight cents, please.
A: (pays)
B: (several minutes later, handing over the bag) Thanks, come again.

It would be hard to imagine speech events more formulaic than transactions in fast food restaurants. So it is particularly interesting that this one goes so bizarrely awry. Why does the innocent prepositional phrase *by itself* receive the complex interpretation that A wants to be handed a fish sandwich naked of paper and unbagged? A later interview—about which, more later—revealed the entirely logical reasoning process that led B to her remarkable inference.

It is precisely the rigidly formulaic structure of this sort of speech event that makes it useful for pragmatic analysis. Everyday language like this wears its principles of organization on the surface, making it easily accessible to analysis. We intend our analysis of this simple text as a demonstration—it is usefully free of the layering of psychologically rich implications of literary texts or the psychotherapeutic interviews Labov and Fanshel (1977) treat. It gives us a way to suggest the minimum essential analytical and theoretical apparatus.

"By Itself": A Common-Sense Interpretation

The fast food worker explained herself very simply:

—She knew her customer Speaker A well: he was a regular, known by his familiar face, if not known by name. He should, she claimed, 'know how to order in a Burger King by now.'
—She took a quick look at A's clothing and general demeanor, and decided that he was a counter-culture type, and environmentalist 'who wanted to save paper.'

But her complex inference seems to circumvent the easier interpretation: that by saying he wanted *a Whaler by itself*, A meant just that: a Whaler, no shake, no fries, no hot apple turnover. We can assume that she was behaving rationally, that she must have employed some sort of decision logic, some systematic process for assigning interpretations to texts. What might that logic look like? And why did she go so far out of her way?

A Simple Account of Gricean Conversational Cooperation

What does it mean to 'know how to order in a Burger King'? Clearly, one knows the meanings of the words, and the meaning relations established by the syntactic structure; this is the competence explained by the usual syntactico-semantic analyses, the domain of traditional linguistic theory. But it is equally clear that the logic that supports the interesting (mis)interpretation here is beyond such formal analyses—syntactic and otherwise.

The Burger King worker's interpretation is a complex inference from the conventional meaning of the sentence uttered, and a body of contextual information guided by principles of text production and interpretation. These are, we assume, the basic categories of a theory of inference.

Grice (1975) proposes that the basis of conversational decision-logic is a general principle for coordinating behavior, a possible universal of social action that he names the *co-operative principle*, (CP for short).

> Make your contribution such as is required, at the stage at which it occurs, by the accepted purpose or direction of the talk exchange in which you are engaged. (Grice 1975, p. 43)

Grice is characteristically unclear about the ontological status of the principle he proposes—principle is usefully neutral on that issue. But his discussion strongly suggests that it is a basic rational strategy for solving complex coordination problems of many types. We concur—if that is what he means.

The Gricean CP might be thought of as a *heuristic procedure* (rather than a set of algorithms) that leads people through the complex problem of coordinating their behavior with the behavior of others who share similar goals and basic cognitive apparatus. The key terms here are *goals*, and *cognitive apparatus*. Grice's principles apply to all *rational, goal-directed, coordinated* behavior—and conversation is simply one of the more elegant examples. Let's try two less elegant, non-linguistic examples:

We are both bakers working over a large cookie-dough mixer. Your job is to add milk to the mix; mine is to add flour. Our goal is to arrive at a properly mixed, moist-but-not-sloppy dough, filling the mixer to the proper line. We both know what proper dough looks like, and the properties of dough as it mixes. The machine is running, and by turns we add our ingredients, decreasing the increments as our batch approaches the mark. With luck (and thanks to our ability to determine the 'required contribution' at each stage of the mix), we get the right amount of properly proportioned dough at the end.

We are auto mechanics installing the oil pan under a car. Your job is to hold the pan securely in place, and to hand me the various bolts (in different lengths) as I work around the flange putting them in place. You watch me, and supply each bolt as I arrive at the relevant hole. With luck, I get the bolt I need just when I need it—never two at once, never the wrong size, and no screws, nails, or other non-bolts or joke-bolts.

In both cases we mutually know the purpose and directions of the task we are engaged in, and the cognitive apparatus and factual knowledge we share: baking principles, and bolting principles, respectively—and the visual scene unfolding before us as the process, or work-exchange, proceeds. We also mutually know (in an extended sense of knowing) the coordination-problem-solving apparatus we both use to order and use the knowledge we share.

Grice expands his co-operative principle as a set of Maxims that constitute it, for the specific case of conversational cooperation:

QUALITY
Try to make your contribution one that is true, specifically:
(i)   do not say what you believe to be false
(ii) do not say that for which you lack adequate evidence

QUANTITY
(i)   make your contribution as informative as is required for the current purposes of the exchange
(ii) do not make your contribution more informative than is required

RELATION
make your contribution relevant

MANNER
(i)   avoid obscurity
(ii) avoid ambiguity
(iii) be brief
(iv) be orderly

Said very simply: the CP and its maxims formalize the guiding heuristics speakers use to form and interpret text; they are constraints on the semantic content and linguistic means offered to meet communicative or interactional ends. As we see, they are not all of the story, but they are, we claim, the basis.

Back to Burger King:
A Gricean Account of a Simple Inference

Recall that we were pondering why *by itself* called for such a complex, inferential interpretation. The restaurant worker's two-part explanation did not address the question directly: She suggested that an experienced customer should "know how to order," and she called up considerable factual, contextual knowledge: dress codes, behavioral interpretation, and so on. Grice explains how she ordered and used this information to form the interpretation—and why she felt compelled to do so in the first place.

Simply put: the prepositional phrase *by itself* was *extra information* at the stage at which it occurs, in light of the accepted purpose and direction of the talk exchange in which these speakers were engaged. In Gricean terms, it was a violation of the Quantity, (ii) maxim: more informative than required. How come? No formal, text-grammatical answer suffices.

There seems to be a fairly rigid procedure for ordering in fast food restaurants, or at least in this one. It is this procedure that the Burger King worker referred to when she suggested that an experienced customer should know "how to order." In the examples we collected, the pattern was remarkably consistent. Without claiming much for the formalism, let us suggest how the procedure works: it constrains each turn of the interaction.

Opening: The worker initiates the interaction, usually with a formula phrase—an indirect request performed via a question:

—Can I help you?

Customer Order I: The customer gets to do one of two things: order the entire order, or simply the entree, followed by a short pause:

—Ah, yeah, I'll have Whopper®, small fries, and a medium Coke.

—Yeah, gimme a cheese Whopper . . .

Clerk's Intervention: The clerk then asks for a *continuation* of the order. In marketing terms, this is 'cross-selling,' a technique for reminding the customer of other options, and perhaps selling more goods. In our 11 recorded fast food interactions, this pattern never varied.

—Anything else today?

—How about some of our new onion rings?

Customer Order II: The customer either continues and finishes the
order, or terminates this turn:

—Yeah, gimme some fries and a small chocolate shake

—No, that's all

Interactions terminated in various ways at this point, depending on the
restaurant. Some asked for payment directly; some asked whether the
customer wanted the order "to go"; some offered apologies, warnings, or
small talk.

What counts as "too little" or "too much" information at any point in
a talk-exchange depends on the nature of that exchange. "Accepted
direction" is the crucial and powerful phrase in Grice's account that
addresses the question of the *nature* of what we variously call *discourse
types,* or *speech-events.* It allows a range of possibilities from rigid
conventionality to open, unstructured, interaction.

Apparently, fast food ordering is rather rigidly constrained. As an
experienced customer, speaker A should not have tried to foreclose the
interaction with his "by itself" phrase; he should simply have waited until
asked for the extension of the order, and then declined. Because both
speakers mutually knew the procedure, it was rational for the Burger
King clerk to assume that the "extra" prepositional phrase was an
information-bearing extension of the expected, conventionally constrained conversational contribution: "He's trying to tell me something; I
wonder what?" The ecological reading follows naturally from her evaluation of the utterance and her contextual knowledge—guided by the
second maxim of quantity. But it is absolutely critical to realize that this
quantity maxim violation is entirely relative to the constraints structuring
the speech event. In fact, all of the maxims are realized only through
interaction with some procedure, some understood purpose or direction
for talk exchanges. In this case, the guiding principles seem to be largely
conventional. They need not be—about which, much more follows.

TOWARD THEORY: AN OUTLINE

First, let's make some of our guiding assumptions explicit:

- We assume that the principles we define for this simple example hold
  for all authentic language; more complex language uses and more
  complicated examples will require more delicate descriptions, but do

not require a radically different epistemology. This runs exactly counter to many language and literary theories—the received New Critical view of literature, for example, which privileges literary texts by postulating different underlying structures.

- We assume that the Gricean apparatus is a basic, cognitive mechanism, and not uniquely linguistic. This view runs counter to various interpretations and applications of Grice which treat his maxims as rules of language, amenable of further specification to account for particular genres or types of language use (cf.: Clark & Haviland 1977, p. 264).

So we have suggested a three-part theory of what speakers know in order to form and interpret texts—and, by extension, to form inferences. The parts are distinct but large; we assume they will require elaborate expansion.

1. *Principles guiding co-operative, rational goal-directed behavior;* the Gricean co-operative principle—in an as-yet-to-be-developed clarified version (re: Levinson 1983, Chapter 3, for a beginning).

2. *Rules of syntax, semantics, and phonology,* the usual generative linguistic account of competence, accounting for speakers' sentence-making and interpreting ability. Some of these rules will probably turn out to be sensitive to pragmatic conditions.

3. *Mutual Knowledge,* an immensely complex body of knowledge shared (or assumed to be shared) by participants in any authentic language-using situation. It's difficult—both from an ontological and a practical/descriptive point of view—to distinguish the kinds. But they include at least these:
   —Factual knowledge; knowing *of* and *about* things, people, concepts, places and so on—the determinant for application of principles of reference, deixis, and definitivization.
   —Knowledge of various law-like regularities, of personality, society, politics, of the physical and social universe generally; the basis of many of our inferences about people's behavior, both reported and the real thing.
   —Conventional knowledge, knowing the various conventions—of language in particular, but also of human behavior generally—which guide and regulate social behavior.

Yes, these are large and vaguely defined claims in complicated and murky areas. Maybe it would be useful to specify what problems we seek to *avoid* with this formulation. Here are two:

- *Speech-acts,* their rules, and questions of taxonomies. On our account, once you have specified the meaning of the words uttered, the conventions, and non-conventional purposes of the "talk-exchange," and the mutual knowledge of the participants, there is no more descriptive work to be done. If this account holds, then it seems that the complex rules of speech-act theory are reifications of observations about the regularities and consequences of language as formal rules.

- *Rules-based accounts of speech-events (Grice's talk exchanges).* Our account is usefully casual about the nature of regularities observed in language use. We recognize that a given speech event may be rigidly conventional; religious ceremonies are, as Searle recognized (and overgeneralized). So are legal procedures. But we aren't certain about Burger King ordering; if it is conventional, it's only partly so, and the conventions are clearly more regulative than constitutive (cf.: Levinson, 1983; Searle, 1969 on rules and conventions). They may be neither: they may simply be predispositions or tendencies to behave in a particular way, based on shared knowledge of human behavior and past experience.

Discourse Conventions and Inferences About Fictional Characters' Acts

A native reader of fiction (Brown & Steinmann, 1979) brings the same knowledge to bear when interpreting the reported acts—speech and otherwise—of characters in written narratives. And she often brings more specific literary conventions as well. Seen this way, the transition between ordinary and literary language is so smooth that the category distinction begins to vanish—and with it the troublesome privileging of literature. Interpreting is interpreting; it simply has different sets of conventions for different genres or speech events.

Much recent reading comprehension research has focused on readers' use of these different types of knowledge—knowledge of concepts (Langer & Purcell-Gates, 1985; Spiro, 1983), subject matter "content" (Holmes, 1983; Marr & Gromley, 1982; Ribovich, 1979), text structures (Anderson, Spiro, & Anderson, 1978; Calfee & Curley, 1984; Carr, Dewitz, & Patberg, 1983; McGee, 1982), or reading strategies (Bruce & Rubin, 1984; Olshavsky, 1976; Phillips-Riggs, 1981) in making inferences about texts. (For a review of prior knowledge research, see Heine, 1985). Our discussion will focus on three types of conventional knowledge: speech-act conventions, social/cultural conventions, and literary conventions, and how readers use this knowledge in making inferences about literary texts.

Speech-act or Conversational Conventions.   Speech-act or conversational conventions define strategies for inferring the meaning of speech events, particularly characters' dialogue (Bach & Harish 1979; Brown & Steinmann, 1979; Hancher, 1983; Labov and Fanshel, 1977; Leech, 1983; Levision; 1983; Pratt; 1977; Searle, 1969; for an annotated bibliography on speech-act analysis of literary texts, see Hancher & Chapman, 1982). Readers use knowledge of these conventions to infer characters' acts, beliefs, goals, or traits as well as narrators' or speakers' role, stance, attitude, or motives (Brown & Steinmann, 1979; Hancher, 1983; Pratt, 1977).

As we have illustrated, readers also use knowledge of politeness maxims (Leech, 1983; Levison, 1983) to infer characters' attempts to "save face" (Brown & Levinson, 1978) or to minimize or maximize costs/ benefits, praise/criticism, agreement/disagreement among themselves (Leech, 1983). For example, if character A says to character B, "you were very generous in your gifts," A is minimizing self-praise. However, character B's response, "Yes, I was," maximizes self-praise, implying immodesty and self-centeredness.

Social/Cultural Conventions.   Social/cultural conventions define ways of understanding what constitutes social and cultural behavior within the "world" of the text (Barthes, 1974; Eagleton, 1983; Fish, 1980; Scholes, 1985). Knowing what is considered as appropriate or inappropriate behavior in certain social contexts or for certain roles helps a reader infer instances of characters' deviating from norms and the social consequences of such deviation. Readers who know the social conventions constituting social roles and appropriate behavior in early nineteenth century British upperclass life can infer, in reading Jane Austen's novels, the potential deviations in accepted behavior that constantly impinged upon the women in her novels.

Readers use their knowledge of social/cultural conventions to infer violations of speech-act conventions and the consequences of those violations. When, for example, a student questions a teacher, the extent to which that speech act constitutes a violation of social norms depends on the social or cultural conventions operating in that teacher's classroom or school. In some contexts, a student may be expected to question a teacher, while in others, questioning a teacher is strictly forbidden.

Given differences in readers' knowledge of social/cultural conventions and their social/cultural attitudes, they will differ in their inferences particularly their perceptions of what constitutes a violation of norms. For example, in a comparison of black and white students' inferences about passage describing a school situation in which a group of black students were "playing the dozens"—exchanging verbal insults—and the principal intervenes to control the students (Reynolds, Taylor, Steffensen, Shirey, & Anderson, 1982), blacks interpreted the incident as "just laughing and joking around," and whites viewed it as a "riot" or "fight." These readers' own knowledge and/or attitudes influenced their inferences as to the cultural meaning of "playing the dozens." Readers who differed in their attitudes towards teaching differed in their inferences about a teacher character (Beach, 1983).

Literary Conventions. Literary conventions constitute the use of literary techniques (characterization, figurative language, plot development, etc.), narrative devices (flashbacks, embedded narratives, false endings, etc.), character types (villains, heroes, foils, etc.), genres (comedy, tragedy, science fiction, lyric, parody, etc.) or language style (Brooks, 1984; Eco, 1979; Iser, 1978; Scholes, 1985).

Readers with a "literary" orientation are more likely to attend to language use as intentional, as deliberately used to imply "literary meaning" (Heath, 1985). For example, knowing that narrative texts typically revolve around an unusual event or complication involving a violation of speech-act or social/cultural conventions (Labov, 1972; Pratt, 1977), a reader may attend to cues such as "you wouldn't believe what happened then" or "it was very, very dark that night" (Labov, 1972) that imply that the narrative has a point and, given its unusual, extraordinary subject, is worth telling (Labov, 1972; Pratt, 1977).

For example, in a *New Yorker* article portraying the lives of five building superintendents (Singer, 1983), the "supers" are telling stories to each other about their jobs. Each of the stories serves as an illustration of a problem, so that the stories themselves, following the Relation Maxim, are relevant to the conversation, i.e., they are not "pointless."

One set of stories concerns complaints, and the point of the stories is that the complaints are, to quote one "super," "getting ridiculous" (Singer, p. 61).

> I had a boss over, a guy from the management office. While he was there, a lady called down and said she had a complaint. What is the complaint? The floor is dirty. Now, I know it is *not* dirty, so I put the boss on the phone. He gets on, she tells him the floor is dirty. He says, "I don't know how that could be, I was just up on your floor and the carpet looked spotless." She says, "Well, it's not *dirty* dirty, but I didn't hear the vacuum." Can you believe it?

Now, here's a second anecdote:

> I get an emergency call at 2 A.M. . . . . A lady says get up here right away. I put on some pants and go up there. Guess what it is? You'll never guess. A

roach. A roach on the floor. Dead. She couldn't sleep with it there. That's the emergency. I had to pick it up and flush it for her.

In the first story, the use of the question, "What is the complaint," the negative, "not" in "not dirty," and the final, "can you believe it" cue the reader to the unusual nature of the complaint. And, in the second story, the question, "Guess what it is," is again used, along with the negative, "never guess," the repetition of "roach," the negative "couldn't sleep" and the ironic "that's the emergency" to dramatize the unusualness of the story.

To some degree understanding the unusualness of each of these events required some elementary knowledge of tenant or employee behavior and the teller's presuppositions regarding "normal" behavior. (Often anecdotes or jokes misfire because the teller has assumed that auditors shared certain presuppositions about "normal" behavior.) Storytellers or writers who are more knowledgable of literary conventions may be better able to employ these cues. Older children's parodies of advertising jingles employed more cues than younger children to signal dramatic narrative aspects of jingles (Geller, 1983). Analysis of autobiographical narratives written by nine-year olds, thirteen-year olds, and adults indicated a steady increase in the use of cues with age (Cooper, 1985). Seventh grade readers who were better readers produced narratives with significantly higher number of cues than did poorer readers (Beach, 1984).

As readers acquire knowledge of literary convention, they improve in their ability to generalize about and evaluate texts (Applebee, 1978; Hillocks & Ludlow, 1984; Landry, Kelly & Gardner, 1982) and their ability to produce narratives (Black & Seifert, 1985; Black, Wilkes-Gibbs & Gibbs, 1982; Vardell, 1983). For example, sixth, ninth, and twelfth graders made increasingly more abstract inferences about detective stories and wrote detective stories with characters, storylines, and characters judged as increasingly more complex (Vardell, 1983).

Literary conventions also consist of conventional inference strategies for understanding texts, for example, the strategy of knowing that "everything counts" in reading a poem (Culler, 1975, 1981; Iser, 1974, 1978; Mailloux, 1982). Understanding a text, as in understanding discourse in a Burger King, involves determining which strategies are most appropriate for understanding a particular type of text or incident within that text (Beach & Appleman, 1984; Harste, 1985; Olshavsky, 1976). As Peter Rabinowitz (1985, p. 420) posits, "my metaphor [for texts] would have to be 'text as unassembled bunk bed from Sears.' It is a concrete thing, but you have to assemble it; it comes with rudimentary directions, but you have to know how to perform basic tasks and must have certain tools at hand; most important, the directions are virtually meaningless unless you know beforehand just what sort of object you are aiming at." A reader may therefore read the same text *as* a "comic novel," a "parody," a "social statement," or an "autobiographical portrait of the author's life." Each of these conventional strategies begin to constitute the text, so that, as Rabinowitz (1985) argues, a mystery story is constituted by mystery-story-reading strategies. This is why openers in texts and social conversation—introductions in conversations, greetings, book or chapter titles, opening sentences—are so important is that they signal how we should experience discourse—which genre strategies we should apply—sales talk, sermon, parody, put-on, lecture, mystery story, romance story, and so on (Eco, 1979).

Moreover, literary conventions not only constitute meaning; they define the conditions for what may serve as an acceptable or intelligent meanings within certain contexts or communities (Mailloux, 1982). Different denominations or religious communities each have their own conventions for interpretating religious texts that constitutes certain boundaries of acceptable meanings. Or, different "schools" of literary criticism adopt certain conventions for what they believe constitutes acceptable or intelligent interpretations. And, as illustrated by Radway's (1984) analysis of a women's "book club" discussions of romance novels, social groups or classrooms functioning as "interpretative communities" (Fish, 1980) may define their own criteria for acceptability.

Within these communities, conventions constitute roles or perspectives for "readers," "students," "teachers," "politicians," "leaders," "wise-guys," "authorities," etc., roles constituted by discourse strategies (Bleich, in press). For example, in an academic context, students define their roles as "critics" by adopting, often awkwardly, the discourse conventions of literary criticism. As Bartholomae (1985) notes, "my students . . . don't invent the language of literary criticism . . . they are, themselves, invented by it" (1985, p. 145).

Readers' knowledge of literary conventions also defines their orientation to the text, how a reader should perceive or evaluate a text as a literary text (Applebee, 1978; Britton, 1984). Readers who assume that they are reading a text "as" a literary text also may assume that a text has a point, adopting what Hunt & Vipond (in press) define as a "point-driven" perspective. Hunt & Vipond compared college students who adopted this more "point-driven" orientation with college students who adopted a more "story-driven" orientation—reading the text simply for enjoyment. They found that the more "story-driven" students frequently evaluated the story, John Updike's "A & P," as "pointless," and therefore had difficulty understanding the story. In contrast, the more "point-driven" students were able to recognize Updike's deliberate use of certain literary techniques to develop a theme.

In summary, readers mesh knowledge of speech-act, social/cultural, and literary conventions to make inferences about literary texts. We now discuss how readers use this knowledge to employ certain basic inference strategies. Given the lack of research on how readers use prior knowledge (Heine, 1985), some of this is only speculation designed to define certain variables that may be examined in future research.

Readers' Use of Interpretative Conventions

In discussing readers' use of conventions in employing inference strategies, we are illustrating their ability to *use* their knowledge—their "knowing-how" competence, rather than their "knowing-that" theoretical knowledge of conventions (Brown & Steinmann, 1979). The fact that readers have a "knowing-how" competence does not necessarily mean that they can articulate their "theoretical" knowledge of literary conventions. As years of developmental research with children's use of syntax and speech acts indicates, children have a "knowing-how" competence to perform certain linguistic feats even though they may have no theoretical knowledge of the language rules or conventions constituting the use of the language (Bloom, 1970; Chomsky, 1972).

Readers acquire this "knowing-how" competence from reading and responding to literature. Rather than directly testing for this "knowing how" competence, it may be assumed that older readers, who bring more background experience in reading and responding to literature, bring more fully developed knowledge of conventions to their reading. In discussing readers' use of "knowing-how" competence, we cite evidence from developmental studies comparing younger and older readers' inferences based on this assumption, and it is only an assumption, that older readers have acquired certain conventions that younger readers have not yet acquired.

Some research (Svensson, 1985) suggests that acquired knowledge of literary conventions is related to ability to interpret texts. Svensson found a steady increase in 11, 14, and 18 year olds' ability to infer the symbolic meanings of poems. He also found that, across age levels, that amount of previous reading of and instruction in literature was related to level of symbolic interpretation.

Applying "Global" Schema.   One of the most basic inference strategies is the ability to apply "global" schema to information in a literary text. Readers instantiate information by "situating" (Chabot, 1985) or contextualizing that information in terms of certain prototypical characters' roles, genre types, or narrative patterns constituted by conventions. Applying this prototypical schema, a reader's attempt to "envision"

(Fillmore & Kay, 1979) larger meanings, integrating or instantiating "local" schema into the more "global" prototypical schema (Langer, 1985; Fillmore, 1981). For example, a reader may conceive of characters' acts in terms of a "hero/villain" relationship, prototypes that imply certain conventional beliefs, traits, or goals for the "hero" and "villain" characters.

In reading the following passage, a reader may envision more "global" meanings for an exchange between Harry "Rabbit" Angstrom and his son in the John Updike novel, *Rabbit is Rich*, (1981, p. 157) by conceiving of their dialogue in terms of conventions constituting father/son social relationships. Angstrom, owner of a Toyota dealership, has just learned that his son Nelson has bought, without his authorization, some convertable used cars:

> Harry: "This isn't some fancy place dealing in antiques. We sell Toyotas. Toyotas."
> The child shrinks beneath his thunder. "Dad, I won't buy any more, I promise. These'll sell, I promise."
> "You'll promise me nothing. You'll promise me to keep your nose out of my car business and get your ass back to Ohio. I hate to be the one telling you this, Nelson, but you're a disaster. You've gotta get yourself straightened out and it isn't going to happen here."
> He hates what he's saying to the kid, though it's what he feels.

A reader could simply infer this as a series of speech acts—that Harry was criticizing and banishing Nelson, and Nelson is promising that he will sell the cars. However, a reader may envision more "global" possible meanings by embedding or situating these inferences into the context of social conventions constituting appropriate father/son relationships. Because fathers usually don't banish their sons or criticize them in such a direct, blunt manner ("you're a disaster"), his act is a violation, given a reader's envisionment of the dialogue in terms of father/son social conventions, of what could be considered as appropriate fatherly behavior.

This would suggest that older readers, who are more knowledgable of social conventions, would be more likely to conceive of or "situate" (Chabot, 1985) characters' actions in terms of more "global" envisionments. These developmental differences were examined in a study comparing eighth graders', eleventh graders', college freshmen', and college seniors' inferences to six specific events in a short story about a reserved adolescent boy who is attempting to develop a relationship with a girl (Beach and Wendler, in press). Subjects' open-ended inferences about characters' acts were rated according to whether subjects inferred acts in terms of physical actions as opposed to social or psychological phenomena. For example, inferences about acts rated as focusing more on physical actions included: "playing ball," "riding her bike," "talking on the phone," "playing basketball," "talking with his father," and so forth. Inferences about acts rated as focusing more on social or psychological phenomena included: "establishing a boy/girl relationship," "backing off/ discouraging," "trying not to get hurt," "expressing negative feelings about self," "gaining confidence."

The college students' mean ratings for degree-of-focus on social or psychological phenomena were significantly higher than the secondary-level subjects' ratings (p <.01). While these differences may represent differences in cognitive stages (Applebee, 1978), they also reflect difference in knowledge of social or psychological phenomena. The college subjects were conceiving of the characters' acts in terms of social conventions constituting "boy/girl relationships," to cite one inference, which triggered attention to problems conventionally associated with the prototype, "boy/girl relationships."

Inferring Prototypical Act/Belief/Goal Relationships. Readers use inferences about characters' beliefs or goals to explain characters' acts (Jose & Brewer, 1984; Rumelhart, 1975; Stein, 1979). In order to infer these beliefs and goals, readers use this prototypical knowledge of typical act/belief/goal relationships defined by discourse conventions. Take, for example, the following dialogue exchange between Mary and Bill, entitled "Story."

1. It was late Friday afternoon.
2. Mary and Bill were alone in the T. A. office going over Bill's paper.
3. Mary looked at her watch.
4. "Bill, this paper could use a little work."
5. "Well, what do I need to do about it?"
6. "You ought to work on it this weekend. Maybe some more work will improve it."
7. "But what do I need to do to improve it?"
8. Mary began to wonder.
9. "Do I really need to tell you?"
10. Bill smiled. "Yes, Mary, I wish that you would."

In order to explain Bill and Mary's actions, a reader may draw on knowledge of social conventions constituting prototypical teacher/student social behavior. For example, a reader may initially assume that as the teacher, Mary's goal is to help Bill with his paper, while Bill's goal is to improve his paper. However, the fact that "it was late" and "Mary looked at her watch" implies that Mary may want to end the conference as soon as possible and go home. A reader may then infer that, in order to maintain her teacher goal of appearing to be helpful while still ending the conference, Mary adopts a relatively indirect and therefore polite form: "the paper could use a little work," as opposed to "work on this paper."

However, when Bill asks her for help, Mary reiterates her request for action, a reiteration that implies a less mitigating and more aggravating stance towards Bill, and, to some degree, her belief that Bill is incompetent. When Bill reiterates his own request, Mary then becomes even less tactful in saying, "Do I really need to tell you," maximizing costs to him.

Up to this point, readers may typically think about these acts in terms of prototypical teacher/student roles and goals, explaining Bill's or Mary's behavior in terms of deviating from ideal teacher/student roles. However, when Bill smiles and reiterates his request for a third time, flouting the Relation Maxim ("be relevant"), some readers may switch schema and begin to reinterpret Bill's acts as flirting with Mary, implying a different set of beliefs and goals. By recalling the initial cues, "late" and "alone," they may now, drawing on knowledge of genre conventions, perceive the story more in terms of a romance narrative. They may then, using a different set of prototypes, conceive of the speech acts from a different perspective.

Readers who are more knowledgable of conventions constituting teacher/student roles or romance genre conventions may therefore be better able to infer beliefs and goals than less knowledgable readers. In a study comparing college and high school students' reasons for characters' speech acts in a comic one-act play about two newly-weds on their honeymoon (Beach, 1985), students' reasons were ranked as representing short- versus long-range goals. For twelve of the sixteen acts, the college students had a significantly higher percentages of reasons ($p < .01$) representing the long range goals than did the high school students. One explanation for this difference is that the college students were more familiar with the social conventions constituting marital relationships in addition to the comic conventions constituting the potential for violation in the characters relationships. Perceiving character acts as part of a comic play may have helped them attend to potential long-range complications in the marriage. A high frequency of the high school students perceived few if any comic elements in the play, so that they were less likely to infer the potential for complications.

Problem-Finding and Problem-Solving Heuristics. As they move through a text, readers, employing their metacognitive skills (Baker & Brown, 1984), are constantly defining aspects of the text they do not understand. For readers, "a little knowledge is a dangerous thing" in that the more readers know, the more likely they are to know that they don't understand potential meanings.

This problem-finding/problem-solving process involves the following steps:

1. recognizing that something in the text disturbs or bothers them, relying on their sense of "felt understanding" to infer the fact that they don't understand something (Baker & Brown, 1984).
2. defining what it is that they don't understand—problem-finding.
3. formulating hypotheses or schema to help them understand what they don't understand (Bruce & Rubin, 1984; Collins, Brown, & Larkin, 1980).
4. reviewing the text to find information relevant to understanding what they don't understand.
5. testing out and revising their hypotheses against prior information in order to settle on a possible solution or explanation (Phillips-Riggs, 1981).

Readers draw on their knowledge of discourse conventions at each of these steps, engaging in heuristics based on discourse pragmatics (Leech, 1983). In order to sense that there are certain things that they don't understand, readers pose questions, using their knowledge of conventions in order to ask, for example, why did character A perform act B which violates maxim or discourse convention C.

Posing these questions evokes potential, more "global" schema, for defining aspects of an incident they don't understand. For example, two short story characters, Jim and Jane, are having an intensive discussion about whether they should get married. In the middle of this conversation, Jim says:

"There's a good movie coming to town this Friday."

Jane replies: "That's interesting."

In responding to this dialogue, a reader may pose the question, why does Jim suddenly switch from talking about marriage to talking about a movie? That sense of dissonance, that something's awry, may have been triggered by knowledge of the Grician maxim, "be relevant." In wondering why Jim does not want to stick to the relevant topic of marriage, a reader may pose other questions—Is Jim trying to avoid the topic? Is he nervous about talking about marriage?, etc.

Similarly, a reader may sense potential questions or problems regarding Jane's reply, "That's interesting." Drawing on knowledge of the Quantity Maxim (Grice, 1975) of saying no more than is necessary, a reader may wonder why Jane is deliberately flouting that maxim. Is she implying that she's really not interested and is irritated at his attempt to avoid talking about marriage? Is she reading Jim's comment as a description of the movie rather than as an invitation to go to the movie, or is she simply agreeing with him?

Once readers define problems in understanding, they formulate and test out optional hypotheses to determine the most valid explanation. In order to test out these hypotheses, they need to determine whether certain meanings will "work" within the context of the social world of the text. As we previously noted, this requires the ability to test the acceptability of their inference according to constraints implied by certain social conventions. In order to determine if an inference about Jim is valid—that he's deliberately switching topics to avoid talking about marriage—a reader considers the larger social context of Jim and Jane's social relationship, meshing knowledge of speech-act and social conventions.

In testing out hypotheses, readers therefore use knowledge of conventions to reduce or limit the range of potential meanings by checking inferences about characters' acts against larger social contexts. To take another example, in the television series, *Upstairs, Downstairs,* the butler, Hudson, says to his master, Richard Bellamy, who is sitting by a fire in the drawing room, "It's cold in here, isn't it." A viewer may infer a number of different hypotheses—that Hudson is describing the room, asking Bellamy to agree with his observation, asking Bellamy to add fuel to the fire, or asking permission of Bellamy to add the fuel to the fire himself.

In order to determine which of these hypotheses is most valid, a viewer tests out optional meanings using knowledge of social conventions constituting upper-class Edwardian society. If a viewer infers that Hudson is simply describing the room, then they may also ask if Hudson believes that Bellamy does not know that the room is cold. A viewer could infer that, given appropriate behavior in master/butler relationships, that it is unlikely that Hudson would impart unnecessary information (a violation of Grice's Quantity Maxim). A viewer may also consider whether Hudson is asking Bellamy to add fuel to the fire. Again, given Hudson's social status, such a request would be irrelevant.

In considering the final hypothesis—that Hudson is implying that he will add fuel to the fire, a viewer may pose the further question, "why doesn't Hudson simply say to Bellamy, 'I'll fix the fire'?" By considering this option in the context of the Edwardian social world, a viewer may recognize that such direct assertions by a butler would violate politeness maxims of generosity (Leech, 1983), so that Hudson would be talking credit for his own action. A viewer may then infer that Hudson opts for the more polite, indirect form of the request, allowing Bellamy to act in his accustomed, superior role.

All of this suggests that readers who may be more knowledgable of certain conventions may differ in their ability to pose questions or detect problems in understanding from readers who may be less knowledgable of these conventions. Assuming that older readers were more knowledgable of the conventions constituting detective stories than younger readers, Beach and Saxton (1982) asked ninth graders, twelfth graders, and college juniors/seniors to list specific aspects of two detective stories they did not understand while they were reading. The college subjects were significantly ($p <.01$) more likely to cite problems in understanding the author's intended meaning and to cite reasons for not understanding these problems, reflecting more presumed knowledge of literary conventions constituting awareness of "intentionality." For example, having inferred that they did not understand why the author focused so much attention to describing a large park in the opening scene of the story, they then inferred a reason—that they did not know enough about subsequent events to understand how the park may be related to a subsequent crime. Having inferred that reason for why they did not understand the author's intended use of the park, they could then use that reason as a schema for reviewing information about the park that may be related to any subsequent crime.

Predicting Story Development.   Readers also use their knowledge of conventions to predict story development or outcomes. Knowing, for example, the social conventions for a "romantic relationship," a reader predicts subsequent developments in a character's relationship. When these expectations are not fulfilled, a reader also knows that they need to revise their expectations. In recognizing the need to revise their expectations, a reader may begin to sense the deliberate use of a literary convention or strategy to "set up" the reader in order to force the reader to examine his or her own attitudes or beliefs (Mailloux, 1982).

A reader may draw on knowledge of these conventions to attend to certain words or phrases that cue potential story development. For example, in responding to the "Story" dialogue between Mary and Bill, a reader may apply knowledge of mystery or romance stories to focus on the words "late" and "alone" in "It was late Friday afternoon. Mary and Bill were alone . . .," words typically used in mystery or romance stories to imply potential violations of social norms.

Readers may then mesh their knowledge of social and literary conventions with knowledge of speech-act conventions to infer implications of characters' speech acts. For example, in the previously-cited study comparing college and high school students' inferences about a comic one-act play (Beach, 1985), the college subjects were more likely infer implications for violation of speech-act and social conventions in terms of potential problems for the newly-weds in their honeymoon. For example, the college subjects were more likely to infer that the bride, in the beginning of the honeymoon, is attempting to test his loyalty to her and that the groom is attempting to placate her in order to order to avoid further fights and enjoy the honeymoon.

In the following dialogue, the bride and groom are on the train going to New York for the honeymoon. The bride says:

> I guess I will take this darned old hat off. It kind of presses. Just put it on the rack, will you, dear? Do you like it, sweetheart?
> Looks good on you.
> No, but I mean, do you really like it?
> Well, I'll tell you, I know this is the new style and everything like that, and it's probably great. I don't know anything about things like that. Only I like that kind of hat like that blue hat you had. Gee, I like that hat.

In this exchange, the bride asks the groom for his opinion about her hat. The college subjects were more likely to infer that rather than simply requesting his perception of the hat, she is really testing his loyalty by seeking his praise.

Then, when he responds, "Looks good on you," the college students were more likely to infer that he flouts the Relation Maxim—deliberately failing to respond to her request as a request about his feelings towards her.

Sensing his disapproval, the bride probes him further, "No, but I mean, do you really like it?" The college subjects were then more likely to infer that the groom, attempting to be tactful, gives a long, irrelevant answer, which violates the Relation and Quantity maxims, further confirming his disapproval.

The college subjects were therefore better able to detect and exploit inferences about violations of speech-act and social conventions than the high school subjects, differences that may reflect differences in knowledge of comic genre conventions.

Creating a "World" for a Text.   Readers also use their knowledge of conventions to define a text's setting in terms of a social world constituted by social conventions. Inferring these norms helps a reader judge characters' actions as adhering to or deviating from these norms. In our Burger King example, knowledge of the ritual ordering pattern was useful in understanding a deviation from that pattern. However, in attempting to predict potential consequences of deviations, readers also draw on knowledge of genre conventions to create fictional worlds as representative of the "worlds" of "mystery," "comedy," "science fiction," "detective," "romance," "adventure" genres.

For example, in reading Jane Austen's *Pride and Prejudice*, a reader draws on not only knowledge of early nineteenth-century social conventions, but also knowledge of the conventions of the comic novel. In that novel, Mrs. Bennet, mother of the main character, Elizabeth, is incessently blathering on, creating some irritation for her daughters and her husband. In the social context of upper class British society, blathering on was a deviation from the laconic, reserved discourse of the gentry. Understanding the "full" meaning of Mrs. Bennet's loquaciousness requires the additional knowledge of the comic literary conventions constituting Austen's novel.

By applying knowledge of these comic conventions, a reader perceives her indiscreet blathering as being used by Austen to portray Mrs. Bennet's character as a foil for her more circumspect daughter, Elizabeth. A reader may also infer that, in Austen's comic world, any dire consequences of Mrs. Bennet's actions are mitigated.

A reader may then use their knowledge of comic literary conventions and social conventions to make inferences about characters dialogue. The process is represented in the following reader's oral "think-aloud" response to the opening episode in the novel in which Mr. Bennet deliberately misunderstands his wife's attempts to get him to visit their new neighbor, Mr. Bingley.

> The novel opens with a tone of comic irony: "It is a truth universally acknowledged, that a single man in possession of a good fortune, must be in want of a wife." And then, as it goes on, this man is "considered as the rightful property of some one or other of their daughters," so a tone is set from the beginning that this is going to be a comedy with a gentle irony. While it may first appear that Mr. Bennet is extremely dense in some of the questions he asks and some of the responses he gives, it becomes clear that he is being deliberately dense just to tease her, in a playful, not malicious way, as you can tell from the entire tone of this chapter.

> You can also tell that Mr. Bennet is not stupid. Some of the questions and responses to Mrs. Bennet initially seem to be stupid, but you later discover that they are really not stupid. Early on when Mrs. Bennet says that that "Netherfield Park is let at last," and asks Mrs. Bennet, "Do not you want to know who has taken it?" Mr. Bennet says, "You want to tell me, and I have no objection to hearing it." That clever retort is an indication that he is going to tease her; it is a kind of opening salvo.

> When Mrs. Bennet says that Mr. Bennet must visit Mr. Bingley because this is a wonderful thing for their daughters, his response is that he doesn't need to go because the girls could go. Now this is totally absurd. In the customs of the times, it would be improper for young women to visit a young man. In order for them to make a visit, it would be necessary for their father or an older man to make the first contact. To suggest that his daughters would go

first . . . we know that he knows better than that, which gives us a clue that
he is teasing.

This reader is able to infer that Mr. Bennet is deliberately flouting the
maxim, "be relevant" in order to tease Mrs. Bennet. She infers such
flouting because she draws on knowledge of "customs of the times"
regarding courtship and the conventions constituting the "comic irony"
in Bennet's dialogue. By inferring that Mr. Bennet knows these conventions that "we know," she recognizes the dramatic irony at work in the
text.

SUMMARY

1. The meanings readers derive from texts vary according to the prior
knowledge of speech-act, social, and literary conventions they bring to
texts, prior knowledge not fully accounted for in reading research on the
effects of prior knowledge on comprehension.

2. Discourse conventions constitute texts and readers' roles; readers
also use them to test the acceptability and intelligence of their inferences.

3. Readers' knowledge of conventions allows them to employ various
inference strategies—to instantiate "global" schema, infer prototypical
act/belief/goal relationships, define problems and expectations, and to
create a "world" of the text.

4. Because readers, particularly readers with different social and
reading experiences, vary in their prior knowledge, their inferences about
texts vary in scope or validity.

TOPICS FOR FURTHER RESEARCH

As we noted, our discussion of how readers use prior knowledge of
discourse conventions to make inferences pointed towards some possible
topics deserving further research.

Content of Inferences.   Much of the research on literary inference
has employed category systems focusing on aspects of the story recalled
or on types of inferences (goal, plan, beliefs, etc.) as opposed to the
content of implied meanings readers derive from texts. As the sample
responses illustrate, readers' open-ended responses represent interesting
and often subtle insights into characters' actions that often are not
captured by "types" categories.

However, analyzing the content of readers' inferences is difficult; it is inherently speculative. If that analysis is to generate group data beyond anecdotal accounts, then some method—for example, the clustering technique employed in the Parker one-act play study—needs to be used and further refined. It may then be possible to distinguish across these types according to the validity, range (short vs. long), relevancy to social or literary contexts, and so on.

Criteria for Discriminating Among Levels of Inferences.   Our discussion suggests that as readers acquire more knowledge of discourse conventions, their inferences become more "sophisticated." Although we do know that some of this is due to level of cognitive development (Applebee, 1978; Vardell, 1983, Walker, 1983), we lack the criteria for determining what constitutes a more "sophisticated" inference. In these examples, so much of the "sophistication" is a matter of greater factual knowledge, but this knowledge is relevant only to the extent that the reader has conventional strategies for applying factual knowledge. Readers' awareness of not only social conventions constituting the "world" of the text, but also of the literary conventions constituting the text, results in what could be defined as an inference reflecting a fuller understanding of the text.

To some degree, judging some responses as more sophisticated than others is presumptuous; it is certainly culture-bound. Moreover, the degree of sophistication may vary according to the interpretative or critical approach employed. What may be deemed as an insightful inference from the perspective of a feminist critic may be labeled as *naive* by a Marxist critic. But this should not surprise us. Reconsider the Burger King example. Although not a literary text, it involves similar interpretative strategies. A rich interpretation of that conversational exchange may not be "right," a right one may not be rich, and in some genres, right may not be at issue.

Thus, different critical orientations or "interpretative communities" define themselves by different conventional ways of interpreting facts, reflecting different social and cultural attitudes and assumptions.

However, much of the inter-critical school squabble concerns relatively high-level literary critical analysis of texts. Differences in younger readers' responses do reflect different levels of understanding consistent with differences in prior knowledge, regardless of differences in their critical orientation. Understanding these differences provides some direction for teachers to help students relate their prior knowledge to their reading. And, teachers may consider ways of organizing a literature curriculum or course around the acquisition of requisite social or literary conventions necessary for interpreting increasingly more difficult texts.

Studying Readers' Heuristics.   Readers acquire problem-solving strategies allowing them to test out alternative implied meanings against social contexts represented in the text. Readers then try to determine which of these alternative implied meanings are the most valid or compelling.

This suggests a learned process in which readers systematically examine implied meanings in terms of characters' beliefs, plans, goals or traits. Further research, drawing on protocol-analysis research employed in problem-solving studies, needs to examine variations in readers' ability to infer and test-out alternative implied meanings.

That research could also examine how readers with different kinds or degrees of prior knowledge attend to certain cues in the texts that signal appropriate social behavior or narrative development. Such research could also examine how textual cues imply or signal the need for readers to shift their schema or adopt new schema as readers strive to understand texts.

REFERENCES

Anderson, R., Spiro, R., & Anderson, M. (1978). Schemata as scaffoling for the representation of information in connected discourse. *American Educational Research Journal, 15,* 85-92

Applebee, A. (1978). *The child's concept of story.* Chicago: University of Chicago Press.

Bach, K., & Harnish, R. (1979). *Linguistic communication and speech acts.* Cambridge: MIT Press.

Baker, L., & Brown, A. (1984). Cognitive monitoring in reading. In J. Flood (Ed.), *Understanding reading comprehension.* (pp. 21-44). Newark, DE: International Reading Association.

Barthes, R. (1974). *S/Z.* New York: Hill and Wang.

Bartholomae, D. (1985). Inventing the university. In M. Rose (Ed.), *When a writer can't write* (pp. 134-165). New York: Guilford.

Beach, R. (1983). Attitudes, social conventions and response to literature. *Journal of Research and Development in Education, 16,* 47-54.

Beach, R. (1984, April). *The effects of reading ability on seventh graders' writing of autobiographical narratives.* Paper presented at the Annual Meeting of the American Educational Research Association, New Orleans.

Beach, R. (1985). Discourse conventions and researching response to literary dialogue. In C. Cooper (Ed.), *Researching response to literature and the teaching of literature* (pp. 103-127). Norwood, NJ: Ablex.

Beach, R., & Appleman, D. (1984). Reading strategies for expository and literary text types. In A. Purves and O. Niles (Eds.), *Becoming readers in a complex society* (pp. 115-143). Eighty-third Yearbook of the National Society for the Study of Education. Chicago: The National Society for the Study of Education.

Beach, R., & Saxton, F. (1982, April). *Problem-solving strategies in response to literature.* Paper presented at the National Council of Teachers of English, Minneapolis, MN.

Beach, R., & Wendler, L. (in press). Developmental differences in literary inferences. *Research in the Teaching of English.*

Black, J., & Seifert, C. (1985). The psychological study of story understanding. In C. Cooper (Ed.), *Researching response to literature and the teaching of literature*. Norwood, NJ: Ablex.

Black, J., Wilkes-Gibbs, D., & Gibbs. R. (1982). What writers need to know that they don't know they need to know. In M. Nystrand (Ed.), *What writers know* (pp. 325-343). New York: Academic Press.

Bleich, D. (in press). *Literacy and social contexts*. Baltimore: Johns Hopkins Press.

Bloom, L. (1970). *Language development: Form and function in emerging grammars*. Cambridge: M.I.T. Press.

Britton, J. (1984). Viewpoints: the distinction between participant and spectator role language in research and practice. *Research in the Teaching of English, 18,* 320-331.

Brooks, P. (1984). *Reading for the plot. Design and intention in narrative*. New York: Knopf.

Brown, R., & Steinmann, M. (1979). Native readers of fiction: A speech-act and genre-rule approach to defining literature. In P. Hernadi (Ed.), *What is literature?* (pp. 141-160). Bloomington: Indiana University Press.

Brown, P., & Levinson, S. (1978). Universals in language usage: Politeness phenomena. In E. Goody (Ed.), *Questions and politeness: Strategies in social interaction* (pp. 56-289) London: Cambridge University Press.

Bruce, B., & Rubin, A. (1984). Strategies for controlling hypothesis formation in reading. In J. Flood (Ed.), *Promoting reading comprehension* (pp. 97-113). Newark, DE: International Reading Association.

Calfee, R., & Curley, R. (1984). Structures of prose in content areas. In J. Flood (Ed.), *Understanding reading comprehension*. Newark, DE: International Reading Association.

Carr, E., Dewitz, P., & Patberg, J. (1983). The effect of inference training on children's comprehension of expository text. *Journal of Reading Behavior, 15,* 1-18.

Chabot, B. (1985). Understanding interpretative situations. In C. Cooper (Ed.), *Researching response to literature and the teaching of literature* (pp. 22-32). Norwood, NJ: Ablex.

Chomsky, C. (1972). Stages in language development and reading experience. *Harvard Educational Review, 42,* 1-33.

Collins, A., Brown, J., & Larkin K. (1980). Inference in text understanding. In R. Spiro, B. Bruce & W. Brewer (Eds.), *Theoretical issues in reading comprehension* (pp. 258-297) Hillside, NJ: Erlbaum.

Clark, H., & Haviland, S. (1977). Comprehension and the given-new contract. In R. Freedle (Ed.), *Discourse production and comprehension* (pp. 253-275). Norwood, NJ: Ablex.

Cooper, C. (1985). *A cross-sectional study of the development of autobiographical writing*. Paper presented at Conference on College Composition and Communication, Minneapolis.

Culler, J. (1975). *Structuralist poetics: Structuralism, linguistics, and the study of literature*. Ithaca: Cornell University Press.

Culler, J. (1981). *The pursuit of signs: Semiotics, literature, desconstruction*. Ithaca: Cornell University Press.

Eagleton, T. (1983). *Literary theory*. Minneapolis: University of Minnesota Press.

Eco, U. (1979). *The role of the reader: Explorations in the semiotics of texts*. Bloomington: Indiana University Press.

Fillmore, C, & Kay, P. (1979). *Text Semantic Analysis of Reading Comprehension Tests*, National Institute of Education Grant Number G-79-0121.

Fish, S. (1980). *Is there a text in this class?* Cambridge: Harvard University Press.

Geller, L. (1983, November). *Children's parodies of advertisements*. Paper presented at the National Council of Teachers of English, Denver, CO.

Grice, H. (1975). Logic and conversation. In P. Cole & J. Morgan (Eds.), *Syntax and semantics, III: Speech acts* (pp. 41-58). New York: Academic Press.

Hancher, M. (1983). Pragmatics in wonderland. In H. Garvin (Ed.), *Rhetoric, literature and interpretation* (pp. 165-184). Cranbury, NJ: Associated University Presses.

Hancher, M., & Chapman, P. (1982). *Speech-act theory and literary criticism: An annotated bibliography.* Minneapolis: Department of English, University of Minnesota.

Harste, J. (1985). Portrait of a new paradigm: Reading comprehension research. In A. Crismore (Ed.), *Landscapes: A state-of-the-art assessment of reading comprehension research, 1974-1984* (pp. 12:1-24). Bloomington, Ind.,: Center for Reading and Language Studies.

Heath, S. (1985). Being literate in America: A sociohistorical perspective. In J. Niles & R. Lalik (Eds.): *Issues in literacy: A research perspective,* Thirty-fourth Yearbook of The National Reading Conference (pp. 1-18). Rochester, NY: The National Reading Conference.

Heine, D. (1985). Readers as explorers: Using background knowledge. In A. Crismore (Ed.), *Landscapes: A state-of-the-art assessment of reading comprehension research, 1974-1984* (pp. 9:1-24). Bloomington, Ind.,: Center for Reading and Language Studies.

Hillocks, G., & Ludlow, L. (1984). A taxonomy of skills in reading and interpreting fiction. *American Educational Research Journal, 21,* 7-24.

Holmes, B. (1983). The effect of prior knowledge on the question answering of good and poor readers. *Journal of Reading Behavior. 15,* 1-18.

Hunt, R., & Vipond, D. (in press). The reader, the text, and situation: Blocks and affordances in literary reading. *Empirical Studies in the Arts.*

Iser, W. (1974). *The implied reader.* Baltimore: Johns Hopkins.

Iser, W. (1978). *The act of reading: A theory of aesthetic response.* Baltimore: Johns Hopkins.

Jose, P., & Brewer, S. (1984). Development of story liking; Character identification, suspense, and outcome resolution. *Developmental Psychology, 20,* 911-924.

Labov, W. (1972). *Language in the inner city.* University Park: University of Pennsylvania Press.

Labov, W., & Fanshel, D. (1977). *Therapeutic discourse: Psychotherapy as conversation.* New York: Academic Press.

Langer, J. (1985). Levels of questioning: An alternative view. *Reading Research Quarterly, 20,* 586-602.

Langer, J., & Purcell-Gates, V. (1985). Knowledge and comprehension: Helping students use what they know. In T. Harris and E. Cooper (Eds.), *Reading, thinking, and concept development* (pp. 53-70). New York: College Board Publications.

Leech, G. (1983). *Principles of pragmatics.* New York: Longman.

Levinson, S. (1983). *Pragmatics.* Cambridge: Cambridge University Press.

Mailloux, S. (1982). *Interpretative conventions: The reader in the study of American fiction.* Ithaca: Cornell University Press.

Marr, M., & Gormley, K. (1982). Children's recall of familiar and unfamiliar text. *Reading Research Quarterly, 18,* 89-104.

McGee, L. (1982). Awareness of text structure: Effects on children's recall of expository text. *Reading Research Quarterly, 17,* 581-590.

Olshavsky, J. (1976). Reading as problem-solving: An investigation of strategies. *Reading Research Quarterly, 12,* 654-674.

Phillips-Riggs, L. (1981). *The relationship between reading proficiency, background knowledge, and inferencing strategies.* Unpublished doctoral dissertation, University of Alberta, Alberta, Canada.

Pratt, M. (1977). *Towards a speech act theory of literary discourse*. Bloomington: Indiana University Press.

Rabinowitz, P. (1985). The turn of the glass key: Popular fiction as reading strategy. *Critical Inquiry, 11*, 418-430.

Radway, J. (1984). *Reading the romance: Women, patriarchy, and popular literature*. Chapel Hill: University of North Carolina Press.

Reynolds, R., Taylor, M., Steffensen, M., Shirey, L., & Anderson, R., (1982). Cultural schemata and reading comprehension. *Reading Research Quarterly, 17*, 348-362.

Ribovich, J. (1979, March). The effect of informational background on various reading-related behaviors in adult subjects. *Reading World*, 253-261.

Rumelhart, D. (1975). Notes on a schema for stories. In D. Bobrow & A. Collins (Eds.), *Representations and understandings: Studies in cognitive science* (pp. 56-84). New York: Academic Press.

Scholes, R. (1985). *Textual power*. New Haven: Yale University Press.

Searle, J. (1969). *Speech acts: An essay in the philosophy of language*. Cambridge: Cambridge University Press.

Singer, M. (1983, October 24). Supers. *The New Yorker*, pp. 61, 66.

Stein, N. (1979). How children understand stories: A developmental analysis. In L. Katz (Ed.), *Current topics in early childhood education, Volume 11* (pp. 149-167). Norwood, NJ: Ablex.

Svensson, C. (1985). *The construction of poetic meaning*. Uppsala, Sweden: Liber Press.

Updike, J. (1981). *Rabbit is rich*. New York: Ballantine Books (p. 157).

Vardell, S. (1983). Reading, writing, and mystery stories. *English Journal, 72*, 42-51.

Walker, G. (1983). *The relationship among cognitive ability, taking an assigned perspective, and type of story idea remembered*. Unpublished doctoral dissertation, The Catholic University, Washington, D. C.

READERS' UNDERSTANDING OF METAPHOR: IMPLICATIONS OF LINGUISTIC THEORY FOR PSYCHOLINGUISTIC RESEARCH

Bess Altwerger

Steven L. Strauss
University of New Mexico

Recent important advances in linguistic theory, cognitive psychology, and the theory of reading have inspired a new wave of investigations into the nature and comprehension of metaphoric expressions. This is because metaphors are recognized by researchers as expressions that arise in the course of special interactions between language structure, context of language use, and strategies of inference. The field of metaphor research can certainly be characterized as optimistic and confident, given the strong pillars on which it rests. Conversely, the "interdisciplinary" nature of metaphor allows researchers to use the study of such expressions as a test of more general hypotheses concerning language, language comprehension, models of the reading process, and so on.

Results of studying readers' understanding of metaphor can be interesting and significant only when the research is securely anchored in an adequate theoretical linguistic description of these figurative expressions. We therefore are concerned here with establishing a theoretical base for studying the role of figurative language in the reading process. This means identifying, on linguistic grounds, the significant properties of metaphor and examining the implications these properties have for research on readers' understanding.

It is necessary to distinguish two broad and distinct domains of figurative language. In one, the meanings of the figurative expressions are not already established by prior convention. In the other, they are established. The former is referred to as *fresh metaphor*, or simply *metaphor*, whereas the latter is referred to as *frozen metaphor*, or *idiom*. The terminology employed reveals an understood connection between metaphor and idiom, namely, that the latter is derived from the former. The transition from metaphor to idiom is normally considered the result of continued use of the metaphor until it becomes "aggrammatized" (Levin, 1977), or "institutionalized" (Grice, 1975), or conventionalized, though there have been suggestions (Nunberg, 1978) that quantity of usage may not be the entire explanation for metaphor freezing. The quality of usage, an admittedly somewhat vague notion at this point, is likely also to be involved.

Consider by way of example the complex expression "bury the hatchet," which we assume was originally coined as a fresh metaphor, meaning "make peace," but which, through continued usage, crystallized its conventional meaning. The possession of a conventional meaning places the expression on a par with simple words of the language. Sometimes a simple word will be used metaphorically, in which case its domain of reference or predication is extended. For example, the word "cold" has been extended from the physical domain, as a description of concrete objects, to the domain of emotions ("a cold person"), though the new meaning for "cold" has become idiomatized. As Hockett (1958) pointed out, the conventional meanings of words and idiomatic expressions are not "deducible" from their internal structure. Just as the meaning of the word "cold" is not entirely predictable from its phonological shape and its syntactic category, so too is the idiomatic meaning of "bury the hatchet" not completely derivable from the meaning of its parts, and from their internal organization.

Metaphors are distinguished from nonmetaphors not only by their novelty, but also by their violation of a rule of language structure or convention of language use. These two types of violations are grounded in Chomsky's (1965) theoretical distinction between linguistic competence and linguistic performance. The former refers to the tacit knowledge of the system of rules and structural principles of one's native language, whereas the latter refers to the actual use of this knowledge in concrete situations, such as reading.

Metaphors that violate rules of semantic structure are called *semantic metaphors*, as distinguished from metaphors that violate conventions governing language use, which are called *pragmatic metaphors*. In a linguistic study of metaphor, Levin (1977) notes that in the metaphoric expression "The stone died," there is a violation of part of the semantic structure of English governing the choice of logical subjects. In this sentence, the verb *die* has a subject that is inanimate, which is a violation of its restriction, logically speaking, to animate subjects. The "semantic selection restriction" of *die* is not being adhered to.

Pragmatic violations are said to contain no internal semantic violation. Rather, the violation involves the relationship between the sentence and the context in which it is used. The sentence, "The old rock is becoming brittle with age" (Reddy, 1969), is internally well-formed, but is metaphoric when used to refer to professor emeritus. In this case, The old rock refers to something that is not its usual referent.

The view taken in much of the linguistic literature has been that a sharp separation must be made between the two types of metaphor. Matthews (1971), for example, claims that semantic selectional restriction violations constitute the necessary and sufficient condition for the existence of a metaphor, although the existence of pragmatic metaphors clearly shows the untenability of this hypothesis (Searle, 1979; Morgan, 1979). Levin also dismisses this position, and although he states that "metaphor is not a purely semantic phenomenon" (p. 94), he nevertheless makes the following remark: "Our aim in discussing pragmatic deviance has been to segregate a class of deviance types from another type, that of purely semantic deviance" (p. 12).

We believe, however, that there is no such thing as a purely semantically deviant metaphor. Semantic deviance in figurative language is at the same time pragmatic deviance. That is, all metaphor-producing violations are violations of conventions of language use. To see this, consider the various possible construals of "The stone died." It may, as Levin points out, be used to refer to an unfeeling person who died, in which "stone" is metaphoric, or to a stone that disintegrated, in which "died" is metaphoric. There may, in fact, be a construal in which both terms are metaphoric, such as "the unfeeling person was overwhelmed with shock."

However, in any particular construal, we can observe a deviance in reference. The word "stone" is used to refer to a person, or "die" is used to refer to the process of disintegrating. It is only when "The stone died" is used in context, with a specific referential intention, that there can possibly be a metaphoric interpretation. By itself, as an abstract linguistic entity considered apart from the context in which it is used, "The stone died" is simply anomalous. We must conclude that all cases of metaphor are pragmatic (involve violations of conventions of use) and that some are additionally semantic (involve violations of rules of logical structure).

In fact, we can even observe that the "freezing" process that turns metaphors into idioms applies to conventions of use, as well as to rules of structure. The idiom "kick the bucket" means "die." Its deviant semantic interpretation has become institutionalized. As has often been observed (Fraser, 1970; Katz, 1973; Newmeyer, 1974), its syntactic behavior has also frozen. "Kick the bucket" cannot be passivized ("The bucket was kicked"), nor can it appear in pseudocleft form ("What was kicked was the bucket"), and still retain its idiomatic sense. Besides the semantic and syntactic restrictions, however, "kick the bucket" is also restricted in its range of contextual settings. One does not normally report the death of close friends or relatives by saying that they have "kicked the bucket," nor do scientists predict when the solar system will kick the bucket.

The significant features of context and the conventions governing use of language in specific settings are absolutely crucial in an adequate linguistic theory of figurative language. Although this is obviously the case for "purely" pragmatic metaphors, which involve the violation of a rule governing the relationship between language and its context (such as reference), it is no less true for "semantic" metaphors, as we have seen. This issue may be clarified somewhat by considering the actual process of meaning-construction.

The construal process for semantic metaphors has been claimed to be based on the application of "transfer rules." These rules transport semantic properties of one term in a metaphor to another term. For example, in Levin's "The stone died," the property animate, included as a condition on the structure of "die," may be shifted to "stone," yielding a semantic structure underlying an interpretation in which "stone" is animate ("the unfeeling person died"). Or, the semantic property 'inanimate' may be transferred from "stone" to "die," yielding a semantic structure underlying an interpretation such as "the stone disintegrated."

The transfer mechanism was originally proposed for generative grammar by Katz and Postal (1964) and was further elaborated by Weinreich (1966), van Dijk (1972), and Levin (1977). Katz and Postal regarded transfer as a strictly grammatical process, to explain certain semantic properties of *nondeviant* sentences. Weinreich observed that the same mechanism could account for properties of deviant, yet interpretable sentences, i.e., metaphor, in the manner previously outlined. It was this insight that van Dijk and Levin expanded upon.

The exact status of the transfer mechanism is a significant issue for a theory of language processing. Is the transfer mechanism a set of grammatical rules that account for abstract, structural properties of sentences, or is it a real-time cognitive operation on linguistic structures? Levin (1977) equivocates:

> On a number of earlier occasions we have stated or implied that the theory should be regarded as constituting a part of the grammar. . . .
>
> It is possible, however, to grant that the linguistic capacity referred to above operates through the medium of the standard grammatical categories and at the same time deny that it represents an aspect of language competence; it may be that the capacity we are speaking of should in fact be reckoned to performance. . . .
>
> At this stage of our knowledge it is not possible to decide definitely concerning certain linguistic capacities whether their explication belongs to one or another component of a general theory of language. It may be that a

theory of metaphor such as has been expounded . . . belongs properly to a
theory of performance. (p. 76)

However, it has been observed by numerous authors, including Levin,
that the transfer rules are not restricted to moving just those semantic
properties that are supplied by the grammar, i.e., the concepts that figure
into the "dictionary definitions" of lexical items (Katz, 1972). Rather,
transfer rules may transfer properties of a more encyclopedic, or connotative, nature. If "The stone died" is interpreted as "the stone disintegrated," then the movement from "stone" to "die" of the necessary,
dictionary, property 'animate' creates a semantic interpretation of "die"
that is close to "cease to exist." But, it is only when encyclopedic or
world knowledge properties are transferred that the particular manner in
which the stone ceases to exist becomes part of the construal. Stones can
normally cease to exist by disintegrating, but not by magically vanishing.
This knowledge is not grammatical knowledge, but rather connotative
knowledge. Hence, the transfer process cannot be thought of as a strictly
grammatical process. Of necessity, transfer rules form a subclass of rules
of language use.

In fact, transfer can take place not only between elements of a
sentence, but between a sentence and its context. When the nonsemantically deviant sentence "The old rock is becoming brittle with age"
(Reddy, 1969) metaphorically refers to a person, we can say that the
property 'animate' is transferred from the context to "the old rock."

The reverse process also exists. Levin points out that semantic metaphors may have interpretations set against the background of the world as
it actually exists, or "phenomenalistic" interpretations, in which the
world itself is altered, and the metaphoric expression is, in a sense,
literally construed. We have already noted interpretations of the first type
("The stone disintegrated"). An interpretation of the second type for
"The stone died" would be one in which we conceive of a world where
stones actually die. The phenomenalistic interpretation involves a tempo-
rary restructuring of belief systems, in which the feature 'animate' from
"die" (more accurately, from its selection restriction) is transferred to the
world in such a way that it now is an inherent attribute of stones.

The transfer process, as just outlined, is an essential component in the
interpretation of all types of metaphor. However, it seems to us unwar-
ranted at this point to insist that an actual transfer or movement of
concepts is involved. An alternative view is to consider the relevant
semantic properties as entering into a relation with each other. The
relation would have to specify an ordering, so as to encode information
that corresponds to the direction of property transfer.

The transfer mechanism, understood now as a system for establishing relations between semantic properties that figure into metaphoric construal, is quite general, in that it applies not only to sentence-internal elements, but to contextual ones as well. There are several possible directions (orders) for the semantic relations, including context to utterance, utterance to context, and utterance to utterance. There are also different formal operations possible in establishing the relations. A semantic property from one term in the relation may dominate over a semantic property from another term, or both may contribute equally to each other. These variations permitted in the transfer system account for the variety of metaphoric interpretations possible for any given expression, such as those mentioned above for the sentence "The stone died." The particular construal selected for a given expression will depend, of course, on its compatibility with surrounding context.

Furthermore, Levin has shown that, except for Aristotle's "metaphor by analogy," the transfer theory is capable of subsuming "the two major classical theories of metaphor" (p. 94), those of Quintillian and Aristotle. Actually, Levin observes that the problem posed by Aristotle's analogy category is precisely that it requires relations established on features of encyclopedic knowledge. Therefore, once we lift the restriction on the transfer mechanism to "dictionary" features, and permit instead more general relations, as we have argued, then even the analogy category falls under its purview.

Ortony (1979) has observed that metaphor involves the elimination of "tension," and we have noted that the tension is caused by some rule violation. The elimination of tension is, essentially, an inferential act that transforms deviance into nondeviance. According to the alternative view of transfer, in which relations are established though not necessarily by a literal transfer of properties, the transfer mechanism would seem to be a component of the theory of inference, in particular, of that part that accounts for metaphoric construal.

This view should not be confused with the "stage" model of metaphor comprehension, (cf. e.g. Searle, 1979) according to which a literal meaning is constructed first, followed by a metaphoric interpretation that eliminates tension. The stage model fails to recognize that readers predict subsequent meanings as they process text, given a rich enough context. These predictions are either confirmed or disconfirmed as readers match the language samples with the meaning predicted. To the extent that inferences are needed for this, the processing of metaphor and nonmetaphor is similar. However, for metaphor, these inferences will involve the various construal processes.

Metaphor involves deviance due to rule violation, and inference that turns the deviance into meaningfulness. Language users simply do not accept anomaly. Grice (1975) has proposed a framework for viewing conversational exchange which sheds light on this notion. Grice points out that conversation is essentially a cooperative activity among the participants. Because of this, the participants must adhere to conversational "maxims," according to which their contributions are to be informative, true, relevant, and perspicuous.

The cooperative nature of conversation, in which meanings are exchanged among the participants, demands that the meanings themselves be such as to promote the success of the exchange. Clearly, the exchange is liable to break down to the extent that anomaly is introduced.

Metaphor may be viewed as arising from the apparent violation of one of Grice's conversational maxims. Semantic deviance is, superficially, uninformative, untrue, irrelevant, and unperspicuous. An expression with pragmatically deviant reference may perhaps be true, but is surely not literally relevant or perspicuous. As Grice notes, metaphor arises when a maxim is "flouted," and the tension created by this type of violation can be eliminated by an appropriate inference, or "conversational implicature." In these terms, metaphoric construal turns superficial maxim violations into meaningfulness, so that the conversational exchange event remains intact. However, it is absolutely crucial to bear in mind that there would in fact be no reason to suspect that a token of linguistic deviance encountered in a communicative setting was intended to be meaningfully interpreted were it not for cooperative adherence to maxims governing the truth, relevance, informativeness, and perspicuity of utterances in language exchange.

Research of readers' understanding of metaphor must be based on a theory that recognizes the essential linguistic properties we have discussed thus far. Therefore, we now turn to several important considerations for conducting research that bring us closer to this goal.

The Gricean principles of conversation just discussed are readily applicable to written language, even though there are important differences between written and oral communication. Writers, for example, do not normally intend to deceive their readers, nor do readers expect writers to be intentionally misleading. The implications for readers' understanding are quite significant. It is only when readers tacitly assume that the cooperative principle and maxims are operative, i.e., when they conceive of reading as an instance of linguistic communication, that they can encounter semantic and pragmatic deviance with the understanding that nonliteral construals are intended. If "The stone died" appears in a text, the reader knows, in virtue of knowledge of the principles of conversation, that the semantic violation is only the surface manifestation of an underlying textual coherence. The cooperative principle has an important part to play in the theory of reading because it enters into the mutual background assumptions and beliefs of the writer and reader.

Although readers' understanding of metaphor presupposes reliance on Grice's conversational principles, we can not always assume that subjects are in fact making use of them. It is a significant fact that, especially as concerns young readers, some traditional methods of instruction have deleterious, rather than beneficial, effects on reading ability. Smith (1982), for example, has stressed that phonics drills and other "skills"-oriented instructional techniques focus readers' attention toward those cuing systems that are least efficient in constructing meaning and away from those that are most efficient. The end product of such instruction often is a reader who regards reading as a complex task consisting of meaningless skills and subskills. The materials that children are exposed to also contribute to a misconception of the nature of reading. Workbooks, words and phrases in isolation, and meaningless sentences such as "The fat cat sat on the hat" lead children to expect nonsense. Reading is not seen as a meaningful, communicative activity. In other words, the Gricean foundation has been destroyed.

It can be reasonably assumed that preschool children who acquire reading ability prior to instruction approach written language as a meaningful conveyor of messages. The print found in their environments is purposeful, meaningful, and functional. Although some children might enter school with an appropriate understanding of written language communication, the materials and instruction discussed previously may override their original notions. Preschoolers' views of oral communication are less likely to be deleteriously affected by school instruction, although they may be altered to include, for example, situations in which questions requiring already known answers are asked anyway. Classroom instruction that disrupts the Gricean foundation for written language communication, although perhaps not for oral language, can result in subjects who perform differently on oral language studies of metaphor comprehension than on comparable written language studies. We must, then, exercise caution in generalizing findings on oral metaphor understanding, which abounds in the literature, to readers' understanding of written metaphor, for which a great deal more research is neded. Exploring young readers' awareness of Gricean principles operating in written discourse seems fundamental to future research of this kind.

Research on metaphor comprehension must make explicit the definitional criteria provided by linguistic theory. Schallert, Reynolds and Antas (1978) found, for example, that fresh metaphoric interpretations induced by prior context required more time for understanding than literal interpretations of the same expression induced by different prior context, though the time difference decreased as length of prior context increased. However, they found that "familiar idioms are processed as quickly as, if not faster than, syntactically and semantically comparable literal language" (p. 21). The linguistic distinction between fresh metaphor and idiom is therefore seen to play an important role in comprehension. Ortony et al. note that idiomatic meanings, unlike fresh metaphoric ones, are "familiar" and "may be stored in much the same way as the meaning of a single lexical item" (p. 26).

It has been pointed out that psychological correlates exist for the rule violations that yield distinct metaphor types. The transfer mechanism just discussed establishes relations between semantic properties of both text and context that underlie construal processes. It is, apparently, a component of the inferential processing required for metaphor. Distinct types of relations are therefore likely to be associated with distinct inference patterns. Hence, research on fresh metaphoric understanding must also distinguish among the metaphor types, just as Ortony et al. distinguish fresh from frozen metaphor to avoid overgeneralizing on the basis of studies of a single type.

In the study previously cited, Ortony et al. select metaphors that are "contextually anomalous whole sentences" (p. 7). For example, the sentence, "Regardless of the danger, the troops marched on," is used metaphorically as a summarizing statement following a passage on children annoying their babysitter. The expression is a (nonsemantically deviant) pragmatic metaphor. Ortony et al. generalize from this example to claims about overall metaphoric understanding. As we have argued, however, the distinctions among metaphor types are significant enough to warrant caution against such moves.

In a later study, Reynolds and Ortony (1980) do show a sensitivity to this issue. They argue that similes (e.g., "John is like a snake") are indeed a type of metaphor. Like all metaphors, they claim, similes are nonliteral comparisons. Evidence presented in support of the hypothesis that "similes [are] understood more easily than corresponding metaphors" (e.g., "John is a snake") (p. 22) can therefore not be attributed to the mere presence or absence of metaphor per se.

Still, differences in comprehension between similes and their metaphorical, non-simile counterparts must be attributed to whatever special property distinguishes the two types of expressions. According to Reynolds and Ortony, similes are "direct" comparisons, whereas their counterparts are "indirect" comparisons. But "directness" is a "general language variable," not restricted to figurative language alone, so the comprehension differences are not due to some peculiar characteristic found solely in metaphors.

It is at this point that the role of an adequate linguistic foundation becomes clear. If similes are indeed a type of metaphor, then, in our view, they must contain some sort of rule violation. If this rule violation is of a different type than that found in the metaphorical, non-simile counterparts, then comprehension differences may be due to a property peculiar to metaphors, rather than to a general language property.

For example, Altwerger (1982) argues that similes are a type of metaphor on the grounds that they violate a rule of discourse. In particular, they contain terms that are superficially irrelevant to the discourse topic. Imagine a passage about an individual named John. Suppose, furthermore, that a sentence such as "John is like a snake" appears, where there has been no prior mention or discussion of the topic "snakes." Then, whereas the term *John* is tied cohesively to previous text, the term *snake* is not (cf. Halliday & Hasan, 1976). This instance of irrelevance demands resolution on the part of the reader. It also points to the crucial role of background text in the determination of simile status. Were "John is like a snake" to appear in a story about John, a snake, and the relative characteristics of both, it would then no longer be a simile.

Our approach to characterizing similes differs from that of Reynolds and Ortony. The latter regard similes as a type of metaphor on the grounds that all are nonliteral comparisons. This implies that comparison is one of the defining criteria of metaphors. In our view, however, the key concept is rule violation, which both similes and metaphoric non-similes possess. The special type of rule violation found in similes suggests that they are strictly pragmatic, non-semantically incompatible metaphors; their counterparts are semantically incompatible as well.

Contrary to what Reynolds and Ortony maintain, however, comparison is not a primitive, defining characteristic of similes and other metaphors. Rather, it is an inference strategy by means of which a contradiction induced by rule violation can be resolved. The theory of rule violations therefore explains why metaphorical language is so intimately concerned with comparisons involving disparate domains.

Given that similes involve a rule violation that differs from that of their metaphorical, non-simile counterparts, comprehension differences between "John is like a snake" and "John is a snake" now might be a function of differences in type of rule violation. Therefore, the question of just how metaphor-specific variables, such as rule violations, interact with general language variables, such as directness, still demands basic research.

Another facet of the problem of making valid distinctions has to do with the existence of self-embedded figurative expressions. Whole, uncontrived texts are replete with frozen metaphors embedded within fresh metaphors, fresh metaphors embedded within frozen metaphors, etc. One example from among the many occurring in the children's story *Sheep Dog* (1966) is the following: "It was fully dark when the alert ears of the larger dog caught the sound of a sharp whistle from the small camp a hundred yards up the wash." The metaphors in this sentence are represented in the Fig. 9.10.

The semantic relations to be established by the transfer mechanism are structurally complex and representable in terms of the hierarchical relations indicated in the figure. Here the main predicate, "caught the sound of," is a frozen metaphor. Its subject, "alert ears," is a fresh, semantic metaphor. The object includes an extended lexical item "sharp," and the locative phrase consists of a special idiomatic use of "up," as well as a possibly extended use of "wash." Examples such as this one testify to the fact that research must go beyond the relatively simple metaphoric structures so often found in passages contrived expressly for experimentation if we are to at all grapple with the problem of *real* readers' understanding. The importance of this point is underscored by findings of Altwerger (1982) in which a large array of distinct metaphor types and type combinations are shown to generate sharp differences in processing strategies.

If research on readers' understanding of metaphor is to be theoretically based, it must involve materials that present metaphors in context. The very nature of metaphor demands this, in that all metaphors, even semantic ones, are dependent on features of context for identification and construal. Metaphors arising from pragmatic, textual, or conversational incompatibilities simply do not exist in isolation.

However, to date, there is a paucity of research on readers' understanding of metaphor which utilizes natural, uncontrived, whole texts. Research which presents metaphor in isolation eliminates information crucially needed by readers for interpretation.

For example, Winner, Rosensteil, and Gardner (1976) used a multiple-choice and open-ended explication task to study 6- to 14-year-olds' understanding of metaphor. Metaphoric phrases were presented *in isolation of any contextual setting* and linked either psychological and physical realms or cross-sensory realms. Examples of these metaphors are "The smell of my mother's perfume was bright sunshine" and "After many

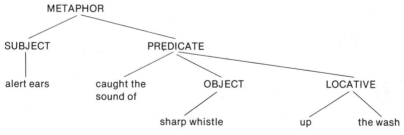

FIG. 9.1

years of working at the jail, the prison guard had become a hard rock that could not be moved" (p. 293). Responses were categorized as reflecting (a) a magical interpretation in which the child creates a fantasy-like context to explain the metaphor; (b) metonymy in which "the link between the two terms of the metaphor is transformed from one based on identity to one based on congruity" (p. 291); (c) primitive metaphor in which both terms of the metaphor are determined to be of the same realm; and (d) genuine metaphor in which features of the terms are from different realms or domains. It was hypothesized that development of metaphoric understanding would proceed through these levels in the order given.

The findings indicated that younger children responded more frequently with magical, metonymic, and primitive interpretations, whereas the genuine metaphor was more frequent in the older children's responses. It was also found that the cross-sensory metaphors elicited more genuine metaphoric responses than the psychological-physical metaphors.

Generalization of these findings, as interesting as they might be, to metaphor understanding in natural settings is not warranted. We learn from this research only how children respond to metaphors in the absence of any situational or contextual support. Findings indicate that children of different ages will supply different types of contexts for interpretation of isolated surface anomalies, and further, that the contexts provided are commensurate with the cognitive and linguistic knowledge they bring to the task. For example, it seems predictable that younger children will be likely to supply magical or phenomenalistic contexts based on their experiences with fairy tales and cartoons which might, in fact, represent a prison guard as a rock-like creature. Furthermore, if Asch and Nerlove (1960) are correct, younger children are more likely to assign a physical interpretation to double function terms such as *hard* used in Winner et al.'s study. This would increase the likelihood of magical, primitive, or metonymical interpretations of the metaphors.

Finally, it is easy to imagine contexts which would render each of the response types perfectly acceptable. It would be interesting to study children's understandings of these metaphors in contexts supporting particular interpretations to find out whether other types of interpretations are imposed on the metaphor at different stages of development. We must resist, however, generalizing the present developmental findings to actual communicative settings.

Results of such research may be more an artifact of the experimental situation than of actual abilities of readers, and reveal little about processing of expressions in more natural settings. As Neisser (1976) has insightfully remarked:

> Cognitive psychologists must make a greater effort to understand cognition as it occurs in the ordinary environment and in the context of natural purposeful activity. This would not mean an end to laboratory experiments, but a commitment to the study of variables that are ecologically important rather than those that are easily manageable. (p. 7).

That is, research must avoid dismembering the setting in which metaphors are produced and understood. Studying isolated variables and skills in order to further our understanding of metaphor is like studying isolated elemental hydrogen or oxygen in order to increase our understanding of water. The compound is radically different from the mixture.

We have emphasized the importance of distinguishing among metaphor types on the basis of a coherent language theory, and of conducting research on the processing of these types as they appear in uncontrived, natural texts. It is clear to us that developments in theories of text will be of particular importance for metaphor research conducted within this framework, by expanding our understanding of just what counts as natural text, and by providing new insights into rules and conventions of language use which may be intentionally violated.

Suggestions on how to proceed already exist. Halliday and Hasan (1976) for example, define text as "a passage of discourse which is coherent in these two regards: it is coherent with respect to the context of situation, and therefore consistent in register; and it is coherent with respect to itself, and therefore cohesive" (p. 23). The rules that construct text tie linguistic terms to each other, as well as to the external context. They further note that while "[u]nder normal circumstances, of course, we do not find ourselves faced with 'non-text' " (p. 23), there are "poets and prose writers who deliberately set out to create non-text" (p. 24), an obvious allusion to the role of rule violation in the creation of metaphor.

We expect that real progress in a theory of metaphor will depend on breakthroughs in our understanding of principles which transcend mere grammatical organization and enter into the realm of language use and the creation of text. We will then be in a position to better comprehend the linguistic creativity not only of the poets and prose writers, but of all language users.

REFERENCES

Altwerger, B. (1982). *A psycholinguistic description of the written language processing of textually embedded metaphoric expressions.* Unpublished doctoral dissertation, University of Arizona, Tucson.

Asch, S., & Nerlove, H. (1960). The development of double function terms in children: An exploratory study. In B. Kaplan & S. Warner (Eds.), *Perspectives in psychological theory* (pp.   ) New York: International Universities Press.

Chomsky, N. (1965). *Aspects of the theory of syntax*. Cambridge, MA: MIT Press.

van Dijk, T. (1972). *Some aspects of text grammars*. The Hague: Mouton

Fraser, B. (1970). Idioms within a transformational grammar. *Foundations of Language, 6,* 22-42.

Grice, H. P. (1975). Logic and conversation. In P. Cole & J. L. Morgan (Eds.), *Syntax and semantics (Vol. 3): Speech acts* (pp. 41-58). New York: Academic Press.

Halliday, M.A.K., & Hasan, R. (1976). *Cohesion in English*. London: Longman.

Hockett, C. (1958). *A course in modern linguistics*. New York: Macmillan.

Katz, J. (1972). *Semantic theory*. New York: Harper & Row.

Katz, J. (1973). Compositionality, idiomaticity, and lexical substitution. In S. Anderson & P. Kiparsky (Eds.), *A festschrift for Morris Halle* (pp. 357-376). New York: Holt, Rinehart & Winston.

Katz, J., & Postal, P. (1964). *An integrated theory of linguistic descriptions*. Cambridge, MA: MIT Press.

Levin, S. (1977). *The semantics of metaphor*. Baltimore: Johns Hopkins University Press.

Matthews, R. (1971). Concerning a "linguistic theory" of metaphor. *Foundations of Language, 7,* 413-425.

Morgan, J. (1979). Pragmatics of Metaphor. In A. Ortony (Ed.) *Metaphor and Thought* (pp. 136-147) Cambridge, Mass.: Cambridge University Press.

Neisser, U. (1976). *Cognition and reality*. San Francisco: Freeman.

Newmeyer, F. (1974). The regularity of idiom behavior. *Lingua, 34,* 327-342.

Nunberg, G. (1978). *The pragmatics of reference*. Unpublished doctoral dissertation, City University of New York Graduate Center.

Ortony, A. (1979, January). *Some psycholinguistic aspects of metaphor* (Tech. Rep. No. 112). Urbana: University of Illinois, Center for the Study of Reading.

Ortony, A., Schallert, D., Reynolds, R. & Antos, S. (1978, July). *Interpreting metaphors and idioms: Some effects of context on comprehension* (Tech. Rep. No. 93). Urbana: University of Illinois, Center for the Study of Reading.

Reddy, M. (1969). A semantic approach to metaphor. *Papers from the Fifth Regional Meeting, Chicago Linguistic Society*. Chicago: University of Chicago Department of Linguistics.

Reynolds, R. E., & Ortony, A. (1980, May). *Some issues in the measurement of children's comprehension of metaphorical language* (Tech. Rep. No. 172). Urbana: University of Illinois, Center for the Study of Reading.

Searle, J. (1979). Metaphor. In A. Ortony (Ed.), *Metaphor and Thought* (pp. 92-123). Cambridge, Mass.: Cambridge University Smith, F. (1982). *Understanding Reading*. New York: Holt, Rinehart, & Winston.

Stovall, J. Sheep Dog. In *Widening Views* (Book VIII) Boston: Allyn and Bacon, 1966.

Weinreich, U. (1972). Explorations in semantic theory. The Hague: Mouton.

Winner, E., Rosensteil, A., & Gardner, H. (1976). The development of metaphoric understanding. *Developmental Psychology, 12,* 289-297.

10

COMPREHENSION AS CONTEXT: TOWARD RECONSIDERATION OF A TRANSACTIONAL THEORY OF READING

Robert F. Carey
Rhode Island College

Jerome C. Harste
Indiana University

Recent studies of comprehension as a cognitive process have focused on the development of models describing the inferred cognitive mechanisms and structures that provide for the proficient processing of connected discourse. A number of these studies (van Dijk, 1973; Kintsch, 1977; Meyer, 1975; Spiro, 1977) have suggested that a significant but underlying part of the text comprehension process is guided by social and contextual constraints.

Halliday and Hasan (1981), among others, have noted that we have had a theory of context far longer than we have had a theory of text (p. 4). Despite this acknowledgement, it has been rare to find a research (or theoretical) study that takes the variable into account in any meaningful fashion. This chapter suggests that contextual constraints must be more effectively accounted for within models of comprehension.

Several researchers (Halliday, 1978, Halliday & Hasan, 1981; Harste & Burke, 1978; Harste & Carey, 1979; Mishler, 1979) have pointed to the need for a more elaborate theory of contextual constraints. This chapter attempts to define several concepts that the authors consider central to a discussion of socio-cognitive context, and in so doing, builds upon the thesis that print is a necessary but not sufficient condition for understanding print processing.

PRINT SETTING

A concept central to our discussion of discourse processing is that of *Print setting,* defined here as the set of linguistic and contextual constraints within any instance of text which operate to reorganize perception and influence behavior.

Written language must be functional or there would be no way to explain its development and use in literate societies (Goodman & Goodman, 1976; Halliday, 1974). It is this functional dimension of written language that also makes it predictable. Print setting encompasses functionality and predictability and is meant to suggest that, in order to understand the cognitive and linguistic processes involved in reading, one must do so in light of the context in which that processing occurs. In an abstracted form, print setting is perhaps best thought of as a set of multimodal cues that synergistically operate to affect cognitive processing.

It is possible, for example, to delineate obvious differences among comprehension data collected from readers in natural encounters with print in comparison to contrived encounters, such as those that typically occur during questioning after reading a selection in the classroom. The salient aspects of print play an important role in determining the meanings to be sought and the specific and general strategies to be utilized in seeking these meanings. Any instance of comprehension data reflects expectancies developed from previous encounters with print. As such, print setting suggests the integral significance of the reader's individual perceptions of the reading process.

As conceived here, print setting is also generative. It is part of a synergistic and cyclical process through which the reader's perceptions of reading are modified and through which his or her expectations are, to some extent, directed. Print setting constitutes a new synthesis: a new "event," characteristically unique and decidedly more than the sum of the specific experiences and expectancies of which it is comprised.

From this perspective, the cognitive structures crucial for seeing are the anticipatory schemata that prepare the perceiver to accept certain kinds of information rather than other kinds, and thus control the activity of looking (Neisser, 1976). Restated more formally, one's conceptualization of reading in a given print setting acts as an anticipatory schema, which directs strategy utilization or perceptual exploration and, consequently, the process of sampling the available print. Which cognitive structures we access in a given situation depends on our past experiences with a given print setting. As a consequence, the process is cyclical: Each new encounter providing the reader opportunity to reorganize perception and bring a new set of anticipatory schemata when this print setting—or one exhibiting some of the same or similar salient features—is again encountered (see Fig. 10.1).

As just implied, the concept of print setting speaks to the notion of the reader's theoretical orientation to reading and the significance of an individual's instructional history in directing perceptions of reading. A covariant of this concept is the teacher's theoretical orientation and its subsequent impact on the reader's perceptions of reading.

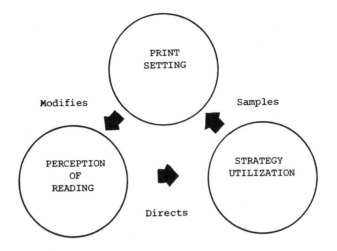

FIG. 10.1 Print Setting

Harste and Burke (1977), for example, have suggested that readers operate theoretically in reading and that student perceptions of reading are strongly influenced by the type of language information focused upon during instruction. They suggest that reader perceptions of reading are identifiable along a continuum ranging from a decoding (phonics), to a skills (words), to a whole language (meaning) orientation to reading. Because the teacher's beliefs strongly affect the instructional decisions made (including how to organize for instruction), the teacher's theoretical orientation often is operationalized as a set of environmental constraints that permeate the classroom to affect language processing.

DeFord (1978) has devised an instrument to differentiate among these organized belief systems. Rhodes (1979) suggests that a variety of reader behaviors are little more than artifacts of instructional history which are identifiable along the aforementioned continuum. Several recent studies have provided support for this view (Feathers, 1980; Siegel, 1980).

It seems appropriate here to note that studies of verbal learning from a schema-theoretic perspective generally do not consider the significance of the print setting. These studies frequently proceed from the perspective of high-level schemata, the assumption being that "background" and amorphous "life experience" direct one's perceptions, i.e., cause a specific schema to be invoked (Anderson, Reynolds, Schallert, & Goetz, 1977). It seems likely that high-level schemata have a significant bearing upon a reader's perceptions, but it also seems clear that these schemata are invoked in the presence of contextual constraints that may have confounded the results of a number of these schema-theoretic studies. Some preliminary data suggesting the validity of this assertion are offered later in this chapter.

Robustness of Perception

Rather than view print processing as dependent on recognition of a set of distinctive features within the print itself, the notion of a print setting suggests that contextual clues operate in conjunction with print cues to make perception more robust than it might be if stripped of context. Context stripping techniques such as tachistosopic presentations of print are quite stringent and fail to recognize the facilitative effect that situational context has on print processing. When it is assumed real reading is being studied, these and similar "context free" approaches lead to potentially fallacious inferences regarding the nature of the process (Mishler, 1979).

Perception can be viewed as residing on a continuum of selection processes, the parameters of which are set by the reader's environment. The reader's perceptions of purpose and the function of reading are the product of those aspects of local and global context that have a bearing on comprehension. This pertains, of course, to processes other than reading; in fact, it seems pertinent to all processes involving sensory-based stimuli.

As Rosenblatt (1969) notes, both Dewey and Piaget, using varying terminology, have addressed a concept similar to robustness of perception. Piaget (1970) describes a process "whereby the organism in each of the interactions with the bodies or energies of its environment fits those in some manner to the requirements of its own physio-chemical structures while at the same time accommodating itself to them" (p. 140). Dewey (1963) observes the same phenomenon: "something, not yet a stimulus . . . becomes a stimulus by virtue of the relations it sustains to what is going on in this continuing activity. It becomes the stimulus in virtue of what the organism is already preoccupied with" (p. 255).

In this view the reader, on the basis of knowledge-of-the-world (e.g., long-term episodic and/or semantic memory), previous encounters with print, and relevant aspect of the cultural and social contexts, selects those aspects of the print environment with which he or she should be concerned. The reader, in short, attends to those aspects of the environment perceived as relevant to the situation.

These situational factors are represented in a variety of ways and are derived from a variety of sources. Some are more or less subliminal, some are patently obvious. But, it is only those relevant factors that the reader perceives as significant to the context of the situation that have a bearing on the meanings to be constructed before, during, and after print processing. Robustness of perception implies, of course, that the reader makes a number of significant decisions prior to sensory contact with print. A variety of situational factors, therefore, conspire to engender comprehension even before "reading," as it is conventionally viewed, occurs.

The school situation is, naturally, a powerful delimiter of the robustness of perception. Certain important expectations, in terms of acceptable behaviors and acceptable meanings, are integrally associated with school settings. Certain meanings that, under different circumstances, might readily be ascribed to a text, are normally not even entertained as possibilities in a school setting. It is in this respect that contexts of culture, situation, and print setting come to bear upon the processing of connected discourse.

Objectifying Contextual Constraints

As previously noted, a number of researchers are aware of the importance of concepts analogous to that of print setting. Rarely, however, have these concepts been objectified or rendered quantifiable in studies of reading comprehension. Indeed, the entire notion of contextual importance retains, as Pearson (1977) might observe, empirical virginity; it is as yet untainted by data.

The reason for this lack of inclusion appears quite reasonable: The means of assessing contextual influence have not been readily available. In general, researchers have perceived local and global context of situation as being a variable—or category of variables—too nebulous to be amenable to empirical investigation. They have noted, quite logically, that the number of separate and palpable influences present in the environment is simply too large to include in any normal, randomized study of the effects of context. In many ways this position is a valid one. When taken in toto, the myriad factors impinging upon one's perceptions of the environment are simply too numerous and interrelated to be considered quantifiable in any meaningful way. As Piaget has asserted, all experience is interpreted.

Recent advances in sociolinguistic inquiry, however, have pointed out that there is no need to consider all the factors present in the environment. In any situation there are some contextual elements that are relevant to the situation and some that are not. Halliday and Hasan (1976) have drawn on work by Bernstein (1971) and Halliday, McIntosh, and Strevens (1964) in suggesting the notion of "register" to describe the contextual factors inherent in discourse processing. They suggest that the linguistic features typically associated with a configuration of situational features constitute register. It is the "set of meanings, the configuration of semantic patterns, that are typically drawn upon under the specified conditions, along with the words and structures that are used in the realization of the meanings" (p. 23).

Register is perhaps best defined in relation to cohesion (a hierarchically comparable concept). Cohesion, as a semantic feature pertaining to relations of meaning within a text, and register collectively define a text and describe its unique texture. The objectification of register, however, provides another problem because a theoretical rationale for describing the relevant constituent elements of register is required. Hymes (1972) for example has posed eight components of the speech situation: form and content of text, setting, participants, ends (intent and effect), key, medium, genre, and interactional norms. Although these factors would certainly seem to delineate any useful areas of inquiry, other systems of examination have also been proposed. Halliday and Hasan (1981), for example using the terminology proposed in Spencer and Gregory's (1964) *Linguistics and Style*, suggest a limited taxonomy at once more abstract and parsimonious: field, mode, and tenor. *Field* is the "total event in which the text is functioning, together with the purposive activity of . . . the writer" (p. 22). Important factors within this concept, then, are the content of the message and semantic intent. *Mode* is the language activity that represents or is associated with a particular communicative event. This element subsumes a considerable amount of relevant information, ranging from the specific linguistic properties of the situation to a number of physical characteristics associated with the particular print setting (e.g., chennal, genre, rhetorical mode, etc.). *Tenor* consists of the interrelationships among the social roles involved in the communicative event, including the relationship between author and reader. In terms of reading instruction, it seems clear that the teacher/student relationship can be an extraordinarily important factor in the comprehension process.

Field, mode, and tenor, then, comprise the register of a communicative event and provide a convenient framework for assessing the various stimuli that the reader selects as important cues from the environment. Naturally each situation is entirely unique (depending on the delicacy of focus that is employed), but it seems likely that, in any case, the features of the situation are relevant at a relatively general level. Given the constraints imposed by the context of culture in which the event takes place, the reader adapts to more or less "typical" situations in a generalized fashion (perhaps along the lines of the "nodes of schematization" suggested by de Beaugrande, 1981). This suggests the theoretical basis for comparing contexts of situation and their relative efficacy in promoting or limiting comprehension.

An important issue in mapping contextual constraints is alluded to previously. The "delicacy of focus" that the researcher or teacher brings to the situation is significant in that it defines the contextual parameters in subtle ways even before the event has been perceived in any coherent fashion. Again, only certain types of information are relevant to the inquiry in process and these are determined by the intent of the observer. The problem here is much like the one encountered by structural anthropologists in attempting to simultaneously observe and describe alien cultures (cf. McCall & Simmons, 1969). In effect, it is the robustness of the observer's perception that determines the relevant aspects of the environment.

It is perhaps worth noting that field, mode, and tenor, as aspects of the print setting, may form a synergistic relationship with the various levels of contextual constraints. There is reason to suppose, for instance, that context-of-culture (Malinowski, 1944), social context (Halliday, 1974) context-of-situation (Firth, 1957; Malinowski, 1944), and print setting form a series of cyclical and interdependent stage processes, each of which has a significant, and perhaps measureable, impact upon each of the others.

In observing language users, in this case readers, from the perspective of social man, it becomes clear that elements are selected from each of the levels noted above. The elements that are selected from context-of-culture, for example, delimit the range of potentially acceptable elements to be selected from the social context. These factors in turn impose constraints on the range of alternatives available to the reader from the context-of-situation in a developing, self-modifying, and increasingly subtle process. When taken as a whole, all of these factors comprise the print setting (see Fig. 10.2).

One important aspect of print setting, especially significant when it is

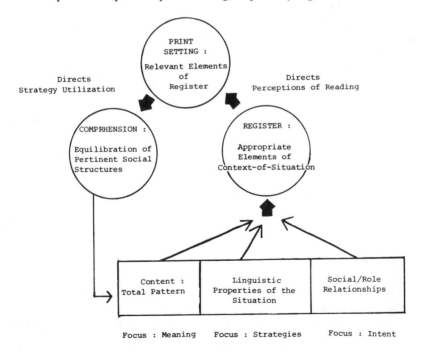

FIG. 10.2 Comprehension as a Function of Contextual Constraints

seen as imposing restrictions on the reader as a fundamentally social being, is the degree of specificity it engenders among the potential meanings encountered by the reader. Tierney and Lazansky (1980) for example, have called the relationship between author and reader an "implicit allowability contract." In this view, the reader and author enter into an agreement regarding acceptable and predictable behaviors. When the author, through whatever means, violates this agreement, the reader is unable, or at times unwilling, to adjust properly and, as a consequence, is unable to comprehend.

Support for this contention is offered by recent studies (Carey, Harste, & Smith, 1981; Smith, Harste, & Carey, 1979) dealing with reader maintenance of ambiguity in the reading of ambiguously written passages. The findings suggest that, in a large number of cases, readers are aware of ambiguity in a reading task and they feel free to adopt strategies which defer semantic encoding pending the resolution of ambiguity.

The study that produced these results was a replication of the landmark study by Anderson et al. (1977) that suggested that high-level schemata (e.g., "background" as identified through a biographical inventory) provide a framework for story interpretation. The study, which required students to read and recall two ambiguously written passages, also concluded that most subjects were unaware of alternate interpretations.

The replication of the study suggested somewhat different conclusions. First, it was inferred that contextual constraints were of first-order significance in the development of an interpretive framework. Second, the results indicated that many subjects were aware of both the ambiguity of the passages and of several alternative interpretations. Because the replication monitored environmental context (the situation in which the tasks were performed) and the original study did not, more complex models of cognitive processing are suggested. Although we can explain a complex process simply, to do so does not change its inherent complexity.

It was not uncommon, for example, for subjects to note in the written protocols that the passages were "unclear" or "poorly written." On occasion the tone of the response approached anger, or certainly frustration, perhaps at having been asked to deal with material with no ostensible resolution. Many of these same responses, however, demonstrated the most accurate recall for the form of the original passage; despite interpolated tasks (which would clearly obviate the retention of the passage as sensory image or in short term memory), these subjects were able to reproduce the passages almost verbatim, very carefully maintaining the original ambiguity.

Several examples from the data collected during the replication study may serve to clarify some of the points being made here. One of the two passages, used in both the original study and the attempted replication, was the following:

> Every Saturday night four good friends got together. When Jerry, Mike, and Pat arrived, Karen was sitting in her living room writing some notes. She quickly gathered the cards and stood up to greet her friends at the door. They followed her into the living room, but as usual they couldn't agree on exactly what to play. Karen's recorder filled the room with soft and pleasant music. Early in the evening, Mike noticed Pat's hand and the many diamonds. As the night progressed, the tempo of play increased. Finally, a lull in the activities occurred. Taking advantage of this, Jerry pondered the arrangement in front of him. Mike interrupted Jerry's reveries and said, "Let's hear the score." They listened carefully and commented upon their performance. When the comments were all heard, exhausted but happy, Karen's friends went home.

Anderson et al. suggested the dominant (e.g., most common) interpretation given to this cleverly constructed passage is that the characters are getting together to play cards, whereas the non-dominant interpretation (common to persons identified as having a music background) is that the reason for the get-together is a night of playing music.

There seems little to argue with in the original study's contention that a musical background would increase the probability of a "musical" interpretation. The replication sought to investigate, however, whether background knowledge and experience had been confounded with print setting. A gross aspect of this notion is that students in music classes, from which part of the sample population was drawn would naturally expect that any print setting encountered in that context would deal with music. As a consequence, these students would be more likely, on the basis of both knowledge-of-the-world and context-of-situation, to interpret ambiguous passages as having to do with music.

The data collected during the replication indicate that this may well be the case. Ancillary effects also were noted, however. As just observed, students tended to at least attempt to preserve the ambiguity of the original passages. When this did not seem possible, subjects were not reluctant to make their frustrations known: "I found this passage incredibly confusing as I felt the terminology was misleading and misused and therefore I had to reread many times and guess at what was trying to be said. Example: You don't 'listen to' a score."

Other, similar examples abound: "Cards may have been used in the game—also, Karen may have been writing notes for a game of 'charades'; passage is not clear as to the name of the game." Examples of several interesting recall protocols may serve to further illustrate the complexity and subtlety of the responses. Consider the following:

Example 1:

This passage is about four friends who get together on a Saturday night. There are two guys and two girls. They play cards for a while and listen to music, after a while things begin to get dull and one of the males begins to gain interest in one of the females. Then they begin to notice their sexual difference and study the "arrangement."

Example 2:

Karen and three of her friends had gathered at Karen's house to play some card game. After not being able to decide what game to play, a table was set up by Jerry, and they played for a while to music from the tape recorder. After a while, when play got more intense, one of the guys asked what the score was. We never were told what it was, but soon the group discussed how they did that night, then broke up and went home.

Example 3:

Every Saturday night, four friends get together. When Jerry, Mike, and Pat got to Karen's house Karen was writing notes in the living room. She put away her cards and went to greet her friends. They couldn't decide what to play until finally Jerry took charge of the situation. Karen played the recorder beautifully. Mike noticed the beautiful diamonds on Pat's hand. After they finished playing everyone went home.

Important findings include the wide divergence and surprising subtlety of some of the interpretations. Several problems were posed by the nature of the data. It was not always clear, for instance, which interpretation was being given to a passage by a subject. The protocols suggest a continuum of response, rather than a series of discrete elements. Subjects tended to interpret the passage along continua ranging from card playing *to* card playing and listening to music *to* listening and playing music *to* playing music, etc. In short, there were no sharp distinctions (or at least relatively few) among the responses, certainly none that were easy for the researchers to categorize.

These findings were consistent with the notion of the reading process as semantic transaction. This conceptualization provides for reading as a dynamic and vital process that denies the supremacy of the author while anticipating shades of subtlety among the interpretations made by readers. In this view, comprehension is much less monolithic than conventional wisdom might suggest. Thus, as has been alluded to previously, each reading act constitutes a unique transactional event of which change, no matter how minor it may seem, is a necessary by-product. The significance of contextual constraints appears obvious and suggests the need for considering these important variables in describing, defining, and modeling the reading process.

The results of studies such as that by Anderson et al., (1977) often may be confounded by the print setting itself. It seems likely, for example, that free recall protocols are significantly influenced by being sought in a school context. Experimental subjects may feel the need to attempt verbatim recall because activities of this sort are common to the school situation. The experimental tasks in this study, for example, closely resemble the kinds of activities required by norm-referenced tests at a variety of educational levels. Students especially may adjust their behaviors according to a scripted scenario arising from their experiences and encounters with print in similar settings; e.g., the most important behavior in these situations is perceived as being detailed recall rather than synthesis and retention of "gist." As a consequence, despite the adequate performance of the subjects on multiple-choice questions following the reading passages, it is not clear whether conventional semantic encoding has taken place. At the very least, encoding may be hindered in the attempt to fulfill what the reader perceives as implicit expectations implicit in the situation.

On the basis of these findings, it seems clear that the concept of print setting has implications for instructional practice and research in reading comprehension. A fruitful example is the case of comprehension measurement, especially with regard to the issue of passage dependency.

A landmark study by Tuinman (1970, 1973) and replications (Pyrczak, 1972, 1974; Allington, Chodos, Domaracki, & Truex, 1977) demonstrated that a significant percentage of comprehension questions on major norm-referenced tests were not passage dependent. The findings suggested that it was possible to perform at acceptable levels of achievement on the tests without having access to the reading passages upon which the questions are allegedly based.

Following these studies, a major broad-based movement in the testing industry has sought to make comprehension questions on norm-referenced tests more passage dependent. A product of this movement has been the wide acceptance of the legitimacy of passage dependency as an important issue in comprehension measurement. The conventional assumption underlying trends in testing now seems to be that a question should be passage dependent if it purports to be valid.

The concepts under consideration here suggest that passage dependency may be a moot issue. In brief, it seems reasonable to suggest that reading comprehension is neither exclusively nor predominantly text dependent. Passage dependency then, may be little more than a red herring, deferring research into more important pre-assumptive questions concerning the possibility of comprehension measurement. These larger questions are dealt with more properly and exhaustively by measurement theorists (Hoffman, 1962; Houts, 1977) and researchers (Farr, 1969). Perhaps the most exacting discussion of this topic, however, is Carroll's (1972) survey of measurement modes and theoretical issues in comprehension assessment.

The specific character of reader dependency on text has yet to be investigated in any thorough fashion. It does seem clear, however, that more difficult types of reading require a greater dependence on the text itself. Lacking data, though, it would be premature to assert any specific level of interactive dependency until other areas of focus, especially the question of pragmatics, have been adequately addressed. The extant evidence suggests that a variety of factors beyond the text but part of the print setting contribute significantly to the comprehension process. This notion points to the consideration of comprehension in terms of speech act theory (cf. Pratt, 1977) with special emphasis on the pragmatics of the process as a unique event. This, in turn, would suggest a need for the re-evaluation of some basic premises underlying a transactional theory of reading, as outlined by Rosenblatt (1938, 1969, 1978).

Comprehension as Transaction

If one accepts the notion that comprehension is a setting for learning generally and reading comprehension specifically, a useful metaphor for this conceptualization is to look upon the setting as transaction. In the heuristic proposed following, a print setting and a mental setting each provide an environment for the other. The mental setting emphasizes the reader in the comprehension process, whereas the print setting accents the role of not only the print but the contexts-of-situation as well. In the encounter, or transaction, between the two, a uniquely new "event" is produced (see Fig. 10.3).

Several key concepts provide the overall framework for Rosenblatt's transactional theory of reading. Her transactional metaphor for describing the communicative process echoes the work of perceptual psychologists such as Ames (1953) and Cantril (1960), and the subsequent formalizations of these conceptualizations by Dewey (1963) and Bentley (1954).

In essence, each semantic "transaction" involving reader and print is viewed as a unique event, amenable to analysis only as an entity in and of itself. The transactional terminology was invoked "to counteract the dualistic phrasing of phenomena as an interaction between different factors because it implies separate, self-contained, and already defined entities acting on one another." Rosenblatt creates an analogue that she describes as "homely," between interaction as an event and "billiard balls colliding. A conceptualization of the reading act, preferable

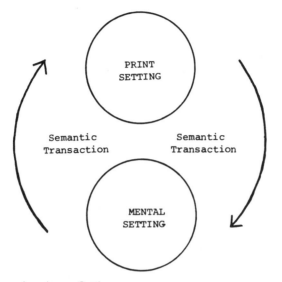

FIG. 10.3 Comprehension as Setting

to interaction, she suggests, might liken the communicative event to the relationship between man and his environment. It makes little sense, from this perspective, to perceive these elements as separate entities "acting" upon one another. Rather, the factors can only be properly considered when they are taken together as a gestalt, when their emergent qualities are perceived as a whole. The notion of semantic transaction, requires a considerably more holistic perception of communication.

In this sense, then, the relationship between reader and text is not linear. It is cyclical and synergistic and must be, in fact can only be, studied within the context in which it occurs. Each of the components of the event constantly undergoes modification in terms of expectations and the implicit allowability contract alluded to above.

Bearing this concept in mind, it may be fruitful to consider similarities between reading as transaction and the psychological field theories introduced by Lewin (1935, 1942). As in the elaborate theory of contextual influence suggested in this paper, Lewin's socio-psychological field was in constant flux: given a change in any one "vector" in the field, the entire field must be redefined as unique. Although Lewin's theories are not, and have not been, fashionable, the holistic nature of his insights does seem to speak directly to the notions of transaction as they have been presented in this review.

A number of disciplines and modes of experimental inquiry would seem to be pointing toward this idea of reading as transaction. Sociolinguistics, psycholinguistics, speech act theory, pragmatics, and cognitive science, all demonstrate recent advances which suggest the likelihood of a more holistic approach to the analysis of communicative events. Because Rosenblatt's notions have yet to be formalized in any systematic fashion, an important goal for comprehension research is that these significant insights be dealt with by theoreticians and model builders in meaningful and productive ways.

REFERENCES

Allington, R., Chodos, L., Domaracki, J. & Truex, S. (1977). Passage dependency: Four diagnostic oral reading tests. *The Reading Teacher, 30,* 369-375.

Ames, A. (1953). Reconsideration of the origin and nature of perception. In S. Ratner (Ed.), *Vision and action* (pp. 37-61). New Brunswick, NJ: Rutgers University Press.

Anderson, R., Reynolds, R., Schallert, D., & Goetz, E. (1977, Fall). Frameworks for comprehending discourse. *American Educational Research Journal, 14*(4), 367-381.

de Beaugrande, R. (1981). *Text, discourse, and process.* Hillsdale, NJ: Lawrence Erlbaum Associates.

Bernstein, B. (1971). *Class, codes and control, Vol. 1: Theoretical studies toward a sociology of language.* London: Routledge & Kegan Paul.

Cantril, H. (Ed.). (1960). *The morning notes of Adelbert Ames, Jr.* New Brunswick, NJ: Rutgers University Press.

Carey, R., Harste, J., & Smith, S. (1981). Contextual constraints and discourse processes: A replication study. *Reading Research Quarterly, 16*(2), 201-212.

Carroll, J. (1972). Defining language comprehension: Some speculations. In R. Freedle & J. Carroll (Eds.), *Language comprehension and the acquisition of knowledge* (pp.   ) Washington, DC: Winston.

DeFord, D. (1978). *A validation study of an instrument to determine a teacher's theoretical orientation to reading.* Unpublished doctoral dissertation, Indiana University.

Dewey, J. (1963). *Philosophy and civilization.* New York: Capricorn.

van Dijk, T. (1973). Text grammar and text logic. In J. Petofi & H. Rieser (Eds.), *Studies in text grammar.* Dodrecht: Reidel.

Farr, R. (1969). *Reading: What can be measured?* Newark, DE: International Reading Association.

Feathers, K. (1980,). *Classroom discourse as semiosis.* Paper presented at the National Reading Conference, San Diego.

Firth, J. (1957). *Papers in linguistics.* London: Oxford University Press.

Goodman, K., & Goodman, Y. (1976,). *Learning to read is natural.* Paper presented at the Conference on Theory and Practice of Beginning Reading Instruction, University of Pittsburgh.

Halliday, M. (1974). *Language and social man.* London: Longmans (for the Schools Council Programme).

Halliday, M. (1978). *Language as social semiotic.* Baltimore: University Park Press.

Halliday, M., & Hasan, R. (1976). *Cohesion in English.* London: Longman.

Halliday, M., & Hasan, R. (1981). *Text and context.* Tokyo: Sophia University.

Halliday, M., McIntosh, A., & Strevens, P. (1964). *The linguistic sciences and language teaching.* London: Longman.

Harste, J., & Burke, C. (1977). A new hypothesis for reading teacher education research:

Both the teaching and learning of reading are theoretically based. In P. D. Pearson (Ed.), *Reading: Research, theory and practice* (26th Yearbook of the National Reading Conference). pp. 32-40 Clemern S. C.: National Reading Conference.

Harste, J., & Burke, C. (1978, July). Toward a socio-psycholinguistic model of reading comprehension. In S. Mour (Ed.), *Viewpoints in teaching and learning: Theoretical and practical considerations in development of reading comprehension. Journal of the School of Education,* Indiana University, *54*(3), 9-34.

Harste, J., & Carey, R. (1979). Comprehension as setting. In R. Carey & J. Harste (Eds.), *New perspectives on comprehension* (pp.   ). Bloomington: Indiana University Monographs on Language and Thinking.

Hoffman, B. (1962). *The tyranny of testing.* New York: Crowell-Collier Press.

Houts, P. (1977). *The myth of measureability.* New York: Hart.

Hymes, D. (1972). Models of the interaction of language and social setting. In J. Gumperz & D. Hymes (Eds.), *Directions in sociolinguistics* (pp.   ) New York: Holt, Rinehart & Winston.

Kintsch, W. (1977). On comprehending stories. In M. Just & P. Carpenter (Eds.), *Cognitive processes in comprehension* (pp.   ) Hillsdale, NJ: Lawrence Erlbaum Associates.

Lewin, K. (1935). *A dynamic field theory of personality.* (D. Adams & K. Zener, Trans.). New York: McGraw-Hill.

Lewin, K. (1942). Field theory and learning. In *The psychology of learning* (41st Yearbook of the National Society for the Study of Education). Chicago: University of Chicago Press.

McCall, G., & Simmons, J. (1969). *Issues in participant observation.* Reading, MA: Addison-Wesley.

Malinowski, B. (1944). The problem of meaning in primitive languages. In C. Ogden & I. Richards (Eds.), *The meaning of meaning* (Supplement I, pp.). New York: Harcourt, Brace.

Meyer, B. (1975). *The organization of prose and its effect on memory.* Amsterdam: North-Holland.

Mishler, E. (1979). Meaning in context: Is there any other kind? *Harvard Educational Review, 49*(1), 1-19.

Neisser, U. (1976). *Cognition and reality: Principles and implications of cognitive psychology.* San Francisco: Freeman.

Pearson, P. D. (1977, November). *Reading comprehension research.* Paper presented at the Great Lakes Regional Reading Conference, Indianapolis, IN.

Piaget, J. (1970). *Structuralism* (C. Maschler, Trans.). New York: Basic Books.

Pratt, M. L. (1977). *Toward a speech act theory of literary discourse.* Bloomington and London: Indiana University Press.

Pyrczak, F. (1972). Objective evaluation of the quality of multiple-choice items designed to measure comprehension of reading passages. *Reading Research Quarterly, 8,* 62-71.

Pyrczak, F. (1974). Passage dependence of items designed to measure the ability to identify main ideas of paragraphs: Implications for validity. *Educational and Psychological Measurement, 34,* 343-348.

Rhodes, L. (1979). Comprehension as an artifact of instructional print setting. In R. Carey & J. Harste (Eds.), *New perspectives on comprehension* (pp.   ). Bloomington: Indiana University Monographs in Language and Reading Studies.

Rosenblatt, L. (1938). *Literature as exploration.* New York: Appleton-Century-Crofts.

Rosenblatt, L. (1969). Toward a transactional theory of reading. *Journal of Reading Behavior, 10,* 31-43.

Rosenblatt, L. (1978). *The reader, the text, the poem: The transactional theory of the literary work.* Carbondale, IL: Southern Illinois University Press.

Siegel, M. (1980,). *Classroom discourse from the perspective of speech act theory.* Paper presented at the National Reading Conference, San Diego, CA.

Smith, S., Harste, J., & Carey, R. (1979). *Schemata, context and comprehension.* Paper presented at the National Reading Conference, San Antonio, TX.

Spencer, J., & Gregory, J. (Eds.). (1964). *Linguistics and style.* London: Oxford University Press.

Spiro, R. (1977). Remembering information from text: The "state of schema" approach. In R. Anderson, R. Spiro, & W. Montague (Eds.), *Schooling and the acquisition of knowledge.* Hillsdale, NJ: Lawrence Erlbaum Associates.

Tierney, R. J., & Lazansky, J. (1980). *The rights and responsibilities of readers and writers: A contractual agreement* (Reading Education Rep. No. 15). Urbana: University of Illinois, Center for the Study of Reading.

Tuinman, J. (1970). *Selected aspects of the assessment of the acquisition of information from reading passages.* Unpublished doctoral dissertation, University of Georgia.

Tuinman, J. (1973). Determining the passage dependency of comprehension questions in five major tests. *Reading Research Quarterly, 9,* 206-223.

11

AUTHOR'S INTENTIONS
AND READERS' INTERPRETATIONS

R. J. Tierney
Ohio State University

T. Raphael
Michigan State University

Jill LaZansky
University of Illinois

P. Cohen
Stanford Research Institute

It is the purpose of this chapter to consider readers' sense of the communicative nature of reading, and the power of that sensibility to drive the inferences they generate. The view of text we are advocating is that the production and comprehension of text are specific acts. As Bruce (1980) suggested, texts are written by authors who expect meaning-making on the part of readers and read by readers who do the meaning-making. Writers, as they produce text, consider their readers—they consider the transactions in which readers are likely to engage. Readers, as they comprehend texts, respond to what writers are trying to get them to do as well as what the readers themselves perceive they need to do. Consistent with these notions we contend that reading and writing are both acts of composing engaged as individuals transact with each other and their inner selves. Furthermore, these composing acts or transactions basically are the same as those that occur daily within the context of negotiations between people.

With this view of text, we believe that most investigations of comprehension to date have given fairly decontextualized accounts of readers' inferencing behavior. Certainly, though detailed analyses attempts have been made to characterize inferencing behavior across familiar and non-familiar text read by readers who differ with respect to topic-related knowledge; and, likewise, there exist systematic schemes for examining inferences generated in response to selected text features (Collins, Brown, & Larkin, 1977; Frederiksen, 1975, 1977b, 1979, Trabasso & Nicholas, 1977; Warren, Nicholas, & Trabasso, 1981). However, these efforts fall short of providing a pragmatic account of these phenomena.

Frederiksen (1977b) alluded to the worth of a more pragmatic-based perspective, suggesting that a theory of inferencing in reading comprehension must not only "specify the types of inferential operations which occur and the discourse contexts in which they occur, but it also must account for the processes which control inference" (p. 319). "What is needed," according to van Dijk (1976), "is a pragmatic component in which rules, conditions and constraints can be formulated based on systematic properties of (speech acts) and communicative contexts" (p. vii). Unfortunately, despite the fact that various scholars (rhetoricians, sociolinguists, theoretical linguists, composition researchers, and computer scientists interested in natural language processing) have converged upon a speech act theory for explaining the pragmatic aspects of language and language processing, there has been little systematic examination of these issues as they pertain to comprehending written discourse. It is with this purpose in mind that this chapter is developed.

With a view to examining the notion that the products of reading and writing are "situated accomplishments" (Cook, 1973), we report our explorations of the interactions between readers and authors as they become environments for each other. We begin by proposing why it is that readers make assumptions about authors. Then a large portion of the chapter is devoted to a description of three investigations, each of which focuses upon the nature of author-reader interactions.

ROLE OF READERS' ASSUMPTIONS

The concept of persuasive speech has evoked the argument that although the attitude a speaker produces in a listener and the nature of the speaker's argument account for much of the persuasive effect speech may have, it is, nonetheless, the character of the speaker that is "the most important of all means of persuasion" (in *The Rhetoric of Aristotle,* 1932). Lawson (1758) attempted to explain this point in the following way. "You cannot be much affected by what he (the speaker) says if you do not look upon him to be a Man of Probity, who is in earnest, and doth himself believe what he endeavoreth to make out as credible to you" (p. 172).

A similar argument has been proposed to explain the persuasive effect of written discourse. The term *ethos*, introduced by Aristotle, is frequently resurrected to describe the character of the speaker that surfaces in text situations, often creating for readers the sense of having been spoken to. The essence of the argument is that the ethos portrayed through a text is integral to the persuasive effect of the text, as it projects to varying degrees the author and his sense of the situation.

Our purpose in raising the issues of persuasive speech is to suggest two notions: First, that as Firth (1957) posits, language is fundamentally "a way of behaving and making others behave;" and second, listeners are compelled either knowingly or intuitively to interpret what is spoken in the context of who is speaking, and thus find their interpretative efforts bound by both a message and its creator. The former notion is not the result of a newly applied logic, nor does it reflect a universal perspective. It is born out of the belief that "a theory of language is part of a theory of action," that in the words of Searle (1969), language is rule-governed intentional behavior, "that speaking a language is performing speech acts, acts such as making statements, giving commands, asking questions, making promises, and so on; and more abstractly, acts such as referring and predicting . . ." (p. 16). The study of what many refer to as *linguistic acts* has become embedded in the larger study of plans and social actions, a theoretical outlook that attributes much of what traditionally has been considered the outcome of knowledge that is exclusively linguistic, to knowledge about how plans are formulated and executed in social settings. The critical assumption here is that understanding plans is crucial to understanding or interpreting actions; in the case of language, knowing why a speaker is saying what he or she is saying is critical to interpreting the meaning of what the speaker is saying.

The second notion, that listeners are compelled either consciously or intuitively to interpret what is spoken in the context of who is speaking, is an outgrowth of the more general argument that discourse is only meaningful in its context of situation; context constituted, in general, "by what people are doing and when and where they are doing it" (Erickson & Schultz, 1977, p. 6). This "doing" (by saying) is both similar to and distinguishable from other "doing" (by saying) as a result of the intentions, knowledge, beliefs, expectations, and interests that shape the plans and goals of speakers, as well as the assumptions of their listeners. That is, just as we can talk about context in terms of what, when, and where "doing" has occurred or is occurring, we also can talk about "doing" in terms of why and how the doing is being executed. Thus, rather than simply a chain of utterances, discourse (e.g., conversation) can be characterized as a matrix of utterances and actions bound together by a web of understandings and reactions (Labov & Fanshel, 1977); and the task of comprehension as forming "a model of the speaker's plan in saying what he said such that this plan is the most plausible one consistent with the speaker's acts and the addressee's assumptions (or knowledge) about the speaker and the rest of the world" (Green, 1980, p. 14).

The application of these two notions to explain text comprehension is not altogether unreasonable or new. Fillmore (1974), for example, in the *Future of Semantics* describes the interpretative efforts of readers in this way.

A text induces the interpreter to construct an image or maybe a set of alternative images. The image the interpreter creates early in the text guides his interpretation of successive portions of the text and these in turn induce him to enrich or modify that image. While the image construction and image revision is going on, the interpreter is also trying to figure out what the creator of the text is doing—what the nature of the communication situation is. And that, too, may have an influence on the image creating process. (p. 4)

Discerning the nature of the authors' plans is tantamount to determining the nature of that communication. For that purpose, readers rely not only on what they may know about a topic (the subject of an author's discourse), but also on what they might be able to infer about why the author is saying what he or she is saying and who the author perceives his or her audience to be. Readers' plans capture that information by linking actions (what an author has done) with goals and intentions (the author's purpose). Bruce (1980) points out that "failure to understand the author's intentions can cause problems for all levels of comprehension, from 'getting the main idea' to the subtle insights expected of skilled readers" (p. 380). This would necessarily be the case because a failure to understand the author's intentions would result in a failure to link the author's actions with his or her purpose. Further, "in cases in which the reader does understand adequately, the ability to perceive the author's intentions can still make the difference between minimally sufficient comprehension and deep understanding of a text" (Bruce, 1980, p. 380). One must ask, then, if readers do infer or imagine "a speaker or set of circumstances to accompany the quasi-speech act" (Ohmann, 1971) how are these inferences about the communicative situation brought into effect.

The data from three investigations reported herein addresses what readers do as they assume different relationships with authors. In the first investigation, the reader–author relationship and its effect upon comprehension are studied against a backdrop of two factors: an author's stance and a reader's prior exposure with the topic. In the second investigation, the effects of topic familiarity and variations in discourse style are studied alongside a detailed analysis of the strategies readers use as different author–reader relationships are established during reading. Our third investigation examines how writers view their counterpart—the reader—and how readers view their counterpart—the writer—in the context of thinking-aloud about what is being written and later read.

Although the three investigations appear disparate, they provide at least some initial support for our overriding hypothesis that the nature of the author–reader relationship has a powerful effect upon what evolves during reading as well as from reading. The studies afford an examination of the negotiations between readers and writers, details of those factors that influence the reader–author relationship.

EXAMINING THE INTENTIONS OF AUTHORS AND THE INTERPRETATIONS OF READERS

The remainder of the chapter describes the three investigations in detail.

Investigation I

In the introduction we made the claim that a reader's perception of the writer has an impact upon that reader's response to a text. Our first investigation (Tierney, LaZansky, Raphael, & Mosenthal, 1979) examined that claim. Taking an essay written by Gerald Faber on student rights, we imposed two sets of four author identities upon the message. One set of four was adapted to an office setting, and included along with a neutral stance, the stance of a corporation executive recently appointed vice president in charge of personnel, a recently dismissed corporation executive, and a clerk typist. The second set of four was adapted to a college setting, and in addition to a neutral stance, included the stances of a recently dismissed college instructor, a recently appointed vice-president in charge of student affairs, as well as a student majoring in social psychology. All eight of the essays were entitled, "Are you a Slave?" (see Example 1 in the Appendix).

Ninety-six university students enrolled in an undergraduate psychology course participated in the study; each student read a randomly assigned essay, "Are You a Slave?", as delivered from one of the eight author perspectives. What followed were a recall task, an importance rating of information included in the essay, and an assessment of likely-to-be-made inferences. In addition, three major sets of probes were developed to identify the perceptions of the author. One set consisted of 20 items designed to measure the extent to which students perceived the author as clear, logical, and informative. Students' responses to the probes were intended to serve as a measure of the perceived "cooperativeness" of the author; for example: Was the author brief and to the point in the presentation of his or her arguments? Were the arguments consistent with the purpose(s) of the text? Students were asked to respond to each of the 20 probes via a rating scale. A second set of probes also consisted of 20 items that required a rating response. The purpose of this second set was to measure the extent to which students perceived themselves to be members of the author's intended audience of readers; for example: Do you think the author was addressing the article to you? Do you think the author highlighted information to which he or she knew you would relate? Those probes were an attempt to measure the perceived "intimacy" of the communication; that is, the extent to which a student felt as though he or she were addressed and understood by the author. A third set of probes required readers to assess the author's age, sex, and political stance, as well as to estimate when and where the essay might have been published.

Two major findings emerged. Although there were no differences in how readers rated what was and was not important, there were differences in how much readers recalled, deemed as likely-to-be-made inferences, as well as large differences in how readers characterized the author in terms of their relationship to him or her. Specifically, there were significant differences between subjects who read one of the four "college scenarios" and those who read one of the four "office scenarios" with respect to three factors: students' perceptions of the intimacy of the communication, $F(1,88) = 20.15$, $p<.01$; students' perceptions of the author's general political stance, $F(1,88) = 4.21$ $p<.05$; and students' perceptions of such physical characteristics of the author as age, $F(1,88) = 16.87$, $p<.01$. Second, when subjects read a version set in what might be deemed the more familiar setting of two (i.e., the college setting), and which reflected a stance more closely aligned to that of our readers (i.e., that of a social psychology major), the readers recalled more information, rated the communication as more intimate, but, at the same time, were more critical of the author's logic and clarity. In contrast, those texts written from the stance of a college administrator or an executive were perceived to be less intimate communications when compared with either a neutral stance, the perspective of a social psychology major, or the disposition of an office worker.

These data suggest that with subtle variation of the author's identity and topic-familiarity, we were able to create variance that we argue is related to different author–reader alignments being established by our subjects. That is, because the variance that surfaced can be accounted for in terms of the existence of different author–reader relationships established in conjunction with the same text written from different author perspectives, we then have empirical evidence that the readers' prior experience with a topic in combination with sense of the author's purposes and goals exerts a powerful influence on the author–reader relationship that develops in the course of text interpretation. That is, the reader's perception of the "doer" (i.e., the author) influenced their interpretation of what was "done."

Investigation II

Our second investigation represented an attempt to examine Bruce's claim that comprehension difficulties may arise from a reader's failure to pursue an author's intentions. Two studies that were run concurrently with one another were initiated. The first study observed the effect of topic familiarity upon the reader's inferencing behavior and their perceptions of the author's intentions. Topic familiarity was controlled for by holding them constant and varying the familiarity of the content. The passages included in Example 2 in the Appendix illustrate how a "building" theme was maintained across passages while individual passages were varied in the familiarity of the particular topic addressed (i.e., building a treehouse vs. building a factory). The second study examined the effect of discourse style (text with and without dialogue) upon readers' perceptions of the author and the reader's inferencing behavior. The passages in Example 3 (see Appendix) illustrate how, for purposes of observing the effect of text, topic was held constant, whereas one aspect of text—the presence or absence of dialogue—was manipulated across passages. This enabled us to look at the effect of different presentations of the same information. Two passages to represent each of the four text types (topically familiar, topically unfamiliar, dialogue, non-dialogue) were developed for a total of eight passages across the two investigations, each passage approximately 300 words in length.

Inconsistent information was then systematically embedded in all passages at both the superordinate and subordinate levels; some instances of embedding occurred at points in the text where the author directly addressed the reader; for example: "try it, I know you will like this game" was replaced with "try it, I know you will hate this game." It was our hope that the inconsistencies would have the effect of "shoving" the author–reader relationship sufficiently to: (a) prompt readers to reflect upon their expectations with respect to authorship; and (b) allow us to observe how the effects of topic and text mode tend to manifest themselves in readers' metacognitive awareness and related inferencing behavior.

Forty-three fifth grade students of varying reading abilities participated in the study. Each student, meeting individually with an experimenter, read silently and recalled orally four passages. Following each recall, students answered selected questions classified as either background knowledge or text-based (Pearson & Johnson, 1978), depending on the passage, then reread orally each selection and responded to a set of predetermined probes. The probes were questions directed at targeted information; targeted information included both inconsistent insertions and ideas that were left as the author had stated them. It was the purpose of the probes to examine whether the reader's awareness of the inconsistencies or procedures for coping with them were related to the reader's perceptions of the author's intentions. At the various interview points, for example, students were asked: "What does ＿＿＿＿＿＿ mean? Does it make sense? What information did you use to figure this out? How much would you rewrite so that it would be easier to understand?" The use of interview probes such as these in conjunction with embedded inconsistencies was an effort on our part to break away from some of the more rigid applications of the error detection paradigm.

Table 11.1 includes a listing of the categories used to classify students' explanations or methods of rationalization for each of the inconsistencies. In addition, we attempted to note the point at which an inconsistency was perceived; that is, whether individual readers appeared to recognize an error during reading, free recall, probed recall, oral reading, the interview, or during debriefing.

Although less than 10% of the readers' free recalls included reference to any item that involved inconsistent information, analysis of the oral reading miscues as well as the interviews indicated that a large percentage of the students were aware of the inconsistencies. In particular, considerably more miscues occurred at the points of the inconsistency than anywhere else in the texts. The interviews indicated that over 90% of the readers either developed a well-reasoned account within which the inconsistencies "made sense," or recognized the inconsistencies as errors.

The results of these two studies suggested that topic familiarity, the presence or absence of dialogue, and the type of the information being interpreted all influenced how a reader interpreted an author's intentions, as well as what the reader did to "make sense" of it. In other words, these data suggested that readers were apt to make different assumptions regarding authorship across different types of texts, and that these assumptions were associated with both the outcomes of their interpretative efforts and the methods they employed to interpret the text message in a plausible way. In particular, readers made different assumptions regarding what authors might legitimately do across these text conditions. In two text conditions (the nonfamiliar and nondialogue conditions) readers, especially poor readers, were less willing to transact an interpretation outside of the mind set that the text was autonomous (i.e., they tended to search the text for a solution to the problem or blame themselves). In many ways, these data support Bruce's (1980) point that "Failure to understand the author's intentions can cause problems for all levels of comprehension, from 'getting the main idea' to subtle insights expected of skilled readers" (p. 380). It is as if to be a successful reader one must be self-initiating—that is, establish one's own goals and rewrite strategies for making meaning. Unfortunately, in certain text situations without a sense of authorship, one can be distracted from so doing.

Investigation III

In I and II investigations, we established: (a) the impact of the author's identity upon reader response; (b) a relationship between an appreciation of an author's intention and comprehension, and (c) a correlation between

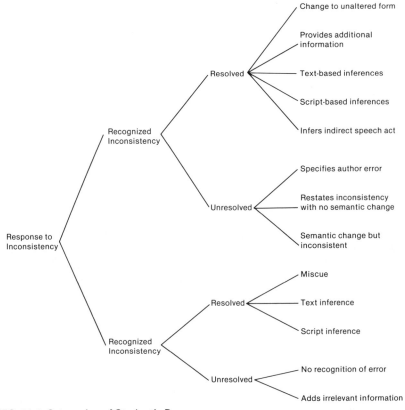

FIG. 11.1 Categories of Student's Responses.

reading strategies and various facets of the author–reader relationship. In our third investigation we examine not only how readers relate to authors, but also how authors relate to readers. Specifically, we explored how a communicative contract is achieved in light of these constraints imposed by the written mode, the author's operationalization of his or her intentions, and a reader's interpretation of those intentions. The data generated for this purpose were gathered in conjunction with a larger study whose purpose was to investigate systematically the ways in which communicative acts were transformed or adjusted to accommodate the requirements of the modality in which they occur. Within the larger study the interactions of pairs of adult subjects were recorded—the expert of the pair providing all necessary instructions to a novice whose task was to assemble a toy water pump. This interaction was recorded across five communication modalities (telephone, teletype, face-to-face, audiotape, and written). To generate an appropriate database for our analyses, we

TABLE 11.1
Example of a Transcript of an Author and a Reader Thinkaloud.

PROTOCOL SEGMENT

Writer	Text	Reader
On the table before we should start with the canister, I suppose. That's the basic piece. No—plunger. Plunger should be better since you have to something in that first, and you can't reach it otherwise. Okay, plunger first. All right. ON THE TABLE . . . IS A PLUNGER . . . WITH A RED cap—oh *RED* TOP. *WITH A*	ON THE TABLE IS A PLUNGER WITH A RED TOP	
RED TOP AND A BLUE CAP AND A GREEN—GREEN whatever, *AND A GREEN—GREEN* END. I think you'll know what I mean. No confusion there, I don't think.	AND A BLUE CAP AND A GREEN END	
		ON THE TABLE IS A PLUNGER WITH A RED TOP, A BLUE CAP, AND A GREEN END. Okay, I just locate this. This is this. Okay, I don't know why—he is probably just going through describing the pieces and if—okay.
There's also a small red plastic item, very simple, which looks like a plug . . . ON THE TABLE. That should be the next piece, since that's an interior one. Okay, ON THE TABLE IS A SMALL RED PLUG— *SMALL* SIMPLE *RED PLUG,* so we won't confuse it with this one. Okay. *A SMALL SIMPLE*—this one has a hole on it. Yeah, that one doesn't. Okay, *A SMALL SIMPLE RED PLUG* WITHOUT A HOLE. *WITHOUT A* HOLE. Okay.	ON THE TABLE IS A SMA LL SIMPLE RED PLUG HOLE	
		ON THE TABLE IS A SMALL SIMPLE RED PLUG WITHOUT A HOLE. Okay, this is— there are several red pieces here, but this seems to be the simplest without a hole. Okay. Now take, I am wondering what to do with it now,
Take the plug. . . . Okay. Take the plug and put it into the interior hole—no—all right, that sounds good enough. If I—I have to specify, though, so he doesn't put it in that hole. Okay. Uh—huh. Take the red		

(Continued)

TABLE 11.1 *(Continued)*

PROTOCOL SEGMENT

Writer	Text	Reader
plug and put it into the AND INSERT IT . . . INTO . . . THE . . . HOLE INSIDE THE GREEN CAP *INSIDE THE GREEN CAP* ON THE PLUNGER. INSERT IT—Have to watch my pronouns here, or else he's not gonna know what I'm talking about. *TAKE THE RED PLUG INSERT IT INTO THE HOLE INSIDE THE GREEN CAP*—tss—redundant . . . *INSIDE THE GREEN CAP ON THE PLUNGER.* And we've already defined what that is.	TAKE THE RED PLUG AND INSERT IT INTO THE HOLE INSIDE THE GREEN CAP ON THE THE -THE- ON THE PLUNGER	
		TAKE THE RED PLUG AND INSERT IT INTO THE HOLE INSIDE THE GREEN CAP ON THE PLUNGER. Okay, he must mean this green cap and this hole here. Like that. *TAKE THE RED PLUG AND INSERT IN THE*—I am just going over this instruction again to make sure that I understood it and that I did it right. And I think that I did. It just seems to be, he is just telling me how to put it together.
Okay. Now we should go to this. All right. That's the next simplest step, since that goes inside that. All right. ON THE TABLE I described a clear plastic tube, one end threaded with two—na. A clear plastic cylinder with threads on one and and two small tubes opening on the side. Okay. That's a fairly clear description. *ON THE* TABLE, hopefully you can see what I mean by it. . . . THE TABLE . . . PLASTIC CYLINDER, WITH THREADS AT ONE END u-u-uh, *WITH THREADS* AT ONE END AND TWO TUBES . . . *TWO TUBES* IN THE SIDE—on the side? *IN THE SIDE.* Okay. Now to clarify things, I better specify which end is top and which end is bottom. Make it easy, I'll say that the threads are the bottom. Therefore, after that I can always refer to	ON THE TABLE IS A CLEAR PLASTIC CYLINDER WITH THREADS AT ONE END AND TWO TUBES IN THE SIDE	

TABLE 11.1 *(Continued)*

PROTOCOL SEGMENT

Writer	Text	Reader
whatever it is goes up, whatever it is goes down. Makes it easier. THE END WITH THE THREADS SHALL BE DEFINED AS THE BOTTOM. . . . *THREADS* . . . yuh . . . AS THE BOTTOM.	THE END WITH THE THREADS SHALL BE DEFINED AS THE BOTTOM	ON THE TABLE IS A CLEAR PLASTIC CYLINDER WITH THREADS AT ONE END AND TWO TUBES IN THE SIDE. THE END WITH THE THREADS SHALL BE DEFINED AS THE BOTTOM. Okay, it appears to be this piece. He is just going through describing pieces that probably need for the next portion of the assembly. Okay.
Okay. Now the next step should be logically the plunger. All right, you take the plunger and we put it inside the clear plastic tube. Put it in the top—okay, we've already defined that—of the clear plastic tube, fitting it all the way in—okay, well, we'll leave that—one step at a time. Okay, fitting it all the way in . . . hup, green end first, green end—fine, so I don't say red end. Looks like the red end would fit anyway. Okay. Hopefully, he can see the idea of the plunger, the red end as being the handle and the bottom end as being the thingamabob humph to press the water up and down. Okay. PLACE THE PLUNGER INTO THE TOP . . . OF THE CYLINDER . . . GREEN END FIRST—t' *GREEN END FIRST.* Tfu-tfu-tfu tfu-tfu-tfu-tfu-tfu-tfu. Actually, it doesn't really matter how far he pushes it in, but . . . suppose it might be more secure if he pushed it all the way in. Uh . . . *PLACE THE PLUNGER INTO THE TOP OF THE CYLINDER. GREEN END FIRST* . . . PUSHING IT DOWN . . . DOWN until it's securely in. I think securely means about the same thing. . . . *DOWN*	PLACE THE PLUNGER INTO THE TOP OF THE CYLINDER GREEN END FIRST

PUSHING IT DOWN | |

(Continued)

TABLE 11.1 *(Continued)*

Writer	Text	Reader

PROTOCOL SEGMENT

Writer	Text	Reader
UNTIL THE GREEN PART IS SECURELY IN—*GREEN CAP IS SECURELY IN.*	UNTIL THE GREEN CAP IS SECURELY IN	PLACE THE PLUNGER INTO THE TOP OF THE CYLINDER GREEN END FIRST PUSHING IT DOWN UNTIL THE GREEN CAP IS SECURELY IN. Okay. If he defined up here the threads as the bottom, then if you put the plunger into the top, that is probably this end then, so *PUSHING IT IN UNTIL THE GREEN CAP IS SECURELY IN.*
All right, the next step should be to fit the blue cap onto it. All right Now, by this point he should've see that it looks very much like a syringe . . . if he's following my directions, or if I'm getting my directions across to 'im. Okay. FIT THE BLUE CAP— *THE BLUE CAP* . . . ONTO THE CYLINDER. And it's rather stubborn—so I better tell 'im to push hard. IT'S A TIGHT FIT. *FIT THE BLUE CAP ONTO THE CYLINDER . . . IT'S A* TIGHT FIT—(laughs)—SO YOU can force it—HAVE TO FORCE IT, ACTUALLY. That's so he doesn't worry about whether or not it's the right piece	FIT THE BLUE CAP ONTO THE CYLINDER IT'S A TIGHT FIT YOU HAVE TO FORCE IT	
		Okay, now this next part says FIT THE BLUE CAP ONTO THE CYLINDER. IT IS A TI—*IT'S* A TIGHT FIT SO YOU'LL HAVE TO FORCE IT. So, this is just eh, another instruction, but it's got a warning in there like that it is a tight fit so that you won't be surprised at the amount of force that it will require to do this. And and be afraid that you are doing something wrong. Okay.

217

initially videotaped the interactions of 25 pairs of adult subjects as they assembled the water pump. Each pair of subjects included a "novice" and an "expert": The novice was unfamiliar with the water pump but was responsible for putting it together; the expert was thoroughly familiar with the water pump and was responsible for providing the novice with instructions for its assembly.

Each pair was assigned to one of the five communication modalities (telephone, teletype, face-to-face, audiotape, or written). Of the five, the interactions that occurred via the face-to-face mode and the written mode are of primary interest for a number of reasons: (a) these two modalities are most disparate in terms of spatial and temporal commonality as well as concreteness of referents; (b) communication within the real world occurs most frequently across these two modalities; and (c) it is specifically the difference between the written and face-to-face modalities that we suspect causes many difficulties for readers. With respect to the other three modalities, communication via telephone and teletype differ from one another only in modality, as they share an absence of spatial commonality and common referential set for participants. The use of audiotype on the other hand, was essentially equivalent to that of written instructions, except for the fact that it was oral, because novices could rewind and stop the tape when they wished but had only the tape upon which to rely.

There were a number of distinctive features of the design of the study that should be noted. First, all subjects were engaged in the same task thus increasing the likelihood that critical differences in discourse attributable to modality would surface. Because the pump assembly task imposed the same goals and subgoals on all subjects, regardless of modality, it was assumed that the structure of the discourse at the level of plans would also be, for the most part, invariant across modalities. Second, this study has been directed at the integration of speech act theory into formalisms for problem solving. This was approached through the development of formal and computer models of the planning and plan recognition of a class of indirect speech acts in task-oriented discourse. Third, an exploratory technique was employed to provide greater access to the intentions of participants engaged in the written mode of communication. This technique involved a "think-aloud" procedure whereby writers engaged in writing were asked to think aloud, or introspect, about what they were trying to get a reader to do or think; likewise, as readers read a text aloud, they were asked to finger point as they read and regressed in the text, as well as to verbalize what they thought the author was trying to get them to do or think. Both readers and writers were taken through a brief training session in which an investigator introduced the technique and its purpose, and monitored the subjects' efforts to implement the technique during a practice warmup. At the onset of the experimental phase, the investigator removed himself from the immediate vicinity of the subjects, and only prodded subjects when a lull occurred in their thinking aloud. The procedure itself certainly has features in common with the think-aloud strategy described by Flower and Hayes (1981), particularly the fact that in the context of both strategies, subjects' thinking aloud occurs at the point of natural pauses, thus allowing the verbalizations to vary in many respects across subjects. Unlike Flower and Hayes (1979), however, our writers and readers were not only given a training and warmup period, but were specifically instructed to specify what they were thinking about one another. This was an important feature, as writers and readers were paired so that their think-alouds or introspective responses would occur in conjunction with the same text. In addition, the video set-up for recording the think-alouds was split-screened to capture what the writer or reader was actually writing or pointing to along with his or her general demeanor. The transcripts, which were then developed, reflected an attempt on our part to merge the responses of paired participants. (See Table 11.1 for an example of the transcripts which were developed. Column 1 details an author's introspective-think-aloud, capitalization was used to indicate when writing occurred. Column 2 includes exactly what was written. The placement of the text alongside Column 1 coincides with its generation. Column 3 includes what the reader thought aloud as he or she read the text. Capitalization was used to indicate the reader's oral reading of the text.)

Broadly speaking, we have attempted to examine how pragmatic aspects of communication are manifested in written discourse, and how they operate so as to maximize the fit between the predictive efforts of writers and the interpretative efforts of readers. For this purpose, we pursued a comparative analysis of the expressed concerns of writers, how these concerns manifested themselves in texts, and were reflected in the reader's think-alouds. In a sense, we looked at written communication in terms of an implicit text, a real text, and an ideal text. An implicit text is what the writer expresses as his or her expectations for the text in terms of the reader's purposes (and expectations) as well as his or her own. A real text is what is actually produced. The ideal is what the reader expresses as his or her expectations for the author and the text. We recognize that our procedures tapped but a portion of this type of data, since a major limitation of the think-aloud procedure was that we would never know if readers and writers made fully explicit their expectations. We could only hope that because the method would foster a more active construction rather than retroactive reconstruction of readers' and writers' intentions, pragmatic aspects of written communication that have been obscure in the past would surface.

For purposes of analyzing the think-alouds, two coding procedures were developed. One coding procedure was used for purposes of recording instances of miscommunications that occurred—along with instances of reader uncertainty and complaint. A second coding procedure detailed: (a) the concerns and information represented in the think-alouds of the writer, (b) the information represented by the text itself, and (c) the concerns and information read or addressed by the reader. In conjunction with the data generated from the other modalities, some interesting findings emerged.

As a result of our interest in "turntaking," we investigated the synchronization of actions across modes. We have been particularly interested in turntaking as it occurred in conjunction with the successful completion of the task. In the face-to-face mode, turntaking of this type usually occurred in conjunction with the visual inspection of each subassembly operation; in the teletype mode, the expert typically used question marks, and the novice responded to each with a "done," "yes," or "okay;" in the telephone mode, the expert used rising intonation to indicate a request for a response (for example, an "okay") from the novice. In the written mode, the author often assumed the role of his or her own reader. As the writer thought aloud, generated the text, and moved to the next set of subassembly directions, the writer would mark his or her composition with an "okay." It was as if the "okay" marked a shift for the expert from a "turn" as the reader to a "turn" as the author.

Our interest in a variety of aspects of the author–reader relationship, has led us to examine information represented in authors' think-alouds against their texts, as well as against their readers' think-alouds. In general, there was not a close match between what authors expressed during think-alouds and what was actually produced as text; however, the match between authors' think-alouds and readers' think-alouds was usually quite close. For example, if an author expressed the need to describe an object by noting a particular attribute of the object (e.g., color), the reader very often would key on this same attribute during his or her think-aloud. This occurred regardless of the fact that other attributes were included in the text as descriptors of this same object. In addition, both authors and readers appeared to understand the function of certain descriptors even when that function was not made explicit in the text. Not infrequently, an author would simply describe an object and, without explicitly cuing, expect the reader to identify, gather and assemble. In contrast, when an object was to be identified but not assembled, authors would explicitly cue the reader to do just that. What these findings suggest is that there may be several conventions which both readers and writers deem legitimate, and for which there exist similar interpretations across readers and writers.

Some of the data that emerged from our analyses of the author–reader think-alouds did not support a relationship between author and reader that was quite so carefully interwoven. First, authors anticipated a great many more miscommunications than actually occurred. Second, although readers' think-alouds evidenced their awareness of author purpose, what they voiced as desirable characteristics of a writer's communication often extended beyond what was represented by the text or addressed during authors' think-alouds. Readers often expressed a sense of frustration due to an author's failure to explain why they were doing what they were doing. Also, readers, were frequently critical of a writers' work, including the writer's choice of words, clarity, and accuracy. Despite those criticisms, however, it was apparent that readers were unwilling to let the tool (the text provided by the author) stand in the way of the successful achievement of their goals, even if it meant taking on the role of an author and revising the text.

The perspective of reader as author and author as reader raises some interesting questions regarding the notion of interaction. The data we have gathered in conjunction with the think-alouds have led us to consider the interaction that occurs during reading as much more than an interaction between text and reader. Rather, it might be more accurately depicted along three dimensions: the "turns" a reader takes with the author, the turns a reader takes with himself or herself as the reader and the turns a reader takes as an author. Certainly the findings that we have shared are preliminary; however, they do point out that the authors' sense of readership and the reader's sense of authorship is not a static but dynamic relationship which changes throughout the development of a text by a writer or its interpretation by a reader. Furthermore, this changing relationship has an impact upon what a reader or writer understands and how they go about making meaning.

DISCUSSION

Across these three investigations we have tried to highlight how readership and authorship manifest themselves. We believe that our data subscribes to the view that the production and comprehension of texts are social events involving transactions similar to those that occur in the context of negotiations between people during conversation. In our first investigation our data suggested that the reader–author relationship is quite susceptible to subtle variations in the identity of the author. In those situations when readers were familiar with the topic and more likely to identify with the author, they are more likely to recall more and, at the same time, be more critical. Our second investigation served to demonstrate how topic familiarity and discourse style influence the relationship established between readers and authors across successful and less successful reading experiences. Again the more successful readers were more self-initiating with respect to their role as readers and their sense of what the author was trying to do. Our third study highlighted how shifts in the author–reader relationship are manifested for both readers and writers. Across the three investigations, then, our findings demonstrate the susceptibility of the author-reader relationship to shifts and the extent to which any reading or writing experience may deteriorate with the demise of the author–reader relationship. In terms of the latter, our findings support a view to reading and writing that suggests that for any reader or writer transactions occur along two dimensions: readers with writers as well as readers and writers with "another self." A successful writer, as he or she composes a text, considers not only the transactions in which his or her readers are likely to engage, he or she is also his or her own reader. Likewise, a successful reader as he or she comprehends a text is self-initiating. Although a successful reader responds reflexively and actively to writers, he or she does his or her own meaning making, engaging in a transaction with him or herself as the writer.

The suggestion that the writer is his or her own reader is not novel. In conjunction with studying the composing process, including revision and the difficulties writers encounter while composing, several researchers have begun to study and discuss the reading that occurs during writing (Atwell, 1980; Perl, 1980; Rose, 1980). Their research suggests, as our data indicates, that writers spend a great deal of time reading and rereading; that the reading that writers do serves different purposes (for example, distancing writers from their own work, problem solving, discovering, and monitoring what has been written); and that the quality of these reading experiences seems to be closely tied to successful or less successful writing products. Although these researchers have begun to define the nature of reading during writing in conjunction with the amount and nature of the text being read and written, less thoroughly investigated is how, when, and why reading proceeds at different moments during a variety of composing experiences. The interaction of what has been written, planned, read, with the writer's other self—the reader—has yet to be fully developed and grounded in theory.

The suggestion that readers are themselves writers is less common. Our data suggested that the responses of readers assumed a reflexive quality as if readers were rewriting the text that they were reading. Sometimes the rewriting appeared to be occurring in collaboration with the perceived author of the text being read; sometimes it appeared as if the reader had decided what he or she needed to know or do and compose meaning with little regard to the reader or the text. These responses to the text appeared to occur as readers became involved in "coming to grips" with their own goals and understandings at the same time as they were dealing with the author's goals, assumptions and suggestions. In general, it serves to remind us that successful reading is more akin to composing than regurgitation of what was stated or merely matching what was written with one's own knowledge.

It is as if the position Petrosky (1982) proposed in his paper, *From Story to Essay: Reading and Writing* serves to acknowledge this point of view:

> one of the most interesting results of connecting reading, literary and composition theory and pedagogy is that they yield similar explanations of human understanding as a process rooted in the individual's knowledge and feelings and characterized by its fundamental "putting together"—its fundamental constructiveness—as the act of making meaning, whether it be through reading, responding or writing. When we read, we comprehend by putting together impressions of the text with our personal, cultural, and contextual modes of reality. When we write, we compose by making meaning from available information, our personal knowledge, and the cultural and contextual frames we happen to find ourselves in. Our theoretical understandings of these processes are converging, as I pointed out, around the central role of human understanding—be it of texts or the world—as a process of composing. (p. 34)

Our position, then, is that central to our understanding the nature of reading is an understanding that reading and writing are social events involving multidimensional transactions between readers, writers, readers as writers, and writers as readers.

REFERENCES

Atwell, M. (1980). *The evolution of text: The interrelationship of reading and writing in the composing process.* Unpublished doctoral dissertation, Indiana University.

Bruce, B. C. (1980). Plans and social actions. In R. J. Spiro, B. C. Bruce, & W. F. Brewer (Eds.), *Theoretical issues in reading comprehension* (pp. 367-384). Hillsdale, NJ: Lawrence Erlbaum Associates.

Collins, A., Brown, J. B., Larkum, K. M. (1980). Inference in text understanding. In R. J. Spiro, B. C. Bruce, and W. F. Brewer (Eds.) Theoretical issues in reading comprehension. (pp. 385-407). Hillsdale, NJ: Lawrence Erlbaum Associates.

Cook, J. A. (1973). Language and socialization: A critical review. In B. Berstein (Ed.) *Class, codes and control* (pp. 293-341). London and Boston: Routledge & Kegan Paul.

Cooper, L. (Ed. and trans.), (1932). *The rhetoric of Aristotle.* Appleton-Century-Crofts.

van Dijk, T. A. (1976). *Pragmatics of language and literature.* Amsterdam: North Holland.

Erickson, F., & Schultz, J. (1977). When is a context? Some issues and methods in the analysis of social competence. *Institute for Comparative Human Development, 1*, 5-10.

Fillmore, C. (1974). Future of semantics. In C. Fillmore, G. Lakoff, & R. Lakoff, (Eds.), *Berkeley studies in syntax and semantics*. Berkeley: University of California.

Firth, J. R. (1957). The technique of semantics. In *Papers in linguistics, 1934-1951*. London: O.U.P.

Flower, L., & Hayes, J. R. (1981). A cognitive process theory of writing. *College Composition and Communication, 32*, (4,)365-387.

Fredericksen, C. H. (1975). Representing logical and semantic structure of knowledge acquired from discourse. *Cognitive Psychology, 7*, 371-458.

Fredericksen, C. H. (1979). Discourse comprehension and early reading. In L. Resnick & P. Weaver (Eds.), *Theory and practice of early reading*. Hillsdale, NJ: Lawrence Erlbaum Associates.

Fredericksen, C. H. (1977b) Structure and process in discourse production and comprehension. In M. A. Just and P. A. Carpenter (Eds.), *Cognitive processes in comprehension*. Hillsdale, NJ: Lawrence Erlbaum Associates.

Green, G. M. (1980, August). *Linguistics and the pragmatics of language use: What you know when you know a language . . . and what else you know* (Tech. Rep. No. 179, ERIC Document Reproduction Service No. ED 193666). Urbana: University of Illinois, Center for the Study of Reading.

Labov, W., & Fanshel, D. (1977). *Therapeutic discourse*. New York: Academic Press.

Lawson, J. (1758). *Lectures concerning oratory*. Dublin.

Ohmann, R. (1971). Speech acts and the definition of literature. *Philosophy and Rhetoric, 4*, 1-19.

Pearson, P. D. & Johnson, D. (1978). *Teaching reading comprehension* New York: Holt, Rinehart, & Winston.

Perl, S. (1980). Understanding composing. *College Composition and Communication, 31*, (4,)363-369.

Petrosky, A. (1982). From story to essay: Reading and writing. *College Composition and Communication, 33, 4*.

Rose, M. (1980). Rigid rules, inflexible plans and the stifling of language: A cognitivists analysis of writer's block. *College composition and communication, 31*, 389–400.

Searle, J. (1969). *Speech acts*. New York and London: Cambridge University Press.

Tierney, R. J., LaZansky, J., Raphael, T., & Mosenthal, J. (1979, Dec.). *Reader, text, and texture*. Paper presented at the National Reading Conference, San Antonio, TX.

Trabasso, T., & Nicholas, D. W. (1977). Memory and inferences in the comprehension of narratives. In F. Wilkenberg & J. Becker & T. Trabasso (Eds.), *Information integration by children*. Hillsdale, NJ: Lawrence Erlbaum Associates.

Warren, W. H., Nicholas, D. W., & Trabasso, T. (1980). Event chains and inferences in understanding narratives. In R. Freedle (Ed.), *Discourse processing: Multidisciplinary approaches*. Hillsdale, NJ: Lawrence Erlbaum Associates.

APPENDIX

EXAMPLE 1
Excerpts from Passages Used in Experiment 1

Passage 1 ARE YOU A SLAVE?	Passage 2 ARE YOU A SLAVE?
At State College, from which I was recently dismissed as a teacher,	At J & B Enterprise, from which I was recently dismissed as Vice-President in Charge of Personnel,
At State College, where I am majoring in Social Psychology,	At J & B Enterprise, where I am working as a clerk-typist,
At State College, where I was recently appointed Vice-President in charge of personnel,	At J & B Enterprise, where I was recently appointed Vice-President in charge of personnel,
. . . the students and faculty have separate and unequal facilities. If a student enters into the faculty dining room, the faculty get uncomfortable, as though there were a bad smell. If a member of the faculty sat in the student cafeteria, they would be looked on with disdain by fellow faculty members. In at least one building there are even restrooms which students may not use. . . .	. . . the office workers and executives have separate and unequal facilities. If an office worker enters into the executive dining room, the executives get uncomfortable, as though there were a bad smell. If one of the executives sat in the office workers' cafeteria, they would be looked on with disdain by fellow executives. In at least one building there are even restrooms which office workers may not use. . . .

EXAMPLE PROBES
Did the text clearly define the author's position on the issue raised in the text?
Was the author brief and to the point in the presentation of his/her arguments?
Were the arguments consistent with the purpose(s) of this text?
Do you think the author was addressing the article to you?
Do you think you could recognize the author by other material he or she has written?
Do you think the author highlighted information to which he or she knew you would
    relate?

EXAMPLE 2
Excerpts from Passages Used in Experiment 2 Varying in Familiarity

Passage 1 THE TREEHOUSE	Passage 2 THE NEW FACTORY
Mary had a problem, and this is the story of how she solved it. There were two things that Mary had always wanted. One was a place to be alone and the other was a place that she could use for bird watching. Mary decided	The Poly Plastic Bag Company has a problem. This is the story of how they solved it. There were two things that the Poly Plastic Bag Company had always wanted. One was a factory of its own and the other was offices that were out

that there was one way she could get both of these things. Her family was renting a home in the big city, and in the back yard, away from the house, they had a large tree. She made up her mind to build a treehouse in that tree. That way she could do the things she wanted to do by herself. . . .

of the city. They decided that they could get both of these things. They were currently renting a factory in a big city. But near a quiet river out of the city, they owned a large block of land. They made up their minds to build a factory on that land. . . .

EXAMPLE 3
Excerpts from Passages Used in Experiment 2
With and Without Dialogue

Passage 3
FLY

Passage 4
FLY

All over the world children like to play different games. In some countries, children enjoy playing a game called "Fly." It gets its name because to play the game you need to be able to leap through the air. Some people say that it is like flying through the air.

The game is very easy to learn and play. The only equipment you need to have is six sticks that are similar in size. The sticks need to be as long as a person's foot and about as big around as a person's thumb.

After the sticks are found, they are placed on the ground. . . .

Lisa and Mike were bored. It was Saturday, and they did not know what to do until Lisa had an idea.

"I know a game we can play that they play in some countries. You know children all over the world like to play different games," Lisa said.

Mike was interested and asked, "What is the game?"

"It is called Fly because to play the game you need to be able to leap through the air. Some people say you have to fly through the air," Lisa said. "You only need six sticks to play it."

It sounded like fun so they decided to try the game. Lisa and Mike gathered six sticks, each one about as long as their feet and as big around as their thumbs. They placed the six sticks on the ground. . . .

PART III

INSTRUCTIONAL ISSUES

Understanding readers' understandings is incomplete without consideration of the contexts and functions of reading. Examples of functions of reading include reading for escape and pleasure, reading for a better understanding of ourselves and our world, and reading for instruction and guidance. The contexts of reading are as varied as human experience. Of late, the varied contexts and functions of reading have been of concern to researchers. For example, Kirsch and Guthrie (1983) have investigated the reading demands of employees at a high technological corporation. The school provides another context of reading and is the focus of the following section.

It is unclear whether reading within school incorporates the functions of reading that are found in society at large. Nonetheless, educators are responsible for teaching children both how to read and how to learn from their reading. This instruction is done within the context of the school and the classroom. Although reading has been going on in schools for a long time, little is known about the actual process; therefore, researchers are asking questions about the reading-related processes that occur in the classroom. This chain of inquiry falls under the rubric of instructional research. Examples of questions asked by instructional researchers include the following: What psychological, sociological, and linguistic principles are related to reading instruction in the classroom? How do teachers design and select instructional strategies to facilitate comprehension? What are the contextual parameters of the classroom? How do teachers respond to the parameters of the classroom? Essentially, instructional researchers investigating reading in the classroom attempt to examine the interdependent factors—the teacher, the curriculum, text, students, and the social systems of the school and classroom—to explain the reading process.

This last section of our book attempts to provide some of the seeds for an understanding of reading instructional research. In all candidness, the field is only in the beginning stages of tilling with the ideas presented within these four chapters. It is our hope that when these seeds are planted and nurtured that we will reap a bountiful harvest of reading-related instructional research.

James Cunningham addresses these concerns in his chapter, "Toward a Pedagogy of Inferential Comprehension and Creative Response." Cunningham's thoughtful contribution reviews research related to the process of inference-making, suggests a terminology to resolve some of the thorny issues confronting reading educators, and provides a pedagogy of inferential comprehension and creative response.

Key to Cunningham's developing pedagogy is the importance of instructional strategies. The second chapter by Jill LaZansky, Frank Spencer, and Michael Johnston focuses on "Reading to Learn: Setting Students Up." These authors review relevant theoretical research and relate that literature to prereading strategies that are commonly offered by reading educators. A significant contribution made by these authors is the notion that strategies need to be evaluated according to certain criteria and selected for their instructionally relevant distinguishing characteristics.

Connie Bridge continues this line of reflection in the third chapter, "Strategies for Promoting Reader-Text Interactions." Bridge critically reviews research on selected strategies that are designed to promote comprehension before, during, and after reading. Her review provides a good background for the development of many research questions.

Finally, Patricia L. Anders and P. David Pearson conclude this book with the chapter "Instructional Research on Literacy and Reading: Parameters, Perspectives, and Predictions." This chapter reviews literature related to the contexts of literacy, discusses seven issues facing instructional researchers, and concludes with recommendations for conducting instructional research.

To reading educators, teacher educators, and instructional researchers, the challenge is clear. Hopefully, these contributions will provide the seeds for planting and harvesting in the field of instructional research.

Kirsch, I. S., & Guthrie, J. T. (1983, May) *Reading practices of adults in one high technology company* (Tech. Rep. No. 6). Newark, DE: International Reading Association.

TOWARD A PEDAGOGY
OF INFERENTIAL COMPREHENSION
AND CREATIVE RESPONSE

James W. Cunningham
University of North Carolina

In many texts it appears that the author has assumed the reader/listener can complete or extend the text and has made such contributions on the part of the processor necessary for a sensible interpretation. Fiction writers, for example, seldom describe every move a character makes; using a paragraph or chapter boundary as the only signal, an author will sometimes have a character be a room or even a continent away from his or her previous location with the reader/listener left to interpolate how that character came to be there. In other texts such completions and extensions may be less necessary but seem to be invited. Some of Poe's stories, for example, almost beg the reader to become coauthor, adding touches of mystery and terror only suggested by Poe. In still other texts, completions and extensions are not necessary for a sensible interpretation nor invited by the author subtly. Instead, they are allowed to occur under the sole authority and impetus of the reader/listener.

In all three of these cases, there are some comprehenders who complete and extend the text and some who do not. If it can be assumed that many who do not can learn to do so, a pedagogy is called for. This chapter is an attempt to move toward such a pedagogy.

BASIC TERMINOLOGY

The most common terms used for the cognitive processes of completing and extending texts and the cognitive products of text completions and extensions have been, respectively, *inferring* and *inferences*. Educators

(Bedell, 1934; Berry, 1931; Dewey, 1935a; 1935b; Gray, 1949; McCullough, Strang, & Traxler, 1946), psychometricians (Carroll, 1969; Davis, 1944; Tyler, 1930), and psychologists (Feder, 1938; Frase, 1972) have long used these terms to refer to text comprehension. Some, however, have used different terms to designate similar if not identical processes and outcomes.

Comprehending ideas that are *implicit* in texts has been discussed and investigated for decades (Carroll, 1927; Gray, 1956, 1960; Robinson, 1966). Gates described a type of reading that requires "thinking with the facts comprehended" (1928, p. 87) an "ability to see beyond the facts actually given" (1935, p. 87). Herber (1970, 1978) has discussed an *interpretive* level of comprehension that appears to refer to interpolating and extrapolating from a literal level of text. Harris and Smith (1976) have defined *creative reading* as "integrating the reading experience into the knowledge of the reader, and producing a response unique to each individual" (p. 296). Blachowicz (1977-1978) has used the term *semantic constructivity* to describe when "children use their knowledge of the world to add to the information found in the text" (p. 189). In a similar vein, Reder (1979) has discussed the role of *elaborations* in prose memory. Both of these latter usages seem to rely, at least in part, on the process referred to as *integration* by Bransford and Franks (1971) or *construction* by Bransford, Barclay, and Franks (1972).

Lowerre and Scandura (1973-1974) have ascribed a type of critical reading to the use of *logical* inference, while Brewer (1977) has distinguished between *logical* inferences and *pragmatic* ones. Logical inferences are necessary given the text and world knowledge while pragmatic inferences are probabilistic and more divergent.

All these terms appear to reflect common concern on the part of their users with the process and product of text completions and extensions during discourse comprehension. Some of the terms, however, also seem to reflect the attitudes of their users toward certain issues.

Issues of Terminology

Terms used to define and discuss a domain of study usually reflect the major distinctions in that domain. The issues of terminology with respect to reader/listener inferences from text center around three important distinctions.

The Distinction Between Literal and Non-Literal.   The term *literal* has been used with two different senses: (a) to mean that which is stated directly in the text or (b) to mean that which is simply, clearly, and solely interpretable on its face (Barfield, 1960). The word for the converse of *literal* in the first sense is *inferential* or *interpretive* whereas the converse of *literal* in the second sense is *figurative* or *metaphorical* (Barfield, 1960). An example will illustrate how confusing it can be to attempt to resolve the two senses of *literal* and their respective opposites. In the sentence, "She steered into the shopping center," *where* she steered is literal information or meaning in either case but *what* she steered is inferential (not literal) and literal (not figurative). In the sentence, "They cloaked their hearts with old regrets," what they did is literal (not inferential) and figurative (not literal). In other words, figurative meaning may be directly stated in the text while meaning inferred from the text may be literal meaning in the sense that it is factual, straightforward and unambiguous!

The Distinction Between Literal and Inferential.   Tyler (1930) reported only a small relationship between the ability to get facts from biology material and the ability to do inferential thinking about that material. Gates (1935) wrote of *literal comprehension* and of a class of readers who are "literal but unimaginative" in that they fail to think beyond the facts given in the passage. He discussed types of questions readers might be asked after reading that are based on the passage but that extend beyond a mere grasp of it. Feder (1938) made a distinction between "reading for information" and "reading for inference," a distinction he claimed was supported by the factorial analysis of that day. Currently, a debate centers around this issue. Some authorities feel that inferential or interpretive comprehension is a different level of understanding above and beyond literal comprehension (Carroll, 1969; Barrett, cited in Clymer, 1968; Flood & Lapp, 1978; Herber, 1970, 1978; Pettit & Cockriel, 1974) whereas others feel that making inferences is an integral part of all language comprehension (Smith, 1971, 1978; Anderson, 1978; Anderson, Reynolds, Schallert, & Goetz, 1977; Bridge, Tierney, & Cera, 1978; Clark, 1977; Noordman, 1979; Parker-Rhodes, 1978; Pearson & Johnson, 1978; Singer & Ferreira, 1983).

The Distinction Between Logical and Pragmatic Inferences.   Strictly speaking, inferring is the process by which conclusions are logically derived from assumed premises, although logicians are not interested in the process but rather in the arguments that result from the process (Copi, 1968). Although some researchers have investigated logical inference during reading in the strictest sense (Lowerre & Scandura, 1973-1974), and others have strictly defined inferences during language comprehension to be only those that are logical derivations from the literal (Carroll, 1969), still others have discussed a *pragmatic* type of inference (Brewer, 1977; Goetz, 1977; Harris & Monaco, 1978). The sentence "They went to pick up a new pup the day after Christmas" yields a logical inference,

"They went on December 26," and a pragmatic inference, "They went to get a young dog." The former inference is necessarily implied by the sentence whereas the latter one is not—they could have gone to get a young seal, for example. Brewer (1977) discusses a "but not test" to distinguish logical from pragmatic inferences:

> If one sentence (or abstract proposition) pragmatically implies another, negating the second statement and conjoining the two sentences with *but* should produce an acceptable sentence. (p. 674)

In the case of a logical inference, an acceptable statement would not be produced. In our example, testing the two inferences would result in these two statements:

> They went the day after Christmas, but they did not go on December 26.

> They went to pick up a new pup, but they did not get a young dog.

Clearly, the former sentence is impossible, even surreal, whereas the second is certainly possible although less probable than the inference it negates. (Another term for pragmatic inferences might be *probabilistic* inferences because, although logical inferences are necessarily implied given the text, pragmatic inferences are only possibly implied given the text and can differ in terms of the probability of their implication.)

A System of Terminology for a Pedagogy of Inferential Comprehension and Creative Response

Anderson (1978) and Pearson and Johnson (1978) write about the role that inferring plays in almost all language comprehension. Anderson, Stevens, Shifrin, and Osborn (1978) read sentences like "Sally looked at the clock in her classroom" to first and fourth graders and then asked them to pick the picture of a clock from three different pictures of clocks and a distractor picture that best matched the sentence they had heard. All the fourth graders and 87% of the first graders picked the appropriate picture for each "clock" sentence even though the task required that the children use the stated locations of the clocks to infer the physical characteristics of the clocks. Even very simple sentences heard by young children seem to be processed in part through the use of inferring. Yet, the logic of Herber (1970, 1978), Estes and Vaughan (1978), and others that activities can be designed of an interpretive or inferential nature that are more challenging than literal activities appeals intuitively to many of us who have planned and taught comprehension lessons to school children. How, then, can this apparent dispute be resolved? Is there or is there not a distinction between literal and inferential comprehension of text?

A resolution of the problem is possible if one grants that there is a distinction between the processes and the products of language comprehension. When one reads or listens to a statement like "She drove home in a hurry," it must be clear that some integration of prior knowledge with textual information is necessary for even a basic understanding. However, to the extent that a cognitive representation of the statement comes to exist in the semantic memory (Tulving, 1972) of the comprehender such as /*The woman came home quickly*/, the semantic product of comprehending can be said to be a literal one containing no inference. More completely, it can be said that the comprehender inferred that the woman drove home in a car or some other vehicle because that inference is necessary to the basic processing of the statement but that because, for the comprehender, the inference contributed no interesting or useful information, it was discarded and a literal product of comprehension was retained in memory. This explanation leads us to the first principle of our system of terminology:

1. *Successful processing of discourse always requires the use of prior knowledge but the product of discourse processing may or may not contain inferences.* This principle raises several questions: What is meant by "product of discourse processing?" What is an inference? When is discourse processing successful? These issues are addressed from the viewpoint of an interactive (Rumelhart & Ortony, 1977) and constructive (Bransford, Barclay, & Franks, 1972; Bridge, Tierney, & Cera, 1978; Frederiksen, 1975a) approach to language comprehension. This approach holds that comprehenders select information from the text and integrate it into prior knowledge structures (schemata) resulting in an internal, semantic interpretation or internal "text" (Cunningham, Moore, Cunningham, & Moore, 1983). The text does not drive the process for the comprehender's background knowledge and purposes for comprehending dictate what text information will be selected for processing and which schemata will be given the task of assimilating that selected information. Conversely, however, the listener/reader does not drive the process for the content and structure of the text constrain what and how semantic interpretations may be arrived at. Any act of comprehension is an interaction between these "top-down" and "bottom-up" processes.

The "product of discourse processing" in the first principle is, then, the semantic interpretation(s) constructed during reading or listening. A semantic interpretation is an internal state, not to be confused with the retellings, answers to questions, recognition responses, and so on, often elicited by necessity from subjects and students by researchers and teachers. These behavior sets are not "products of discourse processing" but rather the evidence researchers and teachers must use to infer the nature and characteristics of the comprehenders' internal states after discourse processing.

"Inferences" are more difficult to define in this context. Certainly, inferences are the chief result of an interaction between reader/listener schemata and text information. A literal "product of discourse processing" would be one that, if it could be compared with the text, would be synonymous in meaning to part of it. A literal comprehension product, however, is not evidence of purely bottom-up processing because, as just explained, prior knowledge may have been used to achieve the literal comprehension product but discarded before the final semantic interpretation was placed in memory. Literal comprehension products are simply those products that have deep structure equivalents in the text. Inferences are those comprehension products which (a) lack deep structure equivalents in the text, (b) are consistent with the text, and (c) complete or extend the text in a way consistent with the comprehender's expectations, purposes for comprehending, and/or knowledge of the world. Only when the semantic interpretation includes new or additional information to that provided by the text, does that semantic interpretation constitute an inference. Yet more than that is required. It can not be said that any information generated by the reader that is not explicitly stated in the text is an inference. Although this definition would meet the first principle, it would not be adequate because it would place too much emphasis on schema-based processes to the detriment of a true interaction. Any procedure for defining a comprehension product as an inference must rule out products that deny the text (misreadings) even though the comprehender may have done some inferring to arrive at those products and included some inferences in those products. In the latter case, I would prefer to call them *misinferences* (Cunningham, 1975).

Just as misinferences can result from an overreliance on schema-based processes while ignoring text information, other misinferences can result from an overreliance on text information while ignoring schematic information. Such misinferences are more difficult to delineate (because schemata are not available for easy scrutiny) but might take the form of interpreting figurative or idiomatic statements too literally or combining parts of texts together because they are juxtaposed even when the integration denies world knowledge or the ability of the comprehender to achieve a meaningful interpretation. This conclusion leads us to the second principle of our system of terminology:

2. *Successful processing of discourse is that which results in a semantic interpretation relatively free of misreadings and misinferences and*

with an appropriate combination of literal and inferential comprehension products given the comprehender's purpose for reading or listening. In this principle, "relatively free" and "appropriate combination" are definitely purpose-bound (Spiro & Smith, 1979). When one is reading a recipe to prepare a delicate dish for the first time when his or her boss is coming to dinner, misreadings and misinferences probably should be totally absent, and inferences probably should be limited to interpolating those behaviors the author of the recipe most likely assumed any preparer of the dish would know to perform. However, when one is reading a long novel as an aid to relaxation and sleep, misreadings and misinferences up to the point of disrupting fluent processing probably do not matter and inferences galore probably flesh out an otherwise modest literary event!

The third principle is:

3. *"Literal comprehension," "inferential comprehension," and "creative response" are not discrete levels of comprehension but are overlapping areas on a continuum of combinations of literal and inferential comprehension products from purely literal (without being misreadings) to purely creative (without being misinferential).* Consider this paragraph:

> The second and third presidents of the United States shared a mutual respect for each other's contributions to liberty. They were close friends in their later years, even though they had once been rivals. They often wrote letters to each other until their deaths.

Let us now examine a series of statements with respect to how they compare with the text:

1. The second and third presidents of the United States shared a mutual respect for each other's contributions to liberty.
2. The second and third presidents of the United States were close friends in their later years.
3. America's second and third presidents admired each other's efforts in the cause of freedom.
4. The second and third presidents of the United States made contributions to liberty.
5. John Adams and Thomas Jefferson shared a mutual respect for each other's contributions to liberty.
6. The second and third presidents of the United States had once been rivals for fame.
7. John Adams and Thomas Jefferson often wrote letters to each other using quill pens.

8. John Adams and Thomas Jefferson were kindred spirits with each other and with their country, dying on the same day, July 4, 1826.

If we pretend that each statement represents a semantic interpretation in the mind of a comprehender after reading or listening to the paragraph, we can see how such interpretations may be said to lie along a continuum from most literal/least creative to most creative/least literal. First, the commonalities of the statements should be mentioned. None of them deny the text or world knowledge, so none of them are misreadings or misinferences. All of them appear to be related to the text in some manner or to some degree although to verify such relationships we might have to consult references external to the text if our expectations, purposes for comprehending, or world knowledge were sufficiently different from those hypothetical readers who arrived at the various semantic interpretations (statements) just given. Finally, if it can be assumed that statement 1 was not merely the result of rote memorization, it is probable that all statements were produced by the same process, i.e., an interactive, constructive process where text information, purposes for comprehending, and reader schemata were interrelated by assimilation and inferring. Different purposes may have resulted in the different products but the processes may in fact have been the same.

Now the differences in the semantic interpretations should be discussed:

Statements 1, 2, and 3. Because all three statements have deep structure equivalence in the text, they are all literal comprehension products or responses. It is apparent, however, that 1 is more literal than 2 and 3. In my opinion, for most readers/listeners 2 is more literal than 3. Although the resolution of anaphora requires some use of prior knowledge on the part of the processor, anaphora ordinarily provides no new information because it is *argument repetition* (Kintsch, 1974) and, therefore, can only result in a literal semantic interpretation. (Those writers who would call statement 2 a bridging inference, Clark, 1977; or a backward inference, Just & Carpenter, 1978; Singer, 1980; Singer & Ferreira, 1983; because it reconciles two sentences from the text by identifying the "given" element, Clark & Haviland, 1977; in the latter sentence as an element in the antecedent sentence are not distinguishing between process and product as we are here.) All three statements are literal, then, but they seem to lie along a continuum within the literal area where 2 has some slightly creative element in it and 3 more still, though not enough that new meaning is expressed!

Statements 4 and 5. Statement 4 is a logical inference necessary to a sensible interpretation of the paragraph even though the paragraph does not say who made the contributions to liberty but merely that these two presidents possessed them. Compared with 3, however, it must be admitted that 4 seems terribly close to a literal statement. Statement 5, however, is clearly not a literal statement, because one who was very proficient in the English language but who knew next to nothing about American history would never arrive at such an interpretation. Again, both statements are logical inferences in that they necessarily follow given the paragraph and world and linguistic knowledge, but they, too, seem to lie along a continuum *within* this area.

Statements 6 and 7. These statements are both pragmatic inferences in that they are possibly, even probably, but not necessarily true. In the case of 6, the two presidents were most definitely political rivals but because the author left the modifier off of "rivals," the reader/listener is free to infer the rivalry in question. In this case, it would be difficult, if not impossible, to prove that Adams and Jefferson were not motivated by the prospect of fame when they entered political life or that they were not jealous, at some point, of each other's fame.

Statement 8. In my opinion, a semantic interpretation like 8 bears so much evidence of schematic information and so little evidence of text information, yet it does not deny or even ignore the text, that it seems to merit the label of *creative* response. Certainly, however, 7 showed much evidence of schematic information, too, and there we are reminded of our continuum again.

Statements 1–5 can collectively be called *text-based responses* whereas statements 6–8 can be called *knowledge-based* or *schema-based responses*. Text-based responses depend on the text and logic for their truth while schema-based responses depend on probability and aesthetics for their truth (see Fig. 12.1).

The fourth principle is:

4. *The dichotomy literal/figurative is not descriptive of comprehension but of language to be comprehended; the dichotomy literal/inferential is not descriptive of language but of comprehension of language.* If a

FIG. 12.1   A continuum of combinations of literal and inferential comprehension products.

text-based		schema-based
literal comprehension	inferential comprehension	creative response
	logical inferences pragmatic inferences	

sentence from an oral or written text such as "Billboards are warts on the landscape" is retained in memory as the semantic interpretation "Billboards are ugly protrusions on the countryside"[1], that is an example of literal comprehension of figurative language because the comprehender's semantic interpretation contains no new or additional information not contained in the text. (The first three statements following our "John Adams and Thomas Jefferson" paragraph exemplified literal comprehension of literal language.) The full range of applications of principle 4 is represented in Fig. 12.2.

Conclusions Concerning Terminology for a Pedagogy of Inferential Comprehension and Creative Response

Although a variety of terms have been used by various theorists and researchers, *inferring* and *inference* have been the most common terms used to label the process and product of comprehenders' completions and extensions of text during discourse comprehension. The distinction between process and product is an important one because the use of prior knowledge is probably involved in all comprehension while the products of that comprehension (what is retained in semantic memory) may be described as literal, inferential, or creative depending on the mixture of textual and schematic elements which make them up. These distinctions, literal versus inferential versus creative, are not distinct levels of comprehension but are labels for overlapping areas on a continuum between purely textual or literal and purely schematic or creative. Because few comprehension products (semantic interpretations) are either purely literal or purely creative, most such products are a mixture of textual and schematic elements. When teachers are teaching students to comprehend

FIG. 12.2   A matrix of combinations of comprehension products and language types.

	literal comprehension	logical inferential comprehension	pragmatic inferential comprehension	creative response
literal language				
figurative language				

[1] I am indebted to Richard Anderson for these examples.

discourse while listening or reading, they are not teaching students to use prior knowledge since all students who can understand spoken language must already know how to do that. What teachers are teaching students to do is to produce a certain type of semantic interpretation, i.e., one with a certain relative mixture of textual and schematic elements. The relative mixture achieved seems dependent on text factors, schema factors, purposes for comprehending, and pragmatic factors including those that the teacher can manipulate and the ones that he or she cannot. With respect to text comprehension, the most useful definition of *inferring* would probably be "the process(es) by which inferences are produced."

The reason for teaching students to produce semantic interpretations of certain mixtures, that is to infer, seems to be to enhance the likelihood that students will be able successfully to process discourse in all those situations that they or others may impose on them in school, work, and life. These semantic interpretations of certain mixtures can be in response to different kinds of language, both literal and figurative in nature.

BASIC PROCESSES

Once it is accepted that literal comprehension, inferential comprehension, and creative reading or listening (in response to either literal or figurative language) do not rely on different processes but, in fact, describe the relative amounts of textual and schematic elements in the cognitive products in semantic memory after comprehension, questions naturally arise as to the processes and factors underlying the production of semantic interpretations of various mixtures.

Issues of Process

"The problem of inference is this: When we read a passage of connected discourse, our understanding consists of much more information than is actually given" (Hintzman, 1978, p. 392).

If, after reading or listening, our understanding contains semantic interpretations or comprehension products that reflect both textual and schematic elements, then two questions become important to answer: When does the mixture of literal and creative occur? and Why does the mixture of literal and creative occur? The answers to these questions have implications for a pedagogy of inferential comprehension and creative response.

When Does the Mixture of Literal and Creative Occur?   A number of people have felt that the mixture occurs simultaneously with the input of the textual information. Bransford and Johnson (1972), for example, have written that "subjects do not simply interpret and store the meanings to sentences per se. Rather, subjects create semantic products that are a joint function of input information and prior knowledge" (p. 718). Because, in this view, subjects do not store sentence meanings as such it is not possible to say that these sentences are only operated on at some later time (during incubation or at output or recall) because the sentences were stored originally in mixed form (Bransford & Johnson, 1973). This view has been supported in research by Frederiksen (1975a) and Potts (1975). In fact, Anderson and Pichert (1977) summarized research to that time by saying that "every established fact about prose recall can be given an encoding interpretation. While some findings can also be explained in retrieval terms, none in the previous literature demands such an explanation" (p. 9).

Several studies that have attempted to deal with the issue of when inferences as products occur have used verification latency experiments in which reaction times necessary to verify statements implied by a passage have been compared to those necessary to verify literal statements from the passage (Goetz, 1977). (Kail, Chi, Ingram, and Danner, 1977, used a variation of this paradigm with answering questions.) The logic here is that if inferences were made on input, there would be no difference in reaction latencies, but if inferences were made during output, reaction latencies would be greater for inferences than for literal statements that, it is argued, were stored at input. Unfortunately, the results of various verification latency experiments have been conflicting (Goetz, 1977). An examination of three experiments employing this paradigm may reveal why previous results have been equivocal.

Stacey (1978) found an interaction between latency differences and delay between text input and question asking. If 17 seconds were allowed to pass for adult subjects between stimulus and question, there was no difference in time needed to answer a literal question or an inferential question, implying that inferences had been made at input. When less delay was allowed, adults required more time to answer the inference questions, implying that inferences had been made at output. Stacey's results, using her stimuli, seemed to support incubation, rather than input or recall, as the period when the mixture between textual and schematic elements takes place. These findings suggest that any verification study which does not systematically control for incubation as a factor may lend itself to confounding of incubation with either the input or the output effect.

Reder (1979), in a careful and well-designed pair of experiments, compared latencies across three factors: prior exposure of inferences, type of inference, and immediate vs. delayed (vs. long delay, in experiment 2). For our purposes, the interesting finding was that latencies for the medium-plausibility inferences were consistently higher than for the high-plausibility inferences regardless of condition on the other two factors. If one examines Reder's inferences, most of the high-plausibility inferences would qualify as logical inferences on the continuum previously discussed, whereas most of the medium-plausibility inferences would qualify as pragmatic inferences or as creative response. This finding, then, suggests that there might be an interaction between degree of mixture of literal and creative and the extent to which that mixture was likely to have occurred at input rather than during incubation or at output or recall. This result would be consistent with the work of Bartlett (1932) and Frederiksen (1975a) who found that the relative amount of non-textual material in recalls increases with the length of the retention period.

Singer (1980) compared the latency of subjects' judgments about statements directly expressed in the text, statements reconciling two sentences from the text, and highly probable, pragmatic inferences. The three experiments described support the conclusion that reconciling two sentences through recognition of argument repetition takes little if any more time than recognition of directly expressed ideas but that recognition of pragmatic inferences takes considerably longer. Singer and Ferreira (1983) obtained similar results using stories.

Taken together the studies of Stacey (1978), Reder (1979), and Singer (1980; Singer & Ferreira, 1983) lend support to the notion that relative mixture of textual and schematic elements may interact with incubation time between input of textual information and occurrence of the mixture. Mixtures that qualify as literal comprehension products or logical inferences may generally occur simultaneously with or soon after reading or listening, whereas pragmatic inferences and creative responses may generally require some significant incubation period. Moreover, the work of Anderson and Pichert (1977) suggests that some mixtures may only occur at output or recall through the application of previously unused top-down retrieval mechanisms or strategies. As Frederiksen (1977) has concluded, it seems that high-level inferential processing units may occur both during input and recall of a text, or even, as Stacey (1978) suggests, during some intervening time. Garnham (1982) has discussed "the omission theory" in an attempt to explain this phenomenon.

Why Does the Mixture of Literal and Creative Occur? The most frequent explanation in the literature for why comprehenders combine schematic elements with textual ones to achieve many of their comprehension products is that these schematic elements fill slots or gaps in the text (Collins, Brown, & Larkin, 1980). At its simplest, this process of slot-filling would operate at the one-word level when comprehenders draw inferences about the meaning of a word from context (Davis, 1944, 1968), or, in a cloze task, infer the meaning of a word-slot from context and then infer again what the most likely word would have been to express that meaning. At a more complex level, this process would supply information not given by the author but which is necessary to provide coherence and continuity to the text (Nix, 1978; Thorndyke, 1976; Tierney, Bridge, & Cera, 1978-1979; Warren, Nicholas, & Trabasso, 1977). Schank (1975) has expressed this view of the role of inference most completely and clearly by suggesting that inferences both fill missing slots in the text and provide texts with unstated, higher level organizations. More extremely, Clark (1977) has confined inferences to being slot-fillers by defining an autho-rized inference that the speaker (or author) intends the listener (or reader) to draw and which provides information that is a part of the message being conveyed. Any inference that was not intended by the author and which does not fill a gap in the message is *unauthorized* and should be discouraged.

If approaching inferences as slot-fillers for gaps in texts seems too text-based, others have approached them as slot-fillers for open variables in schemata. Anderson (1978) has written that the "slots in a schema may be instantiated with information that could be said to be 'given' in the situation, or message, but often slots are filled by inference" (p. 68). This position, supported by Keenan (1978) and others, though similar to that discussed in the previous paragraph, is less text-based because a compre-hender may use textual information to partially instantiate schemata and inferential processes to complete the instantiation when the slots filled by inference are not authorized to be filled or even of benefit to the coher-ence and continuity of the text. A burglar, for example, when reading a classified advertisement by someone wanting Sugar Bowl tickets and giving an address, might fill some schema-slots that, though unauthorized and unnecessary for comprehension of the ad, might prove very profit-able around New Year's Day!

A third, and older, approach to the why of inference does not contra-dict either the text-based or the schema-based slot-filler explanations. It holds that good readers are imaginative (Gates, 1935), and that they have an intrinsic motivation to apply that imagination to any reading task in an attempt to have the fullest possible response (McCullough, Strang, & Traxler, 1946). Their responses, of course, would fill all empty slots in the author's message (Gray, 1949) but there seems to be the feeling when consulting these early reading education authorities that, as long as the response did not contradict or ignore the text, the sky was the limit.

A synthesis of these three related views of why the mixture of textual and schematic elements occurs, couched in the basic terminology out-lined earlier in this chapter, would be as follows. All comprehension involves reader/listener schemata and their instantiation by the comprehender. Moreover, it would be an unusual act of comprehension where all schema-slots were instantiated with given information, leaving no need or opportunity for inferring to complete the schemata. The product of comprehension, however, will be literal if the background information used to fill the slot(s) is not retained in the semantic memory for that comprehension event. If the sentence "Sally looked at the clock in her bedroom" (Anderson, Stevens, Shifrin, & Osborn, 1978) were in a context where the characteristics of the clock were not important to coherence and continuity of the narrative and were not of interest to the comprehender, it is likely that the characteristics of the clock would be inferred from the bedroom context to achieve a subjective sense of comprehension (Anderson, 1978), but be abstracted out of the comprehender's forming semantic interpretation, leaving it literal in nature. In short, then, schematic elements should be included in semantic interpretations of what is comprehended when sense and coherence of the text makes them necessary or when interest, enjoyment, or purpose for comprehending of the reader/listener make them desirable. Schematic elements should not be included in semantic interpretations when they are neither necessary nor desirable.

Processes Underlying Inferential Comprehension Products

Literal comprehension products have deep structure equivalents or equivalence in the text. Inferential comprehension products are those containing a mixture of textual and schematic elements in combinations lacking deep structure equivalents or equivalence in the text, which neither deny nor ignore any part of the text, and which complete or extend the text consistent with the comprehender's expectations, purposes for comprehending, or knowledge. Inferential comprehension products which consist almost entirely of schematic elements are termed creative response. The processes involved in the production of the various relative mixtures are the same in the sense that they are constructive, interactive, and abstractive (Tierney, Bridge, & Cera, 1978-1979). Determining the relative mixture of literal and creative in any one semantic interpretation are several factors: (a) whether the comprehender has structural schemata matching the words, grammatical/propositional structures, cohesion, and staging of the text (Frederiksen, 1975b; Grimes, 1975; Kintsch, 1974); (b) the language-processing strategies available to the comprehender; (c) pragmatic conditions (including teacher-manipulated task variables); (d) the comprehender's purposes for reading/listening; (e) the comprehender's knowledge of the world—conceptual and procedural schemata; and (f) the comprehender's metacognitive/meta-comprehension skills (Baker & Brown, in press). These factors all affect the depth-of-processing (Anderson, 1970; Andre, 1979; Craik & Lockhart, 1972) of text and the willingness or tendency of comprehenders to involve their own conceptual and procedural schemata actively during text processing (Spiro, 1975; Anderson, 1978).

These factors appear to operate and interact in ways that determine comprehension task, criteria for task performance, ability to perform task, and ability to regulate task performance. A comprehension task is an assigned process for comprehending a text, an assigned product to be achieved from or with the text, or both (Cunningham, Cunningham, & Arthur, 1981). The task may have been assigned by a teacher or a superior, by a situation, or by the comprehender him or herself. Thus, it may be said that factors 3 and 4, pragmatic conditions, and the comprehender's purposes for reading/listening, combine to set the task. These same two factors also set the criteria for task performance that could be defined as part of the task itself except that, when the task is an assigned process, criteria for task performance only can be applied by the comprehender through metacognitive introspection, whereas assigned products can be evaluated from without.

Ability to perform the task at or above criteria is determined by factors 1, 2, and 5, the match between text components and the comprehender's structural schemata, the comprehender's language processing strategies, and the comprehender's conceptual and procedural schemata. Ability to regulate task performance is determined by factor 6, the comprehender's metacognitive/metacomprehension skills.

Comprehenders select information from the text and integrate it into prior knowledge structures to achieve an internal, semantic interpretation which meets the criteria for task performance. This constructive process is equilibrated by the metacognitive skills of comprehension monitoring (Baker & Brown, in press) and autoregulation (Gibson & Levin, 1975; Piaget, 1952), which means that the developing product of comprehension is constantly being examined for internal consistency, freedom from misreadings and misinferences, and adherence to criteria for task performance. Clearly, a lack of structural, conceptual, or procedural schemata or insufficient language processing strategies affect task performance, but when the available schemata and strategies are more than sufficient to accomplish the task at criteria, comprehension monitoring/autoregulation determines the mix of textual and schematic elements in the semantic interpretation remaining in memory after discourse processing.

In fact, the relative difficulty of achieving inferential and creative semantic interpretations (even though they both result from the same constructive, interactive, and abstractive processes) probably results from two causes: the presence of schemata sufficient to fill gaps in texts but insufficient to extend texts (Morris & Bransford, 1982), and the increased difficulty of monitoring/autoregulating increasingly creative semantic interpretations. In the second case, literal comprehension products are more easily regulated because one can resort to a reexamination of the text or to one's episodic memory (Tulving, 1972) for the listening/reading of the text. Inferential comprehension products and creative responses, however, must not merely restate a portion of the text, but must be consistent with the text as a whole as well as being true to the knowledge of the world held by the comprehender (Rystrom, 1977). Much more must be taken into consideration. The ability to autoregulate semantic interpretations so that schematic elements consistent with the text and one's knowledge of the world without letting in elements that are misreadings, misinferences, or importations is quite a juggling act, especially if the language is figurative in nature. Many comprehenders keep their semantic interpretations very literal so they can more easily regulate them. These comprehenders apparently receive little discouragement from their teachers in this tendency to overregulate comprehension products towards the literal end of the continuum (Durkin, 1978-1979; Guszak, 1967).

TOWARD A PEDAGOGY

A pedagogy consists of methods, materials, and metamethods (procedures for selecting materials and for selecting, using, and modifying methods to meet needs of specific learners in specific situations). A pedagogy of inferential comprehension and creative response, then, would consist of methods, materials, and metamethods.

Methods

Anyone who has spent much time in public school classrooms will agree that teachers do very little, beyond asking questions, to teach students to be better comprehenders and research has supported this observation (Durkin, 1978-1979). Experience will verify that this condition is only truer with respect to the amount of inferential comprehension and creative reading/listening instruction. Unfortunately, in the case of inferential comprehension and creative response, there is evidence that teachers do not even ask very many of those kinds of questions (Guszak, 1967). If one source of teaching methods is what teachers themselves are already doing, that source seems unlikely to provide us with methods for teaching inferential comprehension and creative response.

Research on teaching inferential comprehension and creative response seems called for. Hopefully, such research would not repeat the mistakes of traditional methods studies (Tierney & Cunningham, 1984). Initial work in this area seems promising (Hansen, 1981a; 1981b; Hansen & Pearson, 1983).

Decision Rules for Conducting Research on Teaching Inferential Comprehension and Creative Response. When one anticipates teaching, testing, or researching inferential comprehension, one is immediately challenged by questions such as "Is this an inference?" and "What constitutes a right (or a wrong) response?" This section presents decision rules based on the conclusions concerning terminology and processes presented earlier in this chapter. These rules provide answers to the two questions just raised plus means for classifying inferences into logical, pragmatic, and creative categories.

In all cases these decision rules are applied (in numbered order) to comprehension products (propositions or statements). In the abstract, these products may be cognitive though in practice they will always be behavioral.

Decision rule 1 is:
No response is acceptable which can not be true if the text is true.

This decision rule is based on the interactive nature of comprehension as is decision rule 2:

An acceptable response must relate directly to the purpose for comprehending.

Comprehending always has both a WHAT and a WHY (Cunningham, Moore, Cunningham, & Moore, 1983) and a response can not be acceptable when it denies either. For example, if a student were asked to predict the ending of a story after hearing most of it, a response that accurately repeated some part of the text like, "He was a European," would be beside the point and thus incorrect by rule 2 though not by rule 1. Decision rule 2 can not always be applied, however, because, in the absence of a stated purpose before comprehending begins, a comprehender can not practically be held accountable to a purpose. These first two decision rules allow the teacher, tester, and researcher to discriminate between acceptable and unacceptable comprehension responses whether literal, inferential, or creative.

Decision rule 3 employs Brewer's (1977) "*but not* test" but with a broader purpose. Brewer used this test to differentiate logical from pragmatic inferences but actually it differentiates between literal statements and pragmatic inferences as well. And because creative responses are types of pragmatic inferences, the test also differentiates them from literal statements and logical inferences. Therefore, decision rule 3 is:

> An acceptable response is text-based if there is a statement in the text which cannot be true if the negation of the response is true; a response is schema-based if there is no statement in the text contradicted by the negation of the response.

For example, the statement "The Indian rode into the west" in response to the text

The Indian rode into the sunset (Rystrom, 1977) is a text-based response because the text can not be true if "The Indian did not ride into the west" is true. The statement "The Indian rode a horse into the sunset" (Cunningham, 1981), however, is a schema-based response because the text can still be true if "The Indian did not ride a horse" is true. This third decision rule allows the teacher, tester, or researcher to discriminate between acceptable responses that are text-based and acceptable responses that are schema-based.

Decision rule 4 is:

> An acceptable text-based response is literal if it is semantically equivalent to or synonymous with part(s) of the text, and a logical inference if it is not.

Decision rule 4 is applied through the use of the "thesaurus and grammar book test" (Cunningham, 1981). An acceptable text-based response is literal if it can be proven using the text, a knowledge of synonyms, and a knowledge of grammar, syntax, and usage; the response is a logical inference if it cannot be so proven. Extending our previous example the statement "Into the sunset the Indian traveled" is literal because it can be proven using the text, a thesaurus, and a grammar book, i.e., it uses synonyms and different syntax from the text but contains no new meaning. The statement "The Indian rode into the west" is a logical inference, however, because no knowledge of language can equate that statement with the text; one must also have the world knowledge that the sun sets in the west before the statement can be proven. Decision rule 4 allows the teacher, tester, or researcher to discriminate between acceptable text-based responses that are literal and those that are logical inferences.

Decision rule 4 is:

> An acceptable schema-based response is a pragmatic inference if average comprehenders (of the type under study) tend to produce it, given a probe; otherwise, it is a creative response.

Decision rule 5 is:

Literal responses are compared with literal responses based on the precision with which they relate to the text and the purpose for comprehending; logical inferences are compared with logical inferences based on the precision with which they relate to world knowledge, the text, and the purpose for comprehending and on conformity with laws of deductive logic.

Decision rule 5 is:

Pragmatic inferences are compared with pragmatic inferences based on the tendency of an average group of comprehenders to produce them when probed and on the probability of their truth given world knowledge and the text; creative responses are compared with creative responses based on the possibility of their truth given world knowledge and the text and on their aesthetic appeal.

A partial agenda of questions to be answered about methods is as follows:

1. Can the teaching of text structure at any level, (word form-classes, grammatical/propositional structures, cohesion, or staging) cause learners to produce more or better inferences (of any or all types)?
2. Can students be taught to write language that evokes inferences and creative responses and, if so, does improved ability to write such language cause them to produce more or better inferences?
3. Can leading students to develop, express, clarify, and respect their own purposes for comprehending cause them to produce more or better inferences?
4. Can developing students' knowledge of the world cause them to produce more or better inferences?
5. Can teaching students to monitor and autoregulate their developing internal "texts" better cause them to produce more or better inferences?

Materials

Materials are of two kinds: texts to be comprehended and texts combined with methods. The latter includes basal readers, workbooks, worksheets, kits, learning machines, and computer-assisted instruction. The methods incorporated in these instructional materials should be evaluated as methods. Therefore, this section only deals with texts to be comprehended.

A partial agenda of questions to be answered about texts is as follows:

1. What are the characteristics of texts that tend to evoke literal responses?

2. What are the characteristics of texts that tend to evoke logical inferences?

3. What are the characteristics of texts that tend to evoke pragmatic inferences?

4. What are the characteristics of texts that tend to evoke creative responses?

5. What is the effect of type of language (literal vs. figurative) on students' ability or tendency to produce inferences?

Metamethods

It is not enough to have methods or materials for teaching inferential comprehension and creative response, though they are important. Procedures for selecting materials and for selecting, using, and modifying methods for specific learners in specific situations are also necessary. Metamethods are methods for using methods and materials.

A partial agenda of questions to be answered about metamethods follows:

1. What criteria (word identification accuracy, word identification speed, literal comprehension, background knowledge) should be used to evaluate the quality of the match between materials and learners when selecting materials for use in inferential comprehension lessons?

2. Are some methods more appropriate for students at one stage of cognitive development than others?

3. What modifications are necessary in methods when teaching students who are reluctant to take risks to produce inferences?

4. Are there sequences for employing methods and materials to develop the ability of students who independently produce inferences of all types?

5. What learning environments are most conducive to having methods of teaching inferential comprehension succeed?

A CALL FOR ACTION

When the amount of theory and research concerning the nature of inferring and of inferences is compared with the amount of theory and research regarding the teaching of inferential comprehension, a tremendous difference is noted. Isn't it time use was made of these theories and research findings to develop a pedagogy of inferential comprehension and creative response? If such a pedagogy is to be achieved, research on inferential comprehension instruction must be seen as a legitimate endeavor and it must be seen as legitimate to begin applying incomplete theories to practical problems. When we are discussing theories, tomorrow never comes, but, when we observe the practice, there is a Dark Age of ignorance.

ACKNOWLEDGMENTS

I would like to thank Richard Anderson, Jill LaZansky, and James Mosenthal for their comments on an earlier draft of this chapter.

REFERENCES

Anderson, R. C. (1970). Control of student mediating processes during verbal learning and instruction. *Review of Educational Research, 40,* 349-369.

Anderson, R. C. (1978). Schema-directed processes in language comprehension. In A. M. Lesgold, J. W. Pellegrino, S. D. Fakkema, & R. Glaser (Eds.), *Cognitive psychology and instruction.* New York: Plenum Press.

Anderson, R. C., & Pichert, J. W. (1977). *Recall of previously unrecallable information following a shift in perspective* (Tech. Rep. No. 41, ERIC Document Reproduction Service No. EP 142 974). Champaign: University of Illinois, Center for the Study of Reading.

Anderson, R. C., Reynolds, R. E., Schallert, D. L., & Goetz, E. T. (1977). Frameworks for comprehending discourse. *American Educational Research Journal, 14,* 367-381.

Anderson, R. C., Stevens, K. C., Shifrin, Z., & Osborn, J. H. (1978). Instantiation of word meanings in children. *Journal of Reading Behavior, 10,* 149-157.

Andre, T. (1979). Does answering higher-level questions while reading facilitate productive learning? *Review of Educational Research, 49,* 280-318.

Baker, L., & Brown, A. L. (1984). Metacognitive skills and reading. In P. D. Pearson (Ed.), *Handbook on research in reading.* New York: Longman.

Barfield, O. (1960). The meaning of the word "literal." In L. C. Knights & B. Cottle (Eds.), *Metaphor and symbol.* London: Butterworth.

Bartlett, F. C. (1932). *Remembering.* Cambridge: Cambridge University Press.

Bedell, R. C. (1934). The relationship between the ability to recall and the ability to infer in specific learning situations. *Science Education, 18,* 158-162.

Berry, B. T. (1931). Improving freshman reading ability. *English Journal: College Edition, 20,* 824-829.

Blachowicz, C. L. Z. (1977-1978). Semantic constructivity in children's comprehension. *Reading Research Quarterly, 13,* 188-199.

Bransford, J. D., Barclay, J. R., & Franks, J. J. (1972). Sentence memory: A constructive versus interpretive approach. *Cognitive Psychology, 3,* 193-209.

Bransford, J. D., & Franks, J. J. (1971). The abstraction of linguistic ideas. *Cognitive Psychology, 2,* 331-350.

Bransford, J. D., & Johnson, M. K. (1972). Contextual prerequisites for understanding: Some investigations of comprehension and recall. *Journal of Verbal Learning and Verbal Behavior, 11,* 717-726.

Bransford, J. D., & Johnson, M. K. (1973). Consideration of some problems in comprehension. In W. Chase (Ed.), *Visual information processing*. New York: Academic Press.

Brewer, W. F. (1977). Memory for the pragmatic implications of sentences. *Memory and Cognition, 5*, 673-678.

Bridge, C. A., Tierney, R. J., & Cera, M. J. (1978). Inferential operations of children involved in discourse processing. In P. D. Pearson & J. Hansen (Eds.), *Reading: Disciplined inquiry in process and practice*. Clemson, SC: The National Reading Conference.

Carroll, J. B. (1969). From comprehension to inference. In M. P. Douglass (Ed.), *Claremont Reading Conference* (Vol. 33). Claremont, CA: Claremont Graduate School.

Carroll, R. P. (1927). *An experimental study of comprehension in reading*. New York: Bureau of Publications, Teachers College, Columbia University.

Clark, H. H. (1977). Inferences in comprehension. In D. LaBerge & S. J. Samuels (Eds.), *Perception and comprehension*. Hillsdale, NJ: Lawrence Erlbaum Associates.

Clark, H. H., & Haviland, S. E. (1977). Comprehension and the given-new contract. In R. O. Freedle (Ed.), *Discourse production and comprehension*. Norwood, NJ: Ablex.

Clymer, T. (1968). What is reading? Some current concepts. In, H. M. Robinson (Ed.), *Innovation and change in reading instruction*. Chicago: National Society for the Study of Education.

Collins, A., Brown, J. S., & Larkin, K. M. (1980). Inference in text understanding. In R. J. Spiro, B. C. Bruce, & W. F. Brewer (Eds.), *Theoretical issues in reading comprehension*. Hillsdale, NJ: Lawrence Erlbaum Associates.

Copi, I. M. (1968). *Introduction to logic* (3rd ed.). New York: Macmillan.

Craik, F. L. M., & Lockhart, R. S. (1972). Levels of processing: A framework for memory research. *Journal of Verbal Learning and Verbal Behavior, 11*, 671-684.

Cunningham, J. W. (1975). *The synthesis of concepts and the nature of inference*. Unpublished doctoral dissertation, University of Georgia.

Cunningham, J. W. (1981). How to question before, during, and after reading. In E. K. Dishner, T. W. Bean, & J. E. Readence (Eds.), *Reading in the content areas: Improving classroom instruction*. Dubuque, IA: Kendall/Hunt.

Cunningham, J. W., Cunningham, P. M., & Arthur, W. V. (1981). *Middle and secondary school reading*. New York: Longman.

Cunningham, P. M., Moore, A., Cunningham, J. W., & Moore, D. W. (1983). *Reading in elementary classrooms: Strategies and observations*. New York: Longman.

Davis, F. B. (1944). Fundamental factors of comprehension in reading. *Psychometrika, 9*, 185-197.

Davis, F. B. (1968). Research in comprehension in reading. *Reading Research Quarterly, 4*, 449-545.

Dewey, J. C. (1935a). The acquisition of facts as a measure of reading comprehension. *Elementary School Journal, 35*, 346-348.

Dewey, J. C. (1935b). A case study of reading comprehension difficulties in American history. *University of Iowa Studies in Education, 10*, 26-54.

Durkin, D. (1978-1979). What classroom observations reveal about reading comprehension instruction. *Reading Research Quarterly, 14*, 481-533.

Estes, T. H., & Vaughan, J. L., Jr. (1978). *Reading and learning in the content classroom*. Boston: Allyn & Bacon.

Feder, D. D. (1938). Comprehension maturity tests—A new technique in mental measurement. *Journal of Educational Psychology, 29*, 597-606.

Flood, J., & Lapp, D. (1978). Inferential comprehension: A grand illusion. *Language Arts, 55*, 188-191.

Frase, L. T. (1972). Maintenance and control in the acquisition of knowledge from written materials. In J. B. Carroll & R. C. Freedle (Eds.), *Language comprehension and the acquisition of knowledge*. Washington, DC: Winston.

Frederiksen, C. H. (1975a). Effects of context-induced processing operations on semantic information acquired from discourse. *Cognitive Psychology, 7*, 139-166.

Frederiksen, C. H. (1975b). Representing logical and semantic structure of knowledge acquired from discourse. *Cognitive Psychology, 7*, 371-458.

Frederiksen, C. H. (1977). Semantic processing units in understanding text. In R. O. Freedle (Ed.), *Discourse production and comprehension* (Vol. 1). Norwood, NJ: Ablex.

Garnham, A. (1982). Testing psychological theories about inference making. *Memory and Cognition, 10*, 341-349.

Gates, A. I. (1928). *The improvement of reading*. New York: Macmillan.

Gates, A. I. (1935). *The improvement of reading* (rev. ed.). New York: Macmillan.

Gibson, E. J., & Levin, H. (1975). *The psychology of reading*. Cambridge, MA: MIT Press.

Goetz, E. T. (1977). *Inferences in the comprehension of and memory for text* (Tech. Rep. No. 49), Champaign, IL: University of Illinois, Center for the Study of Reading.

Gray, W. S. (1949). Basic competencies in efficient reading. In W. S. Gray (Ed.), *Reading in an age of mass communication*. New York: Appleton-Century-Crofts.

Gray, W. S. (1956). *The teaching of reading and writing*. Chicago: Scott, Foresman.

Gray, W. S. (1960). The major aspects of reading. In H. M. Robinson (Ed.), *Sequential development of reading abilities*. Chicago: University of Chicago Press.

Grimes, J. E. (1975). *The thread of discourse*. The Hague: Mouton.

Guszak, F. J. (1967). Teacher questioning and reading. *Reading Teacher, 21*, 227-234.

Hansen, J. (1981a). The effects of inference training and practice on young children's reading comprehension. *Reading Research Quarterly, 16*, 391-417.

Hansen, J. (1981b). An inferential comprehension strategy for use with primary grade children. *Reading Teacher, 34*, 665-669.

Hansen, J., & Pearson, P. D. (1983). An instructional study improving the inferential comprehension of fourth grade good and poor readers. *Journal of Educational Psychology, 75*, 821-829.

Harris, L. A., & Smith, C. B. (1976). *Reading instruction* (2nd ed.). New York: Holt, Rinehart & Winston.

Harris, R. J., & Monaco, G. E. (1978). Psychology of pragmatic implication: Information processing between the lines. *Journal of Experimental Psychology: General, 107*, 1-22.

Herber, H. L. (1970). *Teaching reading in content areas*. Englewood Cliffs, NJ: Prentice-Hall.

Herber, H. L. (1978). *Teaching reading in content areas* (2nd ed.). Englewood Cliffs, NJ: Prentice-Hall.

Hintzman, D. L. (1978). *The psychology of learning and memory*. San Francisco: Freeman.

Just, M. A., & Carpenter, P. A. (1978). Inference processes during reading: Reflections from eye fixations. In J. W. Senders & R. A. Monty (Eds.), *Eye movements and the higher psychological functions*. Hillsadale, NJ: Lawrence Erlbaum Associates.

Kail, R. V., Jr., Chi, M. T. H., Ingram, A. L., & Danner, F. W. (1977). Constructive aspects of children's reading comprehension. *Child Development, 48*, 684-688.

Keenan, J. M. (1978). Psychological issues concerning implication: Comments on "Psychology of pragmatic implication: Information processing between the lines" by Harris and Monaco. *Journal of Experimental Psychology: General, 107*, 23-27.

Kintsch, W. (1974). *The representation of meaning in memory*. Hillsdale, NJ: Lawrence Erlbaum Associates.

Lowerre, G. F., & Scandura, J. M. (1973-1974). Conceptually based development and evaluation of individualized materials for critical reading based on logical inference. *Reading Research Quarterly, 9*, 186-205.

McCullough, C. M., Strang, R. M., & Traxler, A. E. (1946). *Problems in the improvement of reading*. New York: McGraw Hill.

Morris, C. D., & Bransford, J. D. (1982). Effective elaboration and inferential reasoning. *Memory and Cognition, 10,* 188-193.

Nix, D. (1978). Linking-media syntax in children's sentence comprehension. *Journal of Reading Behavior, 10,* 79-89.

Noordman, L. G. M. (1979). *Inferring from language.* New York: Springer-Verlag.

Parker-Rhodes, F. (1978). *Inferential semantics.* Sussex, England: The Harvester Press.

Pearson, P. D., & Johnson, D. D. (1978). *Teaching reading comprehenesion.* New York: Holt, Rinehart & Winston.

Pettit, N. T., & Cockriel, I. W. (1974). A factor study of the literal reading comprehension test and the inferential comprehension test. *Journal of Reading Behavior, 6,* 63-75.

Piaget, J. (1952). *The origins of intelligence in children* (M. Cook, Trans.). New York: International University Press.

Potts, G. R. (1975). Bringing order to cognitive structures. In F. Restle, R. M. Shiffrin, N. J. Castellan, H. R. Lindman, & D. B. Pisoni (Eds.), *Cognitive theory* (Vol. 1). Hillsdale, NJ: Lawrence Erlbaum Associates.

Reder, L. M. (1979). The role of elaboration in memory for prose. *Cognitive Psychology, 11,* 221-234.

Robinson, H. M. (1966). The major aspects of reading. In H. A. Robinson (Ed.), *Reading: Seventy-five years of progress.* Chicago: University of Chicago Press.

Rumelhart, D. E., & Ortony, A. (1977). The representation of knowledge in memory. In R. C. Anderson, R. J. Spiro, & W. E. Montague (Eds.), *Schooling and the acquisition of knowledge.* Hillsdale, NJ: Lawrence Erlbaum Associates.

Rystrom, R. (1977). Reflections of meaning. *Journal of Reading Behavior, 9,* 193-200.

Schank, R. C. (1975). The role of memory in language processing. In C. N. Cofer (Ed.), *The structure of human memory.* San Francisco: Freeman.

Singer, M. (1980). The role of case-filling inferences in the coherence of brief passages. *Discourse Processes, 3,* 185-201.

Singer, M., & Ferreira, F. (1983). Inferring consequences in story comprehension. *Journal of Verbal Learning and Verbal Behavior, 22,* 437-448.

Smith F. (1971). *Understanding reading.* New York: Holt, Rinehart & Winston.

Smith, F. (1978). *Understanding reading* (2nd ed.). New York: Holt, Rinehart & Winston.

Spiro, R. J. (1975). *Inferential reconstruction in memory for connected discourse* (Tech. Rep. No. 2, ERIC Document Reproduction Service No. ED 136 187). Urbana, IL: University of Illinois, Center for the Study of Reading.

Spiro, R. J., & Smith, D. (1979). *Patterns of over-reliance on bottom-up and top-down processes in children.* Unpublished manuscript.

Stacey, R. (1978). A comparison of adults' and children's understanding of and memory for potential inference sentences. *Dissertation Abstracts, 38*(9-b), 4515-4516.

Thorndyke, P. W. (1976). The role of inferences in discourse comprehension. *Journal of Verbal Learning and Verbal Behavior, 15,* 437-446.

Tierney, R. J., Bridge, C., & Cera, M. J. (1978-1979). The discourse processing operations of children. *Reading Research Quarterly, 14,* 539-573.

Tierney, R. J., & Cunningham, J. W. (1984). Research on teaching reading comprehension. In P. D. Pearson (Ed.), *Handbook of reading research.* New York: Longman.

Tulving, E. (1972). Episodic and semantic memory. In E. Tulving & W. Donaldson (Eds.), *Organization of memory.* New York: Academic Press.

Tyler, R. W. (1930). Measuring the ability to infer. *Educational Research Bulletin, 9,* 475-480.

Warren, W. H., Nicholas, D. W., & Trabasso, T. (1977). Event chains and inferences in understanding narratives. In R. O. Freedle (Ed.), *Multidisciplinary approaches to discourse comprehension.* Hillsdale, NJ: Lawrence Erlbaum Associates.

13

READING TO LEARN: SETTING STUDENTS UP

Jill LaZansky
University of Illinois

Frank Spencer
Tuscon Unified School District

Michael Johnston
Tuscon Unified School District

Teachers have long been faced with the dilemma of preparing students to read to learn in ways which deemphasize the vicariousness of learning from prose but which, nonetheless, lead students to interpretations that are instructionally appropriate. Efforts to help the reading teacher deal with this dilemma have resulted in a number of recommendations, including, "preteach new vocabulary by drawing upon concepts already familiar to students" and "prompt students to use their prior experience to predict outcomes cued by story titles". Efforts to help the teacher of a content area deal with this dilemma have led reading educators and content area specialists to recommend the use of several rather distinctive instructional strategies, such as, the advance organizer, the structured overview, and pretesting. These and other recommended strategies for preparing students to read to learn fall under the category of prereading instruction, that is, instruction which precedes students' reading of text material.

The purpose of this chapter is to consider the *notion* of setting students up to read to learn and then the *task* of setting students up to read to learn in the context of content area instruction. Two questions provide the framework for this discussion.

1. What theoretical rationale underlies the notion of setting students up to read to learn?
2. How has the task of setting students up to read to learn been approached in the context of content area instruction?

In the process of addressing these two questions, some light will be shed on the extent to which the theoretical rationale underlying the notion of setting students up to read to learn is borne out in practice.

WHAT THEORETICAL RATIONALE UNDERLIES THE NOTION OF SETTING STUDENTS UP TO READ TO LEARN?

One can assume that setting students up prior to their reading of text material is typically prompted by a desire to have some sort of beneficial effect upon the outcome of students' reading. But this fact alone does not explain why one might expect, for example, that asking students prior to their reading of a story to predict story outcomes based upon the title of the story could have a facilitative effect upon students' understanding and/or recall of the story. This particular expectation can, however, be explained in light of what we now know about the nature of understanding, in particular the influence of what a reader already knows upon what he comprehends and remembers. (What a reader already knows, that is, the knowledge an individual already has prior to encountering unfamiliar or novel information, is frequently referred to as prior knowledge or background knowledge.)

Much of what we do know about the role of prior knowledge in comprehension was uncovered during the seventies when (a) several theories of comprehension and memory were advanced (e.g., Kintsch & van Dijk, 1978; Minsky, 1975; Rumelhart, 1978; Rumelhart, & Ortony, 1977; Schank & Abelson, 1977), theories which attempted to address the role of prior knowledge during processing, and (b) several landmark experiments were carried out (e.g., Anderson, Reynolds, Schallert & Goetz, 1977; Anderson, Spiro & Anderson, 1978; Bransford & Johnson, 1972; Schallert, 1976; Steffensen, Jogdeo & Anderson, 1978), experiments which demonstrated that prior knowledge plays not only a useful role but an integral role in individual efforts to comprehend and remember. In order to understand the notion of setting readers up to read to learn, it is important to understand the point of view regarding prior knowledge that emerged from this body of work.

What follows is a discussion that focuses upon the role of prior knowledge during processing as explained by schema theory, the theory most commonly associated with the work on prior knowledge that appeared in the seventies. Our purpose in addressing the role of prior knowledge from a schema point of view is to provide a theoretical basis or rationale for understanding the notion of setting students up to read to learn and for evaluating how the notion is approached in practice. This discussion of schema theory includes a fairly detailed description of the theory, however it does not include historical background on the concepts that are discussed. Several key experiments are related in order to elucidate particular points that are central to the theory. The discussion begins with a brief description of knowledge as it is presumed to exist in memory.

The Role of Prior Knowledge from the Point of View of Schema Theory

The term "schemata" (Rumelhart & Ortony, 1977) [also "frame" (Minsky, 1975) or "script" (Schank & Abelson, 1977)] is used to refer to highly abstract frameworks of knowledge that operate in a superordinate fashion to interpret information. Individually, schemata are prototypical representations of some aspect of world knowledge, and contain slots or placeholders which can be instantiated through an assignment of values (or information) from either the environment, memory or by default (inferred values) (Anderson, Pichert, Goetz, Schallert, Stevens & Trollip, 1976; Anderson et al., 1978; Rumelhart & Ortony, 1977). Collectively, these frames of knowledge form conceptual networks, and characterize in form and function the situational nature of knowledge and knowing.

Schemata become more definitive, that is, particularized or context-specific representations through contact with new information. The bringing together of knowledge structures and information (input or values) is attributed to an interaction staged by two simultaneously operating procedures: a top-down (or concept-driven) search for values which "fit," that is, meet the variable constraints of a knowledge frame; and a bottom-up (or data-driven) search for a knowledge frame(s) that will accommodate particular values (Bobrow & Norman, 1975; Rumelhart & Ortony, 1977). These two converging searches, in addition to accessing appropriate frames for interpretive purposes, effect the creation of new schemata or the modification of existing ones by means of the interaction they facilitate between existing knowledge and new information, an interaction which is reflected in the interpretation constructed or reconstructed during attempts to comprehend and remember. Central to this theory is the argument that interpretation is a function of the high-level schemata employed during comprehension and recall, as well as the corresponding fit between the selected schemata and information to be learned and remembered.

If, indeed, high-level knowledge structures are integral to interpreting new information, then unsuccessful attempts to select appropriate frameworks should diminish an individual's ability to understand a given set of information. The results of a study by Bransford and Johnson (1972) provide support for this prediction. Subjects were asked to read a paragraph which made the task of selecting an appropriate schemata an especially difficult one for some subjects. The paragraph described the scene of a modern day Romeo, and was written so as to make little sense unless the reader were first shown a picture that depicted the scene described in the text. In other words, the paragraph included information that did not readily fit more than one interpretive frame, and the appropriate interpretation was not an obvious one unless one were cued via an accurate pictorial rendition of the scene. Subjects who were shown the picture accurately recalled much of the paragraph. Subjects who were not shown the picture or who were shown a picture that was inconsistent with the information in the paragraph performed poorly on recall measures. In this highly contrived instance, making *any* real sense of the passage was contingent upon the successful selection of a specific knowledge framework, because few (if any) alternate frameworks would adequately accommodate the given information, and, as reported, unsuccessful selection tended to impair understanding. These results implicate a positive relationship between readers' selected interpretive frames and their ability to interpret new information.

Subsequent research served to extend this finding, exemplifying: (a) the influence of readers' background knowledge upon their selection of interpretive frames; as well as (b) the nature of the influence of selected knowledge frames upon readers' recall of information. The former was addressed in a study by Anderson, et al. (1977) who created passages which individually supported two equally appropriate interpretive frames or schemata. Other studies also have used ambiguous passages, together with biasing titles (Schallert, 1976), as well as embedded character names (Brown, Smiley, Day, Townsend, & Lawton, 1977), for purposes of demonstrating through controlled manipulation the influence of high-level schemata upon interpretive outcomes. In the case of the frequently cited Anderson et al. (1977) study, however, the manipulation was achieved by selecting subjects with differing amounts of knowledge about particular topics rather than overtly cueing selection of high-level schemata. Physical education students and music students were asked to read and recall two passages, each passage designed to support two equally appropriate but topically diverse interpretations. In accordance with the logic of the design, if high-level schemata significantly affect interpretive outcomes, then in this case, subjects' perspective selection should manifest this highly confounding influence in a predictive fashion. Further, if the more familiar a topic (i.e., a perspective) the more developed or elaborate its conceptual representation in memory, then if an interpretive bias were to surface, it would likely surface in the direction of the more familiar topic (i.e., the more elaborate schemata embodying knowledge about the content of the text). The experimenters reported that more physical education students took a wrestling perspective in response to a prison/wrestling passage and a card perspective in response to a card/music passage; music students took the counter perspective in each case. This tendency on the part of the students to interpret a passage in terms of the perspective most indicative of their respective backgrounds of experience resulted in a differential recall of the passages that depicted a strong effect of readers' background knowledge upon their selection of interpretive frames.

Corroborative evidence in this regard emerged from a similar study by Steffensen et al. (1978). Subject selection was again the means for engineering a biasing effect, except in this instance subject selection was based upon differences in cultural background. An important feature of the study was its attempt to distinguish the influence of background knowledge upon comprehension and recall of topically familiar (native) discourse *from* its influence upon topicallly unfamiliar (non-native) discourse. This effort facilitated a differential account of characteristics of recall when the factor of relevant background knowledge was presumed high and when it was presumed low. Rather than using ambiguous passages the experimenters asked subjects from the United States and India to read and recall two letters, one describing an East Indian wedding, the other describing an American wedding. It was reported that subjects read the native passage more rapidly than the non-native passage, recalled a greater amount of the native passage, and produced not only more culturally consistent elaboration when recalling the native passage but more culturally-biased distortions when reading the non-native passage. As in the Anderson et al. (1977) study where subjects' background knowledge proved to be a good predictor of subjects' perspective selection, background knowledge again manifested a biasing influence by facilitating more accurate recall of information important to (typical of) the selected interpretive framework than information which was not characteristic of the prototype.

As the latter results illustrate, interpretive bias can have a debilitating as well as a facilitating effect depending upon the relationship between new information and readers' interpretive frameworks, that is, the match between the information to be interpreted and slots in readers' selected schemata. This circumstance was shown to be no less the case when, in a study by Anderson et al. (1978), both passages used in the experiment assumed presupposed frameworks that were familiar. Selected character names and food items were embedded in each of two passages: a description of "a meal at a fine restaurant," and a description of "a trip to a supermarket." Individual subjects read and recalled one of the two. The experimenters reported that the restaurant setting facilitated greater recall of the food items, and led subjects to more consistently recall which food items were matched in the passage with which characters. Further, when food categories were identified and rated on a scale reflecting the probability of their being included in a restaurant schema, it was found that the restaurant passage facilitated greater recall of high probability food items than did the supermarket passage, but no better recall of low probability items. The authors suggested that although the target information made perfect sense in the context of either of the two passages, it had special significance within the restaurant setting but no particular significance within the supermarket setting. The restaurant scheme would then better accommodate the target values, because it would more likely include slots for the instantiation of these elements than the supermarket schema. The provision of slots within high-level schema has implications for interpretive outcomes, or so suggests the "ideational scaffolding" hypothesis, because when "information fits a slot it will be instantiated as part of the encoded representation for the text" (Anderson et al., 1978, p. 438).

The biasing effects of high-level schemata are probably nowhere more clearly isolated experimentally than in those landmark studies just cited. If collectively these particular experiments build a case for any one argument, it is the argument that "the schemata embodying background knowledge about the content of a discourse exert a profound influence on how well the discourse will be comprehended, learned, and remembered" (Steffensen, Jogdeo & Anderson, 1978, p. 14). In fact as alluded to earlier, the many and varied distortions and intrusions which surface in recall are striking evidence of this confounding of existing knowledge with new information, and according to Anderson et al. (1977) are not unlikely when: (a) a text is incompletely specified and a reader must rely heavily upon existing knowledge to fill in apparent gaps; or (b) when the set of relations a reader expects on the basis of a schema is deliberately distorted by the author; or (c) when the reader simply selects schemata which differ significantly from that of the author; or (d) when a message is capable of being assimilated to more than one high-level schemata, which happened to be the case in the Anderson et al. (1977) study described previously.

Conclusions Regarding Setting Students Up to Read to Learn

What can we conclude about the notion of setting readers up to read to learn in light of what we know about the influence of prior knowledge? First, we can conclude that the notion is a legitimate one if by "setting up" we mean preparing students to process information in such a way that there is an interaction between what students already know and what they encounter in text. In other words, it is reasonable to expect some beneficial effects to accompany setting students up when, as a result of setting up, students are successfully led to select and employ appropriate interpretive frames. Second, we can conclude that any time students are likely to experience minimal interaction between what they already know and what they are going to encounter in text is a time to consider setting them up prior to their reading. Minimal interaction is probably most likely to occur (a) when students are not apt to recognize relationships between new information and what they already know, (b) when students simply possess little knowledge that can be easily or appropriately related to new information, or (c) when students are compelled to avoid or suppress attempts to relate known and new information because, for example, they are in pursuit of predetermined interpretations. Third, we can also conclude that the goal associated with setting students up (i.e., preparing students to process information in such a way that there is an interaction between what students already know and what they encounter in the text) is an important one because when interaction is minimal, not only is individual and/or accurate interpretation sacrificed but the most basic of instructional goals is sacrificed as well: namely, the opportunity to elaborate upon and/or modify existing knowledge.

What can we conclude about how to approach the task of setting students up to read to learn in light of what we know about the influence of prior knowledge? Actually, there are some very important conclusions that can be drawn.

1. The state of students' background knowledge as it relates to (a) the information students will encounter in text material, and (b) the objectives associated with students' reading of text material, should have a bearing upon how students are set up to read to learn.
2. It is important to prepare students to utilize an appropriate framework for interpreting the information they will encounter.

The first conclusion specifies what are prerequisites for setting students up to read to learn: at least some knowledge of students' existing states of understanding, the nature of the content to be read and the objectives associated with the task of reading. These prerequisites are rather self-evident since it would be difficult to make decisions regarding how to go about setting up a group of students if one did not know the specific characteristics of the instructional situation. The second conclusion specifies what is a fundamental aspect of the task of setting students up to read to learn: preparing students to utilize an appropriate framework for interpreting the information they will encounter. From a practical standpoint, what this particular aspect of setting students up entails depends upon the nature of the instructional situation in which students are being set up. First, it may, and frequently does, entail preparing students to use their background knowledge by (a) bringing to students' attention existing knowledge that is relevent, or (b) assisting students in the development of necessary background knowledge. In some instructional situations preparing students to use their background knowledge may require that familiar information which is relevant be cited or possibly reviewed, however, it can require that several concepts unfamiliar to students be taught. Second, preparing students to use an appropriate framework may also entail making students aware of the information they should read to find out about. In other words, it may be necessary to assist students in setting specific purposes for reading. Third, in an effort to prompt students to utilize an appropriate framework, it may also be necessary to address the relationships between new concepts students will encounter in the text and relevant concepts that are already familiar to students.

Is there more to the task of setting students up to read to learn? In other words, is it enough to prepare students to utilize an appropriate framework for interpreting the information they will encounter in order to facilitate the interaction between background knowledge and new information during reading? We argue that it is not always enough. Schallert (1976) illustrated this in part in a study where subjects were not only cued via biasing titles, but both task instructions and exposure duration were manipulated in order that subjects' level of processing would be effected differentially. (By level of processing is meant the degree of semantic analysis. "Depth of processing refers to a hierarchy of stages through which incoming stimuli are processed, where preliminary stages involve the analysis of physical features and later stages are concerned with the extraction of meaning" [Schallert, 1976, p. 622].) Schallert reported that the cues had a facilitative effect on both recall and recognition, but that the effect was restricted to conditions which demanded a more semantic kind of information processing.

In light of these results we have been led to conclude that, generally speaking, it would be not only naive but foolish to assume that students will process information to the extent that they should, just as it would be unwise to assume that students will automatically select the appropriate framework in which to interpret a set of ideas. In other words, the task of setting students up to read to learn should take into account not only students' background knowledge, but the issue of level of processing as well because, for a student, knowing how to approach the task of reading to learn is as essential as knowing how to approach the content. This particular conclusion suggests to us that the task of setting students up should be approached with at least two additional points in mind.

3. The ability of students to meet the particular processing demands

associated with the task of reading to learn should have a bearing upon how students are set up to read to learn.

4. It is important to prepare students to engage in the most appropriate processing of the ideas they will encounter in the text they are being set up to read.

The former point specifies another prerequisite for setting students up to read to learn: a knowledge of students' ability to appropriately process the ideas they will encounter in the text material. The latter point specifies what is a third aspect of the task of setting students up to read to learn: prepare students to engage in appropriate processing of ideas. Translated into practice this may mean alerting students to the type of reading it will take to appropriately address the information they will encounter in the text. It may also mean engaging students in the type of prereading tasks that make appropriate processing demands upon them prior to their encounter with the text they are being prepared to read.

Of what particular significance are the conclusions that have been drawn here regarding the task of setting students up to read to learn? Collectively, the conclusions we have drawn here provide a very basic framework for thinking about the task of setting students up to read to learn. Figure 13.1 summarizes the conclusions in the form of a diagram. What Figure 13.1 elucidates quite clearly is the fact that there are a number of variables associated with the task of setting students up to read to learn. The variables cited in the upper left portion of the figure are characteristics of instructional situations which should have a bearing upon what fundamental prereading objectives are associated with the task of setting students up. Then, as the figure indicates, these two sets of variables, together, should determine how students are set up, that is, the specific strategy for setting students up.

HOW HAS THE TASK OF SETTING STUDENTS UP
TO READ TO LEARN BEEN APPROACHED
IN THE CONTEXT OF CONTENT AREA INSTRUCTION?

Over the years several different strategies have been recommended for purposes of preparing students (typically secondary level students) to read to learn in the context of content area instruction. Some have found their way into instructional settings more than have others. Central to any discussion of the specific nature of these recommendations and their adequacy is an important fact: the fact that there is a great deal of diversity among instructional situations in which it would be desirable to set students up to read to learn.

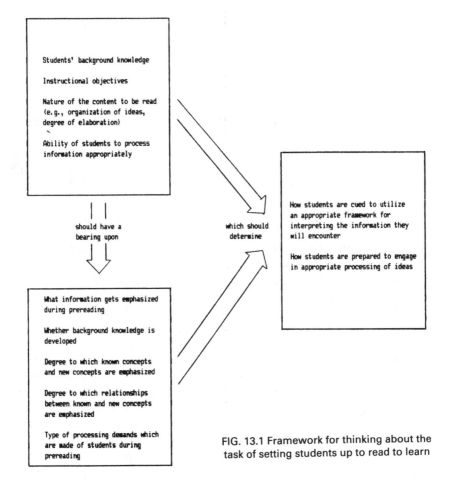

FIG. 13.1 Framework for thinking about the task of setting students up to read to learn

The fact that there is diversity among instructional situations is important because it suggests that many of those factors which should have a bearing upon how students are set up to read (i.e., the type of content that is being studied, the nature of the text material being read, the ability level of students, the nature of students' background knowledge, and the purpose for which students are being set up to read) are likely to vary considerably from situation to situation. This implies a couple of important things: (a) the specific needs associated with setting students up are situational and thus are likely to vary across instructional settings, and (b) what is appropriate for purposes of setting students up in one situation is not necessarily appropriate in all situations.

In light of the diversity that exists among instructional situations it is obvious that the problem of setting students up to read has no single solution. It should come as no surprise, then, that efforts to deal with the problem have resulted in the development of a variety of very different strategies. It should also come as no surprise that differences among the various recommended strategies are due to differences in those variables cited previously in Figure 13.1. To be more specific, the apparent diversity among strategies is due to (a) differences regarding which particular prereading objectives the strategies can be used to achieve, and (b) how the strategies go about facilitating particular prereading objectives.

We examined and compared several strategies that have been recommended for purposes of setting readers up to read to learn. The fact that the strategies do not all approach the facilitation of particular objectives in the same way was quite obvious. For example, we observed that highlighting relationships between particular concepts is sometimes approached using a diagram, sometimes with the aid of discussion, other times a short prepared passage that contrasts ideas is used, while in still other instances compare-contrast exercises based upon relevant information are utilized.

The fact that much of the apparent diversity among strategies is also due to differences regarding which particular prereading objectives the strategies can be used to achieve is a fact that is not so obvious but nonetheless very important. We observed, for example, that some strategies assume the existence of certain prior knowledge and attempt to mobilize it, while other strategies attempt to build background knowledge where none exists. We concluded, therefore, that the strategies are not all based upon the same assumptions regarding students' background knowledge. We also observed that some strategies do no more than highlight known concepts which relate to those students will encounter in the text, while other strategies not only highlight known and new concepts but emphasize the relationships between the two as well. This observation led us to conclude that the strategies do not all emphasize known concepts, new concepts and the relationships between the two to the same degree. It also became apparent as we compared the various strategies that prereading strategies do not all make the same types of processing demands of students. For example, some strategies represent an attempt to really engage students' thinking by requiring them to determine key relationships between concepts, while other strategies do no more than require students to review a few selected concepts that are familiar and that relate to those about which they are to read.

The fact that there are differences among recommended strategies is an important one because it means that no one strategy is applicable in all instructional situations. Furthermore, it implies that practitioners cannot be arbitrary about their selection of a prereading strategy, or for that matter, arbitrarily implement a particular strategy across a variety of instructional situations. The veracity of this circumstance will become increasingly clear as we share our thinking about four strategies, each of which at some point in time has been recommended for purposes of setting students up to read to learn in the context of content area instruction. We selected these particular four strategies for discussion because they differ considerably from one another in terms of how the task of setting students up is approached. Our purpose in singling them out is threefold: (a) to further elucidate how the task of setting students up to read to learn has been approached, (b) to illustrate the idiosyncratic nature of individual strategies, and (c) to highlight the nature of existing differences among strategies. Included in our treatment of each strategy is (a) a description of the strategy, (b) some mention of research addressing its effectiveness, if such research exists, and (c) a critical discussion of the strategy in light of what we assume to be its more notable strengths as a prereading strategy and its more notable weaknesses. Our comments are, for the most part, an outcome of thinking about the strategies in terms of those variables cited in Figure 13.1. Following our discussion of all four strategies we will briefly compare them on the basis of the prereading objectives they can be used to achieve.

Advance Organizer

Possibly the most controversial recommended strategy for setting students up to read to learn is the advance organizer. It is undoubtedly the most theoretically driven strategy as well (with the exception of the structured overview, its distant cousin), since it is based directly upon subsumption theory (Ausubel, 1962), a theory which suggests that meaningful learning is dependent upon the logical relatability of new concepts to a learner's established cognitive structure. The organizer itself is a passage read in advance of material that is to be learned, and is designed to provide a reader with a conceptual framework "which both (a) gives him a general overview of the more detailed material in advance of his actual confrontation with it, and (b) also provides organizing elements that are inclusive of and take into account most relevantly and efficiently the *particular content* contained in the material" (Ausubel, 1963, p. 219). A critical feature of the organizer according to Ausubel is that it is formulated in terms that are already familiar to the learner, but at a higher level of abstraction, generality and inclusiveness than the text that follows. Ausubel draws a further distinction between an expository organizer and a comparative organizer: an expository organizer is a passage that is used with unfamiliar material to provide concepts which will act as subsumers to information the reader is about to encounter;

whereas, a comparative organizer is a passage that precedes familiar material to facilitate the integration of new ideas, as well as increase the discriminability of concepts covered in the passage from readers' existing knowledge.

For almost two decades attempts have been made to replicate the successes of Ausubel's early advance organizer research. Comparatively speaking, results are incongruous (Barnes & Clawson, 1975; Faw & Waller, 1976; Hartley & Davies, 1976; Lawton & Wanska, 1977; Sledge, 1978). In short, the many attempts to operationalize Ausubel's strategy are insufficient evidence to either confirm or discount the facilitative effect of advance organizers. Efforts have been made to synthesize findings associated with these many attempts. However, there is good reason to question these syntheses since in some cases comparisons were made when only one variable was common to the studies compared (Lawton & Wanska, 1977).

One possible explanation for the incongruous results lies in the fact that research has vitually failed to settle upon the form and substance of a well-constructed organizer. Since its initial introduction, organizer research has been criticized both for the development of ill-conceived organizers on the part of many attempting to replicate Ausubel's early work, as well as inappropriate instructional and experimental use of the strategy. But, as Ausubel (1978) points out, "apart from describing organizers in general terms with an appropriate example, one cannot be more specific about the construction of an organizer. For this always depends on the nature of the learning material, the age of the learner, and his degree of prior familiarity with the learning passage" (p. 251). In other words, developing an advance organizer in accordance with Ausubel's general specifications means coming to terms with the rather elusive concepts of abstract, general, and inclusive as they apply to specific text material intended for use with particular learners. From our point of view, this particular circumstance constitutes the single greatest limitation associated with the advance organizer, namely the fact that Ausubel's definition loses much of its definitiveness when examined in the context of a range of readers and texts. This circumstance also explains why the organizer has all but defied systematic replication, as does the fact that when considering its effectiveness, less attention has been given to manipulating features of the organizer then has been given to manipulating other characteristics of the learning environment. The bottom line is this. The advance organizer is a strategy which is theoretically-speaking somewhat promising. The information that appears in the passage is selected on the basis of the particular information students will encounter in the text they are being prepared to read as well as students' existing states of understanding, a circumstance which constitutes probably the greatest strength associated with the advance organizer. However, practically-speaking, an organizer is quite difficult and time-consuming to design in light of the fact that it is a piece of prose which must make sense in and of itself, must represent ideas in terms that are already familiar to students, as well as represent ideas at a higher level of abstraction, generality, and inclusiveness than the text that follows.

We also suspect that in addition to there being good reason to question the practicality of the organizer, there is good reason to question its potential effectiveness as a prereading strategy. In the first place, advance organizers do not address precisely that information which students will encounter when they read the text but rather address information related to but more general than that about which students will read. This being the case, the effectiveness of the organizer is contingent in part upon students' recognition of the relationship between the information they read about in the organizer and the information they read about subsequent to prereading. We question whether it is altogether realistic to assume that students will recognize this relationship.

A second reason to challenge the potential effectiveness of the advance organizer has to do with the fact that the organizer is simply a short passage of prose. As such, we question its ability to facilitate the development of background knowledge where none exists. While it is true that there is little known about the creation of new frames, it seems not only a bit presumptuous but naive as well, to liken the creation of background knowledge with a simple adaption of an imposed framework via a short prepassage. As Anderson, et al. (1978) suggest, when the reader does not possess relevant schemata, there is no good reason to suppose that they can be acquired from a few abstractly worded sentences.

We also question whether a prepassage has the potential to prompt students to engage in appropriate processing of ideas. In other words, can a short prepassage prepare students to address ideas in the way that they should to the extent that they should? We argue that if the task of reading to learn is something students need to be set up to do, asking students to simply read to learn during prereading may not be all that beneficial, especially if how to go about reading to learn is as much a mystery to students as how to approach the content.

Structured Overview

The structured overview is a prereading approach designed to emphasize the organization of content material through the use of two strategies: graphic outline and group discussion. As the strategy was originally conceived, a diagram is constructed by the teacher to depict relationships between selected content vocabulary, a diagram that can take any number of forms depending upon the state of students' understanding, the nature of the content to be diagrammed, and the instructional objectives associated with the prereading lesson. A discussion of the diagram is then used to clarify the relationships between the different concepts depicted in the overview, while promoting their integration within previously learned concepts. Together, the diagram and the discussion purportedly (a) introduce technical vocabulary, (b) represent them conceptually within a logical framework, (c) portray relationships between new vocabulary and previously learned concepts, and (d) clarify learning objectives. Barron (1969) likens the structured overview to the advance organizer.

> The overview assumes the properties of Ausubel's advance organizers. It attempts to relate new content information to relevent subsuming concepts that have previously been learned. At the same time, pupils are given cues as to how the structure of the new unit relates to the structure of the course as a whole. (p. 33)

On the surface the overview would appear to have more going for it than most recommended strategies: it highlights known concepts, new concepts as well as the relationships between the two; it addresses some of the very ideas students will later encounter in the text; it serves as a model of sorts, illustrating one way to go about organizing a set of ideas; it can accomodate a fairly elaborate presentation of information; it uses both visual display and discussion to clarify key concepts and key relationships between concepts. However, the limited number of experimental attempts to evaluate the use of the structured overview both as part of content area instruction and in relation to other prereading strategies (e.g., Earle, 1969, 1973; Estes, Mills, & Barron, 1969; Hash, 1974) provide little support for its effectiveness (Smith, 1978). Therefore, our discussion of the overview is based primarily upon our own observations which, as it turns out, have led us to conclude that the overview is one strategy for which the supposed strengths far outweigh the supposed weaknesses.

Possibly the greatest weakness or limitation associated with the structured overview is the fact that it may not always be appropriate to diagram the relationships between concepts. Why? Some critics suggest that when information covered by a text is already quite explicit and relationships between concepts are easily discernable, imposing an additional outline or organization may interfere with processing (Jenkins & Bausell, 1976). For this reason, Jenkins and Bausell (1976) recommend restricting the use of the overview to materials that tend to be contextually abstract. It has also been suggested that some text material does not readily lend itself to visual display. What is more accurately the case is that the relationships between some sets of ideas can be easily represented in the form of a diagram and are, in fact, much clearer when depicted diagramatically, while other sets of ideas are difficult to represent in a diagram and doing so seems to serve no real purpose.

As far as strengths are concerned, there appear to be several associated with the overview. First and foremost is the fact that the overview strategy can be designed to (a) emphasize new concepts and/or previously learned concepts, as well as (b) depict relationships between concepts. Because this is the case, the overview is a strategy that can accomodate a variety of different prereading objectives. It can be used to assist students in developing appropriate background knowledge prior to their encounter with the text. It can be used to highlight relationships between relevent background knowledge and new concepts when, for example, an author's treatment of a particular topic fails to point out how new information relates to information previously covered by the author or when it may be difficult for students to recognize important distinctions between what they already know and the new information they will encounter. It can be used to depict the most important relationships between ideas students will encounter in the text when, for example, the text is poorly organized. It can be used to compare two or more perspectives of the same topic or issue. In short, the overview is a strategy that can be adapted to meet the needs of a variety of instructional situations.

Another critical characteristic of the overview is the discussion aspect of the strategy, which we consider to be particularly advantageous for several reasons. First, it provides an opportunity for not only detecting misconceptions students may have prior to their encounter with new material, but for clearing up those misconceptions as well. Second, if implemented skillfully, the discussion phase of the overview strategy can serve to engage students in the appropriate processing of ideas. In other words, together with the diagram, the discussion has the potential to prompt students prior to their encounter with the text to begin addressing ideas in much the same way they should once they begin reading the text, if, that is, the discussion is used to teach and set into motion appropriate reasoning.

It is also noteworthy that, unlike many other strategies, the overview can accommodate a very broad as well as a relatively elaborate presentation of information. In other words, an overview can quite easily be used to highlight any number of concepts and depict any number of relationships between concepts. Ausubel (1978) suggests that the overview achieves its effect largely by the simple omission of specific detail. This particular observation suggests to us that there may be a point at which undue elaboration begins to jeopardize the facilitative effect of the overview. Specifically, a highly detailed overview may divert the attention of students away from main ideas, or simply fail to focus upon any particular concepts and/or relationships, and thereby impede the development of specific lines of inquiry which could lead students purposefully through an author's message. It would appear, therefore, that even though, unlike many other strategies, the overview can accomodate a large body of information, the amount of information included in an overview is a factor that must be carefully weighed.

SQ3R

SQ3R is a study method developed by Robinson (1946) to provide students with a systematic approach to reading textbook material. It is a study method that incorporates the use of five different strategies: surveying, questioning, reading, reciting and reviewing. While SQ3R is designed to take students through textbook material, in the process it sets students up prior to leading them through a portion of text. Before commenting on its prereading components, we will briefly describe all the components of the SQ3R method, components which Robinson (1961) suggests are individually reasonably well-founded in research, but which, together as a method, have been subjected to little experimentation (Spencer, 1978).

The SQ3R study procedure requires students to initially *survey* the text material they are about to read by reading and thinking about the title of the chapter, the opening paragraphs, the headings and subheadings, the closing paragraphs, and any questions that appear at the end of the material. The purpose of the survey component is to provide students with an overview of the chapter. Following the initial survey of the text, students are required to locate the first heading (i.e., a topic the appears in boldface print) in the chapter, read it and restructure it into a *question*. The purpose behind the question component of the method is to provide very specific purposes for reading (Forgan & Mangrum, 1976). Students are then directed to *read* the material that immediately follows the heading to find the answer to the question. Once the answer is ascertained students are required to pause, think about the answer, put it in their own words (*recite* it), and make written note of both the question and its answer. This question-read-recite procedure is repeated as many times as is necessary as students make their way through the chapter from one heading to another. When the final heading has been read, restructured into a question, answered, and the answer recited, students are then directed to *review*. This review component requires students to reread all written notes, as well as go back through the chapter, reread each heading and attempt to recall the key ideas associated with it. The specific purposes behind the recite and review components are to facilitate self-comprehension checks and fix information in memory (Forgan & Mangrum, 1976).

Since SQ3R is a multi-strategy approach to textbook reading, it should come as no surprise that it is reputedly a very demanding study method for students to implement. In fact, it has been recommended that each component of the procedure be explained and practiced before students attempt to use the method as a whole (Wooster, 1958). It has also been suggested that the procedure be introduced late in students' high school career to insure better independent application of the strategy by mature readers (Niles, 1967).

What we perceive to be the greatest strength associated with the prereading components of SQ3R (i.e., the survey and question components) is possibly also the greatest weakness: namely, the fact that the strategies of survey and question require students to make use of existing textbook cues before beginning to read. There are at least three notable limitations associated with the fact that, in the case of SQ3R, students are required to base their prereading assumptions upon existing textbook cues. First, in requiring students to rely solely upon textbook cues as they do, the strategies of survey and question encourage a highly text-based search for information. They do not assist students in building appropriate background knowledge when none exists, nor do they directly facilitate the interaction between students' background knowledge and what students are about to encounter in the text. Rather the uninformed student who comes to the text with little or no relevant background knowledge to speak of, is left with no other source of information with which to interact aside from the text itself. Secondly, using textbook headings and subheadings as cues assumes that the headings and subheadings reflect key concepts associated with the topic about which students are to read and the logical organization of those concepts. When this assumption does not hold true, that is when, for example, textbook headings do not accurately depict the author's message or when the questions derived from the headings do not lead students to seek main ideas, the strategies of survey and question may only serve to mislead students. Finally, requiring students to rely solely upon existing textbook cues sets students up to pursue the textbook author's perspective of a topic. The danger in this is that students might be less likely to process ideas in an integrated fashion. In other words, students might be less compelled to relate what they do know to new concepts they encounter during their reading of the text. Students might also be less likely to formulate alternative perspectives of a topic.

There are also a couple of fairly obvious advantages to requiring students to use existing textbook cues. First and foremost, the students need not rely upon some teacher-prepared adjunct for purposes of preparing to read textbook material. Rather, once they become familiar with the strategies of survey and question, students can apply them independently any time anywhere. Secondly, requiring students to use existing textbook cues makes the relationship between prereading and the task of reading to learn a fairly obvious one. We view this as an advantage since when students do not recognize the relationship between a prereading exercise and a textbook assignment (which is sometimes the case), it is less likely that they will apply the fruits of prereading during their efforts to read to learn.

One other characteristic of the prereading phase of SQ3R that we feel has potential merit is the use of questions to direct students' reading of textbook material. While we just previously drew into question the use of chapter subheadings as a basis for questioning, we do consider the use of questions worthwhile in a couple of respects. First, the questions cue students to approach text material with specific purposes in mind. For example, rather than approaching an entire textbook chapter on the Civil War with one rather broad objective in mind, "to find out about the Civil War", students are cued to make their way through the chapter one section at a time with a particular question to guide their reading of each section. The result is that students' reading is likely to be much more purposefully driven because, when the questions are good ones, students know specifically what information they should seek to derive from the material. Secondly, the use of questions to direct students' reading places the notion of inquiry and the notion of reading to learn in coincidence with one another. The advantage to this as we see it is that the role of the reader with respect to the task of reading to learn becomes a bit more defined.

Pretests

The term "pretest", unlike our references to other strategies, alludes to a variety of preinstructional tasks which can vary substantially from one another along several dimensions (e.g., response format, comprehensiveness, task demands), but which collectively share a common goal: assessment. Pretests are typically developed to aid teachers in assessing students' background knowledge prior to the introduction of a new topic and/or new set of concepts. The purpose behind such assessment tends to vary, although typically teachers use pretest results as a basis for making important instructional decisions regarding what gets covered and how, or as a basis for measuring the amount of learning that has taken place as a result of instruction.

Over the years it has been suggested that pretests should not be treated as simply assessment devices. In fact, it has been argued that pretests can have an impact upon subsequent learning in some of the same ways that strategies designed to set students up to read to learn do. As early as 1926, Pressey suggested that in the process of achieving certain assessment goals, pretests also increase students' sensitivity to a learning situation, lead students to evaluate subsequent learning tasks in terms of their apparent relevancy, and serve to categorize learning tasks, thus increasing the likelihood of generalization. It is in light of the fact that pretests are associated with the achievement of certain prereading goals that pretests are included in our discussion of strategies recommended for purposes of setting students up to read to learn.

Research on the topic of pretesting has been extensive, and for the most part, supportive of the facilitative effect of pretests upon posttest performance. However, as several studies have pointed out (in particular research on prequestions), the facilitative effect of a pretest upon posttest performance is highly conditional (Anderson & Biddle, 1975; Hartley & Davies, 1976; Rickards, 1976), apparently a function of several factors, including the following: whether the pretest tests the important information in the text, whether the text is difficult for the learner to understand, and whether the learner is held accountable for *only* the information targeted by the pretest. What pretests apparently do not readily improve is *general* comprehension and recall of prose. Rather, they tend to restrict learning of this type (Anderson & Biddle, 1975) and, like objectives, typically emphasize intentional learning over incidental learning.

We suppose the greatest weakness associated with pretesting as a prereading strategy to be the way in which information is presented (e.g., via short answer questions, true-false items, multiple choice items). We base this particular conclusion on three observations. First, tests tend to provide a less than integrative depiction of information. In other words, it is not always clear from test items how information cited in the items relates to what students already know, or for that matter, how the various concepts or ideas cited in the items relate to one another. Because of this tendency, it would not be surprising if students who based their prereading assumptions upon pretest items found it difficult to select a framework within which the various concepts they encounter in text could be collectively interpreted. Secondly, tests typically target only selected concepts. From a schema point of view this is likely to diminish recall of other information not targeted during pretesting, especially since, in the case of tests, relationships between ideas are typically not intentionally emphasized. Third, while tests typically highlight concepts, they rarely explain or elaborate upon them. As a result, a pretest may be effective when it comes to cueing students to access appropriate knowledge, but it is unlikely that pretests would meet the needs of students who should develop appropriate background knowledge before attempting to read to learn.

As far as strengths are concerned, the most obvious is the fact that pretests typically cite the very information for which teachers intend to hold students accountable. The advantage to this is that students can treat the test items as cues to what they should read to find out about. In other words, the test items can assist students in setting specific purposes for reading.

A somewhat less obvious strength has to do with the assessment aspect of pretests. Specifically, we suppose that the use of pretests for prereading purposes serves to emphasize the role of students' self-assessment prior to reading. By self-assessment we mean a students' evaluation of his or her own existing state of understanding in light of the demands associated with the subsequent task of reading to learn. This is not to say that the forms which pretesting typically assumes (e.g., short answer questions, multiple choice items) serve as models for the process of self-assessment. However, since pretests do represent information in an assessment framework, pretests may represent a more direct approach to inciting self-assessment than most other prereading strategies. In addition, the emphasis upon assessing information prior to reading, especially when coupled with recall subsequent to reading (i.e., posttesting), has the advantage of placing assessment and the task of reading to learn in obvious coincidence with one another. We argue that bringing the less obvious purpose of prereading assessment in coincidence with the more obvious purpose of postreading assessment, highlights the role of evaluating understanding along the road to understanding. However, as we see it, the challenge of designing a pretest which initiates this type of self-assessment lies in using some form of testing to key in on important concepts and their relationships to the broader topic at hand in a way which brings appropriate background knowledge into focus as well. In other words, the challenge lies in designing pretests that not only alert students to what it is they do not know that is relevant, but which also alert students to what it is they do know that is relevant.

Comparative Remarks

We chose to discuss the advance organizer, the structured overview, SQ3R and the pretest because they approach the task of setting students up so differently from one another. As it turns out, they also differ considerably from one another in terms of the prereading objectives they can be used to achieve.

How do the four strategies compare in terms of the task of building background knowledge? Building background knowledge is the prereading objective we probably know the least about because there are still many questions yet to be answered about the process of knowledge acquisition. However, even though our understanding is limited, there is little doubt in our minds that the structured overview is the one strategy of the four previously discussed that could readily accomodate the needs of students who should develop background knowledge prior to their encounter with unfamiliar text material. Unlike the other three strategies, the overview strategy lends itself to not only highlighting new concepts, but explaining them to what ever degree is necessary and relating them to what is already known. In short, because the overview facilitates both a depiction of information as well as a discussion of it, it allows a teacher to do more than draw attention to particular concepts; it allows a teacher to facilitate an understanding of those concepts that are necessary for an understanding of the text students are being prepared to read. While it is true that the organizer was also designed to accomodate the needs of students who should develop background knowledge, as we discussed previously there is good reason to suspect it is not apt to do so.

How do the four strategies compare in terms of the task of prompting students to access existing knowledge? Unlike building background knowledge, alerting students to information they already know that is relevant is a prereading objective that each of the four strategies could be used to achieve. However, it is probably the exception rather than the rule that the strategies of SQ3R and pretesting would, since they are strategies which typically address known information that is relevant only incidentally. In the case of SQ3R, cues regarding relevant background knowledge would have to already exist in the textbook chapter (i.e., as part of chapter headings, opening and closing paragraphs, and/or end-of-the-chapter questions). In the case of pretests, cues would have to exist in the form of test items that, for example, are worded in such a way so as to alert students to the relevancy of particular background information, or that actually require students to make use of known information that is relevant while in the throes of addressing new information. The advance organizer and the structured overview, on the other hand, can and typically do accomodate the task of cueing students to access existing knowledge. However, there are important differences in how these two strategies go about doing it. In the case of the organizer, students are made aware of existing knowledge that is relevant via cues embedded in prose. In the case of the overview, students are made aware via cues embedded in a diagram and emphasized during an oral discussion. Furthermore, unlike the organizer, in the overview the cues typically appear in the context of explicit references to new information students are about to encounter in the text.

How do the four strategies compare in terms of the task of highlighting new information that is important? In the case of the prereading components of SQ3R and pretesting, fairly explicit references are made to information in the text students should attend to or focus upon as they read. However, as noted earlier, these strategies typically do not emphasize the relationships between the ideas they highlight. As a result, students are likely to approach the text with specific purposes for reading in mind, but not with an overall framework in which to interpret individual concepts or ideas in light of one another. The organizer attempts to highlight particular key information in exactly the opposite way. It is designed to cue students to pay attention to particular information by providing a conceptual framework that is more general than those ideas students will encounter in the text rather than by referencing the specific ideas about which students will read. The overview essentially achieves the task of highlighting new information that is important both by providing an interpretive framework *and* by referencing specific concepts students will encounter when they read the text. In the case of the overview, students are typically led to recognize what concepts or ideas they need to focus upon as they read and how to organize the information related to those concepts as they read about them.

How do the strategies compare in terms of the task of addressing relationships between ideas? As far as pointing out relationships between concepts, only two of the four strategies can be said to actually accomodate this objective: the advance organizer and the structured overview. The overview is specifically designed to depict relationships between ideas in a very explicit fashion. Furthermore, it can be used to address relationships between known concepts, between new concepts, as well as between known and new concepts. The organizer, on the other hand, is designed to present familiar ideas in such a way that students have a framework for interpreting new information they will encounter. What this suggests is that relationships between ideas are addressed in an organizer passage, but the relationships are between familiar ideas. Therefore, in the case of the organizer, it is up to the students once they begin reading the text to recognize the relationships between the familiar ideas in the organizer and the new ideas in the text. It is also the case that since the organizer is in fact a piece of prose and not a diagram, the relationships between ideas may be in some instances implicitly rather than explicitly referenced.

How do the four strategies compare in terms of the type of processing demands made of students who utilize them? The advance organizer is probably the least demanding of the four. It requires that students read and comprehend a short prepassage that is formulated in terms that are familiar to the students. The prereading components of SQ3R are somewhat more demanding since students are required to initially seek an answer to the general question, "What is this chapter all about?", and then pose a number of more specific questions, a procedure which serves to assist students in setting specific purposes for reading. In effect, the survey and question components of SQ3R require students to recognize those concepts of which they need to seek an understanding but do not require students to address those concepts in order to understand them during prereading. The overview is more demanding still since it requires that students address the "big picture" with respect to a particular topic or issue (something which students can sometimes be led to do during the prereading portion of SQ3R), as well as address a number of specific concepts related to that topic or issue and the relationships between those concepts. In our view, the overview strategy is typically more demanding than either the organizer or SQ3R because it is the meaning of particular concepts and how those concepts relate to one another that students must grapple with during prereading. As far as the pretest is concerned, it is difficult to say how it compares to the other strategies in this regard since it can take so many different forms.

Summary

There are important implications regarding setting students up to read to learn which can be drawn from research that addresses the influence of prior knowledge upon comprehension and recall. First, the notion of setting students up is a legitimate one if by "setting up" is meant preparing students to process information in such a way that there is an interaction between what students already know and what they encounter in the text they are being set up to read. Second, the notion is an important one because when interaction is minimal, not only is individual and/or accurate interpretation sacrificed, but the opportunity to elaborate upon and/or modify existing knowledge is minimized.

Research also suggests that the task of setting students up to read to learn entails (a) preparing students to utilize an appropriate framework for interpreting the information they will encounter, and (b) preparing students to engage in the most appropriate processing of the ideas they will encounter in the text they are being set up to read. Furthermore, there are a number of variables associated with the task of setting students up to read to learn. Specifically, the nature of students' background knowledge, the nature of the content to be read, the objectives associated with students' reading of text material, and the ability of students to process information appropriately, should be among those aspects of instructional situations that have a bearing upon (a) whether or not an effort is made to facilitate the development of background knowledge, (b) the degree to which known and new concepts are emphasized, (c) the degree to which relationships between known and new concepts are emphasized, and (d) the type of processing demands that are made upon students during prereading. Together, both sets of variables (i.e., the characteristics of instructional situations and the objectives associated with the task of setting students up) should determine the strategy for setting students up, in other words, how students are prepared to utilize the most appropriate framework *and* how students are prepared to engage in the most appropriate processing of ideas.

Over the years, a variety of very different strategies have been developed to cope with the dilemma of preparing students to read to learn. The strategies tend to differ from one another not only in terms of how they go about approaching the task of setting students up, but also in terms of the particular prereading objectives they can be used to achieve. These apparent differences suggest that no one strategy is applicable in all instructional situations. Therefore, a strategy should not be implemented in a given instructional situation without considering the extent to which it can accomodate the particular prereading needs at hand.

REFERENCES

Anderson, R. C., & Biddle, W. B. (1975). On asking people questions about what they are reading. In G. H. Bower (Ed.), *The psychology of learning and motivation* (Vol. 9). New York: Academic Press.

Anderson, R. C., Pichert, J. W., Goetz, E. T., Schallert, D. L., Stevens, K. V., & Trollip, S. R. (1976). Instantiation of general terms. *Journal of Verbal Learning and Verbal Behavior, 15,* 667-679.

Anderson, R. C., Reynolds, R. E., Schallert, D. L., & Goetz, E. T. (1977). Frameworks for comprehending discourse. *American Educational Research Journal, 14,* 367-381.

Anderson, R. C., Spiro, R. J., & Anderson, M. C. (1978). Schemata as scaffolding for the representation of information in connected discourse. *American Educational Research Journal, 15,* 433-440.

Ausubel, D. P. (1962). A subsumption theory of meaningful verbal learning and retention. *Journal of General Psychology, 66,* 213-224.

Ausubel, D. P. (1963). Cognitive structure and the facilitation of meaningful verbal learning. *Journal of Teacher Education, 14,* 217-221.

Ausubel, D. P. (1978). In defense of advance organizers: A reply to the critics. *Review of Educational Research, 48,* 251-257.

Barnes, B. R., & Clawson, E. U. (1975). Do advance organizers facilitate learning? Recommendations for further research based on an analysis of 32 studies. *Review of Educational Research, 45,* 637-659.

Barron, R. F. (1969). The use of vocabulary as an advance organizer. In H. L. Herber & P. L. Sanders (Eds.), *Research in reading in the content areas: First year report.* Syracuse, New York: Syracuse University, Reading and Language Arts Center.

Bobrow, D. G., & Norman, D. A. (1975). Some principles of memory schemata. In D. G. Bobrow & A. M. Collins (Eds.), *Representation and understanding: Studies in cognitive science.* New York: Academic Press.

Bransford, J. D., & Johnson, M. K. (1972). Contextual prerequisites for understanding: Some investigations of comprehension and recall. *Journal of Verbal Learning and Verbal Behavior, 11,* 717-726.

Brown, A. L., Smiley, S. S., Day, J. D., Townsend, M. A. R., & Lawton, S. C. (1977).

Intrusion of a thematic idea in children's comprehension and retention of stories. *Child Development, 48,* 1454-1466.

Earle, R. A. (1969). Use of the structured overview in mathematics classes. In H. L. Herber & P. L. Sanders (Eds.), *Research in reading in the content areas: First year report.* Syracuse, New York: Syracuse University, Reading and Language Arts Center.

Earle, R. A. (1973). The use of vocabulary as a structured overview in seventh grade mathematics classes. In H. L. Herber & R. F. Barron (Eds.), *Research in reading in the content areas: Second year report.* Syracuse, N.Y.: Syracuse University, Reading and Language Arts Center.

Estes, T. H., Mills, D. C., & Barron, R. F. (1969). Three methods of introducing students to a reading-learning task in two content subjects. In H. L. Herber & P. L. Sanders (Eds.), *Research in reading in the content areas: First year report.* Syracuse, N.Y.: Syracuse University, Reading and Language Arts Center.

Faw, H. W., & Waller, T. G. (1976). Mathemagenic behaviors and efficiency in learning from prose. *Review of Educational Research, 46,* 691-720.

Forgan, H. W., & Mangrum, C. T. (1976). *Teaching content area reading skills: A modern preservice and inservice program.* Columbus, Ohio: Charles E. Merrill Publishing Company.

Hartley, J., & Davies, I. K. (1976). Preinstructional strategies: The role of pretests, behavioral objectives, overviews and advance organizers. *Review of Educational Research, 46,* 239-265.

Hash, R. J. (1974). *The effects of a strategy of instructional review, level guides, and vocabulary exercises on student achievement, reading comprehension, critical thinking and attitudes of junior high school classes in social studies.* Unpublished doctoral dissertation, State University of New York at Buffalo.

Jenkins, J. R., & Bausell, R. B. (1976). Cognitive structure variables in prose learning. *Journal of Reading Behavior, 8,* 47-66.

Kintsch, W., & van Dijk, T. A. (1978). Toward a model of text comprehension and production. *Psychological Review, 85,* 363-394.

Lawton, J. T., & Wanska, S. K. (1977). Advance organizers as a teaching strategy: A reply to Barnes and Clawson. *Review of Educational Research, 47,* 233-244.

Minsky, M. (1975). A framework for representing knowledge. In P. H. Winston (Ed.), *The psychology of computer vision.* New York: McGraw-Hill.

Niles, O. S. (1967). Comprehension skills. In W. K. Durr (Ed.), *Reading instruction: Dimensions and issues.* Boston: Houghton-Mifflin Co.

Pressey, S. L. A. (1926). A simple apparatus which gives tests and scores—and teaches. *School and Society, 23,* 373-376.

Rickards, J. P. (1976). Type of verbatim question interspersed in text: A new look at the position effect. *Journal of Reading Behavior, 8,* 37-45.

Robinson, F. P. (1946). *Effective Study.* New York: Harper and Bros.

Robinson, F. P. (1961). *Effective study (3rd ed.).* New York: Harper and Row.

Rumelhart, D. E. *Schemata: The building blocks of cognition* (CHIP Rep. No. 79). La Jolla: University of California, Center for Human Information Processing, December 1978.

Rumelhart, D. E., & Ortony, A. (1977). The representation of knowledge in memory. In R. C. Anderson, R. J. Spiro, & W. E. Montague (Eds.), *Schooling and the acquisition of knowledge.* Hillsdale, N.J.: Erlbaum.

Schallert, D. L. (1976). Improving memory for prose: The relationship between depth of processing and context. *Journal of Verbal Learning and Verbal Behavior, 15,* 621-632.

Schank, R., & Abelson, R. *Scripts, plans, goals, and understanding.* Hillsdale, N.J.: Erlbaum, 1977.

Sledge, A. C. (1978). The advance organizer: A review of research at the secondary level. In

J. L. Vaughan, Jr., & P. J. Gaus (Eds.), *Research on Reading in Secondary Schools, 2*, 41-60.

Smith, A. L. (1978). The structured overview: A prereading strategy. In J. L. Vaughan, Jr., & P. J. Gaus (Eds.), *Research on Reading in Secondary Schools, 2*, 61-80.

Spencer, F. (1978). SQ3R queries regarding relevant research. In J. L. Vaughan, Jr., & P. J. Gaus, *Research on reading in secondary schools, 2*,23-38.

Steffensen, M. S., Jogdeo, C., & Anderson, R. C. (1978). *A cross-cultural perspective on reading comprehension* (Tech. Rep. No. 97, ERIC Document Reproduction Service No. ED 159 660). Urbana: University of Illinois, Center for the Study of Reading.

Wooster, G. P. (1958). *Teaching the SQ3R method of study: An investigation of the instructional approach*. Unpublished doctoral dissertation, Ohio State University.

14
STRATEGIES FOR PROMOTING
READER–TEXT INTERACTIONS

Connie A. Bridge
Department of Curriculum and Instruction
University of Kentucky

Within the last decade, there has been renewed interest in the comprehension of connected discourse. Investigators in the fields of linguistics, cognitive psychology, artificial intelligence, and education have turned their attention to the complex factors involved in the acquisition of knowledge from text. As the evidence from these various studies accumulates, a common thread appears to be running through all of the studies; that is, the acquisition of knowledge from text is affected by characteristics within the text itself but also by characteristics within the comprehender. Furthermore, it is possible to influence to some extent the interplay between textual characteristics and reader characteristics.

The intent of this chapter is to briefly review the literature concerning strategies for promoting interaction between reader and text. Working from a constructivist view that reading involves the construction of meaning by the interaction of one's knowledge of language and the world with the printed message of the author, an attempt is made to draw some tentative conclusions regarding those strategies that appear to promote maximal interaction between the comprehender and the material to be comprehended. It is hoped that some limited educational implications can be drawn for teachers whose goal is to lead their students to improved comprehension.

WORLD KNOWLEDGE

The importance of world knowledge to comprehension can not be overemphasized. As Anderson, Reynolds, Schallert, and Goetz (1976) pointed out in terms of schema theory, the main determinant of the knowledge that a person is able to acquire from reading is the knowledge that he or she brings to the task. If a reader does not possess the relevant schema or does not know how to bring this schema to bear upon the task, the reader will be unable to comprehend the material.

The role of schemata is an important one in comprehension, because the schemata the reader brings to the reading task guides the reader's selective processing of the input data. Schemata can be defined as abstract, stereotyped descriptions of a concept, which exist for objects, actions, events, and sequences of events; they resemble an outline or template with slots for the components and a structural network that defines the relationships between the components (Rumelhart & Ortony, 1977). A schema serves as an interpretive framework, enabling the reader to go "beyond the information given" (Bruner, 1973). Schemata are "hypothesis-driven" and provide an interactive approach to comprehension that allows for the interaction of the schema or pre-existing knowledge structures with the incoming data. It is this interaction that is involved in comprehension of discourse, for even when the sensory data is incomplete, individuals can use their schematic expectations of the variable constraints and relationships to make logical guesses about the unspecified information.

Several recent studies have assessed the effect of students' prior knowledge of a topic upon their comprehension of a passage about that topic. Two related studies by Chiesi, Spilich, and Voss (1979) and Spilich, Vesonder, Chiesi, and Voss (1979) involved an investigation of how knowledge of a given domain (baseball), including the goal structure of the game as well as the states and actions of the game, affected the acquisition and processing of domain-related information. Chiesi et al. (1979) found that subjects with high knowledge of baseball had superior recognition performance, especially for material that was rated more important in terms of the goal structure, needed less information to make recognition judgments, anticipated a higher percentage of goal state outcomes, and were superior at recalling event sequences than were subjects with low knowledge of baseball. These results were interpreted to mean that knowledge of a given topic facilitates the acquisition of new related information and involves a mapping process in which new information is mapped onto one's existing knowledge structure. Spilich et al. (1979) found further support for these conclusions in a study in which high-knowledge subjects and low-knowledge subjects listened to an account of a fictitious baseball game and then were asked to write a summary of the account, a complete recall of the account, and to take a completion test over the material in the account. Both qualitative and quantitative differences were found in favor of the high knowledge individuals. These results were explained in terms of the high knowledge individuals' superior ability to relate the actions of the game to the goal structure and to hold in memory the most important information.

A study by Taylor (1978) revealed that prior knowledge facilitated the comprehension of both good and poor third- and fifth-grade readers. Poor readers, especially, comprehended better when given an expository passage for which they had greater prior knowledge. Taylor concluded that providing material about familiar concepts is particularly important for poor readers. Gordon, Hansen, and Pearson (1978) also found that prior knowledge facilitated the comprehension of second graders reading an expository passage. The readers who had more prior knowledge about the topic of the passage learned more from the sections of the passage where that knowledge was needed for understanding. However, for explicitly stated information for which no prior knowledge was needed, the recall of the two groups did not differ significantly.

A study by Brown, Smiley, Day, and Lawton (1977) involved providing students with prior information before asking them to listen to an ambiguous passage that was about a young tribal hunter from a fictitious tribe and that could be interpreted from differing points of view, depending on the orientation information provided prior to hearing the selection. Each subject received one of three orientations: an Eskimo orientation, a desert Indian orientation, or an irrelevant Spanish orientation, but the investigator did not relate the orientation to the passage itself. A different investigator conducted the second part of the experiment a week after the orientation information was given. The children listened to the recorded passage twice, then their recalls of the story were recorded. After the free recall, the children were asked probe questions designed to test their acquisition of crucial inferences, regarding climate, terrain, the prey, and the rival hunter. The results indicated that the students who had received the relevant orientation information prior to listening recalled more units than those who received the irrelevant orientation. The inferences they generated centered around the type of orientation information provided prior to listening. Brown concluded that children, like adults, use schemata as a framework for comprehending discourse, filling in ambiguous or incomplete sections of a story to make it conform to previous knowledge.

The facilitative effects of stored information upon acquisition of new information was investigated by Wittrock, Marks, and Doctorow (1975) in two experiments with sixth graders in which unfamiliar vocabulary words were embedded in familiar stories. The familiar stories appeared to serve as the context to cue the recall of related memories needed to construct and learn the meanings of the target vocabulary words. In two other experiments with sixth graders, one or two familiar high-frequency words were substituted for lower frequency synonyms in each sentence of a reading text with a corresponding increase of 50% in comprehension and 100% in retention of the story (Marks, Doctorow, & Wittrock, 1974).

Recognition of the important facilitative effects of prior knowledge upon learning from text forces the educator to deal with two major questions: (a) If students lack prior knowledge necessary for understanding a passage, how can the relevant schema be provided? and (b) If the readers possess the necessary schema, how can they be helped to relate their existing knowledge structures to the new information?

BUILDING BACKGROUND

Little empirical research exists regarding ways to build up a background of knowledge related to the topic of the selection to be read. However, typical basal reader lessons commonly suggest the introduction of vocabulary as a prereading step. When the concepts associated with the vocabulary words are introduced along with the written form of the word, this step can serve the purpose of building prior knowledge. Frequently, such lessons also include a section for "building background" or "getting ready to read" that helps to arouse previous conceptual associations and to provide new associations through discussions designed to help students relate the unfamiliar concepts to familiar ones.

Conflicting results have been found in studies investigating the efficacy of vocabulary training on general reading comprehension. Swaby (1977) compared the effects of 15 minutes of oral vocabulary instruction and a 5-minute exposure to a written advance organizer on reading comprehension of target stories. She found that subjects receiving the vocabulary instruction did perform significantly better on experimentor constructed story comprehension questions; however, she did not use a standardized measure of comprehension to see if the effects of the training transferred to other reading situations.

Schachter (1978) compared the relative effectiveness of prereading vocabulary instruction to thematic instruction in which fifth-grade subjects were asked prereading questions related to the theme or topic of the story and were asked to relate the theme to their own past experiences. The vocabulary instruction group was presented with six words and their definitions and instructed to use each word in a sentence. The control group was provided with an orienting statement but did not receive any instruction prior to reading. All three groups read seven stories (one at a session during a 4-week period) and answered 10 comprehension questions and 12 vocabulary items about each story. The thematic instruction group performed significantly better on the postreading story comprehension questions than did the vocabulary instruction group, but the performance of the vocabulary instruction group was significantly better than that of the control group. The vocabulary instruction group also was better able to write definitions of words used in the stories. Neither of the instructional strategies had a significant effect upon subjects' scores on standardized measures of reading comprehension.

Previous studies on the other hand, have failed to find evidence that vocabulary instruction facilitates reading comprehension (Jackson & Dizney, 1963; Pany & Jenkins, 1978). In the study by Jackson and Dizney on the effect of vocabulary instruction on twelfth graders' reading comprehension, the experimental group did vocabulary assignments and a vocabulary workbook, whereas the control group did literature assignments. On standardized tests the vocabulary training group performed significantly better on vocabulary subtests, but not on other measures of reading ability.

Pany and Jenkins (1978) conducted a study involving six fourth and fifth-grade learning-disabled students to determine the effects of three different vocabulary instruction techniques on subjects' scores on vocabulary tests (in context and in isolation) and on a story comprehension test in which subjects wrote the answers to 10 factual recall questions. Students did perform better on the vocabulary measures after receiving vocabulary instruction, but this instruction did not appear to facilitate general story comprehension. Because of the small number of students involved in this study and the fact that they had been labeled *learning disabled* limits the generalizability of the results.

It appears, however, that the results of studies designed to investigate the effects of vocabulary instruction have shown that although students' understanding of the words taught is improved, and in some cases, the understanding of the story from which the words were taken is facilitated, there is no transfer to more general comprehension measures.

Gordon (1979) also found a lack of transfer of facilitative effects to other reading situations in a study in which she attempted to improve fifth graders' comprehension of narrative selections by the use of two intervention techniques. One treatment focused on developing students' background knowledge about the story prior to reading and increasing students' awareness of narrative text structure. The second treatment involved teaching students a strategy for drawing inferences. To insure an equal amount of time spent in teacher–pupil interaction, a control group read and discussed the story and did a variety of related activities suggested in the basal reader guide. The students receiving the background information and text structure training were better able than the control group to answer questions that required the integration of textual information and prior knowledge on the instructional worksheets following the stories, whereas the group receiving inference training outperformed both the expanded content group and the control group on these questions. However, these fifth graders did not spontaneously transfer these inferencing skills to similar experimenter-designed questions on unfamiliar selections.

Another study by Sloan and Pearson (1978) indicated that poor readers' comprehension of difficult technical material was facilitated by almost any type of teacher intervention. More research is needed to investigate the effectiveness of methods of building background for a selection on the comprehension of that selection.

PROMOTING READER–TEXT INTERACTION

Assuming that readers possess the relevant background information, it still is necessary that they activate the relevant schema in order to comprehend the textual material. Teachers who want to facilitate students' ability to acquire knowledge from text must help students employ strategies for actively relating the new information they gain from reading to their previous knowledge structures. This mobilization of cognitive structures prior to reading provides what Ausubel (1968) terms *ideational scaffolding*. Relating the new information to these memory scaffolds also requires active involvement on the part of the students during reading. Finally, after reading, the students must be helped to integrate the new information with the old to form an updated knowledge structure.

The following discussion reviews the research literature on various methods for promoting students' active involvement with text before, during, and after reading. These methods include: questioning, using both teacher-generated and student-generated questions; advance organizers; pictures, both student-generated and experimenter provided; and student-generated summary sentences.

Questioning: Teacher-Generated

One of the conventional methods that teachers have used to enhance student comprehension has been questioning. The type and placement of these questions appear to be key factors in facilitating interaction between student and text. Furthermore, type and placement of questions appear to have some differential effects on subjects of various age and ability levels.

Many of the studies involving questioning have evolved from Rothkopf's (1970) concept of mathemagenic behaviors, which he defines as activities that give birth to learning. The importance of this concept is its emphasis upon what the learner does in the learning situation. That is, what the learner learns is not in simple correspondence to the stimulus being presented, but this stimulus is affected in various ways by the students' own actions (i.e., attention, set, orienting reflex, cognition, rehearsal). The mathemagenic activities determine what will be learned. Although the content and organization of the material is important, in the final analysis it is what the student does with the material that determines what is learned.

This concept has lead to investigations of prose learning in which the students' activities during the reading process were manipulated through the use of instructions or questions. Retention of the textual information was then assessed for the varying questioning conditions. To separate the specific instructive effects of the questions from any possible general facilitative effect from a modified learning set, Rothkopf divided his posttests into two parts: one composed of the inserted questions themselves and the other composed of questions whose answers were independent of the answers to the inserted questions. Thus, he hypothesized that the inserted questions measured intentional learning, whereas the other questions measured incidental learning.

In a comprehensive review of the literature on questioning, Faw and Waller (1976) summarized the results of Rothkopf's initial studies and those of other questioning studies using similar materials and procedures. That is, most of them have involved adult subjects using factual materials and factual questions and immediate posttests with no opportunity for looking back over the material. The results of these studies support the following conclusions:

1. Factual prequestions facilitate intentional learning of the material relating to the questions.
2. Factual postquestions also facilitate intentional learning of the material to which they relate, but also facilitate the learning of incidental material.

That is, both factual prequestions and postquestions tend to increase students' abilities to answer these same questions after reading; however, only postquestions facilitate overall comprehension.

Question type and ability of student tend to alter the effects of question placement. Higher order conceptual questions have been found to have a facilitative effect in a number of studies (Frase, 1970, 1973; Gagne & Memory, 1978, Rickards & Hatcher, 1977-1978; Shavelson, Berliner, Ravitch, & Loeding, 1974; Smith, 1978; Wiesendanger & Wollenberg, 1978).

Rickards and Hatcher (1977-78) in a study of fifth-grade good and poor comprehenders found that poor comprehenders benefited significantly from receiving interspersed meaningful learning postquestions that required them to relate passage details to higher level ideas contained in the questions themselves. The meaningful learning postquestions helped poor comprehenders more than rote learning postquestions, which required them to literally recall specific informational content, or no questions at all. Good comprehenders, on the other hand, did not score significantly differently in any of the three questioning conditions: meaningful learning postquestions, rote learning postquestions, or no questions. For instructional purposes, it is important to note that poor comprehenders presented with meaningful learning postquestions scored as well as good comprehenders in any of the three conditions. Gagne and Memory (1978) also found that low-achieving students benefited significantly from main idea prequestions. High-achieving students, however, scored equally well under conditions of main idea prequestions and general instructions to read carefully. Thus, it would appear that good readers possess adequate strategies for organizing and recalling text, whereas poor readers profit from questions that direct them toward the main idea and toward organizing the details in the text around higher level ideas.

Smith (1978) found that higher cognitive level questions; that is, interpretive questions that required the modification of content by analysis, reconstruction, or inference of relationships, more effectively activated the higher cognitive processes as measured by length of communication unit in the answer.

Wixson (1980) also found that fifth-grade students who received higher level questions, that is, textually implicit and scriptally implicit questions as defined by Pearson and Johnson (1978), recalled as much explicit information and generated more inferred information than students who received textually explicit questions. Children who received unrelated postreading questions generated as much inferred information as students with implicit questions and significantly more than students with explicit questions. In fact, verbatim postreading questions inhibited the extent to which children integrated the textual information with their own knowledge structures.

Faw and Waller (1976) point out that when higher order inserted questions are used, more of the passage content is required in responding. They hypothesize that if several higher order questions were inserted in a passage, then little incidental content would be left. Thus, there would be little incidental learning to measure; and, in fact, its measurement would not be meaningful. They suggest formulating specific objectives regarding the information that subjects are expected to obtain from studying the selection and then writing a posttest to assesss the attainment of these objectives. A sample of these higher order questions could be interspersed throughout the text and their effect observed. Although posttest scores would be a measure of intentional learning, this measure would actually encompass both incidental and intentional learning as it would be assessing all of the information deemed important in terms of the objectives.

Although some of the research on prequestions shows that students are better able to answer these same questions after reading but that there is a limiting effect on overall comprehension, two important considerations must be recognized in instructional situations. In most reading assign-ments, there are certain ideas that the teacher thinks are more important and wants to be sure that students recall. In these situations it would appear to be legitimate to direct the attention of students to these ideas through the use of prequestions. If the previously mentioned suggestion of Faw and Waller (1976) was followed and several higher order questions were used prior to and during reading, then most of the useful information in the passage would be covered. Furthermore, it seems neither neces-sary, possible, nor practical to expect readers to recall everything they read. Thus, teachers should design questions that focus students' atten-tion on important aspects of the selection.

Questioning: Student-Generated

The previously mentioned research on the use of questioning to promote comprehension has employed questions written by the researchers. Yet a desirable goal of instruction is to create independent learners who are capable of controlling their own learning from text. It is toward this end that several authors have suggested that students devise their own pre-reading questions through the use of predicting and previewing strategies (Pearson & Johnson, 1978; Singer, 1978; Stauffer, 1976; Thomas & Robinson, 1972).

In Stauffer's (1976) Directed Reading Thinking Activity (DRTA), the reader is given limited clues about the story content (i.e., title, picture, first paragraph) and then asked to predict what is going to happen in the story. At various logical breaking points in the story, the reader is asked to confirm, reject, or revise previous predictions on the basis of evidence, and to make new predictions as the evidence accumulates. Thus, the reading process becomes an active search for information to confirm or reject the reader's predictions. The purposes for reading evolve from the reader's own questions: Was my prediction right or wrong? How do I know? What evidence was there in the story to prove my prediction right or wrong?

Eliciting predictions prior to reading was also an essential aspect of a strategy developed by Hansen (1979) to facilitate second graders' inferen-tial comprehension by inducing them to integrate textual information with prior knowledge. Hansen selected three main ideas from the story and asked a question about each of the three ideas that required the children to relate the idea to some of their own previous experiences. After discussing these related experiences and writing down their own experi-ence, the students hypothesized a similar event that might happen in the story and also recorded this prediction in writing. Another group of students in the study were asked discussion questions during the guided reading that required drawing inferential relationships. The control group answered questions that had a 5:1 ratio of explicit to inferential questions. After an 8-week period in which 10 stories were taught, children's scores on the dependent measures revealed that the children in the two experimental groups performed better on the comprehension questions immediately following the instructional stories and on a standardized reading comprehension test, but there were no differences in their scores on the other dependent measures: An experimenter-designed test on two selections that was not accompanied by the instructional procedures and a free-recall measure on a story not previously taught. Hansen concluded that eliciting predictions and asking questions that require inferencing facilitates immediate comprehension of stories in which the instructional procedures are employed, but that children may not spontaneously transfer these strategies to other similar stories.

Singer (1978) recommends teaching active comprehension by helping students learn to ask their own questions to guide their own independent processing of a selection. He suggests the use of a phase-out/phase-in strategy that begins with the teacher taking the students through a lesson or chapter in a particular content area while demonstrating what questions to ask. These teacher-posed questions serve to model the thinking process involved in reading and comprehending text. Then the teacher gives another lesson or chapter in which students are encouraged to formulate their own questions before, during, and after reading. Singer contends that the purpose of teaching students to formulate their own questions goes beyond the immediate goal of helping them to select and retain information while reading and leads to the ultimate end of teaching students an active process of reading and learning from text that stresses the reader's own purposes and the interaction between reader and text that occurs when one is reading to satisfy one's own curiosity. An unpublished study by Rhodes is reported by Singer in support of this contention. Rhodes found that students who were taught the active comprehension process did not suffer from the limiting effects of teacher preposed questions and performed significantly better on literal, interpretive, and general questions than control groups who had teacher-posed prequestions or postquestions or no questions.

Getting students to formulate their own questions is also an integral part of Robinson's (Thomas & Robinson, 1972) SQ3R (survey, question, read, recite, review) study technique. After surveying the chapter or unit, using titles, headings, subheadings, illustrations, graphs, charts, and summaries and conclusions, students are directed to turn the headings into questions that should be answered as they read the section under the heading.

Manzo (1969) reported positive results from the use of his Reciprocal

Questioning Strategy (ReQuest). In the ReQuest Procedure, the teacher and student(s) take turns asking each other questions over portions of the text. The role of the teacher is to model higher level questions in an attempt to get students beyond the level of literal recall. The alternate questioning continues until the student's questions set purposes for completing the text.

In view of the constructivist notion that reading involves the construction of meaning by the interaction of one's existing knowledge with the printed message of the author, questions generated by the students prior to and during reading would seem to promote maximum interaction between student and text, but little systematic investigation has been carried out to demonstrate the efficacy of these instructional strategies that use self-generated questions.

Conflicting results regarding the effects of self-generated postquestions have been found in several studies. Andre and Anderson (1979) conducted a study in which subjects were assigned to one of three groups: a questioning-with-training group, an untrained questioning group, and a read–reread control group. Students were taught to construct questions by identifying the main idea of each paragraph and forming questions that asked for new instances of ideas and/or concepts or that involved a paraphrase of a concept in the text. Findings showed that students who generated their own questions, both with and without training, performed better on the comprehension test than students who simply reread the text. The authors hypothesized that students who constructed main idea questions, either with or without training, by determining main ideas and transforming them into questions were involved in a deeper semantic analysis of the text than students who simply read and reread. The benefits of the self-questioning study strategy appeared to be more beneficial for lower verbal ability students.

Frase and Schwartz (1975) also found favorable results for student generated questions in a study in which high school students worked in pairs in studying a text. For one third of the text, they were to ask their partners questions, on another third they were to answer their partner's questions, and in the other third they were to study on their own. The means of the answering and questioning conditions differed significantly from the studying-only group, but not from one another. In a second study involving college freshmen, the students read one section of text and then constructed questions over it; then they simply studied the other section. They scored significantly better on the section over which they had generated their own questions.

Duell (1975) also found facilitative effects for self-generated questions in a study of college students who were assigned to three groups: one that was given the passages, objectives, and a list of objectives and instructions to write questions to match the objectives; a second group that was given the passages and the objectives and told to study them; and a third group that took the test without having read the passages. The group that had generated their own questions scored significantly better than the students who simply read under the guidance of the objectives.

Schmelzer (1975) compared the effects of self-generated questions in prereading, postreading, and interspersed conditions. A fourth condition involved a read–reread condition with no questions. The college students who generated their own questions in a postreading situation scored significantly better than the other groups.

Pederson (1977), on the other hand, in a study of self-generated questions found no significant difference in the comprehension of students in four conditions: one in which they read and answered five factual postquestions, one in which they read and answered five inferential postquestions, another in which they constructed five postquestions of their own, and a fourth group that simply read the passage twice. In a second experiment, using short answer questions in place of the multiple-choice questions and three conditions: experimenter-generated questions, self-generated questions, and repeated readings with no questions, Pederson still found no significant difference between treatment groups. As a result of these findings, Pederson questioned the value of both student-constructed and experimenter-constructed post-questions as a technique for facilitating learning from prose.

Adejumo (1975) studied the effects of self-generated questions, questions generated by other students, experimenter-generated questions, and no questions and found that the group answering questions generated by other students scored significantly better on measures of total and incidental learning and intentional learning than did the self-generated questioning group. On intentional learning, the experimenter-generated question group scored significantly better than the other three groups. Morse (1976) also found that experimenter-generated questions tended to produce greater learning than subject-generated questions. On immediate recall tests, Meader (1975) reported that experimenter-generated questions produced significantly better results than either the student-generated questions or the control group, but this finding did not hold true on the delayed retention test.

Further investigation of the effects of student-generated questions must be carried out before these conflicting results can be explained. A factor that will have to be considered in these investigations will be the amount of prior knowledge of the topic that the student is bringing to the task. A student with a greater understanding of the topic would be better able to judge the relative importance of ideas within the passage, and thus be more apt to formulate questions reflecting upon the important ideas. A study by Miyake and Norman (1979) tested the hypothesis that learners must possess an appropriate level of knowledge as a prerequisite to asking questions about new subject matter. Subjects grouped according to levels of background knowledge were asked to read materials at two levels of difficulty and to orally express all of their questions and thoughts while reading. Subjects with low-level topic knowledge asked more questions when reading easier material than did high knowledge subjects. The reverse situation occurred with more difficult material when trained learners asked more questions than novice learners. These results suggest the need to consider the interaction between prior knowledge and difficulty level of the material when studying the effect of self-generated questions on learning from text. Furthermore, studies by Anderson et al. (1976) have shown that readers with differing perspectives assign different importance ratings to the same ideas depending upon their own point of view. Because there is a natural tendency to construct questions over the content one considers most relevant, it is possible that an experimenter would ask different questions than a student with a less well-developed schema. The age and metacognitive awareness of the students also would affect their ability to generate questions over the relevant aspects of the selection. Older students and students who are able to monitor their own learning might benefit more from self-generated questions, whereas younger students might need the guidance of teacher-generated questions to focus their attention upon the most important ideas within the passage.

Advance Organizers

Another method of facilitating the interaction between the reader's background information and the textual information was developed by Ausubel (1960). He called the technique an advance organizer, which is essentially an outline of the new ideas in the text presented at a higher level of generality and abstraction. Ausubel's advance organizers were designed to "mobilize the reader's cognitive structure" and to aid in the integration of new information into existing knowledge structures. He asked subjects to read either an abstract organizer or an historical introduction prior to reading the passage. On the measures of retention, the group reading the advance organizers recalled more information from the target passage. Students of lower ability and poorer background knowledge benefited especially. Both the advance organizers and the historical introductions were constructed so that no material was included that would directly improve performance of the posttest retention measures. The superior retention of the group having the advance organizers could be attributed to the facilitative effect of the advance organizer upon these subjects' ability to relate the new information to previous knowledge structures.

Crafton (1980) used a strategy similar to Ausubel's advance organizer in that one reading passage was used to enhance students' comprehension of a second related passage. The strategy employed a preparatory passage that contained background information that could be accessed during the reading of the second passage on the same topic. Both fourth and eleventh graders who read two texts on the same topic comprehended the target passage better and generated more inferences than did students who read an unrelated passage prior to reading the target passage. The study demonstrated that reading a background passage can be used as a knowledge-building activity that facilitates comprehension of new conceptual material.

In an extensive review of the research on the use of advance organizers at the secondary levels, Sledge (1978) reported that in the studies in which significant differences were found in favor of advance organizers, the less able students appeared to benefit most from their use. However, the majority of studies reviewed did not find differences supporting the use of advance organizers. It is doubtful, however, that the advance organizers used in the studies conformed to Ausubel's definition of an advance organizer. Before conclusive statements can be made regarding the efficacy of the advance organizer, researchers must conform to the same criteria so that valid comparisons can be made.

Generated Sentence Summaries

In a study designed to test a generative model of learning, which holds that instruction should stimulate relations between the stimuli to be processed and stored knowledge, Doctorow, Wittrock, and Marks (1978) asked sixth-grade students to generate a sentence about each paragraph in the text. Paragraph headings were provided for some of the subjects to facilitate the construction of schemata and the selection of prior knowledge to be associated with the textual information. The generation of the sentences was designed to stimulate the construction of relations between text and prior knowledge. The combined effect of paragraph headings with sentence generation produced the greatest amount of comprehension and recall. Sentence generation alone ranked next in effectiveness for both high- and low-ability readers with inserted paragraph headings ranking third. Low-ability readers especially benefited more from sentence generation than inserted paragraph headings. It was hypothesized that low-ability readers do not spontaneously construct elaborative meanings for text as frequently as high-ability readers who seem able to use paragraph headings to recall related prior knowledge to aid in the comprehension of text. Taylor and Berkowitz (1980) conducted a study comparing the effectiveness of three study techniques on fifth-grade students' comprehension and memory of social studies material assessed by an immediate short answer comprehension test and a 24-hour delayed multiple choice test and free recall. The three study techniques were (a) generating summary statements for each paragraph during reading; (b) completing a study guide consisting of interspersed questions; and (c) answering questions after the entire passage. The summary generation group recalled significantly more propositions in general and more main idea propositions than the other two experimental groups and the control group. No other differences were found on the other comprehension measures. Bridge, Belmore, Moskow, Cohen, and Matthews (1984) also investigated the effects of a sentence generation task on good and poor university readers' ability to recall paragraphs in which main idea statements were explicitly stated in the initial position or omitted. Students' recall of both types of paragraphs was equal when they performed the generation task, and poor readers performed as well as good readers when required to generate a summary sentence. These studies of generated sentences support the facilitative effects of requiring subjects to generate cognitive constructions during reading.

Dee-Lucas and Di Vesta (1980) studied the effects of learner-generated organizational aids on university students' comprehension of an expository text as measured by a free-recall test, a matching test, and a test of passage structure. Half of the subjects were required to generate topic sentences, headings, related factual sentences, or unrelated factual sentences; whereas the other half of the students had these aids provided in the text. The results indicated that organizational contexts and orienting tasks have differential effects upon recall, depending on the type of comprehension measure employed. The generation tasks functioned in a manner similar to prequestions in that they caused the learners to focus their attention upon a certain portion of the text and to learn that portion well at the expense of other information in the text. The variations in context also caused learners to focus on different types and quantities of information in that the contextual aids served to direct students to task-relevant information in the text. Further, the study indicated that organizational contexts and orienting tasks will produce differential results only when they induce subjects to process information that would not have been attended to otherwise. Thus, Dee-Lucas and Di Vesta concluded that the nature of the passage alters the effects of orienting tasks; information that is high in the hierarchical structure of the text or meaningful to the learner will be remembered regardless of the type of orienting task employed.

Day and Brown (cited in Day, 1980) investigated fifth, seventh, and tenth graders, and junior college, and university students' abilities to summarize texts after being instructed in how to apply five rules for summarizing. All ages successfully learned to use the two easiest rules: the deletion of trivia and the deletion of redundancy. Younger students had more difficulty learning the two most complex rules: location of topic sentences and invention of topic sentences when the author failed to provide one. Even college students had trouble inventing topic sentences; thus, in a follow-up study, Day (1980) attempted to train junior college students to apply all five summarization rules. Four conditions were set up in which the explicitness of training varied from (a) a self-management condition in which students were encouraged to write good summaries; (b) a rules alone condition in which the rules were explained and modeled; (c) a rules plus self-management combining rules training and encouragement to self-monitor; and (d) a rules integrated condition in which students were taught the rules and given training in monitoring their use of the rules. Students of both low and average ability in all four training conditions learned the three easiest rules. Students in all conditions improved on their ability to apply the more difficult selection of summary sentence rule, with average-ability subjects becoming more proficient than low-ability subjects. On the most difficult rule, invention of topic sentence, all students found it difficult, but better students gained most from the training. Thus, Day concluded that all subjects benefit from explicit training in summarization rules but that low ability subjects need more training to be successful especially when learning the complex selection and invention rules.

In terms of the constructivist view of the reading process, it is not surprising that tasks that engage students actively in integrating and synthesizing information from the text tend to facilitate comprehension. However, the effects of generation tasks can be altered by the organization of the text as well as by learner characteristics, such as interest, purpose, and reading ability.

Visual Imagery and Pictorial Aids

In search of methods for improving young children's recall of narrative passages, Levin and others have investigated the effects of pictures, both in the form of experimenter-provided illustrations and subject-generated visual images. Guttman, Levin, and Pressley (1977) report that both younger (age 5 and 6) and older (age 9 and above) children's recall of information is facilitated by the inclusion of appropriate visual illustrations. However, older, but not younger, children benefited from instructions to generate their own visual images of the story content. Therefore, Guttman et al. (1977) conducted a developmental investigation of the effect of providing partial pictures and requiring kindergarten, second-, and third-grade subjects to generate visual images of objects not included in the picture. For example, the partial picture for the sentence, "One evening Sue's family sat down to eat a big turkey for dinner" included a family seated at a table set up for dining, but the turkey was not on the table. In the complete version of the picture, everything in the picture was the same except for the inclusion of the turkey on a platter. For each sentence, a "wh" probe was used to assess the child's recall of the item omitted from the partial picture.

For kindergarteners, only complete pictures improved comprehension. Third graders benefited equally from provided partial and complete pictures as they did from instructions to generate their own pictures. The results for second graders, however, were less clear cut. Complete pictures facilitated comprehension significantly more than imagery and control, with partial pictures being neither significantly better than imagery and control, nor worse than complete. Results indicated that the partial pictures aided subjects' recall of objects not actually pictured, but only implied. In addition to the complete and static partial pictures, some subjects were shown dynamic partial pictures that were constructed so as to lead the subject to predict that something really was located behind the screening object or beyond the picture frame. This was done by depicting the activity and movements of the story characters. In the static partial pictures, on the other hand, the characters were shown in a stationary manner. Although there were no differences on recall between static and dynamic picture conditions when measured by the single "wh" probe, there was a difference in favor of the dynamic pictures when propositional recall was assessed by a series of questions. Thus, it was concluded that the implied activities in the dynamic pictures helped the children integrate the entire relationships in memory.

Levin and Pressley (1981) summarized the results of two other studies (Bender & Levin, 1978; Ruch & Levin, 1977), in addition to the Guttman et al. (1977) study and concluded that children who heard the stories accompanied by pictures recalled more information than students who heard stories without pictures. The third graders experienced as much benefit from pictures as the kindergartners and second graders (Guttman et al., 1977). Bender and Levin (1978) found that third graders hearing a longer passage recalled 25% more information when pictures were provided and educable mentally retarded children (ages 10–16) recalled 89% more information.

The use of pictures to provide an organizing context prior to reading has been shown effective by Arnold and Brooks (1976). Reminiscent of the Bransford and Johnson (1972) studies in which a context-setting title facilitated adults' comprehension of an otherwise ambiguous passage, the study by Arnold and Brooks compared the effects of verbal context, pictorial context, and no context on fifth and second graders' comprehension of short passages that needed a disambiguating theme or context in order to be understood. Using a free-recall measure of comprehension in which both explicitly stated information and appropriate inferences were counted as correct, fifth graders appeared to benefit from having a pictorial context, but not a verbal context, provided prior to listening to the passage. Second graders, however, did not demonstrate similar beneficial effects. Again this points out the need for caution in applying the results of a study using subjects of one age group to subjects of another age group.

Although the results of these studies that demonstrate the facilitative effects of pictorial aids seem promising, it is necessary to remember that the studies employed oral presentations of the passages. It has not been demonstrated that pictures accompanying texts to be read by subjects will be equally beneficial. Indeed, earlier studies have found conflicting results. Samuels (1970) found that pictures had a prohibitive effect upon learning to recognize isolated words. Samuels explained his results in terms of the selective attention hypothesis contending that the children were attending to the accompanying pictures rather than to the distinctive features of the words to be learned.

The results of studies of children's comprehension when reading text with and without adjunct pictures have also shown varied results. A study by Halbert (1943) indicated greater recall of important ideas from the story when pictures accompanied the text. However, Vernon (1953, 1954) found no differences in recall and comprehension of texts with and without pictorial aids, and Koenke (1968) found that accompanying pictures did not facilitate students' ability to state the main idea of a paragraph. Miller (1938) found that stories in basal readers with the illustrations removed were comprehended as well as stories in the readers with their illustrations left intact. Weintraub (1960) even found a negative effect on second graders' ability to answer multiple-choice questions when they read paragraphs with pictures present than paragraphs with no pictures.

Levin and Pressley (1981) charge that the failure of several of these studies to detect positive effects was due to inappropriately constructed pictures; that is, pictures that were either irrelevant or weakly related to the target text. On the other hand, the pictorial aids in the studies of Levin and associates were drawn to convey the essence of the content of the passage. Thus, Guttman, Levin, and Pressley (1977) contend that enough evidence has been accumulated to demonstrate the positive effects of illustrations on children's comprehension of prose and that the task that remains is to delineate the nature and extent of picture benefits in terms of amount and type of information retained over time. It also will be necessary to provide adjunct pictorial aids that parallel the content of the text in reading situations as well as in listening situations before definitive conclusions can be reached regarding the effect of pictures on children's comprehension of written discourse.

If the results from the listening studies hold true in studies of reading comprehension, then the following predictions can be made. An appropriately constructed illustration that parallels the printed text could be shown prior to reading as a context-setting device. Partial pictures could be used to induce subjects to predict the missing parts and thus help children integrate in memory the entire relationship. Instructing children to generate their own visual images should be effective in facilitating comprehension at third grade and above. Mentally filling in the missing parts of pictures and generating their own visual images are tasks that require subjects to create cognitive constructions and thus process the information at a deeper level. For younger children, at grade two or below, it may be necessary to supply complete pictures that depict the content of the text. If tentative educational implications can be drawn from the results of the listening studies, then the indications are that students at third grade and above can benefit from strategies requiring their active participation in generating the missing parts of partial pictures or accompanying visual images, whereas younger children may be less able to employ these constructive activities but need to have the illustrations provided for them by the publisher.

Conclusions and Implications

The intention of this chapter was to review the literature regarding strategies that are designed to promote interaction between reader and text. A constructivist view of the reading process holds that readers construct meaning as they interact with the author's message in terms of their own background knowledge. Thus, a strategy that promotes active involvement between reader and text should facilitate improved comprehension if the reader possesses the prerequisite background knowledge.

This review would appear to lead to some tentative implications for teachers, researchers, and publishers:

1. Prior knowledge of a topic facilitates comprehension of passages about that topic.
2. When students lack prior knowledge, teachers must provide this

information before maximal comprehension can occur. Introduction of vocabulary and concepts through discussions and advance organizers have been helpful in several studies mentioned in the previous discussion.

3. Students must be encouraged to relate their prior knowledge to the new information in the text.

   a. Experimenter-provided questions requiring higher level processing of textual information appear to be most effective in promoting the integration and synthesis of new information with existing knowledge structures.

   b. Self-generated questions have been helpful to comprehenders in some studies, but the importance of matching the difficulty level of the material to the knowledge level of the reader must be considered before a student can generate appropriate questions.

   c. Instructing students to generate their own visual images to accompany textual material or to mentally fill in the missing parts of partial pictures also has been effective with students age eight and older.

These implications must be interpreted with caution, as factors within the text, within the reader, or within the contextual situation in which the reading occurs may alter the effects of a strategy. For example, the age and ability level of the students tend to interact differentially with type and placement of questions. Age also affects the ability to generate visual images and missing parts of pictures. Thus, care must be taken in generalizing the results obtained with one age group to another group of older or younger subjects. But with the direction provided in the studies reviewed in this chapter as well as other studies beyond the limited scope of this review, researchers can begin to systematically unravel the remaining threads.

REFERENCES

Adejumo, J. A. (1975). The effects of some structured strategies on the acquisition and recall of instructional prose material. *Dissertation Abstracts International, 36,* 180A. (University Microfilms No. 75-13, 954)

Anderson, R. C., Reynolds, R. E., Schallert, D. L., & Goetz, E. T. (1976). *Frameworks for comprehending discourse* (Tech. Rep. No. 12, ERIC Document Reproduction Service No. ED 134 935). Urbana: University of Illinois, Laboratory for Cognitive Studies in Education.

Andre, M. E., & Anderson, T. H. (1979). The development and evaluation of a self-questioning study technique. *Reading Research Quarterly, 14,* 605-623.

Arnold, D. J., & Brooks, P. H. (1976). Influence of contextual organizing material on children's listening comprehension. *Journal of Educational Psychology, 68,* 711-716.

Ausubel, D. P. (1960). The use of advance organizers in the learning and retention of meaningful verbal material. *Journal of Educational Psychology, 51*, 267-272.

Ausubel, D. P. (1968). *Educational psychology: A cognitive view.* New York: Holt, Rinehart & Winston.

Bender, B. G., & Levin, J. R. (1978). Pictures, imagery and retarded children's prose learning. *Journal of Educational Psychology, 70*, 583-588.

Bransford, J. D., & Johnson, M. K. (1972). Contextual prerequisites for understanding: Some investigations of comprehension and recall. *Journal of Verbal Learning and Verbal Behavior, 11*, 717-726.

Bridge, C. A., Belmore, S. M., Moskow, S. P., Cohen, S. G., & Matthews, P. D. (1984). Topicalization and memory for main ideas in prose. *Journal of Reading Behavior, 16*, 61-80.

Brown, A. L., Smiley, S. S., Day, J. D., & Lawton, S. C. (1977). *Intrusion of a thematic idea in children's comprehension and retention of stories* (Tech. Rep. No. 18 ERIC Document Reproduction Service No. ED 136 189). Urbana: University of Illinois, Center for the Study of Reading.

Bruner, J. L. (1973). Going beyond the information given. In J. M. Anglin (Ed.), *Beyond the information given* (pp. 218-238). New York: Norton.

Chiesi, H. L., Spilich, G. J., & Voss, J. F. (1979). Acquisition of domain-related information in relation to high and low domain knowledge. *Journal of Verbal Learning, 18*(3), 257-274.

Crafton, L. K. (1980). *The reading process as a transactional learning experience.* Unpublished doctoral dissertation, Indiana University.

Day, J. D. (1980). *Teaching summarization skills: A comparison of training methods.* Unpublished doctoral dissertation, University of Illinois.

Dee-Lucas, D., & Di Vesta, F. J. (1980). Learner-generated organizational aids: Effects on learning from text. *Journal of Educational Psychology, 72*, 304-311.

Doctorow, M., Wittrock, M. C., & Marks, C. (1978). Generative processes in reading comprehension. *Journal of Educational Psychology, 70*, 109-118.

Duell, O. K. (1975). Effect of types of objective, level of test questions, and judged importance of test materials upon posttest performance. *Journal of Educational Psychology, 67*, 380-384.

Faw, H. W., & Waller, T. G. (1976). Mathemagenic behaviors and efficiency in learning from prose materials: Review, critique, and recommendations. *Review of Educational Research, 46*, 691-720.

Frase, L. T. (1970). Boundary conditions for mathemagenic behaviors. *Review of Educational Research, 40*(3), 337-347.

Frase, L. T. (1973). Sampling and response requirements of adjunct questions. *Journal of Educational Psychology, 65*, 273-278.

Frase, L. T., & Schwartz, B. J. (1975). Effect of question production and answering on prose recall. *Journal of Educational Psychology, 67*, 628-635.

Gagne, E. D., & Memory, D. (1978). Instructional events and comprehension: Generalization across passages. *Journal of Reading Behavior, 10*, 321-335.

Gordon, C. J. (1979). *The effects of instruction in metacomprehension and inferencing on children's comprehension abilities.* Unpublished doctoral dissertation, University of Minnesota.

Gordon, C., Hansen, J., & Pearson, P. D. (1978, March). *Effect of background knowledge on silent reading comprehension.* Paper presented at meeting of American Educational Research Association, Toronto.

Guttman, J., Levin, J. R., & Pressley, M. (1977). Pictures, partial pictures, and young children's oral prose learning. *Journal of Educational Psychology, 69*, 473-480.

Halbert, 'M. (1943). An experimental study of children's understanding of instructional materials. *Bureau of School Service*, University of Kentucky, *15*(4), 7-59.

Hansen, J. (1979). *The effects of two intervention techniques on the inferential ability of second grade readers.* Unpublished doctoral dissertation, University of Minnesota.

Jackson, J. R., & Dizney, H. (1963). Intensive vocabulary training. *Journal of Developmental Reading, 6,* 221-229.

Koenke, K. R. (1968, February). *The roles of pictures and readability in comprehension of the main idea of a paragraph.* Paper presented at the annual meetings of the American Educational Research Association, Chicago, IL.

Levin, J. R., & Pressley, M. (1981). *Improving children's prose comprehension: Selected strategies that seem to succeed.* In C. M. Santa and B. L. Hayes (Eds.) Children's prose comprehension: Research and practice. Newark, DE: International Reading Association, p. 44-71.

Manzo, A. V. (1969). The ReQuest procedure. *Journal of Reading, 13,* 123-126.

Marks, C. B., Doctorow, M. J., & Wittrock, M. C. (1974). Word frequency and reading comprehension. *Journal of Educational Research, 67,* 259-262.

Meader, J. (1975). Effects of environmental controls on skill development and transfer in prose learning. *Dissertation Abstracts International, 36,* 685A-686A. (University Microfilms No. 75-16, 790).

Miller, W. (1938). Reading with and without pictures. *Elementary School Journal, 38,* 676-682.

Miyake, N., & Norman, D. A. (1979). To ask a question, one must know enough to know what is not known. *Journal of Verbal Learning and Verbal Behavior, 18,* 357-364.

Morse, J. M. (1976). Effect of reader-generated questions on learning from prose. *Dissertation Abstracts International, 36,* 6635A-6636A. (University Microfilms No. 76-8701).

Pany, D., & Jenkins, J. R. (1978). Learning word meanings: A comparison of instructional procedures and effects on measures of reading comprehension with learning disabled students. *Learning Disabled Quarterly, 1,* 21-32.

Pearson, P. D., Hansen, J., & Gordon, C. (1979). *The effect of background knowledge on young children's comprehension of explicit and implicit information.* Urbana-Champaign, IL: University of Illinois, Center for the Study of Reading.

Pederson, J. E. (1977, November). *An investigation into the differences between student-constructed versus experimenter-constructed post-questions on the comprehension of expository prose.* Paper presented at the 28th annual meeting of the National Reading Conference, New Orleans, Louisiana.

Rickards, J. P., & Hatcher, C. W. (1977-78). Interspersed meaningful learning questions as semantic cues for poor comprehenders. *Reading Research Quarterly, 13,* 538-553.

Rothkopf, E. Z. (1970). The concept of mathemagenic activities. *Review of Educational Research, 40*(3), 325-336.

Ruch, M. D., & Levin, J. R. (1977). Pictorial organization versus verbal repetition of children's prose: Evidence for processing differences. *AV Communication Review, 25,* 269-280.

Rumelhart, D. E., & Ortony, A. (1977). The representation of knowledge in memory. In R. C. Anderson, R. J. Spiro, & W. E. Montague (Eds.), *Schooling and the acquisition of knowledge* (pp. 99-135). Hillsdale, NJ: Lawrence Erlbaum Associates.

Samuels, S. J. (1970). Effects of pictures on learning to read, comprehension and attitudes. *Review of Educational Research, 40*(3), 397-407.

Schachter, S. S. (1978). *An investigation of the effects of vocabulary instruction and schemata orientation upon reading comprehension.* Unpublished doctoral dissertation, University of Minnesota.

Schmelzer, R. V. (1975). *The effect of college student constructed questions on the comprehension of a passage of expository prose.* Unpublished doctoral thesis, University of Minnesota.

Shavelson, R. G., Berliner, D. C., Ravitch, M. M., & Loeding, D. (1974). Effect of position and type of question on learning from prose material: Interaction of treatments with individual differences. *Journal of Educational Psychology, 66,* 40-48.

Singer, H. (1978). Active comprehension: From answering to asking questions. *The Reading Teacher, 31,* 901-908.

Sledge, A. C. (1978). The advance organizer: A review of research at the secondary level. In J. L. Vaughan, Jr. & P. J. Gaus (Eds.), *Research on Reading in Secondary Schools, 2*(2), 41-60.

Sloan, M., & Pearson, P. D. (1978). The effect of teacher intervention strategies on poor readers' comprehension of technical matter in a technical-vocational school. *The Journal of Vocational Education Research, 3,* 9-20.

Smith, C. T. (1978). Evaluating answers to comprehension questions. *The Reading Teacher, 31,* 896-900.

Spilich, G. J., Vesonder, G. T., Chiesi, H. L., & Voss, J. F. (1979). Text processing of domain-related information for individuals with high and low domain knowledge. *Journal of Verbal Learning, 18*(3), 275-290.

Stauffer, R. G. (1976). *Teaching reading as a thinking process.* New York: Harper & Row.

Swaby, B. (1977). *The effects of advance organizers and vocabulary introduction on the reading comprehension of sixth grade students.* Unpublished doctoral dissertation, University of Minnesota.

Taylor, B. M. (1978). A comparison of good and poor readers' ability to read for meaning. *Dissertation Abstracts International, 39*(04), 2108-2109A.

Taylor, B., & Berkowitz, S. (1980). Facilitating children's comprehension of content material. In M. L. Kamil & A. J. Moe (Eds.), *Perspectives in reading research and instruction* (pp. 64-68). Clemson, SC: National Reading Conference.

Thomas, E. L., & Robinson, H. A. (1972). *Improving reading in every class.* Boston: Allyn & Bacon.

Vernon, M. D. (1953). The value of pictorial illustration. *British Journal of Educational Psychology, 23,* 180-187.

Vernon, M. D. (1954). The instruction of children by pictorial illustration. *British Journal of Educational Psychology, 24,* 171-179.

Weintraub, S. (1960). *The effect of pictures on the comprehension of a second grade basal reader.* Unpublished doctoral dissertation, University of Illinois.

Wiesendanger, K. D., & Wollenberg, J. P. (1978). Prequestioning inhibits third graders' reading comprehension. *The Reading Teacher, 31,* 892-895.

Wittrock, M. C., Marks, C. B., & Doctorow, M. (1975). Reading as a generative process. *Journal of Educational Psychology, 67,* 484-489.

Wixson, K. K. (1980). *The effects of postreading questions on children's discourse comprehension and knowledge acquisition.* Unpublished doctoral dissertation, Syracuse University.

15

INSTRUCTIONAL RESEARCH ON LITERACY AND READING: PARAMETERS, PERSPECTIVES, AND PREDICTIONS

Patricia L. Anders
University of Arizona

P. David Pearson
Center for the Study of Reading

The world of literacy research is dynamic. Those who are asking research questions, carrying out research, and changing education, both in and out of school, have a rich theoretical and research base from which to work. Indeed, this base is wider in perspective and deeper in richness of thought than any ever available to literacy researchers. The purposes of this chapter are to reflect on the status of literacy instruction and to pose some questions and issues that need careful attention in future research. Our reflections focus on three topics: context, critical issues, and the conduct of reading research.

First, we consider issues related to context effects on literacy generally and reading instruction specifically. This discussion briefly reviews research that suggests that the context in which readers encounter print affects the understanding they create when reading.

Second, we address seven issues that we believe researchers of literacy and reading instruction need to confront: (a) the influence of a teacher's model of literacy on students' literacy attitudes and performance, (b) the functionality of the strategies researchers investigate and recommend, (c) the transfer effects of these strategies for learners as they move from one context to another, (d) the degree to which comprehension instruction should be explicit, (e) the ownership of comprehension strategies, (f) the value of strategies that focus on developing readers' knowledge about their own reading learning behaviors, and (g) the completeness of instructional models.

In the final section of this chapter we discuss the conduct of instructional research. We offer several guidelines to those researchers who share our goal of conducting instructional research that is both ecologically valid and generalizable.

CONTEXTS OF LITERACY

Many literacy-related investigations of the past decade have focused on the many and varied contexts of literacy. These studies have been descriptive, ethnographic, and quasi-experimental. The fundamental question they have addressed is: What environmental conditions influence the quality and quantity of literacy events? Researchers have worked in both the real world of the classroom and the real world of work.

Real World Contexts of Literacy

Among the descriptive studies of the real world of literacy in the work place, those of Mikulecky and his associates stand out (e.g., Harste & Mikulecky, 1984). They have gathered observational and interview data on the reading and writing of adults both on and off the job. The consistent conclusion drawn from these studies is that adults seem to read and write differently, in both quality and quantity, than standardized test results would predict. The implication, then, is that within the context of daily living, both on the job and off, adults are able to negotiate the meanings of what they read and are able to record the language they need to communicate through reading and writing, despite what some tests may indicate.

Kirsch and Guthrie (1982, 1984) observed and interviewed employees in a major manufacturing plant. Their results corroborate the findings of Mikulecky and his colleagues. Kirsch and Guthrie observed 14 employees representing seven job classifications, ranging from semi-skilled workers to professional employees, over a 3-week period in 2- to 3-hour time blocks that varied by time of day and day of the week. Each observation was followed by a 1- to 2-hour structured interview.

The results of their work point out one obvious but important fact: The reading that one does as an adult in the world of work and leisure is very different from the way reading is viewed and taught in school. For example, Kirsch and Guthrie (1982) concluded that most job-related reading is not done from books; rather, it is done from "manuals, handbooks of information, schematics, magazine articles, tables and figures, business correspondence, legal documents, and directions or guidelines" (p. 46). Very seldom did on the job readers read for the gist or general idea of a text; rather, purposes for reading were geared toward "identifying facts, totally remembering information, evaluating and revising a document, synthesizing information from several documents, transforming information into a new presentation, conveying information through conversation with others, or gaining an overview of operations or agreements" (p. 46). Notice that reading is completed for purposes that arise from within the context of the job at hand. Another of the several conclusions reached by Kirsch and Guthrie is that the need to read was neither frivolous nor limited to those employees with professional status. Reading was viewed by the majority of workers as an "indispensible activity" (p. 47).

Kirsch and Guthrie also point out that standardized reading tests, which examine subjects' "comprehension" of text taken from fictional pieces and textbooks, cannot possibly predict the success one will have doing on-the-job reading.

Heath's (1983) findings also lend support to this picture. Her interpretations of ethnographic data suggest that members of a community develop and use the literacy strategies needed to negotiate the meanings of print. She relates example after example of children and adults constructing meanings required for daily life. In many cases, children who were not yet in school or adults who had very limited school experience were able to use both reading and writing in the context in which those processes were needed (e.g., in the grocery store and church).

Carey, Harste, & Smith (1981), in conducting a modified replication of Anderson, Reynolds, Schallert, and Goetz's (1977) demonstration of the influence of prior knowledge on comprehension, uncovered an interesting within-school context effect. They found that in addition to the effect for prior knowledge, college students' understanding of ambiguous passages was influenced by the physical setting within which comprehension was assessed. Specifically, both physical education and music majors responded with stronger prior knowledge biases when they were tested in a gymnasium and a music room, respectively, than when they were tested in a neutral (i.e., English) classroom. Harste, Woodward, and Burke (1984) have described reading as a sociopsycholinguistic process. That is, humans come to know in many ways, and all that is embodied in the reader, the text, and the environment has the potential of affecting the understanding one creates.

In summary, it is apparent that the studies investigating reading in real world contexts reveal certain behaviors and attitudes about reading that have not been highlighted or emphasized in the past. Literacy events exist within contexts and those contexts affect the meaning that is constructed.

School Contexts

A number of researchers have been examining within-school and within-classroom contextual effects, using a variety of methods of investigation and analysis, ranging from thick ethnographic descriptions of teacher–student interaction (e.g., Harste, Woodward, Burke, 1984) to broad-based regression models of the effects of various "levels" of influence (e.g., classroom, building, district) within the "schooling" ecology (e.g., Barr & Dreeben, 1983). Despite differences in methodology, all these studies point to the inescapable conclusion that virtually all aspects of the context in which literacy is acquired affect both attitude toward and performance on literacy tasks.

Consider, for a moment, this litany of findings:

1. Teacher beliefs about language and literacy influence the decisions they make about what to teach students (Harste & Burke, 1977 and Harste, Woodward, and Burke, 1984b; DeFord, 1985).

2. Teachers' expectations about student performance influence the kind of feedback they offer students when they make oral reading errors/ miscues (Allington, 1980; Hoffman et al, 1984) as well as how they interact with students (McDermott, 1977).

3. Teachers' knowledge about students at-home language traditions influences the kinds of interaction patterns they use when teaching minority children (Au & Mason, 1981).

4. Task ambiguity and perceived personal risk influence students' recall performance; that is, high risk and high ambiguity push students toward more literal responses (Mosenthal & Na, 1980).

5. Decisions made at the district level constrain those made at the school level that, in turn, constrain those made at the classroom level; furthermore, all such decisions have an impact on performance (Barr & Dreeben, 1983).

6. The style of leadership embraced by building principals, including how they regard, interact with, and involve in decision-making those teachers with whom they work influences the success of innovations as well as student performance (see Samuels, in press, for a summary).

No matter the level within the school hierarchy or the actors involved in the interaction, it is clear that the social context in which literacy tasks are taught and learned influence both the quality of the literacy experience and the quantity of literacy performance, as measured by either conventional or unconventional assessments.

This body of research tends to support the contention that reading is a social as well as a cognitive act: Literacy is a vehicle for social interaction and this is no less true in the classroom than it is true on the job or in one's favorite reading chair with a good book on a Sunday afternoon.

Implications for Research

This brief review of contexts of literacy suggests implications for researchers investigating literacy development, especially in classrooms.

First, we need to ask the extent to which school reading should resemble real word reading. Harste and Mikulecky (1984) suggest that the two contexts hardly resemble each other at all. They (along with Kirsch & Guthrie, 1982, 1984) imply that the contexts should be similar. If that is true several questions come to mind: (a) What processes involved in the world of work should be incorporated in the classroom context? (b) How would we determine those work related tasks that might be incorporated? (c) Are there steps or phases in such an incorporation? (d) How would such a curriculum be organized and developed?

Second, it seems apparent that current and future research efforts must include consideration for context effects. At the very minimum, researchers need to describe the context(s) in which they conduct their studies. Furthermore, researchers are obligated to examine their results for possible context effects. For example, Osako and Anders (1983) found, in their investigation of the effects of interest on reading comprehension, that high school students have learned to suppress interest when doing assigned reading in the classroom.

Most importantly, researchers should realize, once and for all, that the classical experimental design cannot be employed in classrooms without concern for the contextual constraints existing in those classrooms. Anders, Bos, and Filip (1984) have found, when doing instructional research in classrooms of students identified as learning disabled, that students' learned passiveness affects the success of instructional strategies. Pilot studies must be done. Researchers must establish a relationship with students, and teachers must let their students know that some of the constraints typically operating in the classrooms are going to be suspended on purpose.

Issues that Research on Literacy Instruction Must Face

The past decade of literacy research has witnessed a revival of interest in instruction reminiscent of the period from 1920 to 1940. But the research paradigms, the dominant themes, and the unresolved issues are quite different. The concern for understanding relationships among variables has shifted to a concern for how instruction works in its natural contexts. The emphasis on word identification and early reading has given way to emphasis on comprehension, composition, and how literate individuals monitor and control their learning. Earlier, we were unsure about the populations of readers to which effective teaching strategies applied. Now, as we have progressed in our understanding of instructional processes, we have raised a host of unresolved issues, issues we must resolve if we are to speak to teachers with confidence about the practices we can advocate on the basis of research findings. We preface our discussion of these issues with a disclaimer: In listing these issues separately we run the risk of implying that each is a separate question. We know, to the contrary, that they are all interrelated; they are but different facets of the same phenomenon—the ecology of schooling.

The first issue is: How does the model of literacy learning a teacher brings to the classroom influence students' attitude and performance? We addressed this issue briefly in our discussion of schooling contexts (cf. pp. 161–162), but we think much work remains to be done. We do know that teachers' beliefs influence their decision-making (Harste & Burke, 1977) and the kinds of activities they ask children to do (Tierney, Leys, & Rogers, 1986). And we know that teachers can be reliably classified as possessing different orientations to reading, such as whole language, skills, or phonics (DeFord, 1985). But what we do not know much about is the effect that these beliefs, decisions, and orientations have on children's performance, orientation, or attitudes. Methodologically this is a step we are ready to take, and we suspect that both ethnographers and experimentalists will take it soon.

The second issue is: Will a functional orientation toward strategy instruction prove more effective than an arbitrary orientation? Consider the plight of students who are constantly barraged with assignment after assignment requiring them to find main ideas, underline verbs, correct spellings, distinguish facts from opinions, or write themes about a picture for an audience of one (the teacher). Students rarely are given opportunities in schools to perform literacy tasks for either personally satisfying reasons or for typical socially motivated reasons (e.g., publication). About the only reason we typically offer students for completing literacy tasks is, "because that's the assignment." And grades are virtually our sole source of motivation. But what would literacy tasks look like, and how would performance change, if we set a requirement that we couldn't assign a task or teach a skill unless we could answer the question, "when and why should a student use it?" And what if students selected their own topics for themes or their own reading assignments based on interest, curiosity, prior knowledge, and the need to know? We think this issue of functionality deserves our attention; it may, in fact, turn out to be a pivotal question in instructional research.

The third issue is: What does it mean to "teach for transfer?" The general issue of transfer of performance from a training task or context to a new task has been discussed by researchers for as long as we have held theories of learning. And the issue is still not settled. Traditionally, in instructional research, our operational definition of transfer has been, will the effect observed during training show up on a standardized reading test? We think that it is time to develop a new set of standards for transfer. What we need is to embrace a view of transfer as a continuum of tasks bearing decreasing resemblance to the training task. We illustrate by example: Gallagher (in preparation) recently examined the transfer effects of an instructional strategy designed to help students learn and remember information about insect societies (ants, bees, and termites) by helping them learn how to organize key information into charts. Her first question was how much did the students learn from these texts in which the strategy was embedded? She measured this with a pretty traditional end-of-unit achievement test. Her first level of transfer required students to read and answer questions about a new insect society, wasps. Her second level of transfer was the same task on unfamiliar human society, the Micmac Indians. Her third level of transfer was the same task on a text describing landforms. Consider the underlying logic. If the students learned only the information in the texts, then there would be transfer to none of the passages. If what they learned was a schema for insect societies, then transfer would extend to the wasp passage but no further. If what they acquired was a social structure schema, then transfer would extend to Micmacs but not landforms. Finally, if what they learned was a strategy about how to organize information, then transfer should extend all the way to landforms. It is well-conceived plans for evaluating transfer, like Gallagher's, that we need in our research. (By the way, the strategy did extend all the way to landforms.)

The fourth issue is: How explicit should instruction be? The issue here is that some researchers and practitioners advocate very explicit instruction (Rosenshine & Stevens, 1984). This instruction, commonly called *direct instruction,* carefully directs the teacher and students in learning the skills believed to be necessary for progress in learning to read. Other researchers and practitioners advocate a relatively centrist position. This position has been labeled *explicit instruction* by Pearson and Gallagher (1983). The suggestion here is that teachers should be capable of predicting students' instructional needs and should provide instruction to accommodate those needs. A third position, directly opposed to the direct instruction model is the *inquiry* or *discovery approach.* This instructional paradigm is student centered; instruction is offered by the teacher or other available resources when students are reading text for purposes they have articulated and care about (Goodman & Burke, 1980). Each of these instructional paradigms need further investigation, particularly in terms of two issues.

First, one must ask, what are the contexts and who are the children for which different types of instruction may work? For example, a 5-year-old who wants to have and use his own pair of real scissors needs direct instruction on the use of those scissors. The parent/teacher would want to be sure that the child knew which types of things are appropriate for cutting and which are not, how to carry the scissors when walking, and how to hand the scissors safely to another person. The adult would discuss, model, and provide opportunities for practice within the constraints of proper scissor handling. On the other hand, when the same child asks questions about dinosaurs or dolphins, the parent/teacher can take a much less directive approach: an approach that responds to the child's questions, one that provides possible resource materials, and one that allows the child independence in seeking the answers to the questions he has. Research needs to describe the circumstances in which explicit instruction is needed, both in terms of task characteristics and student interest, background, and ability.

Second, research points to the importance of providing students with explicit routines for monitoring how they are comprehending or how they are proceeding to complete an assigned task. Some students may discover task-monitoring procedures on their own, but we wonder whether it is helpful to explicitly teach unsuccessful readers to monitor their comprehension. We also wonder if explicit task-monitoring strategies might interfere with the self-monitoring that some students seem to be capable of doing on their own.

These two issues, and perhaps a host of others, still need investigation before the explicitness of instruction question can be answered.

Who should control the learning environment is the fifth issue. Generally, this question has not been addressed by instructional researchers in the field of literacy. Few would disagree that a goal of education is to develop mature and independent learners, but few researchers have investigated the process of becoming independent or the sufficient and necessary conditions for independence. Examined from a common sense perspective, one would argue the following: Readers assume independence when they are ready; when something can be accomplished without help, one generally prefers to assume that responsibility. One of our concerns, however, is that some strategies and some management systems may in fact impede the progress of becoming independent and may unnecessarily foster dependence.

The sixth issue is: Should we worry about strategies or metastrategies? Essentially, this question leads from the previous dependence–independence question and overlaps with the issue of transfer. The strategies discussed in the previous chapters by Bridge and LaZansky, Spencer, and Johnston are primarily instructional strategies. The goal of these strategies is to help students understand and learn from their reading. However, we know little about how these strategies might become metastrategies; that is, strategies that the learner may adapt and generalize to her own purposes with other materials. This is a key question that needs immediate attention.

What constitutes a complete instructional model is the last issue. This question, of course, subsumes all the others we have asked and, we suspect, many we have failed to ask. What we want to offer, in closing this section, is a possible model, derived from several sources (most notable, Paris, Lipson, & Wixson, 1983; Pearson & Gallagher, 1983), but still developing. Every instructional strategy teachers and researchers ask students to learn should, we think, answer the following questions:

1. *What?* Students need to know what this thing is you want them to do. They must, in effect, develop a concept of the strategy. And to know what something is, they will have to know what it is not. For example, if they are to learn main ideas, they need an operational definition (by the way, they do not need a dictionary definition) of a main idea and they need to know how a main idea differs from a detail or an irrelevant statement. They need to be able to recognize one when it "hits them in the face."

2. *How?* What all students need desperately is a set of procedures to use when they are asked to apply a strategy. Where do I start? What do I try first? Second? What do I do when I don't succeed the first time? It is exactly this step-by-step procedural information that Durkin found lacking in classroom instruction (1978-1979) and in basal reader manuals (1981).

3. *Why?* The why of a strategy gets us back to the issue of functionality. And we would argue that if you cannot generate a legitimate, understandable reason for asking students to perform a task—one that you can share with them, then perhaps you should not teach it? We believe the why should relate to the purposes for the reading. The purposes for the reading should be for certain types of information, for a literary experience, or for pleasure and escape. The strategy is taught, employed, and practiced because it may help the reader accomplish that functional goal.

4. *When?* We assume that not all strategies were meant to be applied to all texts or to all tasks. Part of the effective use of a strategy is knowing when to ignore it. For example, in teaching about main ideas, we would likely want students to reserve it for informational texts and to forget it when they were reading stories.

To use the language of modern information processing, every instructional episode should address declarative knowledge (that is the *what*), procedural knowledge (that is the *how*) and conditional (after Paris, Lipson, & Wixson, 1983) knowledge (the *why* and the *when*). If we could validate the importance of each of these kinds of knowledge, we would create a revolution in literacy instruction. Indeed, Durkin's work suggests that we seldom address any of these questions; instead, we offer only one component, *practice,* in the form of endless streams of worksheets. The basis of that practice-only approach seems to be that if we can get by with just giving students opportunities to practice tasks, then we can avoid dealing with the what, how, why and when of each strategy we think we want students to learn. But avoiding these questions may turn out to be more costly, both in time and in lost opportunities, than facing these issues squarely in the first place. Indeed, it might turn out that children develop their own strategies which work much better than ours when left to their own devices and when they are working with resources they need to understand for their own purposes.

CONDUCTING LITERACY RESEARCH

Thus far, we have discussed school and society contexts of literacy and we have raised seven issues that we believe are compelling and in need of further investigation. In this concluding section we want to remind ourselves and our readers of certain principles of research that are prerequisite to valuable and generalizable studies.

First, the research questions we ask have always been crucial to the success of any study or series of studies. Traditionally, we have been advised that questions should be elegant—neat, simple, and clear. Although this is still true, it is difficult to ask elegant questions when one is also challenged to account for the many variables to be found in the context of most learning situations. This double bind can be addressed as follows. First, a researcher might begin an investigation by first getting the "big picture." By using observational research techniques one would determine the salient characteristics of any one group. Next, the researcher might intervene with an experimental variable to determine what, if any, effect that particular variable had on the group. Both qualitative and quantitative data should be gathered, analyzed and reported.

Next, the instructional researcher might return to similar groups and gently and systematically alter one instructional or contextual variable at a time to determine the effects of those variables. A lot of instructional research has been generated in the past decade. However, much still needs to be done because too much of the research has not looked carefully and completely enough at the complexities of the teaching and learning environment.

Specifically, instructional researchers would do well to adopt the notion of triangulation from observational research paradigms (Webb, Campbell, Schwartz, & Secrest, 1966) and ethnographic research paradigms (Sevigny, 1981). Methods of triangulation help get a handle on the many variables affecting instruction. In fact, even within experimental circles, there is precedent for something like triangulation. X's concept of converging operations (using multiple data sources to evaluate the strength of a finding) is the experimental analogue of triangulation (see Kamil, 1984).

Next, it is hard to imagine an instructional research study that could be done without first piloting the idea. We are confident that many worthwhile studies have never seen the light of publication because on the first pass no significant differences were found. A pilot study allows the researcher to modify the study so as to maximize the likelihood of finding effects.

Finally, let us start providing as much qualitative data about our studies as we do quantitative data. It may well be that by more completely describing studies, they will become more ecologically valid and generalizable. And, for those who persist in relying on quantitative data as their *primary* evidence, we suggest that, at the very least, qualitative data collected in conjunction with quantitative outcome data will help *explain* why some things worked or did not work. Quantitative data rarely explain.

A second way out of the double bind is to move from the controlled situation of the laboratory where effects have been found into the real world of the classroom. In effect, this is what has been done in many literacy related studies. We are concerned about this methodology because if context effects are as great as they seem to be, the researcher may ignore or affect the classroom environment in ways that are unpredictable. Even so, such a concern should not keep us out of the classroom; instead, it should motivate us to stay in the classroom to try to understand how it works.

REFERENCES

Allington, R. L. (1980). Teacher interruption behaviors during primary grade oral reading. *Journal of Educational Psychology, 72*, 371-372.

Anders, P. L., Bos, C., & Filip, D. (1984). The effects of the semantic features analysis on the vocabulary and comprehension of adolescent learning disabled students. In J. A. Niles (Ed.), *Thirty-third yearbook of the national reading conference* (pp. 162-166), Rochester, NY: National Reading Conference.

Anderson, R. C., Reynolds, R. E., Schallert, D. L., & Goetz, E. T. (1977). Frameworks for comprehending discourse. *American Educational Research Journal, 14*, 367-382.

Au, K. H., & Mason, J. M. (1981). Social organizational factors in learning to read: The balance of rights hypothesis. *Reading Research Quarterly*, 1981, v. 17 n. 1, 115-152.

Barr, R., & Dreeben, R. (1983). *How schools work*. Chicago: University of Chicago Press.

Carey, R. F., Harste, J. C., & Smith, S. L. (1981). Contextual constraints and discourse processes: A replication study. *Reading Research Quarterly*, 1981, v. 16, p. 201-212.

DeFord, D. (1985). Validating the construct of theoretical orientation in reading instruction. *Reading Research Quarterly, 20*, 351-367.

Durkin, D. (1978-1979). What classroom observations reveal about reading comprehension instruction. *Reading Research Quarterly, 14*, 481-533.

Durkin, D. (1981). Reading comprehension instruction in five basal reader series. *Reading Research Quarterly, 16,* (4), 515-544.

Gallagher, M. C. (in preparation). *Acquiring specific information, knowledge frameworks, and independent reading strategies from the discussion of natural science texts.* Unpublished doctoral dissertation, University of Illinois.

Goodman, Y. M., & Burke, C. L. (1980). *Reading strategies: Focus on comprehension.* New York: Holt, Rinehart & Winston.

Harste, J., & Burke, C. L. (1977). A new hypothesis for reading teacher research: Both the teaching and learning of reading are theoretically based. In P. D. Pearson (Ed.), *Reading: Theory, research, and practice,* Twenty-sixth Yearbook of the National Reading Conference. Clemson, SC: National Reading Conference.

Harste, J. C., & Mikulecky, L. J. (1984). The context of literacy in our society. In A. C. Purves & O. Niles (Eds.), *Becoming readers in a complex society,* Eighty-third Yearbook of the National Society for the Study of Education. Chicago: University of Chicago Press.

Harste, J. C., Woodward, V. A., & Burke, C. A. (1984a). Examining our assumptions: A transactional view of literacy and learning. *Research in the Teaching of English, 18*(1), 84-108.

Harste, J. C., Woodward, V. A., & Burke, C. A. (1984b). *Language, Stories, and Literary Lessons.* Portsmouth, NH: Heinemann Publishing Co.

Heath. S. B. (1983). *Ways with words.* Cambridge, England: Cambridge University Press.

Hoffman, J. V., O'Neal, S. F., Kastler, L. A., Clements, R. O., Segel, K. W., & Nash, M. F. (1984). Guided oral reading and miscue focused verbal feedback in second-grade classrooms. *Reading Research Quarterly, 19,* 367-384.

Kamil, M. L. (1984). Current traditions of reading research. In P. D. Pearson (Ed.), *Handbook of reading research* (pp. 39-62). New York: Longman.

Kirsch, I. S., & Guthrie, J. T. (1982). *Conceptual foundations for competencies and practices of reading.* Technical Report #1, International Reading Association.

Kirsch, I. S., & Guthrie, J. T. (1984). Prose comprehension and text search as a function of reading volume. *Reading Research Quarterly, 19,* 332-342.

McDermott, R. P. (1977). Social relations as contexts for learning in school. *Harvard Educational Review, 47,* 198-213.

Mosenthal, P., & Na T. (1980). Quality of children's recall under two classroom testing conditions: Toward a socio-psycholinguistic model of reading comprehension. *Reading Research Quarterly, 15,* 504-528.

Osako, G. N., & Anders, P. L. (1983). The effect of reading interest on comprehension of expository materials with controls for prior knowledge. In J. A. Niles & L. A. Harris (Eds.), *Searches for meaning in reading/language processing and instruction* (pp. 56-60). Rochester, NY: National Reading Conference.

Paris, S. G., Lipson, M., & Wixson, K. (1983). Becoming a strategic reader. *Contemporary Educational Psychology, 8,* 293-316.

Pearson, P. D., & Gallagher, M. C. (1983). The instruction of reading comprehension. *Contemporary Educational Psychology, 8,* 317-344.

Rosenshine, B., & Stevens, R. (1984). Classroom instruction in reading. In P. D. Pearson (Ed.), *Handbook of reading research* (pp. 745-798). New York: Longman.

Samuels, S. J. (in press). Characteristics of exemplary reading programs. In S. J. Samuels & P. D. Pearson (Eds.), *Changing school reading programs: Guiding principles and successful projects.* Newark, DE: International Reading Association.

Sevigny, M. J. (1981). Triangulated inquiry—a methodology for the analysis of classroom interaction. In J. Green & C. Wallat (Eds.), *Ethnography and language in educational settings* (pp. 65-86). Norwood, NJ: Ablex.

Tierney, R. J., Leys, M., & Rogers, T. (1986). Comprehension, composition and collaboration. In T. Raphael (Eds.), *Contexts of literacy*. New York: Random House.

Webb, E. J., Campbell, D. T., Schwartz, R. D., & Secrest, L. B. (1966). *Unobtrusive measures*. Chicago: Rand McNally.

AUTHOR INDEX

SUBJECT INDEX

A

Acceptability, 16, 26
Actualization, 15
Advance organizer, 266–267, 275–278, 295–296
Argument repetition, 236, 241
Assumptions, 206–223
  of listeners, 207–223
  of readers, 206–223
Attention, 19–21, 32, 47–51, 300
  selective, 300
Author-reader relationship, *see* Print setting, author-reader relationship

C

Cognitive processes in reading, *see* Print setting
Coherence, 16, 19, 21, 26, 34, 43, 50, 242–243
Cohesion, 16, 26, 34, 43, 193–194, *see also* Lexical cohesion
Communication modality, 213–222
Composing, 217–223
Comprehension
  comprehension processes, *see* Comprehension processes
  constructive process, 11
  figurative, 231, 237–239
  inferential, *see* Inferencing
  literal, 230–249
  metaphorical, 231

non-literal, 230–232
  purpose-bound, 235
  vocabulary instruction, effects of, 286–287
Comprehension processes, 7–13
  bottom-up processes, 61, 233–234, 257
  expectations, effects of, 11–12
  gist processing, 7, 12, 26, 32
  macroprocesses, 7–13
  phrase boundary, selection of, 10
  prior knowledge, role of, 256–279, 284–302
  processing chunk, formation of, 10
  processing cycles, 8–10
  top-down processes, 61–73, 233, 241, 257
Comprehension strategies, 59–73, 283–302, *see also* Reading, preparation for
  top-level structures, use of 59–73
Comprehension task, 244
Concept formation, 131–138, *see also* Typicality, prototype
  categorization, 131–141
  by attributes, 134–135
  by internal structure, 134–135
  digital category approach, 132
Constructivist view of reading, 283–302
Contexts of literacy, 308–317
  instruction, 313–314
  discovery, *see* inquiry
  explicit, 313–314
  direct, 313
  inquiry, 313
  instructional model, 314–315